Boston Public Library

A new Collection of Voyages, Discoveries and Travels

Containing whatever is worthy of Notice, in Europe, Asia, Africa... Vol. V

Boston Public Library

A new Collection of Voyages, Discoveries and Travels
Containing whatever is worthy of Notice, in Europe, Asia, Africa... Vol. V

ISBN/EAN: 9783744757843

Printed in Europe, USA, Canada, Australia, Japan

Cover: Foto ©Andreas Hilbeck / pixelio.de

More available books at **www.hansebooks.com**

A NEW
COLLECTION
OF
VOYAGES,
DISCOVERIES and TRAVELS:

CONTAINING

Whatever is worthy of Notice, in
EUROPE, ASIA,
AFRICA and AMERICA:

IN RESPECT TO

The Situation and Extent of Empires, Kingdoms, and Provinces; their Climates, Soil, Produce, &c.

WITH

The Manners and Customs of the several Inhabitants; their Government, Religion, Arts, Sciences, Manufactures, and Commerce.

The whole consisting of such ENGLISH and FOREIGN Authors as are in most Esteem; including the Descriptions and Remarks of some celebrated late Travellers, not to be found in any other Collection.

Illustrated with a Variety of accurate
MAPS, PLANS, and elegant ENGRAVINGS.

VOL. V.

LONDON:
Printed for J. KNOX, near Southampton-Street, in the Strand. MDCCLXVII.

OF THE

FIFTH VOLUME.

CONTINUATION of Keyſler's Travels through Germany, Hungary, Bohemia, Switzerland, Italy, and Lorrain; illuſtrated with the remarks of later travellers, page 1

Travels through France, by Sacheverel Stephens, Gent. interſperſed with the remarks of later travellers, 273

Travels through, and an account of the kingdoms of Spain and Portugal; collected from the remarks of the Reverend Mr. Clarke, chaplain to the Earl of Briſtol, when ambaſſador extraordinary at Madrid in 1760, and from other writers: including alſo an authentic narrative of the ſufferings of Iſaac Martin in the Inquiſition at Granada, 327

An account of the empire of Ruſſia; with ſome curious perſonal anecdotes of the Czar Peter I. Collected from the obſervations of Mr. Hanway, and other writers, 434

A brief account of the kingdom of Pruſſia; with ſome anecdotes of king Frederic II. from Mr. Hanway, &c. 469

A COLLECTION OF VOYAGES AND TRAVELS.

CONTINUATION of the TRAVELS
OF
JOHN GEORGE KEYSLER, F. R. S.

BEFORE we enter that long celebrated city of Rome with Mr. Keyſler, it will not be amiſs to attend to the idea Mr. Sharp gives us of the nature of travelling in Italy. He writes thus from Rome.

" We arrived at this place, after a journey of ſeven days, with accommodations uncomfortable enough. Give what ſcope you pleaſe to your fancy, you will never image half the diſagreeableneſs that Italian beds, Italian cooks, Italian poſt-horſes, Italian poſtilions, and Italian naſtineſs, offer to an Engliſhman, in an autumnal journey; much more to an Engliſhwoman.

At Turin, Milan, Venice, Rome, and, perhaps, two or three other towns, you meet with good accommodation; but no words can expreſs the wretchedneſs of the other inns. No other beds than one of ſtraw, with a matraſs of ſtraw, and next to that a dirty ſheet, ſprinkled with water, and, conſequently, damp; for a covering you have another ſheet, as coarſe as the firſt, and as coarſe as one of our kitchen jack-towels, with a dirty coverlet. The bedſted conſiſts of four wooden forms, or benches: an Engliſh peer and peereſs muſt lye in this manner, unleſs they carry an upholsterer's shop with them, which is very troublesome. There are, by the bye, no such things as curtains, and hardly, from Venice to Rome, that cleanly and most useful invention, a privy; so that what should be collected and buried in oblivion, is for ever under your nose and eyes. Take along with you, that in all these inns the walls are bare, and the floor has never once been washed since it was first laid. One of the most indelicate customs here, is, that men, and not women, make the ladies beds, and would do every office of a maid servant, if suffered. To sum up, in a word, the total of Italian nastiness, your chamber, which you would wish to be the sweetest, is by far the most offensive room in the house, for reasons I shall not explain. I must tell you, that except in two or three places, they never scour their pewter, and unless you were to see it, you will not conceive how dirty and nauseous it grows in thirty or forty years. Their knives are of the same colour as their pewter, and their table-cloths and napkins such as you see on joint-stools, in Bartholomew-Fair, where the mob eat their sausages. In these inns they make you pay largely, and send up ten times as much as you can eat. This is almost constantly the fare.—A soop like wash, with pieces of liver swimming in it; a plate full of brains, fried in the shape of fritters; a dish of livers and gizzards; a couple of fowls (always killed after your arrival) boiled to rags, without any the least kind of sauce, or herbage; another fowl, just killed, stewed as they call it; then two more fowls, or a turkey roasted to rags. I must not omit to mention, that, all over Italy, on the roads, the chickens and fowls are so stringy, you may divide the breast into as many filaments as you can a halfpenny-worth of thread. Now and then we get a little piece of mutton, or veal, and, generally speaking, it is the only eatable morsel that falls in our way. I should mention, that pigeons boiled and roasted, often supply the place of some of

the

the abovementioned dishes. The bread all the way is exceedingly bad, and the butter so rancid, it cannot be touched, or even borne within the reach of our smell. We procured, the other day, a pint of cream, and made a little extempore butter, which proved almost as good as any we eat in England, so that the fault seems to lye in the manufacture, and not in the milk; yet such is the force of education and custom, that the people here do not wish to have it better than it is. In Savoy, amongst the Alps, we were often astonished at the excellence of their diet; so great is the disparity between French and Italian cooks, on the Savoy and the Loretto roads.

But what is a greater evil to travellers than any of the above recited, though not peculiar to the Loretto road, are the infinite numbers of gnats, bugs, fleas, and lice, which infest us by night and by day.

You will grant, after this description of the horrors of an Italian journey, that one ought to take no small pleasure in treading on classic ground; yet, believe me, I have not caricatured; every article of it is literally true."—]

If we compare modern Rome, with regard to its present extent, and the number of inhabitants, with several other cities in the world, we shall find many that surpass it; but, when we add the power and influence it has maintained, during so many centuries, over many powerful nations, Rome never had its equal in the world.

It is highly probable, both from ocular demonstration and the accounts of ancient writers, that the walls of the modern city are, in many places, the same with those of the ancient, and their circumferences nearly equal. But the difference between the number of buildings on this spot is very great, one half of modern Rome lying waste, or converted into gardens, fields, meadows, and vineyards; in which the most magnificent structures were anciently erected. You may walk wholly round the city in three or four hours

hours at moſt, the circumference being reckoned about thirteen ſhort Italian miles: whereas a tour round the city of Paris and its ſuburbs will, at leaſt, require ſix or ſeven hours.

It muſt be granted, that the number of inhabitants in ancient Rome exceeded that of the modern, it appearing from Ciacconius, in the life of pope Gregory XI. that, in the year 1376, the whole number of inhabitants in Rome amounted only to thirty-three thouſand. Paulus Jovius informs us, that, under the happy and peaceable government of pope Leo, the number was increaſed to eighty-five thouſand; but in the turbulent times of Clement VII. Rome could boaſt only of thirty-two thouſand inhabitants. In the year 1709 the number of births, at Rome, amounted to three thouſand ſix hundred and ſixty-two; and the whole number of inhabitants to a hundred and thirty-eight thouſand five hundred and ſixty-eight; among whom were forty biſhops, two thouſand ſix hundred and eighty-ſix prieſts, three thouſand five hundred and fifty-nine monks, a thouſand eight hundred and fourteen nuns, three hundred and ninety three courteſans, or licenſed proſtitutes, and fourteen Moors. The Jews were not thought worthy of being included in this computation, though they amounted to about eight or nine thouſand. Five years after, namely, in July 1714, pope Clement XI. ordered an account to be taken by Carraccioli of all the inhabitants in Rome, the number of which, then, amounted to a hundred and forty-three thouſand; whereas Paris contains, at leaſt, between eight and nine hundred thouſand, and London ſtill more, as plainly appears from the yearly bills of mortality. The latter city has, within theſe twenty years, increaſed ſo prodigiouſly, that the difference between London and Paris is ſufficiently evident from taking a view of the latter from the tower of Notre Dame, and of the former from the upper gallery in St. Paul's cupola. With regard to the multitude

multitude of inhabitants; London, indeed, has more open and larger squares than Paris; but Paris abounds with several spacious convents, which are, in proportion, but thinly inhabited. The people have also little employment upon the Seine, whereas the many hundred large vessels, and the almost infinite number of boats and other small craft on the Thames, maintain more people than many large cities contain. We may form some conjecture of the inhabitants of London from the quantity of provisions, there being, one day with another, twelve hundred oxen killed, and upward of twenty thousand sheep every week, beside twelve thousand hogs and calves; as appears from exact registers, and the assurances given the king of Prussia, in 1725, at Herenhausen, by lord Townshend.

The sovereignty of ancient Rome over a great part of the globe seems, indeed, to give it a superiority over modern Rome; but the latter boasts of a monarchy raised by a peculiar sort of policy, and, in respect of the extent of dominions, especially before Luther's reformation, surpasses ancient Rome itself. And I must own, that in external splendor and the beauty of its temples and palaces, modern Rome excels the ancient. In this respect I differ from St. Augustin, who wished, above all things, to have seen *Christum in carne, Paulum in ore, Romam in flore.* "Christ in the flesh, St. Paul preaching, and Rome "in its ancient glory."

The veneration entertained of antiquity, and the natural prejudices of mankind for things lost or absent, make us look upon them in a quite different light from those that are actually present. The beauty of a city does not solely consist in the number of its statues, and the enormous extent of its buildings, of which ancient Rome boasted. No city in Europe can shew any thing equal to St. Peter's church at Rome; and I question whether Nero's golden palace, or any other building in ancient Rome, could be compared with this structure.

If we consider the prodigious sums annually remitted to this city from all countries of the Romish religion, we shall be the less surprised that Rome was able to recover herself after so many severe devastations. A few centuries ago, the power of the pope was so considerable, that not only several kings paid him an annual tribute, but seditions, excommunications, and even deprivation of their dignity were the general consequences of his displeasure. St. Antoninus observes that the words of the royal prophet, Pf. viii. ver. 7, &c. " Thou hast put all things under " his feet, all sheep and oxen, also the wild beasts " of the field, the birds of the air, the fish of the " sea, and whatever it contains," have been literally accomplished in the pope: for, according to this commentator, under him were subjected the sheep, or Christians; the oxen, or Jews; the beasts of the field, or heathens; the fowls of the air, or good and bad angels; and, lastly, the fish in the sea, or the souls in purgatory. The orthodox cannot be offended with this interpretation, they being compared to that innocent creature the sheep; but heretics are little obliged to Urban Cerri, who, in his State of the Romish Church, stiles them unclean beasts, and highly commends pope Innocent XI. for his zeal in persecuting heretics; exhorting him to proceed, by applying, profanely, these words in the Acts of the Apostles, chap. x. ver. 13. " Rise, Peter, kill and eat," to the Roman pontiff.

The pope's revenues must be very considerable, if we only reckon what sums are annually sent to Rome from foreign countries, for dispensations, annates, palls, canonisations, and the like: and the great wealth of such families as have the good fortune to have one of their relations exalted to the papal chair, is a manifest proof that they are prodigious: for, notwithstanding the pope's profuse method of living,
they

they leave behind them confiderable fortunes, both in money and lands; as is well known to be the cafe, with regard to the Ottoboni, Altieri, Chigi, Pamfili, Barberini, Borghefe, Ludovis, and other papal families. It has, in particular, been computed that Urban VIII. defcended from the houfe of Barberini, left his family upward of twenty-four millions of Roman fcudi, about fix millions fterling, which he accumulated, partly from the confifcation of the eftates and effects of about three thoufand unhappy perfons put to death by the inquifition, and partly from other revenues *.

---

* Our readers will doubtlefs be gratified on this occafion by feeing the fees of the pope's chancery, from a book printed about 150 years ago, by the authority of the then pope; being a table or lift of the fees paid for abfolutions, difpenfations, licences, indulgences, faculties and exemptions. It was tranflated many years fince, under the title of, *Rome a great cuftom-houfe for fin*.

ABSOLUTIONS.

For a layman that ftole holy or confecrated things out of a holy place, 10 s. 6 d.

For the prieft that reftores not to the church the holy things he took away, 10 s. 6 d.

For him that reveals another man's confeffion, 10 s. 6 d.

For him who lies with a woman in the church, and there commits other enormities, 9 s.

For him that hath committed perjury, hath wilfully and falfely forfworn himfelf, 9 s.

For him that fecretly practifeth ufury, 10 s. 6 d.

For him that burieth an open and notorious ufurer in Chriftian burial, 12 s.

For a layman for the vice of fimony, 9 s.

For a prieft for the vice of fimony, 10 s. 6 d.

For a monk for the vice of fimony, 12 s.

For him that fimonically enters holy orders, 1 l. 6 s.

And his letters of abfolution from the fimony, 1 l. 4 s.

For a layman for murdering a layman, 7 s. 6 d.

For him that hath killed his father, 10 s. 6 d.

For him that hath killed his mother, 10 s. 6 d.

For him that hath killed his wife, 10 s. 6 d.

For him that hath killed his fifter, 10 s. 6 d.

For him that hath killed his kinfwoman, if they be of the laity, are rated at no more than 10 s. 6 d.

And his letters of abfolution will coft him 19 s. 6 d.

Pope Innocent XII. bears, in his family arms, three cups, which he ordered to be inverted, to shew that he intended not to gather, but pour out and distribute,

with

But if the party so slain be a clerk, a priest, or a clergyman, then the murderer is bound to go to Rome, and visit the apostolic see, 0 l. 0 s. 0 d.

For laying violent hands on a clergyman, or religious man, so it be without effusion of blood, 10 s. 6 d.

For the husband, or wife, who find in the morning, or when they awake, the infant lying by them, to be dead, 9 s.

For the husband who beats, or strikes his wife, being big with child, so as thereupon she comes before her time, and loseth her child, 9 s.

For a woman, who being with child, took medicinal drink, to destroy her birth, or doth any other act, whereby the child being alive in her womb is destroyed, is rated at 7 s. 6 d.

For a priest, or clergyman, that keeps a concubine; as also his dispensation, to save him from being irregular, (which by general and provincial constitutions he incurs) all this together is rated at 10 s. 6 d.

For a layman that keeps a concubine, 10 s. 6 d.

For him that hath defiled a virgin, 9 s.

For him that lyeth with his own mother, 7 s. 6 d.

For him that lyeth with his sister, 7 s. 6 d.

For him that lyeth with his godmother, 7 s. 6 d.

For him that lyeth with any woman that is of his blood, or carnal kindred, 7 s. 6 d.

For him that robs or spoils another, 12 s.

For him that burns his neighbour's house, &c. 12 s.

For him that forges letters testimonial, 10 s. 6 d.

For him that is a witness to such forged letters, 10 s. 6 d.

For him that forgeth any writs of the office of the penitentiary, 12 s.

For him that forgeth letters of privilege, 1 l. 4 s.

For him that forgeth the pope's hand, 1 l. 7 s.

For him that forgeth letters apostolical, 1 l. 7 s.

For him who in a criminal cause takes a false oath, 9 s.

For him that takes two holy orders in one day, 2 l. 6 s.

For him who celebrateth the service of any order he hath not taken, 2 l. 6 s.

For him that procures himself to be promoted to a feigned title, that is, to such or such a benefice, when indeed he hath none, if he confirm with a false oath, 2 l. 9 s. 6 d.

For him that is ordained without letters dimissory, from his own ordinary, 1 l. 8 s. 6 d.

For him that holds many benefices, 2 l. 17 s.

For

ROME.

with this motto, *aliis, non sibi*; but Pasquin put the comma after the word *non*, and by that means intirely changed the meaning, and, indeed, with a great deal of

---

For a king for going to the holy sepulchre without licence, 7 l. 10 s.

For a prince who vowed to visit the holy sacrament, 1 l. 10 s.

DISPENSATIONS.

For a bastard to enter all holy orders, and take a benefice with a cure, 18 s.

To have two benefices compatible, 16 s.
To have three benefices, 1 l. 6 s.
To marry in the 4th degree of consanguinity, 1 l. 5 s. 6 d.
To marry in the 3d degree of consanguinity, 2 l. 6 s.
To marry in the 2d degree of consanguinity, 2 l. 2 s. 6 d.
To marry in the 1st degree, 2 l. 14 s.
To marry her with whom one hath a special kindred, 4 l. 10 s.

For him who having one wife absent, and hearing her to be dead, marrieth another, but she proving to be alive, he notwithstanding desireth to keep and to live with the latter, 15 s.

And moreover there must be a composition with the datary, which will be sometimes 300, 400, 500, or 600 glosses, according to the quality of the persons so married; and the clerk or writer will have 10 s. 6 d.

For a man or woman that is found hang'd, that they may have Christian burial, 1 l. 7 s. 6 d.

For one that entered into his benefice by simony, that he may notwithstanding retain the same, 1 l. 10 s.

For one under age to enter holy orders, and to be made a priest, 2 l. 9 s. 6 d.

For one under age to be ordained a bishop, 2 l. 9 s. 6 d.
To be ordained at any time of the year, 4 l. 1 s.

LICENCES.

For a man to change his vow, 15 s.

For a layman to change his vow of going to Rome, to visit the apostolic churches, 18 s.

To eat flesh and white-meats in Lent, and other fasting days, 10 s. 6 d.

That a king or queen shall enjoy such indulgences, as if they went to Rome, 15 l.

For a queen to adopt a child, 300 l.

That a king, or a prince, may exact contributions of the clergy, 3 l. 15 s.

If the contribution arise to a hundred thousand florins, then for the first thousand he must have 7 s. 6 d.

And

of truth. The court of Rome can considerably increase its revenues, being able to dispose of consecrated reliques, palls, *Agni Dei,* rosaries, indulgences, *Quietus's,*

And for every other florin, 1 s. 6 d.

That a king upon Christmas-day morning, may cause a naked sword to be carried before him, as is carried before his holiness the pope. 11 l. 5 s.

That he that preaches before a king, may give indulgence to all that hear him, 18 s.

That a nobleman may go into a monastery, with a certain number of followers, 18 s.

To receive the sacrament, or be buried in a church interdicted, 2 l. 5 s.

To found an hospital, 1 l. 4 s.

To found a chapel, 1 l. 4 s.

To erect a church parochial, 1 l. 10 s.

To erect a church collegiate, 3 l.

To erect a cathedral church, 3 l. 15 s.

To found a deanry in the same, 1 l. 10 s.

For the prebendary, 1 l. 4 s.

To erect an university, 11 l. 5 s.

To translate it from one place to another, 4 l. 10 s.

To make a city of a town, and therein erect a bishop's see, 75 l.

That a town may have a school kept in the parish church, 2 l. 5 s.

For a city to coin money, 37 l. 10 s.

That a town which hath used green wax in its seal, may use red, 3 l. 15 s.

For a layman to choose his confessor, 15 s.

To marry in times prohibited, 2 l. 5 s.

To eat flesh in times prohibited, 1 l. 4 s.

Not to be tied to fasting days, 1 l. 4 s.

To have a portable altar, 15 s.

To have mass in a place interdicted, 15 s.

To go into a nunnery alone, 18 s.

To divide a dead body into two, that it may be buried in two places, 18 s.

That during the interdict of a town, the officers may have mass and service in a chapel, 3 l. 15 s.

For a town to take out of the church them that have taken sanctuary therein, 4 l. 10 s.

For a priest to say mass in any place, 6 d.

For a bishop to visit, 3 l.

For a bishop to take to himself a year's profit of every vacant benefice for three years, 3 l. 15 s.

To exercise episcopal jurisdiction out of his diocese, 3 l.

To exact a subsidy, or benevolence of his clergy, 1 l. 10 s.

INDUL-

ROME.

Quietus's, and bones out of the catacombs at a cheap rate.

The apostolic chamber manages the lands and revenues belonging to the pope: and in this office the employments are so profitable, that the principal are sold for eighty or a hundred thousand dollars (about 22,500 l. sterling.) The granting and collating of ecclesiastical benefices, dispensations, and the like, are performed in the datary, so called from the usual subscription, *Datum Romæ apud sanctum Petrum*, &c. when the pope resides in the Vatican; and *apud sanctum Mariam majorem*, when in the Quirinal palace. Every instrument, dispatched in the datary, is carried into the secretary's office, the datary being only a kind of department of

INDULGENCES.

For an hospital, or chapel, to last one year, 1 l. 4 s.
For two years, 1 l. 10 s.
For three years, 1 l. 16 s.
For four years, 2 l. 5 s.
For five years, 3 l.
For six years, 3 l. 15 s.
For the remission of the third part of one's sins, 7 l. 10 s.

FACULTIES.

To absolve all delinquents, 3 l.
To dispense with irregularities, 3 l.

EXEMPTIONS.

Of fryars minors from the jurisdiction of their provincials, 2 l. 5 s.
From the jurisdiction of a bishop, during his time, 3 l. 15 s.
And if the abbot will have withal a licence to wear a mitre, it will cost him (by the rate-book of pope John XXII.) 7 l. 10 s.
For a bishop from the jurisdiction of his metropolitan, during his life, 3 l. 15 s.
Of a parochial church from the bishop's jurisdiction, 1 l. 10 s.
Of the parson of a parish from the power of his ordinary, during a suit, 1 l. 10 s.
Of a town from any imposition, 4 l. 10 s.
Of a private person from the same, 2 l. 5 s.
Of a monastery, and convent, from the same, as it is found in the rate-book of pope John XXII. It is taxed at 22 l. 2 s.

Cætera desunt.

N. B. This is only the pope's share.

it. The rota is considered as a parliament, or a court of ultimate appeal. The consistory is the highest assembly where the cardinals have a seat and vote: there is free access into this assembly on particular occasions.

The pope's forces, either by sea or land, make but a poor figure; and you see no soldiers, except in the castle of St. Angelo, in Civita Vecchia, Urbino, Ferrara, and some other small garrisons on the frontiers. The pope's Swiss guards make a handsome appearance, yet serve only for keeping off the crowd at public solemnities. I must needs say, that foreigners find them here civil on all occasions, especially when one speaks to them in German, and calls them landsmen or countrymen: whereas, on the contrary, the same good character cannot be always given to the Swiss at Versailles. And I remember, that a certain Austrian nobleman, of the first rank, being pressed by the crowd, in return to his polite compliment of landsman, received this rude and brutal answer: "To-day, indeed, every bear-leader will call me countryman."

To prevent all disorders in the city of Rome, they have three hundred Sbirri or halberdiers, whose commander is called Barigello. He is distinguished from the others by a gold chain, with a medal of the same metal hanging to it. When he is desirous of being known, he wears the chain about his neck. His employment was formerly in good esteem, but, at present, it is fallen into great contempt.

The figure which the cardinals make is not at all correspondent to that of persons who claim an equal rank with crowned heads. The title of cardinal is pretty ancient, but not in the sense in which it is taken at present. In former times the whole body of the clergy and people of Rome chose their bishops, who was confirmed by the emperor, and sometimes deprived by him for seditious practices. The great reputation in which cardinals were held began under

pope

pope Nicholas II. They had the red hat given them by Innocent IV. in the year 1243, at the council of Lyons. Paul II. conferred the red habit upon them; and for the title of *eminentiſſimus* they are indebted to pope Urban VIII. having, formerly, no other ſtile than *illuſtriſſimi*, like other biſhops and prelates: that they formerly wore woollen and linen caps, appears from Petri Diaconi Chronic. Caſſinenſ. lib. iv. c. ii. p. 428. The red hat is ſaid to be an emblem of their readineſs to ſhed their blood in the cauſe of religion; but we find few cardinals in the liſt of martyrs. It is certain that this whole ſcarlet habit is very becoming; and the dead cardinals are painted red, the better to ſet off their cadaverous countenances. Cardinal Pamfili was buried on the 24th of March, after his body had lain ſome time in ſtate, in St. Agnes's church, *à la Piazza Navona*, and his face painted of a beautiful red colour with vermilion.

In the promoting foreign prelates to the cardinalſhip, the pope regulates himſelf according to the nomination of crowned heads, who profeſs the Roman catholic religion: and this privilege the king of Sardinia obtained by a refined piece of policy, recommending to pope Benedict XIII. Ferreri, a brother of the marquis d'Ormea, whom the pope himſelf would gladly have ſeen inveſted with the purple. I could alſo name a cardinal who owed his promotion to a defender of the proteſtant faith, namely, George I. king of Great Britain, who procured him the nomination of the king of Poland; but the peculiar connections of this affair are beſt known to the preſent biſhop of Namur, formerly the abbé Strickland.

The conclave is the ſcene where the cardinals principally endeavour to diſplay their parts, and where many tranſactions paſs which hardly ſhew their inſpiration from the Holy Ghoſt. It is well known, that, during the election of a pope in 1721, the animoſities ran ſo high, that they came to blows with both their hands and feet, and threw the ſtandiſhes at each other.

other. Davia, Albani, Pamfili, and Althan, moſt diſtinguiſhed themſelves in theſe quarrels; and, therefore, it is not at all ſurpriſing, that among the officers belonging to the conclave, they have one or two ſurgeons. At each election, the emperor, and the kings of France and Spain, have a right of excepting againſt any perſon propoſed for the papal dignity; but this muſt be done before the full number of voices requiſite for that purpoſe is actually declared. While an election may be prevented by cabals or intrigue, recourſe is ſeldom had to an excluſion.

During the whole time of the conclave's ſitting, Rome is filled with paſquinades, and every day copies of them are ſold ſecretly, in the coffee-houſes, to foreigners; but they are generally wretched performances.

It is ſurpriſing that ſome means have not been diſcovered for limiting the duration of a conclave, as ſuch cloſe confinement to perſons, who uſually live in commodious palaces, muſt, eſpecially in hot weather, be extreamly inconvenient. In England, juries are locked up in criminal caſes, without meat, drink, or candle, till they have agreed on a verdict. How far this might be imitated, with regard to conclaves, I ſhall leave others to determine. It would, at leaſt, prevent a great deal of caballing, and render unneceſſary many privileges granted to the conclaviſts, who are two attendants on each cardinal; a ſet of perſons who muſt be all pleaſed, becauſe they are acquainted with the moſt ſecret intrigues. Their favour is of great importance, it being evident from the hiſtory of papal elections, that they have often gained for their maſters the papal throne.

It is ſcarcely to be imagined with what diſpatch each cardinal partitions and contrives, according to his own fancy, the ſmall part allotted him in the conclave for his cell. The whole apartment is not above eighteen or twenty feet ſquare, which is laid out into a dining-room, a bed-chamber, and lobby, for ſervants

vants and conclavists: some make two stories of it, but then the stair-case is very narrow. The cells have no other partition than cloth-hangings; so that, when a large room is divided into many cells, whatever is spoken aloud in any of them, may be heard in all the rest. Hence appears the scandalous falsity which the author of a treatise, intitled *La Guerre d'Italie, ou Memoires du Comte D——*, is guilty of, in saying, that the young cardinals in the conclave divert themselves with their mistresses, give little concerts, singing and dancing themselves, like wanton boys.

I have already observed that no cardinal has the liberty of chusing his cell, but must content himself with that assigned him by lot. But when any cardinal refuses to attend the election, his cell remains unoccupied. The cardinals created by the late pope, and his other dependants, have the hangings and furniture of their cells of a dark-violet colour; but others have green. The former, likewise, are dressed in purple, during the time of the conclave. The chapel of Sixtus IV. is fitted up for the scrutiny and adoration, and in it is a stove for burning the suffrages or voting billets.

Each conclave costs the papal treasury about two hundred thousand scudi; nor have foreign princes any reason to desire frequent conclaves; particularly the emperor, who always sends an ambassador extraordinary, and also defrays the charges of the German cardinals, who on this occasion retire to Rome: so that each of the two last conclaves is said to have cost him upward of two thousand Rhenish guilders. During the conclave, many disorders and violences are daily committed, especially in the country; where foreigners, who have no connection with the candidates, and consequently should have nothing to fear, would act very imprudently, not to retire to their lodgings before it is dark. Twenty or thirty murders are generally committed in the streets of Rome, during the sitting of the conclave.

Before

Before I conclude my description of the papal court, I must observe, that proteſtants are not admitted to an audience, if they refuſe to kiſs the pope's foot. Clement I. was, however, leſs ſcrupulous in this particular, and, when ſuch proteſtants withdrew, would give them his bleſſing, adding, *Ad minimum non nocebit*, " It will, at leaſt, do no harm." No perſon is admitted to the pope with a ſword or cane; nor muſt any preſume to wear gloves in his preſence; for, when the Swiſs guards, who walk before the pope, obſerve foreigners with their gloves on, they immediately order them to pull them off.

On Maundy Thurſday, ſeveral religious fraternities, and a numerous proceſſion of others, among whom ten or twelve were maſked, came to St. Peter's church and ſcourged their naked backs with thongs tagged with iron. It was eaſy, from the quantity of blood on the pavement, to diſtinguiſh the place where they ſtood. Whether theſe were voluntary ſelf-tormentors, or whether this flogging penance had been enjoined them for ſome enormous crimes, I ſhall not pretend to determine: but, be that as it may, a lighted torch was carried behind them, and often applied to their backs, to ſtop the great effuſion of blood. Benedict XIII. forbid ſuch proceſſions, as not proper to be allowed among Chriſtians; but, as no pope was then elected, every perſon followed his own opinion. How the fantaſtical prieſts of Bellona, Iſis, and the Dea Syriæ diſciplined themſelves, is ſufficiently deſcribed in ancient hiſtory.

From the Tribuna, over the ſtatue of St. Veronica, near the altar Maggiore, is ſhewn a piece of Chriſt's croſs; part of the iron of the ſpear with which he was pierced, and, laſtly, an impreſſion of our Saviour's bloody face on a linen cloth. The name of St. Veronica is, in all probability, derived from the fable of the *vera Icon*, or true image of Chriſt; and Mabillon *(in Præf. Muſæi Ital.)* conjectures, that this ſpurious ſaint acquired the name from a painted face of Chrift, and the Greek words φέρω, I bear, and εἰκὼν, an image.

On Good Friday, fome of our company, following a great concourfe of people, came to a fubterraneous chapel belonging to the jefuits, which, as foon as they had entered, was immediately locked. The fathers diftributed to each a knotted fcourge, while another of the fraternity, at the altar, made a long harangue on our Saviour's fufferings, and concluded with faying, " that the leaft we could do was, by his example, to chaftife our flefh and blood." He then exhorted his audience that, in performing this holy duty, " they would not fpare the old Adam." The lights were now put out, and the Litany fung, during which time the audience continued fcourging and whipping themfelves. The exhortation and fcourgings were three times repeated. I fuppofe the intention of putting out the lights was, that fome might not fcourge themfelves too feverely, and the modefty of others who ftripped themfelves, might not be expofed by their ftripes. The proteftants who entered with the crowd, were not difpleafed with the darknefs, as they were not inclined to lacerate their bodies for the benefit of their fouls; and, at the fame time, did not think it advifable to make themfelves known. The difcipline being ended, the fcourges were returned, and the doors thrown open.

On the fame day was expofed, in the Greek church, a wooden model of Chrift's fepulchre; the bifhop affifted the reft of the clergy in finging the antiphone, with a round tiara on his head.

Turks and Jews are ufually baptifed on Eafter-Eve in the Lateran church, and great numbers of ecclefiaftics are at the fame time admitted into holy orders.

Thofe who are defirous of feeing Rome, would do well not to poftpone it till after the middle of Lent, becaufe, from that time till Eafter, moft of the fine altar-pieces are covered.

Vol. V.   C   The

The city of Rome has suffered so much from the ancient Gauls, Vandals, Heruli, Ostrogoths, Visigoths, and German troops; especially from the latter in the year 1527, headed by Charles of Bourbon, that it is said to have been sacked or pillaged seven times: this, however, is certain, that the surface of the ground on which Rome was originally founded, is surprisingly altered by their frequent ravages. It is difficult, at present, to distinguish the seven hills, on which Rome was anciently built, the low grounds having been filled up by the ruins of whole streets; so that we sometimes ascend an eminence celebrated by the ancients without perceiving it. Antiquity informs us, that the ascent from the street to the Pantheon or Rotundo consisted of thirteen steps; whereas now the whole area about it is upon a level with the pavement of the temple. The basis and inscription of Trajan's pillar is lower than the adjacent ground, so that it will be requisite, for preserving that part of the pillar, to support the ditch made round it with a wall. It is common in digging deep for the foundation of houses, &c. to discover pillars, statues, and fragments of ancient buildings; and, in some places, they have even found the pavement of the old city, twenty or thirty feet below the present surface of the ground. And this alteration of the surface has, likewise, in all probability, affected the salubrity of the air.

The stupendous common-sewers by which the filth and dirt of the ancient city was conveyed in the Cloaca maxima, have, indeed, still many passages for conveying away the soil and water; but the greatest part of these are stopped, and the Cloaca maxima itself is in bad order. This must needs cause a putrefaction in the air, which is too sensibly perceived by those, who, by digging deep into the earth, happen to discover an aperture of such an obstructed sink; there being several instances of workmen who have left

their

their lives from the putrid effluvia, notwithstanding all their care and caution. The same alterations are visible in other parts of the country, especially those near the sea; several fine cities and palaces being anciently erected there, and frequented, as the most healthy spots in time of pestilence; which are now quite the reverse, part of the sea-coast being a wet marshy soil, and the air so bad, that during the summer season, several of the convents are forsaken, the monks removing to some more healthful situation. The land, even in the neighbourhood of Rome, is but badly cultivated, and, in the night-time, covered with fogs and igneous vapours. These must have been uncommon in the time of the ancient Romans; for Livy often mentions such phænomena as prodigies, or omens: and, in the Roman mythology, they occasioned propitiatory sacrifices and offerings. Mineral sulphur is often dug near Rome, in the form of white earth, and afterward purified by sublimation. Vitriol is found here in abundance, and that found in the copper mines, is called Roman vitriol. There are alum works in the neighbourhood of Rome; arsenic, also, abounds here. From these works and mines rise many noxious effluvia, which never affected ancient Rome, these minerals being then unknown, or suffered to remain in the bowels of the earth.

Perhaps, a concurrence of all these circumstances have contributed to alter the temperature of the seasons, particularly with regard to the mildness of the winters, for some time observed in this climate. Some passages in Horace intimate, that during the winter in his time, the streets of Rome were filled with snow and ice: and it appears from the sixth satire of Juvenal, that it was not uncommon to see the Tiber frozen over: whereas, at present, the winter must be remarkably cold for snow to lie a day in the city; and, with regard to the Tiber, no person can remember its being frozen.

The alterations in the adjacent countries have also proved prejudicial to the Tiber; its mouth or efflux into the sea is almost choaked up with mud and sand; and its bed very much contracted by filth and rubbish from the houses situated on its banks: so that a strong south-wind is often the cause of its overflowing its banks, and causing great inundations in Rome, and the adjacent country. The papal chamber has, indeed, employed one Cornelius Mayer, a Dutchman, to erect proper works for confining the river to its channel, and to clear it in some places; but this cannot be compleated at once. Some are of opinion, that if the course of the river could be turned into another channel, many curious pieces of antiquity, as well as immense riches, thrown into it during the misfortunes of Rome, would be found. The water is generally so foul, that it is not even fit for horses to drink, till it has stood two or three days to settle.

The inhabitants of Rome are very cautious of their health, especially during the heat of the dog-days. And it is affirmed, that no inhabitant of Rome can, without manifest danger, sleep within fifteen or twenty Italian miles of the city: so that, in travelling to Rome, they take care, in the last day's journey, not to put up within that distance. Even in the city, they seldom change bed-chambers for another in the same house. To remove from one house to another, betwixt St. Peter's and All Saints-Day, is supposed to be attended with so much danger at Rome, that no tenant or lodger can be obliged to leave a house within that term.

The south-east winds, blowing over the Pontini fens, would still be more pernicious to the city, if it were not defended by the woods on the mountains of Albano and Tusculum. It is, however, evident, that the inhabitants of Rome make too much ado about the unwholsomeness of their climate, and the dangers attending the heats of the summer. Strangers,

gers, who never take half the precautions, enjoy as good a state of health as the natives. How many cardinals come to Rome in the midst of summer from distant countries when a conclave is to be held, without so many timorous fears, and return as well as they came, without suffering for their negligence? And surely no one will pretend that heat has any respect of persons. This chimerical danger seems to have been unknown in the time of Cicero, from whose epistles it appears, that he frequently resided at Rome in the summer months, and took many journies to and from that city.

It cannot, indeed, be denied, but that, after the north wind has continued a long time, and suddenly shifts to the south, or a strong south wind arises with cloudy fogs, health is precarious at Rome; but this evil is not peculiar to that city, all Italy is equally obnoxious to it. From the vernal to the autumnal equinox, Rome generally enjoys a clear serene air; the soil is good, the mountains pleasant, and the thin air from the hills corrects the thicker vapours rising in the vallies or lower ground. Few cities can equal Rome for large fountains, which, by continually throwing up water, give a freshness to the air; and, the inundations of the Tiber being now provided against, the inhabitants are in a fair way of being eased of their apprehensions, with regard to the summer heats; especially as Leo X. and Urban VIII. ordered several of the sewers or Cloacæ to be repaired, and made other regulations, for rendering the city and its neighbourhood more clean and salutary. The quarters about the Quirinal and Trinita del Monte are the most healthy parts of Rome; for which reason, foreigners generally chuse to lodge, especially in the latter, as the coffee houses and taverns are chiefly situated near the Piazza di Spagna.

That Rome, of itself, is not unhealthy, may be gathered from the great age, to which not a few of its inhabitants arrive; and even some judgment may be be formed of this from several cardinals, who have reached their eightieth year. Some affirm, that one third of that reverend body have reached that term, and without feeling any of the infirmities commonly attendant on that feeble stage; whence it may also be concluded, that the ancient Romans did not live so abstemious as the modern, few such instances being recorded in the ancient historians. Add to this, that the manner of living at Rome is at present much more agreeable than it was in former ages, hardly a day passing, but one may have an opportunity of visiting polite assemblies of persons of distinction of both sexes. But unmarried ladies have not here the same liberty of appearing in public, as in other countries; for, throughout all Italy, they are confined in nunneries till they are either old or married.

The carnival diversions at Rome are much more elegant, except to those who delight intirely in debauchery, than those at Venice, where people stroll about in mean masquerade habits, in company with infamous courtesans; whereas, at Rome, none but women of character dare appear on the Corso, without being exposed to the danger of a very severe treatment, in case of a discovery. These diversions last only the eight last days before the beginning of Lent, and then but from two till six in the afternoon; hence the people of Rome say, that their carnival lasts no more than twenty-four hours. The place of meeting is the Corso, a fine street running in a straight line, from the Porta del Popolo, eleven hundred geometrical, or about two thousand seven hundred and twenty common paces. Every person is at liberty to appear with or without a mask, on foot or in a coach, according to his own inclination. The coaches follow each other in two rows. The principal nobility of Rome are carried in splendid triumphal chariots, which give a grand appearance to their diversions. Sbirri are posted in different parts to prevent any disturbance, and their barigello, or captain, rides up
and

and down uncovered, without putting on his hat, till toward evening, when he has obtained an order for the horse-races, a sport no where to be seen but in Italy and England.

The nobility here, like the English, value themselves upon keeping horses of uncommon swiftness. In Italy, most of their race-horses are from Barbary; but the English are of their own breed, having no occasion for those of foreign countries. But there is still a greater difference in these diversions of the two nations; in England they take particular care that the riders are exactly of the same weight; whereas, in Italy, the horses run alone, being trained up for this purpose. On their sides and backs are leathern straps, fastened on with pitch, and under these iron balls set with strong sharp points, like the rowel of a spur, which continually prick the horses, while they continue in motion; they also fasten another spiked ball, of the same kind, under the horse's tail. Between five and eight horses stand in a row on the Piazza del Popolo, waiting, with great impatience, for the signal, which is commonly given by dropping a rope stretched across the course; immediately, upon this, they set off, and fly like an arrow from a bow along the Corso, through an incredible number of spectators, the coaches forming a lane on each side of the street. The prize, which is generally a piece of brocade, of about seventy or eighty scudi in value, is commonly given to the grooms. The people are entertained with such races every day during the carnival.

The summers are very tedious at Rome, every one keeping close within doors all day, and taking a nap at noon. Whence it is a common saying among the Romans, " That none then walk the streets but " dogs, fools, or Frenchmen." The people here, from the warmth of the climate, are excessively fond of cool clear spring-water and iced liquors; for which purpose, the quantities of snow gathered from the mountains, and preserved in their ice-houses, are of

great

great service. In Rome they use several sorts of water for drink; but it is only in some convents that river-water is used. Rain-water is saved in cisterns, and, though troublesome to keep clean, yet is looked upon as very wholsome: beside this, they have well-water; also, water is conveyed into the city, at a great expence, from distant parts, by means of aqueducts. As I never saw any city so badly provided, in proportion to its extent, with good water to drink as Paris; so, on the contrary, I believe that no city surpasses Rome for multiplicity of clear and plentiful fountains.

Several among the ancient Romans distinguished themselves by magnificent aqueducts. The three principal aqueducts, at present in being, are those of Aqua Virginea or Trevi, Aqua Felice, and Paulina. The first was repaired by pope Paul IV. The second comes from the neighbourhood of Palastrina, twenty-two miles distant, and is a work which does honour to the illustrious reign of pope Sixtus V. who expended a million of scudi upon it; and called it *Il Condotto dell' Aqua Felice*, from Felix, the name he assumed while a monk, before he had ascended the papal throne. It discharges itself in Rome at the Fontana di Termine, which stately work Sixtus V. also built under the direction of the cavaliere Domenico Fontana. It consists of three arches, supported by four pillars of the Corinthian order, and discharges the water through three large apertures. Over the middle arch is a fine statue of Moses striking the rock with his rod; in a basso-relievo on a second compartment, Aaron is represented leading the people to the miraculous springs that gushed out in the wilderness; and, in the third, Gideon trying his men by their drinking the water. Below stand four lions, two of which, in white marble, were done by Flaminius Vacca; but the other two, of Oriental granate, were brought hither from an ancient temple of Serapis. All the four lions eject water in continual streams.

The Aqua Paulina, which owes its name to its reſtorer, pope Paul V. divides itſelf into two capital channels, one of which ſupplies mount Janiculus, and the other the Vatican and the neighbouring parts. It is brought hither from the diſtance of thirty miles, and principally diſcharges itſelf through the fountain behind the church of St. Pietro Montorio, ſtanding on the ſummit of mount Janiculus, anciently called Aurelius, at preſent Montorio. Its ſtately portal was the joint gift of Fontana and Maderno. Among its five ſtreams three of them are ſo plentiful as to look like rivulets, and have a ſufficiency of water to turn three mills.

In 1690 pope Alexander VIII. added new decorations to this fountain, and the area round it; and is worth viſiting, were it only for the fine proſpect it affords over the whole city. From theſe large reſervoirs of water ſeveral other ſmaller ones are ſupplied, of which a particular deſcription would be tedious. Beſide the public fountains, there is ſcarcely any houſe or garden of note without private ſprings and water-works for amuſement.

In autumn, the time of their vintage, the commonalty abandon themſelves to a licentious jollity, the fruits of which generally appear the May or June following; it being obſerved, that more children are brought to the hoſpitals, during theſe two months, than in all the other ten months of the year.

The winter diverſions at Rome are plays and operas; the latter, during the carnival, are performed on three theatres, the Aliberti, Capranica, and Al Theatro Nuovo. The firſt, which has its name from its founder count Aliberti, has a pit large enough to contain nine hundred ſpectators. This is ſurrounded by ſeven galleries one above another, in each of which are thirty five boxes, in all two hundred and forty-five. I cannot recollect ever to have ſeen a theatre capable of holding ſo numerous an audience.

A tra-

A traveller, both in Rome and all other foreign countries, ought to be on his guard, and rather to speak too little than too much. At Rome there are a certain set of fellows, who inform the government of every thing done or said in the city. This they do with unblemished character and an easy conscience, the calling of an informer or spy not being without a patron or saint, namely, St. Alexis. They do not, however, seem to be very careful in observing the behaviour of strangers, because they spend large sums of money annually in the country. At the meeting of the host, and other processions, the protestants need not fear any of those brutal insults, which, in other countries, they sometimes meet with from the bigotted persecuting spirit of the vulgar. If an Italian sees a stranger not complying with the prescribed genuflections, he only considers him as an infidel or heretic. Even in the *Missa Spiritus Sancti*, and the presence of many cardinals, several protestants remain standing at the elevation of the host, without the least insult from the catholic Swiss guards in waiting, as is usually practised at the chapel royal at Versailles. During Lent, or other fast-days, the protestants never fail of meeting with butchers meat at most taverns or houses of public entertainment, without the trouble of procuring a licence for eating it.

The Roman catholics themselves cannot, indeed, be said to be here very strict observers of their fasts, and on Saturday use this expedient to eat meat for their supper; they wait till the clock strikes twelve, and then consider it as a Sunday morning's breakfast, which doth not come under the church's prohibition.

I have often been surprised to hear some Roman catholics, at public ordinaries, launch out with such freedom against the jesuits and the pope's usurpations, in civil matters, over the rights of several potentates, especially the emperor and princes of the empire. A certain papist once declared, that he never passed by the palace of the Crescenti family without putting off
his

his hat, as a token of veneration for that glorious man, who dared to drive a turbulent pope out of Rome, though his magnanimity met but with indifferent returns. I do not care to repeat the name he was pleased to bestow on the emperor of Germany, for suffering the pope to grow so powerful at Rome.

During the conclave, a multitude of manuscript pasquinades against the deceased pope and cardinals were sold at coffee-houses, for half a paola a sheet. These satirical pieces took their name from an old mutilated statue, near which was formerly the shop of one Pasquin, a bantering inquisitive taylor or shoemaker. At present the proclamations are stuck up on this statue, on which is also an inscription, with a mark above eight feet from the surface of the ground, shewing the height of the water, during an inundation of the Tiber, in the time of pope Clement VI.

With regard to the public stews, I question the truth of some accounts, concerning the revenues accruing to the pope's treasure from the milk-tax, as it is called. They who make the number of these prostitutes amount to twenty thousand, do not consider, that all the females in Rome, young and old, scarce amount to fifty thousand. Those wretched creatures who give in their names, age, country, and family to the barigello of the sbirri, in order to be entered in a book for that purpose, are, in general, such despicable objects, that, at Naples, and other places, their practice would not defray the small tax to which they are subject. Perhaps the small sum produced by this tax never goes farther than the hands of the sbirri, part of whose province it is, to take care that none of the monks and priests enter these forbidden places; and that, in Easter week, during Advent and Lent, and other fasts and festivals of the church, these prostitutes receive no company. I have been assured, from good hands, that their number does not exceed eight hundred. In the time of pagan Rome they lived together, and the places of their evening
rendezvous

rendezvous were called, by Tertullian, *Consistoria Libidinum Publicarum*, "The statutes for the public "prostitutes;" which expression agrees with the *Institoria Matronarum*, mentioned in Suetonius's Life of Nero, chap. xxvii. Over their stews or fornices, from which the word fornication is derived, was written the name of the courtezan, and her price. Among the ancients it was not permitted, or, at least, not usual, for those prostitutes to make their public appearance before evening, or the ninth hour of the day; and this appears to be the reason why Persius gives the name of Nonaria to one of that sisterhood. Their dwellings were known by a lamp or candle burning at their door. And, at present, it is customary at Rome to keep a lamp burning in the street before the door of one of these registered prostitutes, which is taken away while she entertains a visitor. In Spain it is known by a sword, which the gallant always leaves at the door.

Rome is not more profligate in this respect than other populous cities; for here are several excellent institutions, made intirely with a view of reclaiming prostitutes from their unhappy state of life: they live together in one quarter of the city, and are debarred from the communion, while they publicly continue in that profession, and should they happen to die in it, they are denied Christian burial. In some parts of Italy, they are obliged, at certain times of the year, to repair to a particular church, and hear a sermon, in which, by a lively representation of their vicious lives, they are exhorted to forsake them; and such as are prevailed upon, by the preacher's argument, and in token of their remorse, kiss a crucifix handed about, are immediately taken into a convent for that purpose. This is generally done on Holy Thursday; but most of these poor wretches are so hardened as to persist in their prostitution, till, by the approach of old age, and utter decay of their usual trade, they are warned to look out for some other way of subsistence. This
also

also brings to mind an order of pope Gregory XIII. which enjoins, that the Jews at Rome shall, every Saturday evening, during Lent, send a hundred men and fifty women of their community to the oratory della S S. Trinita, not far from the Ghetto or particular quarter assigned them for their residence, in order to hear a discourse on the Christian religion. The number of Jews in Rome amounts to nine thousand, and, by an order of pope Paul IV. the men are obliged to wear a piece of red cloth in their hats, and the women the same, in their head-dresses, to distinguish them from Christians. Formerly, the Jews might reside where they pleased in Rome; but the last mentioned pope, who was no friend to that people, confined them to a very narrow quarter, not far from the Tiber, where they generally live in a very miserable and slovenly manner.

All sorts of provisions are much cheaper and better at Rome than in many other parts of Italy; however, wine is not included in the rate you pay for your board, but every one provides his own at a pretty reasonable price. Esculent and all other kinds of vegetables are to be had at Rome all the year. The fruits are excellent, particularly the Perugean melons, which surpass all others. Such as are desirous of early fruit send for it to Naples, from whence they bring those forced cherries which make a part of the entertainment usually given by the pope to the cardinals on Holy Thursday. Though the Neapolitan fruits are soonest ripe, yet those of Rome are allowed to have the finest flavour.

A stranger cannot well be without some carriage in Rome, and during the carnival, they charge upward of fourteen paoli a day for it; but, in summer, they may be had under nine. Few chairs or sedans are to be met with, and none for a single person. There is also another inconveniency, they have no lamps to light the streets in the night-time; and, as I am finding fault with Rome, I must add, that the manner of drying their linen seems very disagreeable to me; for this is not only done out of their windows, but upon lines extended from one side of the street to the other; and what a mean appearance this has in a city, otherwise so splendid, any one may easily judge.

Lastly, with regard to the figure which the pretender to the English crown makes at Rome, I must say, that it is mean in every respect. The court of Rome, indeed, has issued an order, that all their subjects should stile him king of England; but this is no more than an empty title, which even many of the Italians make a jest of. For, when they speak to strangers whom they take to be none of his friends, they sometimes, with a mixture of civility and satire, call him, *Il rè di qui*, "The king here," meaning Rome; but, when they speak of the rightful possessor, they stile him *Il rè di qua*, "The king there upon the spot," meaning England.

The chevalier de St. George, the title by which he is generally known, has an annual pension, from the pope's treasury, of twelve thousand scudi, or 3000 l. and, though the private donations, annually remitted to him by his adherents in Great Britain, may probably amount to as much more, yet all this falls far short of supporting the dignity of a person, who would appear like a king, and expects to be treated as such.

The pretender is remarkably fond of seeing his image upon medals: and no doubt, were kingdoms to be gained by tears (which he shed very plentifully in 1708, after the miscarriage of his attempt in Scotland) he would have found work enough for his medallists. Not to take any notice of the medal lately struck for him, I shall give you that which is at present in hand, as it will shew that his life affords but very few illustrious actions; since, to find a subject for another medal, they are obliged to go a great many years back to the birth of his eldest son. On one fide is reprefented the buft of the pretender and his confort, with this legend:

Jacob. III. *R. Clementina R.*

On the reverfe appears a lady holding a child in her left arm, leaning on a pillar, the emblem of conftancy, and pointing with her right hand to a globe, on which are drawn England, Scotland, and Ireland; the legend is:

Providentia Obftetrix.

And underneath:

Carolo Princ. Valliæ.
Nat. Die ultima.
A. M.DCC.XX.

The chevalier generally comes abroad with three coaches, and his whole court confifts of about forty perfons. He lately affumed fome authority at the opera, by calling *encore* to a fong that pleafed him and fome others. After a confiderable paufe, this order was at laft complied with. This is the only time he is known to have affected the leaft power; and a compliance of this fort is no more than what the claps of half a dozen of the fpectators may at any time procure. Upon his coming into any affembly, no Englifh proteftant ftands up, and even Roman catholics pay him their compliments very fuperficially. His pufillanimity and licentious amours certainly leffen him in the efteem of every perfon.

M. S———, who pretends to be an antiquarian, and has the title of a Polifh counfellor of ftate, narrowly obferves every ftep taken by the pretender and his adherents, and maintains a clofe correfpondence with the Britifh miniftry. While the pretender continued at Bologna, he had hardly any news to fend, and being himfelf no longer neceffary, his remittances were likely to be withdrawn; but the pretender's return gave him an opportunity of continuing his fervices. The principal motives which induced the pretender to return to Rome were intereft and neceffity; which gave rife to an obfervation, that no ftricter friendfhip could

could exist than that between the pretender and Mr. S——, neither of them being able to live without the other. The King of Great Britain is dreaded at Rome, notwithstanding the great distance of the two kingdoms, on account of his powerful fleets.

The pope, when considered as a temporal prince, has great influence on the affairs of Italy; and as those of Europe are often connected with them, he is sometimes under a necessity of treating with the British court: but, as this cannot be done in his own person, a third hand is employed to carry on the negociations. This was formerly done by the cardinal for the imperial affairs at Rome; but, since the misunderstanding betwixt the courts of London and Vienna, by the cardinal protector of France.

[Dr. Smollet gives a more familiar and less favourable representation of Rome, both ancient and modern, than we are usually led to conceive of it. He observes—'Strangers that come to Rome seldom put up at public inns, but go directly to lodging-houses, of which there is great plenty in this quarter. The Piazza d'Espagna is open, airy, and pleasantly situated in a high part of the city, immediately under the Colla Pinciana, and adorned with two fine fountains. Here most of the English reside: the apartments are generally commodious and well furnished; and the lodgers are well supplied with provisions and all necessaries of life. But if I studied œconomy, I would chuse another part of the town than the Piazza d'Espagna, which is, beside, at a great distance from the antiquities. For a decent first floor and two bed chambers on the second, I paid a scudo (five shillings) per day. Our table was plentifully furnished by the landlord for two and thirty pauls, being equal to sixteen shillings. I hired a town coach at the rate of fourteen pauls, or seven shillings a day; and a servitore di piazza for three pauls, or eighteen-pence. The coachman has also an allowance of two pauls a day. The provisions at Rome are reasonable and

and good, especially the vitella mongana, which is the most delicate veal I ever tasted, but very dear, being sold for two pauls, or a shilling the pound. Here are the rich wines of Montepulciano, Montefiascone, and Monte di Dragone; but what we commonly drink at meals is that of orvieto, a small white wine of an agreeable flavour. Strangers are generally advised to employ an antiquarian to instruct them in all the curiosities of Rome; and this is a necessary expence, when a person wants to become a connoisseur in painting, statuary, and architecture. For my own part, I had no such ambition. I longed to view the remains of antiquity by which this metropolis is distinguished; and to contemplate the originals of many pictures and statues, which I had admired in prints and descriptions. I therefore chose a servant, who was recommended to me as a sober intelligent fellow, acquainted with these matters: at the same time I furnished myself with maps and plans of antient and modern Rome, together with the little manual, called *Itinerario istruttivo per retrovaire con facilita tutte le magnificenze di Roma e di alcune citta', e castelli suburbani.* But I found still more satisfaction in perusing the book in three volumes, intitled, *Roma antica, e moderna,* which contains a description of every thing remarkable in and about the city, illustrated with a great number of copper-plates, and many curious historical annotations. This directory cost me a zequine; but a hundred zequines will not purchase all the books on these subjects.

Dr. Smollet farther remarks,——" Our young gentlemen who go to Rome will do well to be upon their guard against a set of sharpers, (some of them of our own country) who deal in pictures and antiques, and very often impose upon the uninformed stranger, by selling him trash, as the productions of the most celebrated artists. The English are more than any other foreigners exposed to this imposition. They are supposed to have more money to throw away;

and therefore a greater number of snares are laid for them. This opinion of their superior wealth they take a pride in confirming, by launching out into all manner of unnecessary expence: but what is still more dangerous, the moment they set foot in Italy, they are seized with the ambition of becoming connoisseurs in painting, music, statuary, and architecture; and the adventurers of this country do not fail to flatter this weakness for their own advantage. I have seen in different parts of Italy, a number of raw boys, whom Britain seemed to have poured forth on purpose to bring her national character into contempt: ignorant, petulant, rash, and profligate, without any knowlege or experience of their own, without any director to improve their understanding, or superintend their conduct. One engages in play with an infamous gamester, and is stripped, perhaps, in the very first partie; another is poxed and pillaged by an antiquated cantatrice; a third is bubbled by a knavish antiquarian; and a fourth is laid under contribution by a dealer in pictures. Some turn fiddlers, and pretend to compose: but all of them talk familiarly of the arts, and return finished connoisseurs and coxcombs to their own country. When you arrive at Rome, you receive cards from all your countryfolks in that city: they expect to have the visit returned next day, when they give orders not to be at home; and you never speak to one another in the sequel. This is a refinement in hospitality and politeness, which the English have invented by the strength of their own genius, without any assistance either from France, Italy, or Lapland. No Englishman above the degree of a painter or cicerone frequents any coffee-house at Rome; and as there are no public diversions except in carnival-time, the only chance you have for seeing your compatriots, is either in visiting the curiosities, or at a conversazione. The Italians are very scrupulous in admitting foreigners, except those who are introduced

as

as people of quality: but if there happens to be any English lady of fashion at Rome, she generally keeps an assembly, to which the British subjects resort.—

Nothing can be more agreeable to the eyes of a stranger, especially in the heats of summer, than the great number of public fountains that appear in every part of Rome, embellished with all the ornaments of sculpture, and pouring forth prodigious quantities of cool delicious water, brought in aqueducts from different lakes, rivers, and sources, at a considerable distance from the city. These works are the remains of the munificence and industry of the ancient Romans, who were extremely delicate in the article of water: but, however, great applause is also due to those beneficent popes, who have been at the expence of restoring and repairing those noble channels of health, pleasure, and convenience. This great plenty of water, nevertheless, has not induced the Romans to be cleanly. Their streets, and even their palaces, are disgraced with filth. The noble Piazza Navona is adorned with three or four fountains, one of which is perhaps the most magnificent that Europe can produce, and all of them discharge vast streams of water: but, notwithstanding this provision, the piazza is almost as dirty as West-Smithfield, where cattle are sold in London. The corridores, arcades, and even stair-cases belonging to their most elegant palaces, are depositories of nastiness; and, indeed, in summer, smell as strong as spirit of hartshorn. I have a great notion that their ancestors were not much more cleanly. If we consider that the city and suburbs of Rome, in the reign of Claudius, contained about seven millions of inhabitants, a number equal at least to the sum total of all the souls in England; that great part of ancient Rome was allotted to temples, porticos, basilicæ, theatres, thermæ, circi, public and private walks, and gardens, where very few, if any, of this great number lodged; that by far the greater part of those inhabitants were flaves, and poor people who did not enjoy the conveniencies of life; and that the ufe of linen was fcarcely known; we muft naturally conclude they were ftrangely crouded together, and that in general they were a very frowzy generation. That they were crouded together appears from the height of their houfes, which the poet Rutilius compared to towers made for fcaling heaven. In order to remedy this inconvenience, Auguftus Cæfar publifhed a decree, that for the future no houfes fhould be built above feventy feet high, which, at a moderate computation, might make fix ftories. But what feems to prove, beyond all difpute, that the ancient Romans were dirty creatures, are thefe two particulars. Vefpafian laid a tax upon urine and ordure, on pretence of being at a great expence in clearing the ftreets from fuch nufances; an impofition which amounted to about fourteen pence a year for every individual; and when Heliogabalus ordered all the cobwebs of the city and fuburbs to be collected, they were found to weigh ten thoufand pounds. This was intended as a demonftration of the great number of inhabitants; but it was a proof of their dirt, rather than of their populofity. I might likewife add the delicate cuftom of taking vomits at each other's houfes, when they were invited to dinner or fupper; a beaftly proof of their naftinefs as well as gluttony. Horace, in his defcription of the banquet of Nafiedenus, fays, when the canopy under which they fat fell down, it brought along with it as much dirt as is raifed by a hard gale of wind in dry weather.

> ———" *trahentia pulveris atri,*
> *Quantum non aquilo Campanis excitat agris.*"

I might obferve that the ftreets were often encumbered with the putrifying carcaffes of criminals, who had been dragged through them by the heels, and
precipitated

precipitated from the Scalæ Gemoniæ, or Tarpeian rock, before they were thrown into the Tiber, which was the general receptacle of the *cloaca maxima*, and all the filth of Rome. Beside, the bodies of all those who made away with themselves, without sufficient cause; of such as were condemned for sacrilege, or killed by thunder, were left unburned and unburied to rot above ground."—

I believe the moderns retain more of the customs of the ancient Romans, than is generally imagined. When I first saw the infants at the *enfans trouvés* in Paris, so swathed with bandages, that the very sight of them made my eyes water; I little dreamed, that the prescription of the ancients could be pleaded for this custom, equally shocking and absurd: but, in the capitol at Rome, I met with the antique statue of a child *emailloté*, exactly in the same manner; rolled up like an Ægyptian mummy from the feet. The circulation of the blood, in such a case, must be obstructed on the whole surface of the body; and nothing at liberty but the head, which is the only part of the child that ought to be confined. Is it not surprising that common sense should not point out, even to the most ignorant, that those accursed bandages must heat the tender infant into a fever; and must hinder the action of the muscles and the play of the joints, so necessary to health and nutrition!—

It is diverting to hear an Italian expatiate upon the greatness of modern Rome. He will tell you there are above three hundred palaces in the city; that there is scarce a Roman prince whose revenue does not exceed two hundred thousand crowns; and that Rome produces not only the most learned men, but also the most refined politicians in the universe. To one of them, talking in this strain, I replied, that instead of three hundred palaces, the number did not exceed fourscore; that I had been informed, on good authority, there were not six individuals in Rome who had so much as forty thousand crowns a year, about ten thousand pounds sterling; and that to say their princes were so rich, and their politicians so refined, was in effect a severe satire upon them, for not employing their wealth and their talents for the advantage of their country. I asked why their cardinals and princes did not invite and encourage industrious people to settle and cultivate the Campania of Rome, which is a desart? Why they did not raise a subscription to drain the marshes in the neighbourhood of the city, and thus meliorate the air, which is rendered extremely unwholesome in the summer, by putrid exhalations from those morasses? I demanded of them, why they did not contribute their wealth, and exert their political refinements, in augmenting their forces by sea and land, for the defence of their country, introducing commerce and manufactures, and in giving some consequence to their state, which was no more than a mite in the political scale of Europe? I expressed a desire to know what became of all those sums of money, inasmuch as there was hardly any circulation of gold and silver in Rome, and the very bankers on whom strangers have their credit, make interest to pay their tradesmen's bills with paper notes of the bank of Spirito Santo? And now I am upon this subject, it may not be amiss to observe, that I was strangely misled by all the books I consulted about the current coin of Italy. In Tuscany, and the ecclesiastical state, one sees nothing but zequines in gold, and pieces of two paoli, one paolo, and half a paolo, in silver. Beside these, there is a copper coin at Rome, called bajocco, and mezzo bajocco. Ten bajocchi make a scudo, which is an imaginary piece; two scudi make a zequine; and a French loui' d'or is worth about two zequines.

Rome has nothing to fear from the catholic powers, who respect it with a superstitious veneration, as the metropolitan seat of their religion: but the popes will do well to avoid misunderstandings with the maritime Protestant states, especially the English, who

being

being masters of the Mediterranean, and in possession of Minorca, have it in their power at all times, to land a body of troops within four leagues of Rome, and to take the city without opposition. Rome is surrounded with an old wall, but altogether incapable of defence. Or if it was, the circuit of the walls is so extensive, that it would require a garrison of twenty thousand men. The only appearance of a fortification in this city, is the castle of St. Angelo, situated on the further bank of the Tyber, to which there is access by a handsome bridge; but this castle, which was formerly the *moles Adriani*, could not hold out half a day against a battery of ten pieces of cannon properly directed. It was an expedient left to the invention of the modern Romans, to convert an antient tomb into a citadel."——

Mr. Sharpe does not represent Rome in a much more advantageous light than Dr. Smollet, though their accounts greatly confirm the testimony of each other.——

" We passed, says Mr. Sharpe, the Campania of Rome, the unwholsomeness of which is held in such horror, that no foreigner, nor any Italian, if he can possibly avoid it, lies on the road there. Accordingly it will be conceived, there is very indifferent accommodation in the Campania, on which account, we found it necessary to keep our post-horses all night at a shabby inn, half-way to the post-house, before you arrive at the Campania, as preferring dirty beds and dirty provisions, to no beds, no provision, and a pestilential climate. The Romans, when they travel post on this road, usually set out from Rome early enough to reach Terni the first evening; or, if they must lie one night in the Campania, when the days are short, it is at Castel-Nuovo, a little above thirty miles from Rome. It grieves one to behold so fine a country as the Campania might be made, by a plentiful population, now almost a waste and barren desart. There is a part of the road within twenty miles

miles of Rome exceedingly well paved with large stones of flat surfaces; but the grass rises betwixt their interstices; so little is now trodden that path which leads to the city of Rome, once so mighty, so populous, and so frequented.——

A man, on his first arrival at Rome, is not much fired with its appearance; the narrowness of the streets, the thinness of the inhabitants, the prodigious quantity of monks and beggars, give but a gloomy aspect to this renowned city. There are no rich tradesmen here, who, by their acquisitions, either ennoble their sons, or marry their daughters into the houses of princes. All the shops seem empty, and the shopkeepers poor; not one hackney-coach in so large a town, a notable proof there is no middle station betwixt those who always ride, and those who always walk. This is the first impression; but turn your eye from this point of view, to the magnificence of their churches, to the venerable remains of ancient Rome, to the prodigious collection of pictures, and antique statues, to the very river and ground itself, formerly the habitation of that people, which from our cradles we have been taught to adore, and, with a very few grains of enthusiasm in your composition, you will feel more than satisfied.

The surface of modern Rome is certainly more elevated than it was in ancient times; such an alteration must happen in the course of ages, to every city which has been often destroyed by time and fire, as all the rubbish is seldom removed; but the ancient pavement in which Trajan's pillar stands, shews the elevation in that place not to be above seven or eight feet; and, I am informed, some of the triumphal arches are not above three or four feet in the ground. The Tarpeian rock is still of such a height, that, should a man be thrown from it, his bones would be in the greatest danger, though there would be no certainty of breaking his neck; nor, indeed, would it be certain, though the rock were ten or fifteen feet

feet higher, as some have supposed it in the time of the Romans, when this kind of execution was in vogue: I should imagine, therefore, they had some method of dispatching the delinquent, when death did not immediately ensue from the fall; perhaps an executioner was at the foot of the rock, ready to give the *coup-de-grace* in case of that event, which, I imagine, would often happen, though the rock had been of twice its present height. Men, in falling from high places, are sometimes killed on the spot, but more frequently languish a considerable time before death. I conclude, therefore, from these considerations, that there is no greater alteration in the site of Rome than what I have mentioned. The most remarkable change is this, that the *Campus Martius* was, in the time of the ancient Romans, an open area, and now it is covered with houses.——

Were an antiquarian to lament over any fall, any metamorphosis of ancient Rome, perhaps it might be the present state of the Forum, where now there is, every Thursday and Friday, a market for cows and oxen, on the very spot where the Roman orators were accustomed to thunder out their eloquence in the cause of their clients, their country, and their gods: accordingly, the Forum now is known by the name of *Campo Vaccino*.

Surrounding the Forum are many vestiges of antique grandeur; triumphal arches, remains of temples, the ruins of the imperial palace, the Campidoglio, &c. all bespeaking the magnificent state of Rome in the times of the emperors. The great amphitheatre called also *Il Colosseo*, where the spectacle of combats was exhibited, is also in its neighbourhood. In this place the spirit of modern Rome seems to prevail over that of ancient Rome; for where the wild beasts and gladiators formerly entertained seventy or eighty thousand spectators, you now see a few miserable old women and beggars, who are praying at the

feet

feet of fourteen small chapels, which represent the fourteen mysteries of our Saviour's passion.——

I am now, continues Mr. Sharpe, where the sovereign is a priest; at a time of the year too, when the priesthood displays all its pomp; and I assure you, it is a trial for the patience of reason. We very well know, from the history of the church, what tyrants they have been formerly, before the laity dared to assume the prerogatives of civil liberty: and, that they do not yet abate one jot of their presumption, you may learn from a passage or two I lately met with, in a book printed at Naples, since the commencement of the present century. Believe my candor and veracity, when I give you my word, that I do not strain the sense in the translation.—— In a chapter upon the article of confessors, the author (a priest) says, "A confessor partakes both of the nature of God and of man; with God, he is a man; with man, he is God."——Again, "Jesus Christ, to absolve man, suffered infinite agonies, and even death itself; whilst a confessor, by only lifting up his hands, acquits the guilty sinner."

The pope and his council have come to a resolution, upon the death of the pretender, to have no more concern in this business, and not only do not acknowlege the title of the present pretender, but have forbidden all the princes and cardinals here to visit him; so that he sees only two or three friends, and leads a recluse and melancholy life. We this morning saw him at St. Peter's church; he came there, attended by three gentlemen and seven servants, to pay his devotions: there was hardly one in the church but ourselves, so that we had the opportunity of examining his person and behaviour very minutely. When I first saw him on his knees, I felt some compunction, which went off by degrees, as I became more certain, from his gestures, of the extreme bigotry and superstitious turn of his mind.

After he had prayed at one altar (for it was not to hear mafs) he walked to another, and prayed a fecond time, kneeling in both places on the hard pavement. I never faw any one more ftedfaft in prayer than he appeared, not allowing his eyes to wander one moment from either the altar, the ground, or the book in his hand. During this tranfaction, reafon fuperfeded my pity, and I felt a kind of exultation in reflecting we were not under the dominion of a prince fo fond of images and hierarchy. Now I have feen him before the Virgin Mary, I can believe all that was faid of his grofs attachment to popery, when he was with us in 1745. His revenues are faid to be very ftrait, not exceeding four thoufand pounds a year. His ftature is very elegant; but his face is a little bloated and pimpled, as if he had drank too much, a vice laid to his charge, but, perhaps, without good grounds. I am told, his brother the cardinal, refents the conduct of this court more than he himfelf does; perhaps as his heart is more fet upon propagating the true faith in the realms of Great Britain; for, however enthufiaftic the prince, as he was called, may be in his perfuafion, the cardinal is much more fo; and poffibly he may think his brother deprived of all hopes by this ftep. I have had fome converfation with a very fenfible ecclefiaftic here, who knows every thing which paffes, both in the pope's and the pretender's palace. I afked what name the pretender goes by at prefent? to which he could hardly give an anfwer, as he fays they fo ftrictly obferve the prohibition not to ftile him king, that he is never mentioned; or if, by chance, they are obliged to fpeak of him, it is under the abfurd appellation of Prince of Wales."———

Rome has not been in fuch a political uproar thefe laft fifty years as at this prefent juncture. One would imagine his holinefs had the promife of Peter's pence once more from our fide of the water, fo devoted does he feem to the court of England: laft Wednefday,

day, he banished from Rome four heads of colleges here, for having admitted mass to be said before the pretender under the title of king: but without a compliment to England, it was incumbent on the pope, in support of his edict and prerogative, to make an example of the offenders. The interest of the Stuart family, by length of time, seems to be almost worn out in the court of Rome; and at this instant, the power of England is considered to be so respectable, that, it is affirmed and believed, the council were unanimous in refusing to acknowledge Mr. Stuart's pretensions; and, in consequence of this refusal, to give out an ordinance prohibition to the cardinals, princes, &c. forbidding them to see him, but as a private gentleman; which, in other words, is the same as to declare, he shall keep no company but that of his domestics. It is said, the measures would not have been so severe, had not the cardinal of York behaved, on this occasion, with so unseasonable an obstinacy. It is thought the pretender himself would have acquiesced and waited for better times; but the cardinal has been, and continues to be furious; a little more indignation and disloyalty will certainly drive both the brothers from this asylum. The cardinal, in a memorial he delivered to his holiness, praying him to acknowlege his brother's title, amongst other arguments, advances that he has nothing to fear from the power of the English; for that the present race of Italians are not degenerated in the least from their ancestors, the ancient Romans. I do not know how the allegation will affect Englishmen; but, I assure you, the Italians themselves laugh aloud, when they are told the story; so ridiculous does the expression appear in their eyes.——

You will conclude from this account, that, for the future, the Stuarts will be a disagreeable weight on the pope's shoulders; and that, if the pretender have the least spirit of a man in him, he will bid adieu to Rome,

ROME.

Rome, and rather take sanctuary in Constantinople, amongst Mahometans, than remain in a city amongst papists, for whose tenets his family have forfeited three such glorious kingdoms."——It is time now to return to Mr. Keysler.]

Young travellers who have generally the least taste for learning, arts and sciences, meet with so many things in Rome to attract their curiosity, that they may pass away their time without having recourse to frivolous diversions, debaucheries, or idle company. The variety of objects daily seen here afford sufficient topics for conversation in coffee-houses and taverns; so that double entendres, which often prove of more prejudice to youth than gross obscenity, are not so frequent here as in France. The natural temper of the inhabitants greatly contributes to this; for allowing the Italians to exceed other nations in voluptuousness, and particularly in some detestable vices, yet they observe more secrecy, and never publish their own infamy, as is common in France, till their passions are subsided by time, and experience has taught them better. In France, they have even the effrontery to boast of *bonnes fortunes,* as the term is, which never fell to their share; and topics of this kind are carried to great lengths in public companies, and even the ladies are solicitous to indulge a strain of pleasantry on these subjects. For it must be remembered, that most of them would rather be thought to want virtue than wit. Young travellers are so taken with this gay humour, that they imagine it the principal accomplishment they are to acquire in France; and even at Rome, those who come from Paris are as readily known as a bird by its note. But I will take upon me to affirm, that the general conversation at Rome is less offensive than in other large cities; and I have met here with several persons well versed in the arts and sciences, who often gave rise to useful and entertaining disquisitions. But they generally are productive of two parties; the one giving the preference to the curious pieces of antiquity still extant in painting, sculpture, and architecture, and the other to those executed by modern artists. The controversy never extends to other sciences.

The parish-churches, in the Roman Catholic parts of Christendom, were, in the pontificate of Paul IV. computed at two hundred and forty-eight thousand, and the convents at forty-four thousand. And, as succeeding ages have rather increased than diminished the number of these structures, it is natural to conclude that Rome, being the residence of the visible head of the Roman Catholic church, must be crouded with churches, in proportion to the number of its inhabitants. It would not be an easy task to give a catalogue of all the convents, chapels, oratories, hospitals, seminaries, &c. in Rome, beside eighty-two parish-churches: it will therefore be sufficient to mention those only which more especially deserve attention.

The church of St. John de Lateran is one of the four churches enjoined to be visited in the *annus sanctus*, or year of jubilee; and on that account, here is a gate walled up, which, at the commencement of the jubilee, is opened by the cardinal archpriest. This door or gate is easily distinguished by the gilt brass crucifix upon it; but something smaller than that of St. Peter's church. The bronze gates, at the entrance, belonged formerly to an ancient temple of Saturn in the Roman Forum, but since converted into a church, and dedicated to St. Adrian.

Plenary indulgences on the feast of St. John the Baptist, are to be had here for twenty-nine thousand years. In the middle isle of the church stand twelve large statues of the apostles, each of them formed out of a single block of white marble, and executed by the best masters. These statues are separated from each other by two noble pillars of verde antico, over which are basso relievos, and above these several pictures of the prophets. The image of our Saviour
in

in mofaic work, faid to have efcaped the flames of feveral fires untouched, is placed over the gallery; and it was pretended that it was irradiated with a glory at the confecration of this church, which hath one part of its name from that of St. John the Baptift, and the other from the Roman martyr Plantius Lateranus, put to death by Nero, who had a garden here. It is however dedicated to our Saviour. Here are likewife two ftatues, faid to be the firft that ever were made of St. Peter and St. Paul. And another in a kneeling attitude, with a manly face, wrinkled with age, but no beard; is fuppofed by fome to be pope Joan, and by others Nicholas IV. It is reprefented in a papal crown, and done in white marble. On the high altar is a fmaller table of wood, on which St. Peter is faid to have read mafs. At prefent none but the pope officiates there, unlefs by virtue of a written licence from his holinefs; and this is only granted for one mafs. The relics that are kept in this papal altar, are the heads of St. Peter and Paul; the hair and garment of the Virgin Mary; the linen towel with which Chrift wiped his difciples feet, after wafhing them; his purple robe, which is fprinkled with his blood; the cloth that covered his face in the fepulchre; fome of the blood and water which flowed from his fide; and a fragment of the barley bread, wherewith he fed five thoufand men.

On the altar Del SS. Sagramento, is a tabernacle, compofed of feveral precious ftones, finifhed by that great artift Pomp. Targoni, who contrived the famous dyke at Rochelle, and immortalifed his name for his great proficiency in feveral arts. Before this altar are four fluted pillars of brafs gilt, and four others of the Corinthian order, of green and white marble, on the altar-piece. The former are faid to be taken out of the temple at Jerufalem by Titus Vefpafian, and brought to Rome. Others allege, that Auguftus had them caft out of the brafs Roftra of the fhips taken from Cleopatra and Mark Anthony.

thony. While others believe they were brought by Sylla from the temple of Jupiter Olympicus in Afia; and others, that Domitian caft them to adorn the capitol. But, be this as it will, they are faid to be filled with holy earth, out of the fepulchre of Chrift, fent from Jerufalem by Helena, the mother of Conftantine the Great.

In the chapel of St. Thomas are preferved two boards of the ark of the covenant; they are indeed fo much decayed by time, that one cannot tell what wood they are, nor how they came to be depofited in this place. Here is alfo fhewn a table of odoriferous wood, on which Chrift is faid to have inftituted his laft fupper. It feems to have been formerly covered with filver, for feveral ftuds of that metal, here and there, are ftill remaining in it. The table itfelf is fo fmall, that it will hardly contain two perfons on each fide. Some, indeed, affirm the table had originally two leaves, which folded on one another. But, after all, I think it might as well have been let alone, as it is evidently too fmall for the above purpofe. They alfo fhew here the rods of Mofes and Aaron. A piece of the latter is likewife fhewn at St. Vitti's church, in Prague; and the Sainte Chapelle, at Paris, glories in having the rod of the former entire. All thefe relics are, at any time, fhewn in the Lateran church for three paoli; but, on Holy Thurfday and St. Thomas's day, they are publicly exhibited. Notwithftanding above twenty popes are interred in this church, two monuments are erected only to their memory; one to that of Martin V. of the Colonna family; and the other to Alexander III. of the family of Pandinella.

From the facrifty is a paffage to the cloifters of the convent, which, on the fide toward the inner court, is decorated with an elegant variety of fmall white marble pillars. At one end is an altar, ornamented with antique mofaic pillars; and through the marble leaf of it is a round hole, faid to remove all doubts

of

of transubstantiation; for any priest, who, through unbelief or ignorance, should reconsecrate an host already consecrated, he would soon be convinced of his error, by that individual host escaping his hands, falling through this aperture, and sticking on a pillar beneath the altar, in the form of a spot of blood.

Here is likewise a large porphyry pillar, said to be the very same on which the cock stood and crowed when St. Peter denied his master. They also shew the pillar on which the standards were fixed, when sentence was pronounced on Christ; together with a fine table of porphyry, on which the soldiers threw the dice for our Saviour's garment. But the most valuable curiosity here is the coffin of St. Helena, the mother of Constantine, formed out of one single piece of porphyry, decorated with large basso-relievos of horsemen, and several other figures. I must not pass over in silence those chairs or stools in the gallery, called *Sellæ Stercorariæ*, or *Exploratoriæ*. Why they are placed here I do not pretend to know. They are two in number, and between them is a chair of white marble, something higher than the other; both are of porphyry, or rather of *pietra egizzia rossa*, a species of Egyptian stone, neither so beautiful nor so hard as porphyry. One has a round arm or elbow; but that of the other is broken off. Before I had seen them, abbot Bencini of Turin assured me, that they are no other than the common chairs of the ancient Romans, in which a hole had been made, and lined with wood, as more proper for the purpose, by reason of the coldness of the stone; but on viewing them, I did not find them at all adapted to that purpose. Neither could they serve for close-stools, the back aperture being too small and incommodiously placed. Perhaps they were used in bagnios, and fires put under them for fumigation; but this conjecture is exploded by Marefius. In my travels I have met with divers chairs of antiquity, but none which had any resemblance to these. That the popes, formerly, at their taking poffeffion of the Lateran church, were placed in one of thefe ftools or chairs, their writers themfelves allow; and Mabillon alleges, that it was done as an act of humility, alluding to the words fung at this ceremony, *Sufcitat de pulvere egenum, & de ftercore erigit pauperem, ut fedeat cum principibus, & folium gloriæ teneat:* " He raifes the needy from the duft, and the poor from the dunghill, that they may fit with princes, and poffefs a throne of glory." Hence thefe chairs were called *fellæ ftercorariæ*. This opinion is fupported by Bellarmine and Chementellius; the latter indeed has the affurance even to deny that there is any aperture at all through the feat. The indecent examination of the pope's fex, which fome have fo merrily defcribed, may perhaps be fabulous; but it was not firft propagated by Proteftants. It came originally from the Roman Catholics themfelves, who often ufed it in their fatires againft their pontiffs.

The hiftory or fable of pope Joan, was well known before Luther was in being, as is evident from the manufcripts of Anaftafius Bibliothecarius and Martinus Polonus: the teftimony of the latter I found in an old book, in the library at Utrecht; and alfo in another, formerly belonging to the abbey of St. Bavo, at Ghent, and now in the city library of Haerlem; where he fays that he exactly tranfcribed this chronicle from the Florentine library.

In the fquare before this church and palace is a beautiful fountain, and the largeft obelifk in all Rome, being, without the pedeftal, and the large iron crofs on the top of it, an hundred and twelve feet high; two of the fides nine feet and an half wide, and the other two eight feet at the bafe. It was formerly of one entire block of *pietra egizzia*, or red granate, and ftood in the *circus maximus*, but was ruined in the hoftile commotions of war, and broken into three pieces. However, Sixtus V. in the year 1588, had the pieces brought hither, and re-erected by Fontana. The Egyptian

Egyptian hieroglyphics on it afford room for many speculative conjectures among the learned.

On the other side of this square is the Lateran hospital, a noble structure, in which are, at all times, several hundred sick, of both sexes, in divers wards, and the greatest care taken of them. Here is also the *Scala Sancta*, or stairs which Christ so often ascended and descended in the house of Pontius Pilate, before he was crucified. This relic is said to have been sent by the devout Helena from Jerusalem to Rome; and that it lay unregarded in the old palace of the Lateran, till Sixtus V. who ordered it to be placed in a regular building, erected on purpose by Fontana. The front of it has five doors, the entrance to so many stairs; the two on each side has thirty steps of free-stone, but those in the center, as being the most holy, are of white marble, and contain twenty-eight stairs; which, by the frequent ascending and descending of pious persons, are worn to that degree, that they have been obliged to fix boards over them; for, without this caution, those stairs would have been soon worn through. They are not ascended with the feet, but the knees only, and therefore may be said to have been kneeled through. They descend by the side-stairs, on which they are permitted to step. They repeat, on each step of the *scala sancta*, a *pater noster* and an *ave Maria*; by which means, an indulgence for three years and forty days is obtained. At the top of these stairs is the *Sanctum Sanctorum*, being a small chapel, in which the chief relics of the Lateran palace are deposited. The chief of these is the εἴκον αχειροποίητον, or picture of our Saviour, begun by St. Luke, but finished by angels, whence it is said not to have been performed by the hand of man. It is painted on a board of palm-wood, and is framed with plates of silver set with jewels, having before it a plate of crystal. No person who scruples to pay the required adoration to this picture can obtain a sight of it; nor are any women ever admitted

mitted beyond the iron grate, behind which it is kept. Mahomet, by placing his women before the windows of paradise, has shewn the same severity toward a sex, not esteemed deficient in devotion.

From a catalogue of these relics, I have extracted the following: 1. Several pieces of stone from the mountains of Golgotha, Sinai, and the Mount of Olives. 2. A piece of the stone of the sepulchre of our Saviour, on which the angel sat. 3. Several of the bones of the holy innocents. 4. A variety of missal garments, made by angels. 5. A napkin used by our Saviour at his last supper. 6. A large piece of the sponge on which the vinegar was offered to Christ on the cross. 7. The chair in which he sat at eating the paschal lamb. 8. Some napkins, with which the angels wiped the sweat from the face of St. Laurence, as he was broiling. These, and many other relics, are deposited under the high altar, in the *Sanctum Sanctorum*, on the architrave of which is this pentameter verse:

Non est in toto sanctior orbe locus.

" No place in the whole world is more holy."

This altar is looked upon as so holy, that even the pope himself is not permitted to officiate at it; there being two chapels contiguous to this for that purpose, as is observed by Soresinus, in his book of the *scala sancta*.

In St. Maria sopra Minerva, the formidable court of inquisition, which is detested even by all rational Roman Catholics themselves, is held every Wednesday. The general of the Dominican order always presides there, next to the bishops. Three congregations of the holy office sit every week; the first in the palace of the inquisition; the second at Alla Minerva, where the processes are regularly digested, to be laid before his holiness at the third meeting,

ing, which is held at the palace where the pope refides. The number of cardinal-inquifitors is not fixed; fometimes there are twelve or more : thefe are affifted by feveral divines and officers; but they are not fo ftrict in Italy as in Spain and Portugal; the Italians not being fo weak as to intruft them with fuch abfolute power. Their rigour is remarkably abated toward foreigners, thofe belonging to cardinals, and fuch as are under the protection of foreign minifters.

The palace of the inquifition, together with the prifon of thofe unhappy perfons who fall under its difpleafure, is in another part of the city, not far from St. Peter's. But what paffes within the walls of that ftructure, is as little known at Rome, as the tranfactions of the feraglio are at Conftantinople. Boards are placed before moft of the windows, like thofe in a great many nunneries.

The bleffing and curfing of printed books likewife depend chiefly on the Dominicans : the *Maeftro del Sacro Palazzo*, without who'e permiffion no book is to be printed, nor read when prohibited, together with the fecretary of the congregation *dell' Indice*, of whom a licence muft be obtained for reading a prohibited book, even out of the jurifdiction of the city of Rome; being both of this order. The council of Trent firft publifhed an *index librorum prohibitorum*, or a catalogue of prohibited books, and of the dangerous paffages in others permitted to be read. This is now continued from time to time by the *Congregatio Indices*.

Ill Sagro Monte della Pieta was infituted to prevent the extortions of ufurers, by which the diftreffes of the poor are fo extreamly aggravated in other countries. Here you receive two thirds of the value of the pledge; and, if it does not exceed thirty fcudi, or crowns, no intereft is paid; but if more, two per cent. only. If the pledge is not redeemed in eighteen months, it is publicly fold, and the overplus referved for the owner; but this sale may be prevented by only renewing the obligation, which is done without trouble or expence. For supporting this fund, which, beside relieving the distresses of the poor, affords a sustenance to several people, legacies have been left by popes, and other persons of rank. There is also a particular fraternity, who take care that every thing is conducted in the most equitable manner.

I am now come to St. Peter's, in the Vatican, which, for largeness and beauty, may well be called the metropolitan church of Rome, Italy, and even the whole world. Here we evidently see to what an amazing pitch the Romish church, so fond of external pomp and splendor, hath, within two centuries, carried its favourite scheme; namely that of captivating the senses, and inspiring the minds of the ignorant with awe and submission to the clergy. Fontana the younger, in his account of this church, observed, that in his time, which is above forty years ago, it had cost above eighty millions of Roman scudi. Pope Leo X, by his impatience of forwarding this stupendous structure, occasioned those flagrant abuses by the sale of indulgences, which raised so great a clamour among the more rational part of mankind. This it was that gave Tezel and Luther room to continue their hostilities against the papal see; and how far th y have proved prejudicial to it, consequences have sufficiently shewn.

Nothing can be more magnificent than the area before the church. The monument of Scipio Africanus, said to have been a pyramid larger than that of C. Sestius, still remaining, was removed in the time of Alexander VI. to enlarge this area; and certainly the eye has lost nothing by the alteration. The oval colonade round it has four rows of large pillars, forming three separate walks. The extent of this area may be reckoned from the shortest diameter, intercepted between the two fountains and the obelisk, which is a hundred and eighty common paces; and

its

its longest diameter, from the beginning of the colonade to the front of the church, is four hundred paces. Some prints represent a colonade directly facing the church; but there is, in fact, no such thing; the area being clear and open to the entrance of the church. This colonade consists of three hundred and twenty pillars, of Tivoli free-stone, which are so large that three men can hardly fathom them. On the roof, which is flat, stand eighty-six statues of saints, all of them twice as big as life, and designed by Bernini. The area is adorned with two stately fountains; and in the center stands that vast obelisk, formerly belonging to Nero's palace, near this place. This lofty obelisk was first dedicated to the sun by Sesostris king of Egypt; and in the time of Caligula, brought to Rome in a very large ship, the dimensions of which are described by Pliny, lib. xvi. cap. 40. Its four sides terminate at the top in an obtuse angle; neither is it embellished with hieroglyphics generally seen on Egyptian obelisks. The weight of it is said to be nine hundred and ninety-two thousand seven hundred and eighty-six pounds; and its height eighty feet, exclusive of the base. It was erected by Fontana, under pope Sixtus V. who, in all other respects, was a great benefactor to the city of Rome. In order to raise this obelisk out of the ground, where it had been, as it were, buried, Fontana contrived forty-one machines, with iron rollers and large ropes. All the powers of these machines were applied at once, by means of eight hundred men, and a hundred and sixty horses. This could not be effected in less than eight days; and to bring the obelisk to the place where it now stands, though only three hundred paces from the spot where it lay, was a labour of four months; but the greatest proof of Fontana's skill in mechanics was displayed on the 10th of September, 1586, when this stupendous mass was raised by means of his machines, which consisted of fifty-two powers; all which were at once applied by particular signals, of founding a trumpet and striking a bell. Being raised to a proper height, it was fixed on its basis amidst the acclamations of the people, ringing of bells, and the discharge of the cannon at St. Angelo's castle.

Fontana, if we may credit report, by confiding too much in his calculations of the power of his machines, had almost totally miscarried; the ropes having stretched much more than he expected, whereby the obelisk could not be raised high enough to be fixed on the pedestal. During this perplexity, an obscure person is said to have called out to the engineers to wet the ropes, which being accordingly done, the obelisk was raised the height desired. Fontana compleated this work (the expence of which amounted to thirty-seven thousand nine hundred and seventy-five scudi, or crowns, exclusive of the crucifix and pedestal) in six months. It is fixed on the backs of four lions, without any cement, its own enormous weight being abundantly sufficient. The lions are of bronze gilt, and placed on the pedestal. The foundation is very broad and deep, and consists entirely of small pieces of brick, tiles, and flint, cemented together with very strong mortar. The cross on the top is of brass gilt, seven feet high; and in it, they say, is contained a piece of the true wood of the real cross: and whoever, in passing by it, says a *Pater-noster* and *Ave Maria*, for the prosperity of the Romish see, is intitled to an indulgence of ten years and ten times forty days.

Several medals, struck on this occasion, are laid in the foundation; the same was done by pope Alexander VII. on the 25th of April 1661, at laying the first stone of the colonade round the area.

The steps from the area to the portico of the church are called *Limina Apostolorum*; and it is said, that Charlemagne ascended them on his knees, when he was going to be crowned in St. Peter's church. But Rome is not at present remarkable for observing ceremonies

remonies of this kind; it is not indeed impoffible but an old woman or two may be often feen practifing such devotions, in order to fecure a place in the happy manfions of eternity. On one fide of thefe fteps is the ftatue of St. Peter, and on the other that of St. Paul, both done by Minio di Fiefoli. At the top of thefe fteps, before the entrance of the church, is a grand portico, which might, at any other place, be itfelf confidered as a church; being two hundred and fixteen feet in length, and forty in breadth. Four doors open into the church from this portico; but the fartheft, on the left-hand, is walled up, being opened only every twenty-fifth year, or that of jubilee, when the pope himfelf performs the ceremony with a hammer. The populace kifs the brafs crofs faftened on this door, with fuch devotion, that the lower part of it is become much paler than the other. No woman was formerly permitted to enter at the fartheft door, on the left hand; but they have, long fince, repealed this abfurd order.

 The form of this fuperb and beautiful church is that of a Latin crofs, and the proportion, with regard to the length, breadth, and height, fo accurately obferved, that the eye does not perceive any of thefe dimenfions to be remarkably large, notwithftanding the whole, when taken together, is prodigious. The middle ifle is about thirty-three common paces in breadth, and the whole length of the church two hundred and eighty-eight; of which, the diftance between the entrance and the center of the cupola is one hundred and eighty.

 The whole length of the ftructure, according to a geometrical computation made by the chevalier Carlo Fontana, including the breadth of the portico and the thicknefs of the walls, is nine hundred and feventy Roman palms, or about feven hundred and twenty-two Englifh feet. I fhall here obferve, once for all, that a Roman palm is eight inches and three lines.

The

The famous temple built by Solomon, confifted of feveral large courts, and was profufely adorned with gold and filver; but the principal building was far from being equal to St. Peter's at Rome. The church of St. Paul in London is a grand piece of architecture, but far from being equal in dimenfions to that of St. Peter; being, according to Chamberlain, fix hundred and ninety Englifh feet in length; and, according to Colin Campbell, in the firft Volume of his Vitruvius Britannicus, which feems the moft accurate menfuration, its length is no more than five hundred and twenty Englifh feet: whereas, that of St. Peter, according to the fame author, is fix hundred and fifty Englifh feet, exclufive of the portico; but, in both, the thicknefs of the walls is included. According to my own menfuration, St. Peter's is two hundred and eighty-eight common paces in length, and St. Paul's two hundred and twenty-two; and from the front to the center of the cupola, one hundred and twenty-four; the length of the crofs ifle, from the north to the fouth door, one hundred and fifteen; and, in other places, forty-fix fuch paces: The diameter of the cupola fifty-three, and the circumference of the firft gallery one hundred and fifty-fix common paces. A wooden model of St. Peter's church is placed in one of the upper apartments of St. Paul's, but fo inaccurately performed, that thofe, who from thence make a comparifon between the two ftructures, will be wretchedly deceived.

But notwithftanding all the care that has been taken in erecting the church of St. Peter, it has, like all human performances, a mixture of defects; but inftead of enumerating them, or examining whether all of them are juftly founded, give me leave to refer to the introduction prefixed to Mr. Campbell's Vitruvius Britannicus.

The cupola of St. Peter is, by all, acknowledged to be a prodigy of art and grandeur; and, at a confiderable diftance, impreffes on the mind a very magnificent

nificent idea of the city in which it is erected. The height, from the pavement of the church to the top of the crofs, four hundred and thirty-two Englifh feet; the circumference of the dome fix hundred and twenty, and the infide diameter one hundred and forty-three Englifh feet, being equal to that of the Pantheon. I meafured round the firft gallery of the cupola, and found it two hundred and fourteen common paces.

This fpacious dome was erected by the architects Jac. de la Porta and Dominico Fontana. during the pontificate of Sixtus V.; but the whole honour, both of the undertaking and defign, is due to Michael Angelo. Some perfons, praifing the rotunda, an antique ftructure, as a work which the moderns would never be able to equal, that great artift replied, that he would not only build a dome of equal dimenfions, but alfo erect it in the air; an affertion which he afterward fully performed. The defigns for the mofaic ornaments in the cupola were drawn by Giofeppe d'Arpino, among which, thofe of the evangelifts, in four large oval compartments, are particularly admired.

This wonderful fpecimen of human art is fupported by four pillars, each ninety palms in diameter, and each adorned with a ftatue of white marble, twenty-two palms in height, exclufive of the pedeftal. Bernini was feverely cenfured for making the niches for thefe ftatues in the four pillars which fupport the cupola, and efpecially for the ftairs, which are carried by their foundation to the *facre grotte*, as they have all a great tendency to weaken the ftructure: and foon after, a fiffure was difcovered in the cupola, occafioned by a violent clap of thunder. Bernini was never remarkable for affability, fo that it is not furprifing he had few friends to oppofe the torrent of popular clamour againft his temerity, as the caufe of this unhappy accident; and perhaps, his fuccefs in removing and erecting the fuperb obelifk

in

in the Piazza Navona, was the chief motive that saved his head. Michael Angelo, who drew the designs for this dome, was apprehensive of an accident of this kind; and therefore desired, with the greatest earnestness, that neither these four pillars, nor their foundations, should have the least alteration. How prudent it would have been to have followed that great man's advice, the unhappy consequences have too evidently demonstrated; as every lover of architecture must be concerned to see this fissure in so grand a structure, and which seems to approximate as near the summit of perfection as is possible for any of the works of mortals to arrive at. This fissure in the cupola was, in the year 1700, considerably enlarged by an earthquake; but its great height renders it scarcely discernible from the pavement of the church, unless you are previously informed of it; but, from the upper gallery, you will plainly see two large fissures or clefts opposite each other, and one of them covered with a cramp of iron four or five inches broad. A tribuna or gallery is erected over each of these statues, from whence, at some particular festivals, a great variety of relics, kept in a particular chapel, are exposed to public view.

In the vaults under the pedestals of each of the four statues is an altar, on which the principal actions of the saint, whose statue is placed over it, are represented in mosaic work, by Fabio Christofori, after the designs drawn by the famous Andrea Sacchi. A flight of stairs leads down under these four altars to other subterranean vaults, full of excellent mosaic; wood and canvas being no proof against the dampness of the place. The mosaic, now placed in these subterraneous apartments, was formerly the pavement of the old church. These vaults are crowded with the tombs of saints, too sacred to be broken or removed, and are therefore inclosed with a wall, which renders it impossible to see any thing without a torch.

The

ROME.

The floor, they say, appears still the same as it did in the time of Constantine the Great, and consists of porphyry and other pieces of marble. Here was also interred Christina, queen of Sweden; and near her monument is a white marble statue of Christ, in the old Gothic taste; and on every side are the stone coffins of popes and cardinals, who flourished in former ages. Adrian IV. lies in a very large coffin made of a single piece of granate, brought out of Egypt at the same time with the Vatican obelisk, and supposed to be the largest of that kind and form in the world.

Directly under the center of the cupola is the *altaro maggiore*, or high altar, which first attracts the eyes of the curious; and, according to the ancient custom, fronts the tribuna. So that, when the pope says mass, his face is always turned toward the east, or grand entrance. Over the altar is a canopy of gilt bronze, embellished with four angels and a crucifix, supported by four large twisted pillars of brass, cast by Gregorio Rossi, from a design of Bernini. Their weight is ten thousand and fifty pounds. The medal from whence they were cast, formerly covered the dome of the Pantheon. The four pedestals are of marble, finely executed by Francisco Fiammingo.

[According to Dr. Smollet,——" the altar of St. Peter's choir, notwithstanding all the ornaments which have been lavished upon it, is no more than a heap of puerile finery, better adapted to an Indian pagod, than to a temple built upon the principles of the Greek architecture. The four colossal figures that support the chair, are both clumsy and disproportioned. The drapery of statues, whether in brass or stone, when thrown into large masses, appears hard and unpleasant to the eye; and for that reason the ancients always imitated wet linen, which exhibiting the shape of the limbs underneath, and hanging in a multiplicity of folds, gives an air of lightness, softness, and ductility to the whole. These two statues weigh 116257 pounds, and as they sustain nothing but

but a chair, are out of all proportion, inasmuch as the supporters ought to be suitable to the things supported. Here are four giants holding up the old wooden chair of the apostle Peter, if we may believe the book *De Identitate Cathedræ Romanæ*. The implements of popish superstition, such as relics of pretended saints, ill proportioned spires and bellfreys, and the nauseous repetition of the figure of the cross, which is in itself a very mean and disagreeable object, only fit for the prisons of condemned criminals; have contributed to introduce a vitious taste into the external architecture, as well as in the internal ornaments of our temples. All churches are built in the figure of a cross, which effectually prevents the eye from taking in the scope of the building, either without side or within; consequently robs the edifice of its proper effect. The palace of the Escurial in Spain is laid out in the shape of a gridiron, because the convent was built in consequence of a vow to St. Laurence, who was broiled to death like a barbecued pig. What pity it is, that the labours of painting should have been so much employed on the shocking subjects of the martyrology. Beside numberless pictures of the flagellation, crucifixion, and descent from the cross, we have Judith with the head of Holofernes, Herodias with the head of John the Baptist, Jael assassinating Sisera in his sleep, Peter writhing on the cross, Stephen battered with stones, Sebastian stuck full of arrows, Laurence frying upon the coals, Bartholomew fleaed alive, and a hundred other pictures equally frightful; which can only serve to fill the mind with gloomy ideas, and encourage a spirit of religious fanaticism, which has always been attended with mischievous consequences to the community where it reigned."———]

But, to proceed in a regular description of this church, I shall return to the main entrance; where, against the two first pillars, opposite one another, are placed two large vessels for holy water, of yellow marble,

marble, each supported by two angels of white marble. Each veffel, as well as the angel which fupports it, is of an entire piece. The work is large, beautiful, and finely executed by Auguftino Cornachini.

St. Peter's church contains about 180 large pillars of marble. Innocent X. incruftated the fquare pillars with red marble, and adorned them with medallions of the popes, executed in white marble, together with doves of the fame ftone in baffo-relievo, having green branches in their bills, the arms of that pontiff. The pavement is entirely of marble, and in the church are twenty-nine altars. The neatnefs and order in which every thing in this church is kept, are remarkable; on the leaft appearance of any duft, either on the walls or cieling, perfons are drawn up in a machine for that purpofe, to take it away; fo that the whole fabric has the appearance of one juft finifhed. They do not think it fufficient to take away the duft by brufhes or beefoms, but wipe the feveral parts with pieces of linen, whereby they are effectually cleaned, and at the fame time the work in no danger of being hurt: fifty perfons are conftantly employed in this office. As they are fo very careful to keep every part of this ftructure clean, I could not help wondering that birds are fuffered to fly about in it, efpecially pigeons, of which I faw feveral. I will not, however, pretend to determine, whether this was owing to the difficulty of catching them, or a fuperftitious regard for that bird.

The great thicknefs of the walls, and the fmallnefs of the windows, render the church fomewhat dark and damp; and the latter has been found of fo much prejudice to pictures, painted either on wood or canvas, that they have found it abfolutely neceffary to fupply their places as they decay, with pieces of mofaic work, which may be termed unperifhable.

The

The materials used by the moderns in these works, are small pieces of glass, tinctured with all the different degrees of colour, like the fine English worsted, used in needle-work.

The glass is first made into thin plates, and afterwards cut into long pieces of different dimensions. Some of these pieces, used in figures seen only at a distance, as on roofs and cielings, appear to be nearly of a finger's breadth; but the more elegant pieces are formed wholly of glass pins, if I may be permitted to call them so, nearly of the size of a common sewing needle; so that above two millions of such pins are required to finish a portrait four feet square. When these pieces are finished, they are polished in the same manner as looking-glasses; after which they appear like pictures painted with the most brilliant colours, and covered with a glass. The ground on which these vitreous pieces are arranged, is a kind of paste, composed of calcined marble, fine sand, gum-tragacanth, white of eggs and oil. This continues for some time so soft, that there is no difficulty either of placing the pieces, or altering any which may have been improperly inserted; but, by degrees, it grows as hard as marble, so that no impression can be made on the work. The paste is first spread in a frame of wood, which must not be less than a foot in breadth and thickness, if the piece be any thing large. This frame is fastened with brass nails to a plate of marble, or a slab of stone; and, as some of the capital pieces are twenty feet by fifteen, and this ground of paste nine inches thick, and the pins or studs of the same length, some idea may be formed of the weight of such a piece. Those designed for cielings, or places where they are viewed at a distance, are not polished; but those performed for the decoration of altars, &c. the greatest care is taken to give them every advantage. The studs of several colours are deposited in cases, and placed before the artist, in

the

the same manner as letters are before a compositor, in a printing-house; and they are so very accurate in imitating the most beautiful strokes of the pencil, that the difference seems to consist only in the colours of the copy, being more vivid and brilliant than those of the painting. Several popes have followed the example of Innocent XII. in leaving proper funds in order to defray the expences of copying the several paintings which adorn St. Peter's church in mosaic; and, as these funds are continually increasing by private legacies, they will soon be able to decorate the several altars with this beautiful work.

How much this curious art has been improved during the two last centuries, may be easily seen, by comparing the coarse works in some of the old cupolas of the chapels in St. Peter's church, with the other pieces lately erected there. The studs in these old works are made of clay burnt, and the surface only tinctured with various colours; but they are to be gradually removed, and their places supplied by the more elegant performances of the moderns. It is also necessary to distinguish the mosaic of the moderns from that called Florentine work, which consists of sparks of gems, and minute pieces of the finest marble, by means of which, birds, flowers, &c. are imitated, in the same manner as cabinet-makers inlay any work, with a variety of figures in wood in different colours; and hence it is called *Pietre pretiose commesse*.

But no traveller should content himself with viewing the vaults and church of St. Peter; for the upper parts of that structure are furnished with objects, the sight of which will sufficiently compensate him for his trouble of going up to the globe on the top. The first winding ascent or stair-case, if indeed it can be called so, the entrance of which is near the Capella del Coro, has not any steps, so that a horse may ascend or descend it without difficulty. It was built in this manner, in order to carry provisions and materials to the workmen above, on asses. After going up about two hundred and eighty steps above the first ascent, you enter a gallery in the church near the cieling; it has no baluftrade, but so broad that you may walk in it without any danger. Here the mosaic portraits appear of an enormous size, though, from the pavement of the church, they seem to be no larger than life: for instance, the length of St. Peter's keys is no less than thirty-three Roman palms.

The inner gallery of the cupola is still much higher; and from thence the gigantic statues of our Saviour and the twelve apostles appear in their true dimensions. The grand cupola or dome may be properly said to be double, the stair-case running between them; and you ascend eighty steps from the inner, before you reach the surface of the upper dome: but they are both concentric, the concavity of the outer cupola answering exactly to the convexity of the inner. After ascending twenty-two steps higher, you arrive at the outward gallery of the cupola, round which is a baluftrade of iron. Round the cupola are many fine pillars, seven spans and a half in circumference, and twenty-four spans in height. The intervals between them are filled with glass windows, which admit the light into the great cupola. These pillars also support the inner dome, over the convex superficies of which you ascend twenty three steps higher, holding by a rope instead of a baluftrade, which brings you to the top of the grand cupola, where the lanthorn is fixed, which has an opening toward the city; and from whence you have a prospect of the sea, though forty miles distant from Rome. On the evening of St. Peter's day this place is illuminated with nine lamps.

You next ascend a wooden ladder of fourteen steps, and then another of iron, of twelve; at the top of which you enter, through a very narrow passage, the copper ball placed on the top of the cupola. They
say

say this ball will contain thirty-two persons; but I am persuaded the number is too large, unless they are stowed as close as ballast in a ship. The diameter intercepted between the cross iron hoops, which bind the work together, is twelve common spans, or about eight feet; some make it eleven palms, or eight feet and one third. This ball, and the cross placed on the top of it, being nineteen palmi, or fifteen English feet and a half high, were cast by Sebastiano Torrisano.

All persons, every time they duly visit this structure, are intitled to an indulgence of six thousand years; nor can this be well doubted by those who believe St. Peter to keep the door of the happy mansions above, as his intercession must doubtless have great weight in procuring admission. This great apostle is said to have caused a spring to burst out in a miraculous manner, near St. Martha's church, which still continues; the water is used in the bakehouse of the pope, near the Vatican, and the bread made there for his holiness is reckoned the best in the whole city.

The spacious palace of the Vatican joins to the north side of St. Peter's church. This palace is said to contain twelve thousand five hundred and twenty-four apartments; and the governor assured me, that there were in it eleven thousand two hundred and forty-six chambers, twenty-two courts, and twelve hundred hearths, or fire-places. We have, however, no other authority for this, than the assertions of the pope's officers and domestics, which they found on a wooden model of this palace, not now to be seen; for it cannot be supposed that any traveller can have either opportunity or inclination to examine into the truth of the account. Antonio Sangallo made an accurate and beautiful model of St. Peter's church, which cost above thirty thousand crowns; but it is now lost. This sum, how great soever it may appear, is vastly less than what the king of Portugal expended

expended in a model of this cathedral; which is said to have cost near a hundred thousand dollars, about twenty-three thousand three hundred and thirty-three pounds sterling. In this exquisite model every particular ornament of the original was represented in miniature, even to the gems.

The Vatican palace having been built and inlarged at different times, no proportion or symmetry is observed in the several parts of which it consists; and, to avoid damaging the fine area before the cathedral of St. Peter, no portico has been erected in the front.

When his holiness gives audience, the cardinals and ambassadors sit on chairs; princes on three cushions laid on the floor; but other persons kneel. On each side of the papal throne, in the chamber of audience, is a stool, covered with red, which, they say, are intended as seats for kings; but, they seem, during the two last centuries, to despise the honour.

In the back-part of the Vatican is the sacristy or wardrobe, and from the many fine pieces of painting, and costly furniture for altars, and other rich vestments, is well worth visiting. It, however, contained formerly more rich moveables than at present, the most valuable having, some time since, been removed into the castle of St. Angelo, where it is not easy to obtain a sight of them.

In the Palazzo Vecchio, or old Vatican palace, is the famous Vatican library, which was removed hither by order and under the care and inspection of pope Sixtus V. Of late, none but members of the sacred college are invested with the office of chief librarian, to which is annexed a salary of an hundred golden crowns a month. His chief deputy has, beside an allowance of bread and wine, six hundred crowns a year; and the other under librarians, four hundred and fifty crowns each.

Among the curiosities, generally shewn to strangers, is a manuscript of Virgil, written in the Literæ Unciale, supposed to be of the fourth or fifth century.

The

The historical pictures in this manuscript have been published in copper-plates by Bartoli, and with an elegancy far beyond the original. The text is not without some palpable errors. Here are also manuscripts of Terence with representations of the Personæ, or masks used by the ancient comedians; and the manuscripts of Henry VIII. of England, *de Septem Sacramentis.* Burnet himself acknowleges that the love-letters to Anne Bulleyn are written with that prince's own hand. Here are also some leaves of ancient paper made from the bark of trees; some writing tablets of the Romans; a manuscript copy of Pliny's Natural history, adorned with fine miniature paintings; another, of Dante's works; the original copy *De Errore Profanarum Religionem,* by Minutius Felix; also several breviaries, missals, and martyrologies, elegantly written. Some of these manuscripts are finely illuminated, among which is that of Julius Clovius; the original of Baronius's Annals, in 12 folio volumes; a Greek manuscript of the Alexandrian chronicle, together with some manuscripts of Onufrius, Ligorius, Thomas Aquinas, Charles Borromeo, and others. Here is also a Hebrew translation of the Homilies of Clement XI. finely written; a volume of hieroglyphical figures; a very ancient fragment of Dion's history; and a great number of Oriental manuscripts, in Arabic, Chinese, and other Eastern languages. But, in my opinion, the most valuable of them all are a manuscript copy of the Septuagint translation of the Old Testament, in Greek, and a copy of the New Testament, written in Greek capitals, without accents, reckoned, both with regard to beauty and antiquity, equal to the Alexandrian manuscript in the royal library at London, and which, some assert, was written in the sixth century; a large unbound Hebrew manuscript of the Bible; the gospels of St. Luke and St. John, written in the tenth century, and bound in ivory; a Greek copy of the Acts of the apostles, written in letters of gold, which was

presented

presented by Charlotte, queen of Cyprus, to pope Innocent VIII. It was formerly adorned on the outside with jewels, but the soldiers, at the sacking of Rome by Charles of Bourbon, took them off.

The Vatican library was enriched with a great number of Syriac, Arabic, Persian, Turkish, Hebrew, Samaritan, Armenian, Ethiopic, Greek, Egyptian, and Malabrian manuscripts, by pope Clement XI. purchased by that pontiff in Egypt, when the Coptic patriarch was desirous of uniting the Romish and Eastern churches. The lovers of Oriental literature will be apprised of the importance of these manuscripts, when the account of them, by Joseph Simon Asseman, a native of Syria, and copyist in the Vatican library for the Arabic and Syrian languages, is finished. The whole library consists of five rooms, beside the two galleries already described; so that the number of volumes must be very great; but, being kept in cases, it is impossible to form an idea of it by the eye, and it has never been ascertained. The library is not, however, remarkable for printed books, their whole number scarcely amounting to twenty thousand; but, with regard to valuable manuscripts, it is allowed to excel any in Europe; some make the number of these to be above twenty-five thousand.

The Vatican librarians are allowed to read all prohibited books, which are deposited in a place by themselves. The expence of seeing this valuable collection amounts to about eight or nine Paoli, or four shillings sterling.

The Vatican palace, as we have already observed, joins on one side to the cathedral of St. Peter; the other is connected by a colonade to the castle of St. Angelo. Alexander VII. who is no great honour to the papal see, erected this colonade, which proved of no service to pope Clement VII. when the city was surprised by the imperial army, in the year 1527; for one of the soldiers shot at him, as he was running along this passage to shelter himself in the fortress.

The

The castle of St. Angelo was anciently the place where the remains of the Roman emperors were interred; being built for that purpose by the emperor Adrian, the Mausolæum of Augustus, on the other side of the Tiber, being then filled with urns; and hence is acquired the name of Moles Hadriani. In the center of this structure is a large round tower, which was formerly decorated with a great variety of marble pillars and statues; but the Roman soldiers broke most of them down, and used them in their defence against the Goths, when they attacked the city. On the top of this tower, the Pigna, now in the Belvedere gardens, was placed. In the reign of Gregory the Great, the city of Rome being visited with a pestilence, the pictures of the Virgin Mary, painted by St. Luke, were carried in a grand procession; and the pope, as they pretend, saw an angel standing directly over this castle, who, immediately, on the pope's looking up, sheathed his flaming sword. The pontiff, considering this as a certain sign that the divine wrath was appeased, caused a chapel to be erected to the honour of the angel, and the place itself to be called Castellum S. Angeli. In the Franciscan convent of St. Maria Ara Cœli, they shew a stone, on which the angel left the impression of his foot. As the city of Rome was destitute both of a citadel and regular fortifications, it was thought necessary to form this castle into a place of defence; and, accordingly, Urban VIII caused it to be fortified in the modern manner, with five regular bastions, ramparts, moats, and other works. The garrison is composed of two hundred regulars, and seven hundred citizens; the latter rarely do any duty, though they enjoy several privileges, particularly that of wearing a sword. The apartment into which Clement VII. retired, from the disturbances he had himself occasioned, by provoking Charles V. is, at present, appointed for a state prison, having a small window which looks into a chapel, through which the persons confined in this apartment may hear mass. At the entrance of this prison is a trobochetto, or trap-door, through which a prisoner may be let down, unexpectedly, into a deep dungeon, and meet with inevitable death; but it is at present covered with an iron grate.

In this castle, beside the state prisoners, are confined such prisoners as the inquisition does not chuse to leave in the Palazzo della Inquisitione, in the city; the populace, at Rome, always making a general gaol-delivery on the death of a pope: for which reason, as soon as any pope is given over by his physicians, they always remove those who have committed any notorious crimes, together with those from whom any danger is apprehended, into the castle of St. Angelo, into which no stranger is admitted during the vacancy of the papal throne. On the top of the tower of this castle is a pedestal, which anciently supported Adrian's Pigna, whose place is now supplied by the statue of an angel in white marble, near twelve feet high, performed by Montelupo. Four brass cannon are mounted on the platform, one of which queen Christina fired, out of a frolic, against the Medicis palace on Monte Pincio; and, in an iron door of that structure, the mark of the ball is still visible. Four or five paoli is the whole expence of viewing the castle. Before you enter the castle, you pass over that grand bridge, called by the ancients Pons Ælius.

The Rotundo, so called from its figure, has supported itself against the attacks of time, better than any structure built by the ancient Romans. And it is surprising, that neither this remarkable temple, the pillar of M. Aurelius, the Mausolæum of Adrian, nor the Septigonium of Severus, should have been represented on any medal struck by the ancient Romans. Pliny tells us, that this edifice was at first dedicated to Jupiter Ultor by M. Agrippa; but afterward to all the deities, celestial, terrestrial, and infernal; whence it was termed Pantheon. The roof of it, according to to some authors, was at first covered with silver, but carried away by the soldiers during the confusions of the city; and that Constantius carried with him to Constantinople the most beautiful statues with which it was adorned. But, notwithstanding these misfortunes, a vast quantity of brass was found about it in the pontificate of Urban VIII. who formed from it the grand altar in the cathedral of St. Peter, together with several pieces of ordnance, which he placed in the castle of St. Angelo. It is surprising he did not also take the superb bronze gates, which are eighteen feet four inches broad, and thirty-six feet high, especially as they are much too large for the edifice, and were, in all probability, designed at first for some other. Pasquin, however, did not let the pope's stripping the Pantheon of its ornaments pass unnoticed, for the following satirical words soon appeared: *Quod non fecerunt barbari Romæ, fecit Barbarini,* "What "the *barbarians* spared, the *Barbarini* took away."

It is evident from the niches still remaining, that the statues of the gods were placed in this structure; and Pliny tells us, that the statue of Venus was adorned with pendants which were made from the pearl spared by Cleopatra at the extravagant entertainment she gave to M. Anthony. It must not, however, be supposed, that this temple contained statues of all the gods worshipped by the Romans, for they amounted to several thousands, and, consequently, could not all be placed here; but all structures, dedicated to more than one particular god, were termed Pantheons. Dio tells us, that before the entrance of the Rotunda, the present name of this edifice, were anciently two statues, one on the right hand, and the other on the left; the former representing Augustus, and the latter Agrippa. The outside of this structure is intirely built of Tivoli free-stone, but the inside is incrusted over with marble.

The roof of the Rotunda is a round dome, destitute both of pillars and windows, seventy-two common
paces

paces in diameter; some say the inside is only one hundred and thirty-two feet, exclusive of the wall, which is eighteen feet thick; but even this is greater than the height, which is ascended by an hundred and ninety steps. . This church has no windows, but a large aperture in the center of the dome, thirty-seven feet and a half in diameter, admits a sufficient quantity of light to illuminate every part of it. It is paved with porphyry and large square stones, placed in a declining position toward the center, where the rain-water is carried off by a sewer, covered with a stone full of holes.

[Dr. Smollet expresses his opinion of the Rotunda as follows.—' I was much disappointed at sight of the Pantheon, which, after all that has been said of it, looks like a huge cockpit, open at top. The portico which Agrippa added to the building, is undoubtedly very noble, though, in my opinion, it corresponds but ill with the simplicity of the edifice. With all my veneration for the ancients, I cannot see in what the beauty of the Rotunda consists. It is no more than a plain unpierced cylinder, or circular wall, with two fillets and a cornice, having a vaulted roof or cupola, open in the center. I mean the original building, without considering the vestibule of Agrippa. Within side it has much the air of a mausoleum. It was this appearance which, in all probability, suggested the thought to Boniface IV. to transport hither eight and twenty cart-loads of old rotten bones, dug from different burying-places, and then to dedicate it as a church to the blessed Virgin and all the holy martyrs. I am not one of those who think it is well lighted by the hole at the top, which is about nine and twenty feet in diameter, although the author of the Grand Tour calls it but nine. Before the time of pope Alexander VII. the earth was so raised as to cover part of the temple, and there was a descent of some steps into the porch: but that pontiff ordered the ground to be pared away to the very pedestal or

base

base of the portico, which is now even with the street, so that there is no descent whatsoever. Pope Urban VIII. removed the large brass beams, which supported the roof of the portico. They weighed 186392 pounds; and afforded metal enough not only for the pillars in St. Peter's church, but also for several pieces of artillery. What is more extraordinary, the gilding of those columns is said to have cost forty thousand golden crowns: sure money was never worse laid out. Urban VIII. likewise added two bellfrey towers to the Rotunda; and I wonder he did not cover the central hole with glass, as it must be very inconvenient and disagreeable to those who go to church below, to be exposed to the rain in wet weather, which must also render it very damp and unwholesome. I visited it several times, and each time it looked more and more gloomy and sepulchral.]

Of the catacombs those of St. Sebastian are the most spacious, and least impaired by time, of any in Rome. They, in some places, consist of several stories, or passages lying one under another; and, the soil being dry and sandy, they were obliged to prop it up here and there with brick-walls. You frequently ascend and descend in these subterranean caverns, and, in many places, are obliged to stoop in going through them. These passages are not above two or three feet in breadth, so that two persons cannot walk abreast, except in some chambers which are between four and six feet broad, and from six to eight in length. In these, according to some, the primitive Christians performed their religious exercises. It is prohibited, under pain of the severest excommunication, to take any thing away from this place; but, I imagine, heretics do not consider themselves as bound by any such prohibition. In both sides of the wall are repositories or cavities, a span, or a span and a half high, and between four and five long, some of which are empty, and stand open; and others walled up with brick, or a small marble stone, on which are

some-

sometimes inscriptions. As I happened to be the last of our company, and, therefore, not so narrowly observed by the monk, who attended us with a consecrated wax-taper, I took down one of these marble-tablets, which was about two fingers thick, and I found in the cavity an human skeleton intire, though not very large; for I met with few of these repositories capable of containing a full grown person at full length. Three or four of these commonly lie over one another; and those cavities in which two or more bodies may be deposited, are called *Bisoma, Disoma, Trisoma, Quatrisoma,* &c. In one place I observed a large stone coffin; and without the church is another in marble, decorated with basso-relievos, representing some histories of the Old and New Testament, which, they say, was taken out of the catacombs. In another place I observed a large and intire earthen urn with a narrow neck, found and intire. In different places of the walls are small glass bottles, but only the bottom part of most of them remained. In some of these I observed a blackish sediment, which, they pretend, is the blood of the martyrs buried here, but, perhaps, may be only the sediment of oil used in the lamps. These glasses resemble the lachrymatories of the ancient Heathens, in which they preserved the tears shed at the funerals of their departed friends; and, also, those of the women hired to weep on such occasions. On the bottom of one of these phials, a friend of mine at Nurenberg shewed me a very beautiful gilt picture, representing a child with a bulla about its neck, and led by its mother. Over the painting was a glass to preserve it from the damp. On another lacrymatory, in the possession of the same gentleman, is the following inscription: *Vivas dulcis anima pie Zeses.* But this picture is not so well executed as the former, the whole work appearing to be modern, and in the Gothic taste. Both these glasses were a part of the Strozzi cabinet, and found in the catacombs. In the year 1716, the celebrated senator Buonatori,

Buonatori, published, at Florence, a work intitled *Offervatione fopra alcuni Frammenti di Vafi antichi di Vetro, ornati di Figure, trovati ne Cimiteri di Roma,* &c. in which a particular defcription is given of feveral paintings on fuch phials; fome of which were done by Heathens, and others by Chriftians. The words *Pie Zefes* are confpicuous on feveral of them; but the rules of grammar will not admit, as fome pretend, that they mean *Pie Jefu*; and the opinion of thofe, who believe them to be a mixture of Greek and Latin not unufual among the Romans in common converfation, feems more plaufible. Befide thefe large cavities are feveral fmall holes, like thofe in pigeon-houfes, along the fides of the catacombs, in which the ancients placed their urns, fome fingly, fome two or three together; and thefe places were called *Columbariæ ollariæ* and *Hypogæa.*

Upon comparing feveral infcriptions which cafually prefented themfelves to my view, without any particular fearch, together with an obfervation I made on the fmallnefs of the fkeletons, I think the conjecture, that, among the ancient Heathens, children were often buried, inftead of being burnt on funeral piles, as was cuftomary with regard to adults, was rendered very plaufible.

Thefe fubterranean paffages have very intricate communications with one another; but ftones are erected in the middle, to direct thofe who vifit them, in their way. A traveller, who would furvey all the catacombs belonging to St. Sebaftian's, muft travel twenty Italian miles at leaft; as appears from a plan of them in the convent, which agrees with the copper-plate print of Paul Arhinghis, called *Roma Subterranea,* where are alfo draughts of the catacombs of St. Hermes, St. Pancrace, St. Agnes, St. Agatha, St. Lucinea, &c. Every one of thefe catacombs, and feveral others, to the number of thirty, have all their fubterranean paffages of fuch extent, that all of them, taken together, are faid to extend above an

hundred

hundred Italian miles; but many of them are so greatly decayed that they are obliged to be walled up, several persons having lost themselves in these subterranean labyrinths. Beside the accounts of Bossii and Arhingi, another was published at Rome, intitled *Osservazione sopra i Cimeteri di Sante Martiri entichi Chriſtiani di Roma*, in two volumes folio, in 1720. That many Christians are interred in these subterranean passages no one will deny; but it does not by any means follow, that these caverns were originally the work of Christians, or that they served for retreats in time of persecution. For, not to mention the vast disproportion of such works to the small number of Christians, how was it possible to convey away the many thousand cart-loads of earth and sand, taken out of these catacombs, with such privacy as to escape the notice of the Heathens? If we candidly inspect the catacombs at Rome, it will appear, that these subterranean passages were originally the Puticuli, mentioned by Horace, Varro, and Festus Pompeius, where only the bodies of slaves, and those whose circumstances would not permit their friends to be at the expence of burning them on funeral piles, were deposited. The digging up puzzolana, a kind of sand, very useful in making mortar for building, of which there are vast strata in many parts of Italy, particularly without the city, may have given rise to this expedient for burying the dead. In process of time, persons of a higher rank were interred here; for the Romans, even before Christianity prevailed, often interred their dead, as is evident from several monumental inscriptions still visible in the catacombs, which begin with the letters D. M; and others, where the express words *Diis Manibus* are engraved at full length; words which would have been looked upon with horror by a Christian.

Another proof, that this was not a burying-place for the primitive Christians, I gather from the great number of lachrymatories found in these catacombs,

and

and ufually placed by the Heathens near their dead, being filled with their own tears, and thofe of the hired mourners, or *præficæ*: as is evident from the expreffions frequently to be met with on tomb-ftones: namely, *Tumulum lacrymis plenum dare; ponere cum lacrymis; cum lacrymis & opobalfamo udum condere*, and the like: concerning which confult Guthier *de Jure Manium*, lib. i. c. 28. p. 173; and *Cafal*, p. ii. c. 21. *de Urb*.

Before the church of St. Theodore is a fhort thick pillar, or Pagan altar and *cenforium*. The brafs fhewolf, now in the capitol, was alfo dug up here; and hence it is fuppofed to have been the temple of Romulus and Remus. It feems that the Heathens ufed to bring their children afflicted with diforders hither, and rub them againft the ftatues of thefe twin brothers, who had been fo miraculoufly preferved; and the ancient matrons, even for fome time after the eftablifhment of Chriftianity, continued this fuperftitious cuftom. To reform this abufe, the temple has been confecrated to St. Theodore, and to this day a particular mafs is read here every Thurfday, after which the fick children are brought to the altar, where a monk lays his hand upon them, and ftrokes their faces with a relic of St. Theodore; and, by virtue of this ceremony, the child is certainly expected to recover or die within feven days. The papifts call this putting away the leaven of heathenifm, and turning it into a practice of Chriftian devotion. This brings to my mind a certain Romifh author, who, in relating, with the higheft encomiums, the zeal of the jefuits in propagating Chriftianity, tells us, that in fome parts, the excrement of oxen were held in fuch veneration, that the inhabitants anointed their heads with it when hot, and left it there to dry. This cuftom the jefuits did all in their power to obliterate, but finding all their endeavours proved abortive, they turned it into a Chriftian ceremony by fprinkling the unction, before it was applied, plentifully with holy water.

St.

St. Silveſtro in Campo Marzo, or in Capite, has an impreſſion of the face of Chriſt, which, according to Euſebius, our Saviour himſelf made on a piece of white linen, and ſent to Abgarus (by that father called Agbarus) king of Edeſſa; the painter ſent from that country being unable to take it, on account of the dazzling brightneſs of Chriſt's countenance. The truth of this whole affair reſts intirely on the relation given of it by Nicephorus Caliſtus, who lived about the middle of the fourteenth century. This impreſſion of our Saviour's face is, indeed, preſerved, though rarely ſhewn, in the convent of the nuns of St. Clare, near their church; but one muſt be contented with a copy of it in a baſſo-relievo of white marble, placed on the left hand of the high altar. If this be a true repreſentation of Chriſt, he was of a very melancholy aſpect; his hair reſembles a wig, and he appears with muſtaches and a long beard. Under this baſſo relievo, is a marble buſt of John the Baptiſt, having a like beard reſembling that above, but a more meagre countenance. Oppoſite to this is the monument of St. Silveſter.

The church of St. Silveſter boaſts of having the heads of St. John the Baptiſt; but though five popes have declared in favour of this church and convent, yet the canons of Amiens maintain that they alone are in poſſeſſion of the Baptiſt's real head; and Du Cange has, in ſupport of their claim, publiſhed a long and very learned diſſertation.

In the churches are many curious pieces in painting, architecture, and ſculpture, yet a greater variety of theſe may be ſeen in the palaces of the Roman nobility; who ſpend the principal part of their fortunes in decorating the villas with ornaments of this kind, that foreigners may be induced to viſit them, and extol their magnificence in diſtant countries. I have more than once obſerved, that between twenty and thirty rooms, in the lower and beſt ſtories of a palace, have been magnificently adorned merely from oſtentation,

tation, while the owner and his family have confined themselves to the upper story. As the elder branch of a noble family lives in this manner, it may easily be supposed, that none of the outward splendor, usual in other countries, is to be expected among the inferior branches. For a younger son of the richest families in Italy, as those of Colonna, Pamfili, Ludovisio, and others, has, beside board, lodging and apparel, no more than forty or sixty scudi a month; which allowance not being sufficient for him to make any great figure, he is obliged to have recourse to the church, in order to procure to himself some rich benefice. From this attention to outward grandeur, more than real conveniency, it often happens, that the Italian palaces are not the most commodious dwellings, and passages of communication from one apartment to another are frequently wanting. The floors are generally of brick, marble being looked upon as unwholesome in damp and cold weather, and boards they do not keep sufficiently clean. The looking-glasses, to correspond with the other rich furniture, ought to be finer and larger; the locks on the doors should be more elegant than common, and the hangings newer and in greater number. They have, indeed, in the last particular, begun to make some improvements; for, at present, the palaces of Barbarini, Caroli, and Altemps are decorated with very beautiful Brabant tapestry.

[Dr. Smollet remarks, that " the churches and palaces of these days are crowded with petty ornaments, which distract the eye, and by breaking the design into a variety of little parts, destroy the effect of the whole. Every door and window has its separate ornaments, its moulding, frize, cornice, and tympanum; then there is such an assemblage of useless festoons, pillars, pilasters, with their architraves, entablatures, &c. that nothing great or uniform remains to fill the view; and we, in vain, look for that simplicity of grandeur, which characterises the edifices of the ancients. A great edifice, to have its full effect, ought to be *ifolé*, that is, detached from all others, with a large space around it: but the palaces of Rome, and, indeed, of all the other cities of Italy, which I have seen, are so engaged among other mean houses, that their beauty and magnificence are in a great measure concealed. Even those which face open streets and piazzas are only clear in front. The other apartments are darkened by the vicinity of ordinary houses; and their views are confined by dirty and disagreeable objects. Within the court there is generally a noble colonnade all round, and an open corridore above: but the stairs are usually narrow, steep, and high: the want of sash-windows, the dullness of their small glass lozenges, the dusty brick floors, and the crimson hangings laced with gold, contribute to give a gloomy air to their apartments; I might add to these causes, a number of pictures executed on melancholy subjects, antique mutilated statues, busts, basso-relievos, urns, and sepulchral stones, with which their rooms are adorned. It must be owned, however, there are some exceptions to this general rule. The villa of cardinal Alexander Albani is light, gay, and airy; yet the rooms are too small, and too much decorated with carving and gilding, which is a kind of gingerbread work. The apartments of one of the princes Borghese are furnished in the English taste; and in the *palazza di colonna connestabile*, there is a saloon, or gallery, which, for the proportions, lights, furniture, and ornaments, is the most noble, elegant, and agreeable apartment I ever saw."]

I have often considered that the Romish religion, by affecting exterior splendor, adds greatly to the improvement of sculpture and painting. Nor will this be throught strange, if we reflect how numerous those pieces are in churches and convents, there being, at least, fifteen thousand pieces of the Lord's Supper, and above fifty thousand of the annunciation in Italy. The painters must, therefore, be continually

ally endeavouring to obtain a superiority in that art, and to recommend them for beauty in colouring and expression. What great improvements may be expected, when we consider that the history of the Bible is to be executed by an ingenious artist? What scope has he there for exerting the strength of his imagination, and the exquisite command of his pencil? Opportunities of this kind are not to be expected in protestant countries, as they do not admit of pictures in public places of worship; and temporal princes have generally other ways of spending their revenues, without erecting superb structures, and decorating them with statues and paintings; whereas convents are frequently possessed of more money than they can dispense with, and it is likewise certain, that whatever is spent on churches, will be reimbursed ten-fold by the profitable resort of pilgrims and others: add to this the daily legacies procured by the artifices of the priests for building and ornamenting their churches. Here all are desirous of an ecclesiastic in their last moments, and his business is to exhort the dying person to perform some good works, and leave his effects to the church; for they say our Saviour tells us, "That "whatever good is done to the least of his brethren, "he will look upon it as done to himself;" and one order of the Franciscans have been so very humble, as to stile themselves *minimi*, the least; which gives them a better title to charitable legacies. What will not a profligate wretch, who hath amassed riches by all manner of oppressive and indirect means, do, when on his death-bed, to attain the happy mansions of eternity? Purgatory is also an inexhaustible fund to the clergy. It is hardly credible what envy and rancour the different orders entertain against one another, and their artifice and assiduity in drawing the silly sheep from one fold to another; and one of the most infallible expedients, for this purpose, is the glaring pomp and magnificence of a church. It must indeed be owned, that this emulation in building and decorating them is very advantageous to the people, as it employs a great number of hands, and confequently promotes the circulation of money; which is infinitely better than to let it lie dead in immenfe treafures, or to let the convents acquire all the landed eftates. That jewels, indeed, which have no fixed or current value, to the amount of fo many millions, fhould fhine as ufelefs offerings in the church of Loretto, is very wrong, but much better than that fociety fhould be deprived of fo much ready fpecie.

Several having given fo ample a defcription of the ancient ftate of Rome, I fhall not now dwell on that fubject, but refer the curious to Roffi, Pinaroli, de Seine, and other authors; and fhall therefore only add to what has already been defcribed, a fhort account of fuch principal remains of antiquity, as are, at prefent, to be feen at Rome, and which have not yet been mentioned.

The amphitheatre of Titus has been honoured by Martial with a pompous epigram; and, though the injuries of time have greatly defaced it, yet it cannot, even now, be beheld without aftonifhment. The whole edifice is of Travartina ftone, and has four galleries above one another, adorned with pillars of the Doric, Ionic, Corinthian, and Compofite orders. According to Eutropius and Caffiodorus, five thoufand, or, if Dio, lib. 66, may be credited, nine thoufand wild beafts, of various kinds, were killed, in its area, at the dedication of it. This grand ftructure retained part of its ancient fplendor, in the time of Paul III. about the year 1534, when it confifted of eighty arches, four of which, larger than the reft, ftood oppofite one another, at right angles, being the four grand entrances. Its circumference was a thoufand fix hundred and twelve geometrical feet, the external figure circular, but the infide elliptical or oval. Titus employed twelve thoufand Jewifh captives at the building of it, and expended immenfe fums upon it. The exact dimenfions of this ftupendous work may be feen in Vitruvius and Lipfius, as alfo in Maffei's elaborate treatife

treatife *de Amphitheatris*, where he fhews, that amphitheatres, built with ftone, were far from being fo common as is generally imagined; that, except Rome, Verona, and Capua, there was not a city, in all Italy, that could boaft of one. Hiftorians have often confounded the words, *amphitheatrum*, *theatrum*, *circus*, *ftadium*, and *arena*, ufing one for another. It is evident, indeed, from Tacitus, *Annal.* iv. that wooden amphitheatres were built in feveral parts of the Roman empire; for he relates, in the place cited, the fall of one at Fidena, not far from Rome, in the time of Tiberius: this accident was occafioned by the great numbers of fpectators, the weaknefs of the materials, and defect in the workmanfhip; fifty thoufand were killed or hurt; or, according to Orofius, and Suetonius, about twenty thoufand loft their lives in that amphitheatre.

The wild beafts were not, according to the opinion of fome, kept in the arched places, under the firft row of feats, the amphitheatres being neither fpacious enough, nor of proper ftrength for that purpofe; but were brought from diftant places to the Arena, from whence they were turned loofe from their cages. The amphitheatre at Rome is called Colifco, or Colofeum, rather for its furprifing magnitude, than from the coloffus that ftood before Nero's golden palace. In the year 1725 a plan and elevation of this furprifing ftructure, begun by Vefpafian, and finifhed by Titus, was publifhed at the Hague, in a large folio, with feveral copper-plates, by Carlo Fontana. A great quantity of ftone has been taken from this ancient ftructure, for the building of the palaces of Farnefe, St. Mark, and the Cancellaria; but fome pretend, that thefe ftones were only fcattered and feparated from the building, by ftorms of rain, tempefts, or earthquakes, not one of them being taken from the edifice itfelf. But, be this as it may, the area is now overgrown with grafs and weeds, and not the leaft care taken to keep it in repair.

In most of the stones on the outside of this amphitheatre, are holes of three or four inches diameter. Some are of the opinion, that, when the popes resid d at the Lateran palace, markets and fairs were held there, and that these holes were made in the walls by the chapmen, for fixing their booths or stands; but there is a strong objection against this opinion, as the holes are made at so great a height, that they could not be of use on such occasions: others imagine these holes were made when the edifice was first built, and that the iron cramps and braces, for binding the stones together, were inserted in them, and fastened with melted lead. This method of binding stones together is mentioned by Thucydides, lib. iv. and Vitruvius, lib. ii. cap. 8. and the marquis Maffei observed holes, of the same kind, not only in the triumphal arch at Susa, but even in the stones of edifices which had remained untouched; and on applying the chissel, in order to separate them, he found iron braces fastened with lead, which could not but confirm him in his opinion of the use of these holes. Whether, during the many ravages the city of Rome has undergone, the enemy thought proper to carry away the lead and iron; or whether the poor herdsmen, whose cattle used to feed near this place, for want of other employment, took the trouble of forcing them out; is not easily determined. Cassiodorus (lib. iii. 31.) indeed informs us, that, so early as the time of Theodorus, it was found necessary to decree punishments for those who should steal the lead and iron from the walls of ancient structures.

According to the most exact computation, the number of spectators this amphitheatre could contain, did not exceed thirty-four thousand, exclusive of those in the upper gallery; I cannot therefore imagine, why some authors should endeavour to impose so flagrantly on their readers. Ammianus Marcellius, in his sixteenth book, says, that eighty six thousand persons sitting, and twenty thousand standing,

might

might have a full view of the sports exhibited in this amphitheatre. The same author, lib. xvi. cap. 16. calls this edifice a prodigious amphitheatre, built of Tiburtine stone, to a height almost beyond the reach of the human eye.

Betwixt the amphitheatre and the triumphal arch of Constantine the Great, is a pillar, which, on the account of the water springing out of it like a fountain, is called *Meta sudans*, and seems to have been intended for the use of the people when heated at the games; but this fountain appears, from a passage in Seneca's letters, to have been in being even so early as the time of Nero. It has been several times repaired, though, at present, it makes but a mean appearance.

The triumphal arch of Constantine the Great shews that sculpture, even in that emperor's time, which was above a hundred years before Rome fell under the power of the barbarous nations, was greatly declined. Nor are the medals, struck since the time of Caracalla, comparable to those of the emperors who flourished before him. Hence the beauty of some pieces in this triumphal arch incline me to think, that they are the works of an earlier date, and belonged to some other ancient monument, perhaps to the triumphal arches of Trajan or Domitian. That, at least, some of the basso-relievos, now on Constantine's arch, were originally on that of Trajan, cannot be doubted, together with the eight mutilated statues, whose heads, according to Paulus Jovius, Lorenzo de Medicis privately broke off, and conveyed to Florence. This arch stands in the Via Appia, at the junction of the Celian and Palatine mounts; under the main arch are these words, *Liberatori urbi*, " To " the deliverer of the city " And on the other side, *Fundatori quietis*, " To the author of public tran- " quillity."

The way from hence, over the Campus Vaccinus, to the Capitol, leads through the triumphal arch of

Titus Vespasian, which is in very good condition, and has, on that side facing the Coliseum, an inscription, from whence it plainly appears, that it was erected on the death of the emperor. This superb piece of antiquity consists only of a single arch, on which is represented, in basso-relievos, the river Jordan, the golden candlestick with seven branches, the tables of the law, two jubilee trumpets, the table of shew-bread, and other utensils of the temple at Jerusalem: from whence some light may be thrown on the Jewish antiquities, as is shewn at large by Reland, in a particular treatise, published at Utrecht in 1717, intitled, *De spoliis Templi Hierosolymitani in Arcu Titiano Romæ conspicuis*. This triumph is also celebrated in another inscription found at Rome, which, in all probability, formerly belonged to this arch.

In the Forum Romanum, or, as it is now called, the Campus Vaccinus, beside the remains of temples, is one of the largest basons, or vases, of a single piece of granate, that ever was found in Rome; it is of a circular figure, and twenty Roman feet in diameter: some conjecture, that it was used in the ancient baths; but, at present, it only serves as a water-trough for sheep and oxen.

The most perfect remains of the Cloaca Maxima, or large common-sewer built by Tarquinius Priscus, are on the left hand near the temple of Janus Quadrifrons, in the Forum Boarium. It was sixteen feet in breadth, and twelve in height, and several other drains emptied themselves into it. That such conveniencies greatly contributed to the healthfulness of the air, is beyond dispute; but whether an advantage accrued to the public treasury from them, as some pretend, is not so certain. One of its passages is carried under the church of St. Stefano alle Corozze, and through the garden of signor Tiberio Genci, into the Tiber. In the gallery of the garden is a mark, with an inscription, shewing how high the water of the Tiber rose in the year 1686. From this place is the best prospect of the remains of the ruined bridge, called Pons Senatorius. With regard to the inundations of the Tiber, which, in all ages, have done such considerable damages to the city of Rome, Lancisi, the pope's physician, is of opinion, that they proceed from the following causes. 1. The force of the sea repelling the influx of the river. 2. The strong and continual south-winds. 3. The obstructions at the mouth of the river. 4. The great number of bridges built upon it, whereby the current is obstructed. 5. The ruins of several bridges and other buildings, the stones of which have fallen into the Tiber, and rendered the bottom of the river very unequal. 6. The great number of mills erected on it; and, 7. The tenacity observed in the water of the Tiber.

The Columna Antonina, which stands in the Piazza di Colonna, is a hundred and eighty-five feet high, and embellished with bass-reliefs, representing the principal actions of Marcus Aurelius. This column is thirty-five feet higher than that of Trajan: within it are stairs winding in a spiral line, the light being admitted through fifty-two small windows, and consist of a hundred and ninety steps, which lead to a square gallery surrounded with iron balustrades, from whence there is a delighful prospect. About fourteen feet above this gallery, is a statue of St. Paul fourteen palms in height, and of gilt brass, erected by pope Sixtus V. who also repaired the whole column, and caused several inscriptions to be cut on the pedestal. This whole column consists of no more than twenty-eight pieces, whence an idea may be formed of the enormous size of the stones. The figures on the upper part of the column are larger than those of the lower; this being the only piece of antiquity where the rules of perspective, with which the ancients were but little acquainted, have been observed. Montfaucon has inserted a great many of its bas-reliefs in his *Antiquité Expliqué*, tom. iv. P. I. But the fullest account of of this pillar is in a treatise, intitled, *La Colonna di Marco Aurelio*, &c.

The Columna Trajani, or Trajan's pillar, which is of a much larger diameter, and adorned with bas-reliefs of a more elevated kind, and bolder execution than that of Antoninus, makes a very grand appearance. The beauty of this column is also augmented by a noble pedestal, representing a rock, and embellished trophies of armour, shields, &c. It stands in a square hole, seven or eight feet deep, the sides of which are supported by brick walls, six or eight feet above the foundation. This evidently shews the great elevation of the ground, and that, by the many ravages and devastations, this famous city has undergone, its situation is raised much higher than it was when this pillar was first erected. The bas-reliefs are carried round this pillar, and from the bottom to the top, form twenty-three spiral circumvolutions: they represent the expedition of Trajan against Decebalus, king of the Dacians, and contain near two thousand five hundred figures; but without the least regard to perspective, those in the rear appearing as large as those advanced in the front, and seem to be raised, in order to present themselves the plainer to the spectator's view. The spiral stair-case within consists of one hundred and eighty steps, and receives light by means of forty-three windows or apertures, properly disposed. The urn, which formerly contained Trajan's ashes, and was placed on the top of this pillar, has been removed, and its place supplied by a statue of brass gilt, representing St. Peter. This pillar is of marble, and consists of thirty-four pieces only; the pedestal is formed out of a single block; the base consists of eight, the torus of one, the shaft of twenty-three, and the capital of one.

The Mausolæum or Augustus, in the Strada Pontifici, behind the church of St. Rocca, is a circular building; the area is filled up, and converted into a garden.

garden. In the center of it is a statue of Augustus, and the outside of this structure is in good condition; but the inside so greatly decayed, that no idea can be formed of its ancient magnificence.

The remains of the emperor Serverus's tomb are without St. John's Gate, on the road to Frescati; and those of the Mausolæum of Cicelia, daughter of queen Creticus Metellus, and wife to the rich Crœsus, in the Via Appia, beyond St. Sebastian's church. The latter resembles an old decayed tower, and is now called Capo di Bove, from the number of ox-heads represented in bass-reliefs on this edifice. When these parts of Italy were the seat of war, the enemy often made use of this tower for a place of arms, or a fortress.

On the side of the Porta, or St. Paul's gate, is the pyramid of Caius Cestus, one of the seven Epulones. This structure, which is built with bricks, and incrusted with marble, is a hundred and ten feet high; and each side of the base is eighty-one feet and a half. At the entrance of this pyramid, are two marble pillars, and within, an oblong apartment, with an arched roof, and a Victory painted in each corner. A particular account and description of this pyramid may be seen in Falconieri's Dissertation, annexed to Nardini's *Roma Antiqua*.

Not far from hence, toward the city, is the Mons Testaceus, or Doliolum, vulgarly called Il Testaceo. This hill consists intirely of the fragments of broken earthen ware, or pot-sherds, brought hither from the city, and is an hundred and sixty feet high, and half an Italian mile in circumference. Some vintners have lately dug wine-vaults here, and as the wine is kept perfectly cool in the summer, they have a great demand for it.

The obelisks near the Lateran, St. Mary Maggiore, St. Maria sopra Minerva, in the Vatican, before the Rotunda, in the piazza Navona, in the villa Medicea, in the villa Mattei, and some others are

all

all of Egyptian granate, and of such enormous size, that it is not a little surprising how the ancient mechanics, who were ignorant of the improvements of latter ages, could move such prodigious masses from place to place. With regard to the ships and floats on which they were transported from Egypt to Italy, Pliny and Suetonius may be consulted. Some of the learned will not allow these obelisks to have been dug out of the quarries in one single piece, but suppose the ancients were possessed of a secret, either as it were of casting them, or working the materials into a certain texture, which, being moulded into a proper form at the place where it was to be erected, was there dried, either by air or fire; but, if this had been really the case, how came Heliogabalus's design of erecting a column of extraordinary design and height, with a stair-case within it, to be frustrated? For Lampridius tells us, that this project came to nothing, merely for want of a block of granate suitable to the emperor's vanity.

The ruins of Pompey's theatre, which, according to Pliny, would contain forty thousand spectators, are now inclosed in the Orsina palace.

In the *Notitia Imperii*, we are told, that the number of temples in ancient Rome amounted to four hundred and twenty; but now it would be no very easy task to ascertain the proper situation, even of the tenth part of them.

I shall conclude this description of the city of Rome with observing, that whoever would see all the above-mentioned curiosities, must be very industrious to dispatch them in six weeks, and also previously furnished with proper information to reap the advantage proposed to himself from such a survey.

The gates of Rome are never shut, so that, at any hour, either of the night or day, one may go in or out at pleasure. In travelling from this city to Naples, the best method is to ride on horse-back, as the cheapest way of travelling. I would not advise
any

any perfon to go from Rome to Naples with the vetturini; for, though they go by the road lying over Monte Caffino, and confequently an opportunity offers of feeing the celebrated abbey of Benedictines on that mountain, yet it is attended with the mortification of being detained five days on the road, and paying them, befide, an extraordinary price for the time they lofe on this occafion.

Between Rome and Torre di Mezza Via, which is the firft relay, are ftupendous ruins of feveral aqueducts. Velletri is three ftages from Rome, and fituated on a hill; it was anciently fo famed for its excellent vineyards, that Pliny, lib. xiv. c. 6. reckons the wines, produced from them, among the beft about Rome; but they have fo much degenerated fince, that they are, at prefent, fo fharp, as to be hardly drinkable, till they are previoufly boiled.

On the left hand, near Cifterna, which is the fourth ftage from Rome, ftands the fine palace of prince Caferta. Sermonetta lies in a marfhy and unhealthy fituation. In Pliny's time it was called Palus Pomptina; but, inftead of twenty-three towns, which, in his time, ftood on this track of land, only a few fcattered houfes are now remaining. Strabo, *Geogr.* lib. v. obferves, that the air of this diftrict was reckoned very unhealthy in former times; and Silius Italicus calls it Campus Pomptinus peftifer; and, as the extenfive fens, and ftagnating waters, which before impregnated the air with thefe noxious particles, are now confiderably increafed, it muft be more unhealthy than ever.

Tarracina, anciently called Anxur, the laft town in the papal dominions, is fituated at the brow of a hill. The whole country, hereabouts, has the appearance of a delicious garden; and therefore it is not at all furprifing, that the ancient inhabitants fhould pay their adoration to Priapus, the patron of gardens; as it appears they did, from the images of that deity, in feveral places.

Juft

Just beyond Terracina are the ruins of the temple of Janus; the palaces of Julius Cæsar, Adrian, and other remains of antiquity; particularly the 'Via Appia, which here extends from Mola to the river Garigliano. This famous road derives its name from Appius Claudius, the censor, who extended it from Rome to Capua, at his own expence. It appears from Tacitus, Strabo, and Horace, that it was carried as far as Brundusium; but they make no mention of the person by whom it was continued. The stones of this pavement are about a foot square, and so hard and firmly cemented, as to have endured the continued frictions of carriages for several hundred years: it is twenty palms broad, and consequently sufficient for two carriages to go abreast. From Terracina there is a fine view of the sea to the right, which is so near the road, that, at the distance of an Italian mile from that town, there was a necessity of breaking down a piece of rock to clear the way, which there runs close by the sea. Three miles further, on this road, is the frontier wall of the kingdom of Naples, called Portello, which extends itself, according to some, from the hill to the sea, or, at least, to a fort, where, in time of war, the Neapolitans have a garrison.

In going from Rome to Naples, it is requisite to be furnished with a passport, which will be given by the imperial minister, or the cardinal-agent, gratis; and, in returning from Naples to Rome, another passport must be procured from the viceroy: in both of them is specified the time of their continuing in force. The ecclesiastical state, and kingdom of Naples, are distinguished by giving the appellation of La Campagna to the former, and Il Regno to the latter: but the difference between them is sufficiently visible; the kingdom of Naples being much more populous, and better cultivated than the papal territories.

It is with pleasure, that I recollect the elegant prospect, all the way, from Fondi to Iteri: the country, on the right, produces garden-stuff, flax, and corn, interspersed by rows of vines, the upper branches of which are interwoven in a very beautiful manner. This prospect terminates with the sea, by which means this charming scene is diversified by a multitude of Tartans, and other vessels sailing on it. The prospect on the left hand is not at all inferior, being variegated with vines, olive and mulberry-trees, lofty cypresses, and orange-groves, and terminated by a distant chain of mountains.

The first town, on this side, in the Neapolitan dominions, is Fondi, which, in the year 1534, suffered extreamly by the attempt of Hariaden Barbarossa, to carry off the beautiful Julia Gonzaga, countess of Fondi, with a view of presenting that celebrated beauty to the grand signor: however, if the story, related of her, be true, her modesty was of a most savage nature. They say, that a gentleman, who rescued her in her shift, at the utmost hazard of his life, was afterward assassinated by her desire, merely because he had seen her almost naked. Had this execrable murder been committed by her husband Vespasian Colonna, in a fit of jealousy, so natural to the Italians, the lady would, in a great measure, have been innocent; but surely she must now be considered as more notorious for her cruelty, than famous for her chastity. Barbarossa, being disappointed of his prize, vented his rage in pillaging and destroying the town, not even sparing the tombs of the two dukes of Colonna; beside exercising the most horrid acts of cruelty, he carried many of the inhabitants into slavery.

Mola is an imperial port, and has a custom-house and a garrison, which is relieved weekly from Gaeta. Near Mola are the ruins of a palace, which, according to some inscriptions said to be found in it, belonged to Cicero; but the grotto and subterranean vaults were very much damaged, in the prefent century, by the imperialifts, who, during the fiege of Gaeta, made this place their magazine. It was on a journey from hence to fome other place, that Cicero was affaffinated by that ungrateful monfter Popilius Lænas, whom that orator's eloquence had faved from the gallows. The fortrefs of Gaeta is fituated three Italian miles from Mola, and is an hour's paffage by water: it derives its name from Cajeta, Æneas's nurfe, who, according to Virgil, lib. 7. both died and was buried here.

On the Monte della Trinita the Benedictines have a church, near which is a large fiffure in the rock, from the top to the fea; faid to have been made miraculoufly, at the time of our Saviour's paffion. This opinion is founded upon modern, and confequently fufpicious tradition, and is abfolutely contradicted by thofe who confine all the miracles, which the holy fcriptures mention to have accompanied the death of Chrift, intirely to the country of Judea. But, whenever this earthquake happened, the effect of it is really furprifing: the chafm is between four and five feet broad near the furface of the fea, and ftill wider at the fummit. You pafs through it, by a flight of fteps, to a little chapel, called del Crociffifo, from whence there is a beautiful profpect of the fea. From the chapel to the church above, are fifty-nine fteps, of which fifty-one are in the cleft of the rock; from whence, to the landing-place, are eighteen more. The monks prefent ftrangers with little pieces of the rock, and to thefe Roman catholics pay a very great veneration, and give a fmall offering, or alms, to the fathers; who, in return, affure them, that they are now poffeffed of an infallible cure for the head-ach, the epilepfy, hard labour, and other diforders. Ships, as they pafs by the lower chapel, generally falute it with a gun, and, lying upon their oars, either pay their devotions, amidft fome mufic, or fend a-fhore a fmall pecuniary offering to the convent, at leaft equivalent

valent to the expence of a falute. It is even faid, that Turkifh veffels have often fent a fum of money to the monks, in confequence of vows made for their prefervation in ftormy weather, upon directing their devotion toward this chapel.

The Francifcan convent here boafts of its having been the refidence of the founder of that feraphic order, as they term it. Without the Porta di Ferra, is fhewn the place, on the fea-fhore, where St. Francis ftood, when he preached with fuch energy, that the very fifhes miraculoufly raifed themfelves above the furface of the water, liftening to his voice. The tower of the cathedral is faid to have been built by Frederic Barbaroffa, by way of expiation for the crimes he had commited. Contiguous to the door of the caftle, which ftands on a hill, is fhewn the body of the famous Charles, duke of Bourbon, with a lower jaw of wood, inferted to fupply the place of the natural one, long fince decayed. As this nobleman was killed in ftorming Rome, and confequently under the pope's excommunication, and openly in arms againft the holy fee, his remains were denied burial in confecrated ground; and to leave him unburied, or depofit his body among the common people, did not feem confiftent either with his high rank, or the eminent fervices he had performed for the emperor; the Spaniards, therefore, determined to dry his corpfe like a mummy, and place it here, fo that it is not at all furprifing, that his face has contracted a black colour. He ftands in a clofet, with yellow boots on, and red facings; the ftockings, which come but a little above the boots, are bordered with fine lace. In 1719, general Prampere, governor of the city, had this fkeleton new cloathed in blue, with filver trimmings, placed a fword by his fide, a cane in his hand, and a hat and feather on his head.

Notwithftanding the eulogies made on this famous warrior after his death, it is well known, that a Spaniard,

niard, in whose house he had taken up his quarters, set fire to it the next day after his death, to efface the memory of its having harboured a traitor. Formerly the officers of this garrison, on public rejoicings, used to take off the duke's skull, and drink healths out of it; but this savage custom having given rise to several quarrels, some of which were productive of unhappy consequences, it was intirely prohibited.

Old Capua, the pleasures of which quite enervated Hanibal's army, lies two Italian miles from the New, on the right hand toward Naples. Of its ancient magnificence, nothing remarkable now remains, except some few ruins of an amphitheatre; it having successively felt the barbarous ravages of the Vandals, Ostrogoths, and Longobards, who levelled every thing with the ground. The distance between New Capua and Naples is sixteen Italian miles; and the road lies through as charming a country as most in Europe. The country on each side is finely diversified with gardens, vineyards, and corn-fields. In some places the vines climb up the lofty trees planted on each side of the road, and, by interweaving their luxuriant branches with those of the tops of the trees, form a kind of beautiful festoons. In the months of February and March, seven stages in a post-chaise can hardly be travelled from morning till night; but, in the long days of summer, the journey from Rome to Naples, which is seventeen stages and a half, is performed, with ease, in two days.

[The kingdom of Naples is bounded on the north-east by the ecclesiastical state; but on all other parts, by the Mediterranean and Adriatic. Its extent from the south-east to the north-west, is 280 miles; and from north-east to south-west, from 96 to 120 miles.]

On account of its fertility, Naples is justly termed an earthly paradise; for it abounds with all sorts of grain; the finest fruit and garden-productions of every

every kind; 'rice, flax, oil, and wine, in the greateſt plenty and perfection. In Calabria are gathered large quantities of manna, and, both here and in other parts of the kingdom, ſaffron, equal to the Oriental in value, is produced.

This kingdom alſo affords alum, vitriol, ſulphur, rock-cryſtal, marble, and ſeveral ſorts of minerals. The wool is excellent both for fineneſs and ſtrength; and it produces ſilk in ſuch abundance, as to ſupply foreign countries with its manufactures of that kind. Its wine diſputes the preference with the richeſt and moſt noted climates for that commodity. It has noble and numerous flocks and herds of cattle, and, particularly, the Neopolitan horſes are ſo famous, that the bare mention of them is ſufficient. Beſide theſe productions, the greateſt part of which is exported, and the returns made in hard coin into the kingdom; the trade in ſtuff, and excellent ſoap, is a conſiderable fund of wealth. I muſt not omit here a particular kind of manufacture, which is principally carried on at Taranto and Reggio, and took its riſe from a ſort of hairy or woolly filaments growing on a certain ſpecies of ſhell-fiſh; out of which materials, the inhabitants, having found out a method of cleaning and preparing them, at preſent knit waiſtcoats, caps, ſtockings, and gloves, reputed warmer than thoſe of wool*. This ſtuff, indeed, falls far ſhort of ſilk in ſoftneſs and fineneſs; but, on the other hand, it always retains a particular gloſs. The natural colour of this ſhell-wool is an olive-green; the muſcles on which it grows, are found in great plenty about the iſlands of Malta, Corſica, Sardinia, and in the gulph of Venice.

Among the natural curioſities of the kingdom of Naples, may be accounted alſo the *lapis Phrygius*, or *Pietra fungifera*, as it is commonly called; which,

---

* A ſhell, with a pair of gloves of this manufacture, are to be ſeen in the Britiſh Muſeum.

when laid in a shady and damp place, spontaneously produces, in a few days, fungi, or champignons, according to the magnitude of the stone; and these may be eaten. But it is a mistake to imagine, that this vegetable is produced purely from a stone; the lapis Phrygius being no other than a conglomerated hard assemblage, composed of earth, rotten boxwood, and the filaments of several plants, under which the champignon-seeds lie concealed, and these so very minute, as, of themselves, to be hardly distinguishable from dust, unless by the help of a microscope. But that, even in this natural production, fungi are generated from homogeneous seeds, is evident from hence, namely, that, if a fungus be not left to ripen so long on such a stone till it has shed its seeds, the stone, at last, quite loses its vegetative quality. Warm water is poured upon this lapis Phrygius, particularly to forward the vegetation of the seeds; for it penetrates into the smallest interstices, dilates the pores of the stone, causes a fermentation in the inclosed sap, and thus warms the seeds, that they speedily germinate. Spring is the season for these stones, when in their natural position on the earth, to produce champignons; but, if laid in pots, and covered with some earth, in order to impart the necessary moisture to them, they yield them at all times of the year. They are met with in great plenty, and of all sizes, in the lower parts of the ecclesiastical state, and further on near Fondi, Gaeta, Iteri, about Naples, and other parts of that kingdom*. The warmth of the climate, and richness of the soil in Italy, is very proper with a suitable moisture previously given it to produce truffles, potatoes, morels, champignons, and the like vegetables, of an uncommon largeness.

 The fiery eruptions of mount Vesuvius, often strike a terror into the neighbouring country; but as

---

* An account of the mush-room stone, was published some few years since by Dr. Hill.

MOUNT VESUVIUS with its Eruption

MOUNT VESUVIUS.

every thing which feems to be noxious, brings alfo fome advantage with it; fo this mountain, by the fulphureous and nitrous particles with which it manures the ground, and the heat of its fubterranean paffages, contributes, not a little, to its uncommon fertility: the fame effect is obfervable from mount Ætna, in Sicily. Thofe are obferved to be the moft fruitful parts, where great quantities of fulphur, falt, faltpetre, and other minerals are found. But, where there are no fiery volcanos in fuch places, the fermentation and ebullition of thofe inflammable fubftances would be productive of the moft dreadful effects: whereas, at prefent, they find fome vent, and make frequent difcharges. As it is found alfo from experience, that this country is fubject to fewer earthquakes, and thofe lefs fatal in their effects, after the eruptions of the fubterranean matter through the mouth of Vefuvius; fo the inhabitants are not at all alarmed at feeing the vernal explofions of this mountain, when they are not violent; nor is the air, by that means, rendered more unhealthy; but, on the contrary, Barra, lying at the foot of Vefuvius, and near the fea, is remarkable for its falubrity, beyond many other places.

The upper part of Vefuvius is, indeed, intirely covered with afhes and ftones, but its lower parts produce three forts of coftly wine, namely, Vino Greco, yellow mufcadel, and the well known Lachrymæ Chrifti, as it is called: the fecond fort has the moft agreeable flavour, but will not bear any long exportation. At Pietrabianca, a bottle of it is fold at a carlin and a half, or about fix-pence. The vino Greco is the produce of vines tranfplanted hither from Greece, and which have anfwered very well. The Lachrymæ Chrifti takes its name from the drops of juice which fall from the grapes when full ripe.

This year, as early as the end of February, mount Vefuvius began to emit flames. The fmoke might be feen about three ftages diftant from Naples, and rifing rising directly up in the air like a large black pillar, till the wind had broke and dissipated it. This happened every three or four minutes, after which time, the top of the mountain might be plainly seen, till a new eruption came on, for a few minutes, casting out the ashes, stones, and smoke. The various agitations of the smoke, by the wind, have caused some persons to imagine, that they beheld several kinds of frightful figures, so that it is not surprising, that, according to Dio Cassius, lib. xvi. in Vespasian's time, a variety of giants was seen in it. The smoke is not immediately dispersed as soon as it comes out of the mountain, but expands itself in long streaks thro' the sky, resembling thick clouds: in the night-time, almost after every explosion, a short fiery pillar was seen to shoot up from the mountain, but extinguished before it fell down again. Probably, this effect only proceeded from the ignited stones thrown up in a perpendicular direction, the greatest part of which, especially in calm weather, fall down again into the caverns whence they issued. After waiting, to no purpose, for eight days, till the eruptions of the mountain should abate, at the expiration of which time, it was rather to be apprehended that they would become stronger, and last longer, than I proposed to stay at Naples; on the 14th of March I resolved to set out and visit this mountain, notwithstanding its fiery explosions.

The parties, to go upon such an expedition, must not be over numerous, as not only hackney-horses are scarce at Naples, but the peasants (whose assistance is absolutely necessary on such occasions) living on the mountains, are too few to attend on a large company. The distance from Naples to the foot of Vesuvius (here commonly called Monte di Somma, either from Plutone Summano, or from its height or summit, called Summita, or from an adjacent manor called Somma) is five Italian miles, including the circuit round the bay, to the foot of the mountain, from whence

MOUNT VESUVIUS.

whence to the fummit is near three miles farther. It feemed formerly to have been confecrated to Jupiter Tonans, as appears from an infcription at Capua, mentioned by Parrini, *Jovi Vefuvio Sacrum*. D. D.

Mount Vefuvius, like Parnaffus, confifts properly of two hills or mountains; though that which lies on the right, as you return from Naples, only emits fire and fmoke. The valley betwixt thofe hills is about a mile long, and extremely fertile; the height of the burning fummit, which is the loweft of the two, is computed to be eleven hundred fathoms above the furface of the fea. This mountain, by a fudden eruption, in the year 1631, laid wafte all the neighbouring country; and a warning, or caveat, was cut in ftone in the Latin tongue, and fet up at Refina, a village within three miles of Naples, to admonifh the inhabitants to fly in time, when threatened with an eruption.

This unfortunate event, in 1631, reached three miles on the fea-coaft, namely, to Torro del Greco, whereby three convents, and other buildings, were entirely deftroyed.

From Refina, the acclivity of the ground increafes; but you may ftill continue on horfeback. Here are feveral ftones fcattered about, as memorials of its former devaftations, and are half calcined; but the greateft part of them have been gathered by the peafants, to make fences for inclofing their vineyards. It is aftonifhing to think of the impetuofity by which fuch huge bulks of four or five hundred weight have been thrown feveral Italian miles diftant from the hill.

At laft you arrive at the afcent of the mountain, where it is impoffible to ride any farther, being covered with afhes and cinders. Here the horfes are left to the care of the fervants, and fhoes fubftituted for boots, for the more expedition on foot. Near this a hermit hath made himfelf a mean habitation, where he continues till the danger of the mountain becomes

becomes so formidable as to drive him away. As travellers return from the mountain fatigued, this hermit stands ready with a flask of wine to refresh them, for some trifling gratuity, as his order does not prohibit him from taking money.

The peasants of the adjacent villages swarm here to attend strangers, and often more than are necessary; which makes them so assiduous, that they often quarrel with each other for their chance, as it may be called. A traveller ought, therefore, to carry fire-arms on these occasions, they being a base thievish crew, and wear at their sides a sort of cutlass. They are, beside, so void of shame, that while the travellers are resting themselves, they jeer one another with their obscene and villainous pranks. During the short time we continued at the skirts of the mountain, they boasted they would conduct us to the top; nay, to the very mouth of this vulcano; but the higher we ascended, the more timorous they grew, and at every little blaze which issued from the mountain, implored the assistance of the Virgin and St. Januarius; telling us the danger we were exposing ourselves to: so that we were obliged to encourage them to keep up their spirits. They wear leathern belts, which travellers take hold of, in order to render their ascent more easy. If the two peasants who go before, are not strong enough to drag them up, one goes behind and shoves. Every prudent person ought to agree first, before he engages these hirelings, and, at dismissing of them, to add a small gratuity, as they have otherwise been known to have proceeded to a mutinous rudeness.

The mountain being steep, and covered with black ashes, the ascent is very difficult; for the ashes cause you often to slide several steps downward; and, in places clear of ashes, the ruggedness of the cinders is attended with equal difficulty. That sulphur lies here a foot deep, as a certain author asserts, I never could perceive; but among those drossy clods and cinders,

MOUNT VESUVIUS.

cinders, I met with fome red and yellow fubftances, feemingly impregnated with fulphur. You cannot follow in the fteps of your guide, the afhes filling up the impreffion made by the foot.

It has often been known, that from this volcano has iffued a flood of lava, or compofition of fulphur, metals, minerals, and the like, to the great damage of all the contiguous parts. The fcoria of this ejected matter lies ftill one layer or ftratum upon another, with large ftones projecting above the furface, which, in their courfe along the fiery river, were ftopped by their inequalities, and fixed in the melted matter, gradually hardened; for had the ftream been intirely fluid, it would have fettled and cooled in a more uniform furface. In the year 1694, the country was vifited with one of thefe fiery rivers of lava, and the burnt ftones, though forced under the melted matter with poles, immediately emerged again. Thefe ftreams or currents are not thrown up from the mountain, like the ftones, but pour down, as from an inclined veffel; fo that it feems as if fuch an effufion muft proceed from the whole cavity, the receffes of the mountain of melted fubftances being abfolutely full. Some, from a pretended calculation, have afferted, that during the eruption in the year 1694, fo great a quantity of this igneous matter was difcharged, that in fome places the furface was fixty ells above the furface of the ground; and that if the whole had been accumulated in one mafs, it would have equaled, in bulk, the mountain from whofe bowels it was emitted.

About half way from the fummit of the mountain, we met with ftones at leaft an hundred weight, glowing hot, which, when broken, had exactly the appearance of red-hot iron. They contained a heat fufficient to fet paper on fire; and our guides affirmed, that they had juft been ejected from the mountain. I faw about ten or fifteen of thefe, but none either tumbling

down

down the mountain, or in motion in the air. As we proceeded farther, our ears were saluted with the most horrid noise, resembling the explosion of a whole battery of cannon at a distance; and under our feet we perceived a rumbling, like the continual boiling of a large cauldron. Upon making a hole in the ashes some inches deep with a stick, a sensible heat was immediately emitted, and, in some places, greater than one's hand could bear. At several places we perceived the smoke to issue out, as it were, through small fissures. I was at a loss, for a long time, what to make of little round holes that appeared in great numbers about the size of those made by the finger; but, at last, I found them to be receptacles for wasps and hornets, who, finding themselves oppressed with cold, retire hither in the night-time. At last, after many weary steps, we reached the place where the largest volcano was formerly situated; but it is now not only choaked up, but by frequent eruptions covered with a round pile of ashes and lava. Here the increase of heat was very sensible, especially at every explosion, when the ashes flew so strongly in our faces, that we were obliged to hold something before them, to defend our eyes. The ground also was so hot under our feet, that the flag burnt the very soles of our shoes: here our ears were not alarmed with the dreadful noises we heard when ascending the mountain, but every eruption was attended with a whizzing noise, like that of a great number of rockets thrown up at once. The multitude of stones, the clouds of smoke, and other materials thrown up into the air, resemble the springing of a mine, and totally obscure the sky. Most of the stones, especially when of any considerable weight, fall again perpendicularly into the abyss from whence they were projected, and, probably, this is often repeated, till they are, at last, thrown without the verge of the aperture. Great quantities, however, fall on the sides, and roll down with such a hideous noise as to strike the spectator

with

with terror. As the wind drives the smoke, ashes, and stones generally more one way than another, a person has thereby an opportunity of chusing a favourable station; but, if the eruptions are violent, you cannot approach any side with safety. We could perceive no flames in the day-time, and, very possibly, the heat we felt, at each explosion, proceeded from the melted lava and ignited stones projected into the air, which, at night, appear like red-hot bullets.

According to Pompeius Sarnella, bishop of Bisceglia, the upper mountain first appeared on the 26th of September 1685. I imagine we might have about eight hundred paces still to ascend over sharp stones and deep ashes: but, at the time we were at the foot of the mountain, the eruptions succeeded each other every two or three minutes, so that we must have stood out upward of eight shocks before we could have reached the top. But the hazard, which continually increases, the nearer you approach to the summit of the mountain, becoming evidently greater, and it being impossible to persuade the peasants, our guides, to proceed any farther, we agreed to return. In all probability, had we ventured to the aperture of the mountain, we should have seen only smoke and vapour. It is, therefore, very ridiculous for travellers to pretend, that, during an eruption of the mountain, they have been at the top, and, looking down the hollow abyss, have observed it all on fire, and running together, with great violence, like the ebullition of sulphur, bitumen, and metal in a furnace. Some ingenious friends, of unquestionable veracity, who have been, several times, at the top, when the mountain was still, have assured me, that, by reason of the smoke, they could but very seldom see the bottom of the cavity; and, when they did, it was subject to great variation, for sometimes it was of a prodigious depth, and, at other times, hardly more than a hundred feet, according to the diversity of the rising or falling of the melted matter from the last eruption,

by

by the induration of which, the bottom is formed. Some travellers are so daring, as to venture a considerable way down into the cavity; but actions of this kind can be productive of no real advantage, and, about two years ago, proved fatal to an English gentleman, who lost his life by his temerity. If, soon after an eruption, a stone be rolled down the aperture, it is followed by a frightful noise, and a cloud of smoke. It is two hours labour to climb to the top of the mountain, but you return much easier, and in less time; for one often slides down upon the ashes upward of four paces at a step. Some days afterward, as the wind sometimes drives abundance of ashes into the city of Naples, they have recourse to processions, and the invocation of St. Januarius, in whom, as their guardian upon all such occasions, the inhabitants repose a particular confidence: though, of late years, for their better security, they have given him the archangel Michael as an associate. Their devotion, it must be allowed, is very well grounded, if what they say be true, that, immediately upon the meer exposing of the saint's head, after the proper supplications have been offered to him, the wind has shifted, and the smoke been, consequently, removed from the city, and the fury of the burning eruptions abated: so that it is not at all surprising, that the governor of the Capella del Tesoro, belonging to the cathedral where the reliques of this saint are preserved, has caused a large medal to be struck, on one side of which is St. Januarius, and on the reverse are the two phials, in which his miraculous blood is kept, and under them a garland.

Sextus Aurelius Victor, and other historians, who affirm, that it was in the reign of Vespasian, the fiery eruptions of mount Vesuvius were first observed, may be easily confuted from Strabo, who lived in the time of Augustus: and it is also false, that Pliny the elder lost his life on this mountain. For, from the account given by Pliny the younger, concerning his

uncle's

MOUNT VESUVIUS.

uncle's death, it is evident, that he was far enough from Vesuvius, and being very fat, and troubled with an asthma, he was suffocated by the gross and sulphureous air.

Since the birth of Christ, historians have recorded upward of twenty memorable eruptions of mount Vesuvius; but it is probable, that, during all that time, the number must have been much greater: one of the most violent was that just mentioned, which happened in the reign of Titus Vespasian, and destroyed the two cities of Herculaneum or Heraclea, and Pompeii, which formerly stood near Naples.

Dio Cassius says, that the ashes, during that eruption, were driven as far as Africa, Syria, and Egypt, and even at Rome the sun was darkened by them.

The great variety of minerals, and other substances, thrown out by Vesuvius, is a sufficient proof of the internal constitution of this vast hollow, and whence its fiery eruptions arise. For, upon mixing quick sulphur and filings of iron together, and kneading them to a paste, with the addition of a little cold water, this mass is not only immediately heated, but it breaks out into a perfect flame. Lemery had once an artificial volcano, of this sort, in his garden at Paris, which spontaneously took fire; and modern chemists have carried their improvements so far, that by the bare mixture of two liquids, previously prepared for that purpose, they can produce flame. When the sea is calm, a great deal of petroleum is often found floating on its surface, at Resina Torre, (two small places near mount Vesuvius and the sea) which the fishermen take up with pieces of sponge, and sell to the apothecaries. That mount Vesuvius has a communication with the sea, experience plainly shews, the waters being surprisingly absorbed, in 1681, as a prelude to the eruption of the mountain, so that several vessels, afloat before, were left dry. Also, by what happened in the year 1698, when the sea suddenly ebbed twelve paces, and the mountain discharged a large

large torrent of bituminous matter; on the return of the sea to its former height, and a ceſſation of the igneous diſcharge, great quantity of ſhells, and other teſtaceous ſubſtances, were found along the ſhore, half burnt, and emitted a ſulphureous ſmell. Parrini and Boccome affirm, that, in a violent eruption of mount Veſuvius, hot ſea-water, fiſh-ſhells, and ſea-weeds, have been ejected by that mountain.

This volcano, however, affords ſeveral freſh ſprings, of which ſome are conveyed to Naples, by a beautiful aqueduct, to the great conveniency of the inhabitants. Theſe waters have not the leaſt heat in them, and a cold wind is felt to blow from ſeveral fiſſures and chaſms of the mountain. I ſhall further remark, that, though a new hill has riſen on the ſummit of Veſuvius, over its former aperture, yet it is ſtill leſs than its former height; of this we have an ocular demonſtration. The ſame may be ſaid of mount Ætna.

The climate of the city of Naples, and the ſouth part of that kingdom, is ſuch, that little or no winter is perceived there, and garden-ſtuff and vegetables are in ſeaſon all the year: ice is ſeldom ſeen in the level country, or plains; and, in the laſt five years, ſnow was known to fall but twice, and then it diſſolved as ſoon as it touched the ground. The inhabitants of the mountains make it their buſineſs to gather ſnow, and carry it to Naples, where it ſupplies the want of ice for cooling their liquors. The extream ſummer heats never fail of being tempered with cool breezes in the evening, which are ſpent in taking the air on foot, and in carriages, after being confined, within doors, during the ſultry heat of the day.

It will not be difficult to form a proper eſtimate of the fertility of this kingdom, and the riches of the country; for, conſidering how long it has been under a foreign government, which, by contributions, troops, wars, and other circumſtances, muſt neceſſarily have drained it of large ſums, yet it is ſtill in a much better condition than many of the ſtates in

Italy;

Italy; and capable, by proper meafures, of affording new fources of wealth. The tobacco-farms, alone, produce near thirty thoufand ducats annually; but, amidſt its fertility, and other natural advantages, the kingdom of Naples labours under many heavy inconveniencies. Befide the calamities it is fubject to, from the frequent eruptions of Vefuvius, it alfo fuffers greatly by earthquakes, particularly the fouthern borders of the kingdom, in all parts of which are aſtoniſhing remains of cities, once famous in hiftory, but now almoſt without a name.

Another difagreeable circumſtance, but common to moſt parts of Italy, is occafioned by the fwarms of lizards, efpecially of the green kind, which abound almoſt every where: in the fpring, hundreds of thefe are feen baſking themfelves on the roofs, and crawling up and down the walls, fo that no door or window can be left open, without the room being filled with them: the green lizards are very nimble, and have a fine, bright, fleek fkin, and beautiful eyes, but are intirely harmlefs. About Fondi, Capua, and Gaeta, are a noxious kind of lizards, vulgarly, but improperly, called tarantulæ, whofe bite or ſting is attended with great danger: they are brown, larger than the green fort, and, when deprived of their tails, refemble a toad. The fcorpions are a greater nufance; they harbour not only in old walls, and under ſtones, but infeſt houfes in this country, fo that, in fome places, it is cuſtomary to make bedſteads of poliſhed iron, and to place them at fome diftance from the wall, to prevent thefe vermin from getting into the beds. It is true, they feldom hurt, unlefs they are firſt aſſaulted, which may eafily happen, either by turning one's felf in bed, or moving a leg or arm in one's ſleep: the fureſt remedy againſt the ſting of thefe noxious creatures, is to bruife the animal, and bind it faſt on the wound; or, if that cannot be done, the beſt way is to foment it with oil of olives, in which dead fcorpions are infufed, applying warm bandages to the part; and, at

the

the same time, to give the patient theriaca, with generous wine to raise a gentle perspiration. This oil is likewise a specific against the sting of the spider solifuga, in the northern parts of Italy: this creature has little or nothing of that venom which appears in the hotter climates, in Malta and Africa. The venom or poison of the viper hath also the same gradations, according to the proximity of the country to the equator. Modern authors have asserted, that the scorpion being surrounded by fire, and perceiving the flame to approach nearer, and the heat more intense, and finding no way to escape, turns up his tail, and strikes himself in the head. This assertion appeared to me very suspicious, and made me think, that this pretended suicide was no more than the natural motion of the animal on such occasions. Being at Naples, I was resolved to bring this vulgar error to the test of repeated experiments, which proved that it was only a mere fiction.

Another plague, peculiar to the kingdom of Naples, chiefly in the southern parts, is the tarantula; so called from the city of Taranto, in the neighbourhood of which they abound, and are the largest and most venomous. Pliny and other writers call them *phalangius*. The person bit by this spider is called, by the Italians, *Tarantolati*; and their extravagant vicissitudes of shrieking, sobbing, laughing, dancing, are very well known. Few of these patients can bear the sight of black or blue, but seem delighted with red and green objects: they are also seized with an aversion to eating fruit and vegetables. A melancholy silence, and a fixed eye, are the first symptoms by which the bite of the tarantula discovers itself: music is then immediately called in to the assistance of the patient, to rouse him to a violent motion, and, by that means, to procure a strong perspiration; but neither the same tunes, nor the same instruments answer the same purposes, with regard to the different patients. The tarantolati dance and skip as long as there is any venom left to be expelled: this exercife and cure fometimes takes up five or fix days. It is not to be fuppofed, that they are continually dancing for fo many days; but when nature is exhaufted, and the mufic fufpended, the patient is put to bed, well covered, and fuch cordials given him, as promote perfpiration, and chear the heart. The patient, upon his recovery, remembers nothing of what paffed during the diforder. If the cure be not perfectly effected, and the poifon intirely expelled, the fame fymptoms never fail to return the fucceeding year, efpecially during the fummer heats; and fome have laboured under thefe terrible diforders at intervals, for ten, twenty, or even thirty years, and others during their whole lives: nor are inftances wanting of perfons, who, meerly from a fenfe of their incurable diforder, or from its melancholy effects, have deftroyed themfelves. Women, on account of their long cloaks harbouring fuch vermin, are more liable to be bit than men: the bite of a tarantula caufes a fmall red fwelling, not unlike that occafioned by the fting of a wafp. In the dog-days, and during the intenfe heats of fummer, the tarantula is moft dangerous, efpecially thofe found in the plains; for thofe found in Tufcany do not produce fuch mifchievous effects as that kind found in Apulia.

In the ifland of Corfica are neither wolves nor vipers, whereas its tarantulas and fcorpions are extreamly venomous.

But, among the worft creatures in this fine country, fome reckon its inhabitants in general, who are of a treacherous, diftruftful, cruel, and unfteady difpofition. Though it is no eafy matter to give national characters, it is certain, however, that the hiftory of Naples, almoft beyond any other, yields numerous and deplorable inftances of the extream depravity of human nature. Tophana, the noted female poifoner, from whom the Aqua Tophana took its name, is ftill in prifon here, and moft ftrangers, out of curiofity, go to fee her: fhe is an old little woman, who had belonged

belonged to some religious sisterhood, for which reason her life has been spared; though she sent many hundred people out of the world, and, in particular, was very liberal of her drops, by way of alms, to married women, who would, it may well be supposed, have no great regret at getting rid of disagreeable husbands. From four to six drops of this liquid is a quantity sufficient to do a man's business, and some affirm, that the dose may be ordered so as to take effect in a determinate time. This water is still privately made at Naples, under the name of Aquetta di Napoli. But since lemon-juice has been found to be a kind of antidote against this water, it is not now in such high repute. But all the antidotes, hitherto found out, presuppose the potion to have been recently administered, or, upon any suspicion, previously guarded against by such preservatives.

The voluptuous manner of living among the inhabitants of this country has been remarked even in ancient times. With regard to the present times, it must be allowed, that in no place are the abandoned licentiousness and impudence of prostitutes carried to so great a height as in this city. This entirely corrupts the young people; and even the clergy, not being subject to the civil power, and connived at by their superiors, lest the sacred function should suffer the smallest disparagement, are but indifferently careful to set a good example.

The common people in this country are so lazy, as to prefer beggary or robbing to labour. But in the city of Naples they are more industrious, and several manufactures flourish among them. It is a common, saying here, that the viceroy, in order to keep this country quiet, must take care to provide three things which begin with an F, namely, *feste, farine, forche*, feasts, meal, and gibbets; the people being excessive fond of public diversions, clamorous upon any scarcity of corn, and seditious, unless awed by examples of severity. Among the public entertainments, is the procession, with four triumphal cars, on the four Sundays

Sundays immediately preceding Lent; the firſt loaded with bread, the ſecond with fleſh, the third with all kinds of veg-tables, and the fourth with fiſh. Theſe are piled up almoſt as high as a houſe, with a band of muſic on the top, and guarded by armed tradeſmen, till they are given up to be pillaged. But what draws the greateſt concourſe of people at Naples, is the caſtle of Cocagna, or Cucagna, as it is called; which is a regular piece of fortification, and faced all over with quarters of meat, ſhins of beef, bacon, geeſe, turkeys, and other proviſions, with which the country of Cocagne is imagined to abound. This ſpectacle is annually exhibited, and on each ſide of the caſtle is a fountain running with wine for a whole day; a party of ſoldiers is planted to guard the works till the viceroy appears in his balcony, which is the ſignal for the populace to take the place by ſtorm.

The Neapolitan nobility uſually ſpend ſome years in a frugal retirement on their eſtates in the country, that they may make a more ſplendid figure, for a while, in the city: for which reaſon they are always running into extreams, though their fortunes are not conſiderable enough to ſupport ſuch profuſion. They are ſo numerous, that in the kingdom of Naples are reckoned a hundred and nineteen princes, a hundred and fifty-ſix dukes, a hundred and ſeventy-three marquiſſes, forty-four counts, and four hundred and forty-five barons, all vaſſals to the crown. A ſpot of land, from which many of them have the title of marquis, has hardly an income of fifty dollars a year.

The number of regular forces now quartered up and down throughout the kingdom, amounts to four thouſand men, which is very far from being ſufficien to keep this nation in awe, in caſe of the approach of any enemy.

With regard to the currency of coin in this country, a Spaniſh piſtole, or an old French Louis d'or, go here for forty-five carlini. The papal money is alſo current, and three paoli are equal to four carlini.

By a ducat, simply so called, is meant an imaginary coin of account, equivalent to ten carlini.

The city of Naples lies in 41° 20′ north latitude. Its walls, which mostly consist of hard, black, quarry-stones, called Piperno, are nine Italian miles in circuit; but, including the suburbs, between eighteen and twenty miles. Though Naples has not such fine palaces as Rome or Genoa, it has not many such mean houses, as, in other cities, disgrace the most beautiful streets. The roofs of the houses are flat, and surrounded with elegant balustrades. The streets are also very well paved, and mostly consist of broad free-stone; but they have no slope from the middle, or kennels to carry off the water. The best street, for breadth and length, is la Strada di Toledo, but not a single palace, of any note, is to be seen in it. It is between twenty and twenty-three common paces broad, and five hundred in a straight line, after which it runs in a gentle curve. Were the streets lighted at night, it would be both an ornament to the city, and a great security in walking through them.

[Mr. Sharpe is very full in the particulars he gives, and the remarks he makes, respecting the city and inhabitants of Naples; a few of which we shall select.

" The road from Rome to Naples is bad enough, the inns are still worse; nay, worse than those on the Loretto road; for, in the town of Loretto, there was good accommodation; but all the way to Naples we never once crept within the sheets, not daring to encounter the vermin and nastiness of those beds. I attempted to please myself with the conceit of travelling the same road that Horace did in his journey to Brundusium: but my sensations were too strong for my fancy. The swampy soil and marshes on the right-hand, with a string of barren mountains on the left, for scores of miles together, may amuse, but cannot delight a traveller. Did we not know that ancient Italy was infinitely more populous than it now is; did we not know that populousness renders a country

country rich and chearful, I should have suspected those masters of the universe had, in their haughtiness, and, from a contempt of all other nations, called theirs the Garden of the world: for, beautiful and fertile as some parts of it are, the amazing quantity of barren mountains, extending from almost the one extremity to the other, should seem to deprive it of that character: and, however bold the assertion may appear, I think England a better resemblance of a garden than Italy; and should not hesitate to oppose our verdure and inclosures, to their myrtle and orange-trees, which last, by the bye, are not to be seen in the winter, except in the southern parts of Italy.

Whilst I was in England, I never heard the words northern climate pronounced, but they conveyed to me an idea of barrenness and imperfection. I had always conceived, that vegetables and garden fruits attained a flavour and savourineſs in the more southern climes, unknown to the latitude of $52°$; but, to my great surprise, I do not find that any of their herbage is equal, in taste and sweetness, to that which grows in our gardens; and, what is still more surprising, few of their fruits excel ours; I believe none, except their water-melons, their grapes, and their figs.——

From Capua, (about four miles from the ruins of the ancient Capua) the road to Naples is very pleasant; the gardens and vineyards on each side are well cultivated; however, the district of Capua does not answer to the idea we have of its luxury in the times of Hannibal, if I may judge from the great difficulty I found of procuring a morsel of dinner in that town.

Some parts of the Alps exhibit a most delightful and tremendous prospect, and were the first great object I met with amongst the marvellous. I think the city of Venice floating on the water, with its beautiful adjacent islands, may be ranked as the second; and I will venture to mention St. Peter's as the third, though

though it partake not of beauties derived from nature, being a meer work of art; but, above all, I admire the heavens, the earth, and the fea of Naples. The iflands, the mountains, the bay, the buildings, and the flope on which the buildings ftand, render the view of this city enchantingly pretty. Since my arrival, we had bluftering weather, and more thunder and lightning than I ever knew in July, in our latitudes; but the fea is fo fheltered that there is no horror in the fcene, and the ftreets are fo well paved, that they become clean and dry in a few hours after a deluge. I can imagine, and am told, that the heats of the fummer are dreadful, but, thank God, they are not to be my concern; I am to enjoy the fweets only of a Neapolitan winter, and, as far as I can judge, they are unfpeakable to a man who fuffers in his lungs from moifture and cold. Damps are little known in this place, neither furniture nor walls fuffer from that circumftance; and for temperature of the air, fuffice to inform you, that, in order to write this letter comfortably, I chufe to open the windows. Could an afthmatic man jump from London to the lodgings I have taken, though at any rifk of his neck, he would do well to venture; but I cannot fay it would be worth while to go and return as we do, through fo much filth, and fo many fufferings from bugs, lice, fleas, gnats, fpiders, &c.——

You tell me, two or three hufbands are lately feparated from their wives, and bemoan the degeneracy of the age in thefe inftances. We here read with aftonifhment that the examples are only two or three in fo large a kingdom. Were Italians to feparate either on the account of indifference or gallantry, there would be almoft as many divorces as marriages. It appears to us, that, becaufe fome feparate where there is no affection others may remain together becaufe there is affection, a paffion in a manner almoft unknown betwixt hufbands and wives in this climate. When I pafs fo fevere a cenfure on the ftate of matrimony.

mony in these kingdoms, do not believe that I speak from a spirit of detraction, or without good grounds: I believe I can much more satisfactorily solve this phænomenon, than the ingenious Montesquieu does the different characters of different nations, from the various latitudes in which they are situated, &c. How is it probable the husbands and wives should have any esteem, much less love for each other, when they are always brought together without the least participation of their own? The fathers never consult the liking of the young people, but look forward to the endowments of the next generation, which are comprised in two words, fortune and family. All that I have here said is so literally true, that it very seldom happens the parties know one another before the marriage articles are drawing up, and, perhaps, do not visit twice, before the day of consummation.

Bad as the above system is, it would not be sufficient to diffuse universal unhappiness through the domains of Hymen: chance and good sense would now and then render this sort of union agreeable, and even friendly; but that abominable and infernal fashion of taking a cicesbeo so soon after they have quitted the altar, is a never-failing measure to estrange whatever affection might otherwise have sprung up. Many people in England imagine the majority of cicesbeos to be an innocent kind of dangling fribble; but they are utterly mistaken in the character; nor do I find that it is understood here that the ladies live in greater purity with their cicesbeos than with their husbands; and, generally speaking, with much less. To say the truth, I myself have seen princesses, dutchesses, and their cicesbeos, visiting with the same unconcernedness, as an honest citizen and his wife do; nor, after a little habit and use, do they afford me more matter of speculation. To give you an idea in one word, how much the mode of inseparableness is established, suffice it to say, that if you invite five ladies to dinner, you of course lay ten plates, as each, for a certainty, brings her cicefbeo with her. You are not to imagine, that when I speak of an invitation of ladies, that a single woman is ever thought of: nor are there more than two unmarried ladies in this metropolis, who visit; all the others are locked up in monasteries.

Children here have very little tendency to support the friendship and harmony of the married state; with us, the joint interest of both father and mother in their little ones, with perhaps the blended features they each discover in their progeny, does not contribute in a small degree to heal any accidental breaches, or at least, to make them live on good terms for the sake of their posterity. In Italy, a certain knowlege of every wife's attachment to a lover, extinguishes all social affection, and all fondness for the offspring. It is only the eldest born, who the husband is sure belongs to him; and for that security, it is generally requisite, the birth should take place the first year, as the women seldom hold out longer without a cicesbeo; indeed how should they? for a husband will not wait on his wife to a public place, and it is not the fashion for women to go, as in England, without men. I have been told, by a grave Neapolitan old gentleman, the fault is intirely on the side of the husbands, who are fickle from the nature of the climate, and cannot continue constant to their wives many months; so that the poor women are driven into this measure: but, whether the practice arise from levity or compulsion, the consequence is dreadful to society, if there be any real delight, any charms in virtue, and mutual love.——

Mr. Sharpe gives us the following account of the theatres at Naples. —" A stranger, upon his arrival in so large and celebrated a city as Naples, generally makes the public spectacles his first pursuit. These consist of the king's theatre, where the serious opera is performed, and of two smaller theatres, called Theatro Nuovo, and the Theatro de Fiorentini, where

where they exhibit burlettas only. There is alſo a little ſhabby kind of a play-houſe, where they perform a comedy every night, though the drama has ſo little encouragement at Naples, that their comedies are ſeldom frequented by any of the gentry, but ſeem to be chiefly an amuſement for the populace.

The king's theatre, upon the firſt view, is, perhaps, almoſt as ſtriking an object, as any man ſees in his travels. The amazing extent of the ſtage, with the prodigious circumference of the boxes, and height of the cieling, produce a marvellous effect on the mind, for a few moments; but the inſtant the opera opens, a ſpectator immediately perceives this ſtructure does not gratify the ear, how much ſoever it may the eye. The voices are drowned in this immenſity of ſpace, and even the orcheſtra itſelf, though a numerous band, lies under a diſadvantage. Upon the whole, it muſt be admitted, the houſe is better contrived to ſee than to hear an opera. It is not to be omitted, amongſt the objections to the immenſe largeneſs of the houſe and ſtage, that, in windy weather, you would imagine yourſelf in the ſtreets, the wind blows ſo hard both in the pit and boxes; and this ſeldom happens without cauſing colds and fevers.

There are ſome who contend, that the ſingers might very well be heard, if the audience were more ſilent; but it is ſo much the faſhion at Naples, and, indeed, through all Italy, to conſider the opera as a place of rendezvous and viſiting, that they do not ſeem in the leaſt to attend to the muſic, but laugh and talk through the whole performance, without any reſtraint; and, it may be imagined, that an aſſembly of ſo many hundreds converſing together ſo loudly, muſt entirely cover the voices of the ſingers.——

An Engliſhman wonders at this behaviour of the Italians; he comes with a notion that they are all enthuſiaſtically fond of muſic; that there is ſomething in the climate which gives them this propenſity, and

that

that their natural genius is nurſed and improved by a muſical education: upon enquiry, he finds his opinion almoſt groundleſs; very few gentlemen here practiſe the fiddle, or any other inſtrument, and all the young ladies are placed in convents, where they remain until they marry, or take the veil, and where muſic is no part of their education; whereas, in England, the fine ladies have alſo an acquired taſte, the effect of aſſiduity and cultivation.——

It will be natural, then, to aſk, after this account, how it happens that Italy furniſhes all Europe with muſicians? The anſwer is, that the infinite quantity of muſic exhibited in their churches and chapels, provides bread, though the wages be ſmall, for a prodigious number of performers; and, as trade is deſpicable, and laborious employments are held in deteſtation, parents are induced to bring up their children to this profeſſion, which they can do at a ſmall expence: for there are ſeveral hundred youths brought up to muſic, in their conſervatorios, or charitable foundations. Now, where there are ſo many hundreds in continual practice, it is not ſtrange that emulation and genius ſhould, every now and then, produce an excellent performer, who, if he be well adviſed, will certainly ſet out for England, where talents of every kind are rewarded ten-fold above what they are at Naples, except in the ſingle inſtance of the firſt claſs of opera ſingers, who are paid extravagantly.

Notwithſtanding the amazing noiſineſs of the audience, during the whole performance of the opera, the moment the dances begin, there is a dead ſilence, which continues as long as the dances continue. A ſtranger, who has a little compaſſion in his breaſt, feels for the poor ſingers, who are treated with ſo much indifference and contempt: and I find, by their own confeſſion, that however accuſtomed they are to it, the mortification is always dreadful; and they are eager to declare how happy they are when they ſing

in

in a country where more attention is paid to their talents.

From the regard shewn to the dances, a person would suppose that a superior excellence was to be expected in this art; but Naples does not, at present, afford any very capital performers, nor do the dances which have been brought on the stage this season, do much honour to their taste. They are, in general, tedious, with incidents and characters vulgar and buffoonish.

The Neapolitan quality rarely dine or sup with one another, and many of them hardly ever visit, but at the opera; on this account they seldom absent themselves. It is customary for gentlemen to run about from box to box, betwixt the acts, and even in the midst of the performance; but the ladies, after they are seated, never quit their box the whole evening. A lady receives visitors in her box one night, and they remain with her the whole opera; another night she returns the visit in the same manner. In the intervals of the acts principally betwixt the first and second, the proprietor of the box regales her company with iced-fruits and sweet-meats. Beside the indulgence of a loud conversation, they sometimes form themselves into card parties; but, I believe, this custom does not prevail so much at present as it did formerly. There is a notion in England, that the Italians frequently sup in their boxes, and that, by drawing the shutters in front, they may be in private; but there are no such shutters, and the practice of supping is so rare that I have never seen it.——

The two burletta opera houses are not in much request, except when they happen to procure some favourite composition, the grand opera being the only objects of the Neapolitans; which, indeed, has such pre-eminent encouragement, that the others are forbidden by authority, to bring any dancers on their stage without a special licence, lest they should divert

vert the attention of the public from the king's theatre. I muſt not omit a ſingularity, in relation to the women dancers at Naples, that, in conſequence of an order from court, in the late king's time, they all wear black drawers. I preſume it was from ſome conceit on the ſubject of modeſty, but it appears very odd. I ſhall not enter into any detail of the two houſes; but their dreſſes, ſcenery, and actors, are more deſpicable than one could poſſibly imagine.

The play-houſe is hardly better than a cellar, and is really very much known by that name, being uſually called the *cantina* (cellar.) You deſcend from the ſtreet down ten ſteps into the pit, which holds ſeventy or eighty people when crouded, each of which pays a carline, that is four pence halfpenny, for his admittance. There is a gallery round the pit, which is formed by partitions, into ten or twelve boxes. Theſe boxes holding four perſons conveniently, let for eight carlines. Under theſe diſcouragements it will not be difficult to conceive that the ſcenes, the dreſſes, the actors, and the decorations of the houſe, muſt be very indifferent: it will not, however, be ſo eaſy to imagine the ſhabbineſs of the audience, which chiefly conſiſts of men in dirty caps and waiſtcoats in the pit, for the boxes are generally empty. All the Italian gentlemen and ladies are very indelicate in the article of ſpitting, never making uſe of a handkerchief, or ſeeking a corner for that purpoſe; but in the *cantina*, their naſtineſs is offenſive to the laſt degree, not only ſpitting all about them, but alſo on every part of the wall, ſo that it is impoſſible to avoid ſoiling your cloaths. This habit is carried by ſome to ſuch exceſs, that I cannot but aſcribe the leanneſs of many Neapolitans, and the ſallowneſs of their complexions, to the abundance of this evacuation.

The drama is ſo little cultivated in Italy, that I believe they ſeldom or never act a tragedy; at leaſt, I have

I have never yet heard of such a representation, nor has it been my good fortune to see a comedy of more than three acts. The principal entertainments seem to arise from double entendres and blunders, mistaking one word for another, and even from dirty actions, such as spitting or blowing the nose in each others faces; just as we see practised in England on the stages of mountebanks, and on the outsides of the booths in Bartholomew-fair: but what appears most essential to the delight of a Neapolitan audience, are two or three characters, such as Punch and the Doctor's man, who speak the dialect of the lower people, which is unintelligible to a foreigner, however well he may understand pure Italian; and it is chiefly by these characters that the company is recreated.

It would conduce much to the improvement of the manners and literature of this people, were some of the quality to give their protection to the stage. It cannot be doubted that a Mæcenas would now, as formerly, in the same climate, call forth the poetic spirit; and it is a little wonderful this event does not take place, as there is a kind of propensity amongst them to patronize comedy : for, during the carnival, there are three or four plays represented several nights, by private persons, and by convents, at their own expence, which meet with great applause. They perform with remarkable humour and exactness; nor do the fathers scruple to wear women's dresses, and appear in very lascivious characters.——How extreamly capricious, that the same mother-church should suffer her sons to play at Naples, and deprive the poor French comedians of Christian burial at Paris!"

His remarks on the people are no less pertinent and amusing.---" The populousness of Naples is so remarkable, that a stranger, the first time he passes through some parts of the city, would imagine the people were assembled in the streets on some extraordinary occasion; but the truth is, that some thousands

sands of the populace (called the Lazoroni, or Black-Guards) have no other habitation than the streets, and much the greater part of the other portion, having no employment, either from the want of manufactures, or their natural propensity to idleness, are sauntering in the streets from morning to night, and make these crouds, which are not seen in other places, but upon festivals, elections, &c. It is computed that Naples contains three hundred, or three hundred and fifty thousand inhabitants; and I suppose it is the only metropolis in Europe which furnishes its own inhabitants. All the others are supplied with people from the provinces, the luxury and expensiveness of large cities being so great an impediment to marriage, and populousness, that they would all, in the ordinary course of nature, be depopulated in a few years, were they not annually recruited from other parts. But in Naples the case is different, from a singular custom amongst the gentry of hiring married, in preference to unmarried servants. In Paris or London, very few servants can hope to be employed who are not single, and therefore an infinite number of this class of people pass their lives in celibacy; as the instances are but rare in those cities where footmen and maid-servants can support themselves after marriage by a different occupation.

In Naples it is almost an universal fashion to keep their men-servants at board wages, not admitting them to sleep in their houses; this naturally leads them into marriage, as it gives them a settlement so essential to the character required by all ranks of masters. But what seems still more to facilitate matrimony, in this order of people, is the prodigious number of young women ready to accept the first offer; for in Italy they are not taken into service as in England: a nobleman who keeps forty men-servants, has seldom more than two maids. This circumstance, with the difficulty a woman has to acquire her living here by any other means, is the reason

son why they seldom make an objection to the certain poverty attending matrimony. The swarms of children in all the streets inhabited by the poor, are such as will necessarily result from this practice; and as a married couple, though they have six or seven children, never occupy more than one room, the extream populousness of Naples must, consequently, follow from such causes.———

The Lazeroni, or black-guards, are such miserable wretches as are not to be seen in any other town in Europe; perhaps amongst the ashes of our glass-houses in London you may find some not unlike them; but here the number is said to be six thousand, not one of which ever lies in a bed, but upon bulks, benches, &c. in the open streets; and, what is scandalous, they are suffered to sun themselves, a great part of the day, under the palace walls, where they lie basking like dirty swine, and are a much more nauseous spectacle. Being almost naked, they suffer extreamly in cold weather, and were the climate less mild, they would certainly perish. The convents at Naples are rich, and make a practice of distributing broth and bread, once a day, to the poor who apply for charity; and it is meerly by this charity that the Lazeronis principally subsist, though by pilfering and begging, some of them acquire enough to appear healthy and robust.———

I can venture to declare, that the streets in London appear like a desart, compared with many in Naples. But if I wonder at the fullness of their streets, how shall I describe their Vicaria, their Westminster-hall? If I remember well, Mr. Addison says, that when a Neapolitan does not know what to do with himself, he tumbles over his papers in order to start a law-suit; but, sincerely, if the kingdom of Naples were as extensive as the commonwealth of Rome, when at its highest pitch of glory, and every cause were to be tried in the capital, the thousands of lawyers you see here would answer to that idea; but

how

how they are supported is to me a problem. The first time I went to the Vicaria, I was mortified to have set out so late from home, finding the streets crouded with advocates in their way to dinner; but notwithstanding the difficulty of threading the multitude, who were pouring out in such numbers, I found, when I had pushed into the hall, almost as much pressing as we usually meet with the first night of a new play in our London theatres. What a blessed country, where all who are not princes or beggars, are lawyers or priests!

The manner of burying their dead in Italy is at first very shocking to an Englishman. Their custom is, to carry the corpse, drest in his usual wearing apparel, with his face exposed, on an open bier, through the streets, to the church where the service is read; after which it is stripped, and at a convenient hour buried; but there is a pride and rivalship among the middling rank of people, in dressing out their dead children for this exhibition, which is truly ridiculous. The other day there passed under our window the body of a boy, about eight years old, whose figure and face were as hideous as the small-pox could make them: would you believe, the parents had dressed him in a fine laced hat, bag-wig, blue and silver cloaths, &c. and, above all things, had not forgot to stick a sword on! I do not in the least doubt but the friends found a real consolation in the prettiness and richness of the corpse, and were amongst their neighbours more occupied with this idea, than with that of the eternal absence of the child.——I have not had the good fortune to meet with an Italian yet, who is well enough read in the history and customs of his country, to inform me of the origin of this practice; but I should conjecture, that it was at first designed to prevent foul play. The reality of every man's death is now evident to the whole parish; and I suppose some such imaginary evil was the ground of this conceit; but it is a fashion I must condemn;

for

for the aspect of death should never be suffered to become familiar to the common people, with so much brimstone in their veins as the Neapolitan mob have; ——but there are ways to render men capable of butchering a man and hog with the same *sang froid*. One would think, that at Naples the police had cultivated this art; for the most atrocious parricides are seldom punished here. I think the last four years have furnished but four examples of executions; and as if a fatality were to attend all their judgments, two of the four proved afterward to have been innocent. If a murderer touches a church wall (and many walls are church walls in this city) before he is seized by the officers, holy church will not admit him to be hanged."——]

The harbour of Naples is spacious, and, for its greater safety, has a mole, about five hundred paces in length, and also a light-house. The large harbour, or *Porto della Cita*, is divided by the mole from the Darsena, which is behind the *Castella Nuovo*, where commonly lie four galleys, the sailors and soldiers of which are obliged, every Lent, to come to confession, and receive the sacrament. After the devotions of the first galley, follows a day of rest; after those of the second, a like interval, and so on. In the evening, when the procession, usual on such solemn occasions, is over, or when the host is exposed, all the galleys honour it with a salute.

[Mr. Sharpe's account of the galley-slaves runs thus. ——" The slaves in the gallies are chained two and two, and may be thought to suffer from lying on the decks; but their condition is far preferable to that of many of the poor, who lie in the streets; beside that they have a certain allowance of bread from the king, and even some cloathing; but above all, and what renders the life of a poor Neapolitan happy, they are, in a manner, exempt from labour, for very few are employed in cruizing, or other business: what work they do aboard the vessels, is chiefly for their own benefit, and I may say, luxury. If a taylor, a shoemaker, or any other handicraftsman earns a few pence, he puts it into his pocket, and purchases some rarity, the government, as I have intimated before, furnishing him with bread. The galleys lie very near my lodgings, and I have diverted myself with speculating on the lives and manners of these slaves. The Neapolitans are not a gay mercurial people, but those aboard the gallies are by no means graver than those out of the gallies; and a man who has visited them so frequently as I have done, will never afterward, when he means to picture extreme misery, represent it as the proverb does, in the shape of a galley-slave. I have seen a musician aboard, entertaining them with vocal and instrumental music, whom I supposed one of their gang; but, upon enquiry, found he was a poor man, they paid for his performances when they were disposed to be merry: and I do not doubt but this poor man stiled those we call wretches, his good masters. If then so sober, so phlegmatic a nation as Italy, finds such delights aboard a galley, what do you think of the lively skipping Frenchmen in the gallies at Marseilles?"]

Naples is provided with many fountains, which are a very great ornament to it, though the water in most of them is but indifferent. The finest among these is that of Medina, opposite to the *Castello Nuovo*, the upper bason of which is supported by the three Graces. The Neptune standing upon it with his trident, and several other figures eject great quantities of water.

Of all the palaces in Naples, the chief is that of the viceroy; and, with regard to its beauty, it is a sufficient encomium to say, it is the work of that celebrated architect, *Car. Fontana*.

Castello del Nuovo has its name from its oval figure, and stands in the water on a rock, joined to the continent by a bridge, two hundred and twenty paces in length.

length. It is said, formerly, to have joined to the firm land, and was anciently the palace of Lucullus; but altered to its present form by the Norman kings, on which account it was for a long time called the Norman castle. The castle is supplied with fresh water by means of some stone conduits, supporting several marble figures, representing animals of all kinds   The water is conveyed from the city under the bridge to the castle, where there is a reservoir for receiving it.

The third castle, which commands the city of Naples, is that of St. Elmo, or St. Eramo, so called from a church dedicated to that saint, which formerly stood on this spot. It stands upon an eminence toward the west, and is in the form of a star, with six rays. The fortifications were chiefly erected by Charles V.

The subterraneous passages of this place are very spacious, and hewn out of a rock, so that they are bomb proof; and, on that account, a great quantity of military stores are deposited here. The castle can likewise be supplied with provisions from *Castello Nuovo*, by means of a subterraneous communication, at present walled up. In the upper part of St. Elmo's castle, are seven cisterns for receiving water; and under the vaults a reservoir large enough for two gallies to sail in. The water in the latter is always extreamly cold, and is drawn from it by a bucket.

The arms of the city being a horse, there formerly stood one of brass near the church of *di Santa Restituta*, of an extraordinary size; the vulgar have a notion that it was cast by Virgil, whom they will have to have been a magician. They had also superstitious notions of the great efficacy it had in all distempers incident to horses, which were brought from all parts, and led round this statue: so that, at last, in the year 1322, Maria Caraffa, archbishop of Naples, to abolish so silly a custom, destroyed the statue, and from the metal cast a large bell for the cathedral.

cathedral. The head is still entire, and reserved as a memorial in the Caraffa family, among a collection of statues and bas-reliefs. Charles, king of Naples, having made himself master of the city after eight months siege, ordered a bit to be put in the mouth of this horse, as an emblematical representation of his having tamed the Neapolitans.

To such influence, respect, and opulence, have the clergy of this kingdom attained, that more than once they have been ready to seize the civil power, and intermeddle with affairs quite foreign to the cure of souls. But with regard to outward ceremonies, the devotion of the Roman Catholics of this kingdom is not so violent as in many provinces in Germany: at the elevation of the host in the churches, or in the streets, when carried to a sick person, none of any other religion is compelled to kneel to it. They make little difficulty with travellers about eating flesh in Lent; on the contrary, the inn-keeper's first question is, even before they have alighted, what the company would please to eat; and, in some places, fish, and the like meagre meals, are not so acceptable to an host, as from these he cannot make out any considerable bill.

The vivacity and acuteness of the Neapolitans (as they do not always meet with a satisfactory solution of their scruples in religion, and want an opportunity of better information, either by books or verbal instruction) sometimes carry them into wild systems, and very often into atheism; and the more they are under a necessity of concealing their notions of this kind, the deeper root they take, so that it is with great difficulty that any of these are reclaimed.

Most of the churches here have, indeed, but ill-contrived roofs and sorry fronts; and most of the marble monuments within them fall very much short, in extraordinary size, of those frequently to be met with at Rome; but, in other respects, with regard to their beauty and richness, hardly any other Roman Catholic

Catholic country can equal them; fo that only the jewels and coftly altar-furniture, amount to feveral millions of dollars. It muft be acknowleged, to the honour of the clergy here, that they are extreamly complaifant to ftrangers, and give themfelves a great deal of trouble to gratify their curiofity, in fhewing them every thing. It would be a work of time to fee all the churches, the number, both of the parochial and conventual, amounting to three hundred and four.

S. Agnello is famous for a crucifix in the chapel belonging to the family of Monachi, which reproached a debtor for denying, fome little time afterward, a fum of money he had formerly borrowed in its prefence.

Behind the high altar, in the cathedral, which is detached from the reft, and entirely of a fine red porphyry, are two filver doors before the fhrine, where is kept the head of St. Januarius, with two glafs or cryftal phials, containing fome of his blood, which is faid to have been gathered up by a Neapolitan woman, the very day that faint fuffered martyrdom. The external form of thefe reliques is drawn on the outfide of the filver tower or fhrine: befide the three ufual times in the year, for expofing them to the veneration of the people, the like is alfo done on emergent occafions of famine, peftilence, violent earthquakes, or any other public calamities, in which the favourable interpofition of St. Januarius is thought neceffary. The pretended liquefaction of the dried blood in the phials, as foon as brought near the head, is a thing very well known; and particularly every firft Sunday of May, trial is made with it; the Neapolitans being ftrongly perfuaded, that on the fuccefs of this miracle depends the whole profperity both of the king and country throughout that year: whereas, from the blood failing to liquefy, they have the moft dreadful apprehenfions, and immediate recourfe course is had to processions, public flagellations, &c. in order to avert the impending danger.

The substance in the phials is of a brownish red colour, and looks like balsam of Peru, which may easily be liquefied. On the day this miracle is to be performed, the blood is placed amidst a great number of lights; when the phial which holds it, being within another smaller, and about an inch in length, is applied to the mouths and foreheads of vast numbers of people, who croud to have that happiness; the priest, all the time, turning it a thousand different ways: so that, by the warmth of his hand, the heat of the lights, the effluvia from such crouds of people, in a hot season of the year, and lastly, the warm breath of the devotees, who kiss it, together with other circumstances, it may easily be imagined, that a previously condensed fluid may be restored to a state of liquefaction. At length, however, the priest cries out, *Il miraculo e fatto.* "The miracle is performed." But this miracle is not peculiar to the blood of St. Januarius; the like is also said to be done by that of St. John the Baptist, St. Stephen, St. Pantaleon, St. Vitus, and St. Patricia, in the respective churches of Naples, where these reliques are kept, and commonly on the days dedicated to those saints. Over the entrance of the old vestry, belonging to the above-mentioned *Capella del Tesoro,* is a bust of St. Januarius, in touchstone, before which are two small phials, half filled with a red kind of liquid. The silver statues, chandeliers, lamps, altarcloths, and other utensils, with which the new chapel is crouded, are valued at upward of a hundred thousand scudi.

S. Genuario extra Mœnia, or *ad Fores,* is also called *ad Corpus,* the body of St. Januarius having been first interred there; and close by it is the entrance into the catacombs, which, of the four hitherto discovered at Naples, are the most spacious and best preserved.

Such

Such as are of opinion that thefe fubterraneous
vaults were made by the primitive Chriftians for
places of retreat, from the violent perfecution of the
Pagans, may eafily be confuted from a bare infpec-
tion of the Neapolitan catacombs, which are hewn
out of a rock; and confequently fo great a work
could not have been done privately, or without a
vaft expence: not to mention, that during the fuperiority of the Pagans, the number of Chriftians,
either in Rome or in Naples, was not fo confiderable
as to accomplifh it in a fhort time. The fandy foil
at Rome, perhaps, would not admit of making thefe
fubterraneous paffages wider than what we actually
find them; but in the neighbourhood of Naples, the
cafe is quite otherwife, where the work was formerly
carried on through a rock; they are not only very
lofty, and arched, but fo broad, that fix perfons a-
breaft may walk in them.

That the Romans buried their deceafed, long before the eftablifhment of Chriftianity, is beyond difpute; nor could the Chriftians want fuch fpacious re-
pofitories for their dead. The bodies are here depofited along the fides of the wall, in fmall cavities, in
five or fix rows one over another, and the cavity, when
full, was clofed up with a marble flab or tiles; but
as moft of thefe are now removed, fewer Heathen infcriptions are to be found here than in the catacombs
at Rome. The bones, faid to be thofe of the primitive Chriftians, have been removed into the confecrated vaults of the churches; the bones that now
lie heaped up here being chiefly the remains of thofe
who died of the plague in the year 1656. At the
entrance of the firft vault, in St. Genario's catacombs,
is a marble bas-relief of St. Januarius, in a reclining
pofture, to point out the fpot where this faint has
been buried fo many centuries. Behind it is the
marble feat of St. Severus, contiguous to the grave
wherein he was firft depofited.

Near

Near this are the tombs of Agrippina, Corenzo? and other faints, together with a mofaic altar placed in a fmall cavity in the wall. They tell you, that in moft places there are three paffages, conftructed one over another: but be this as it may, thofe branching out are very narrow, and in many parts walled up, to prevent robbers from making ufe of them as their retreats. Here is one particular vault of fuch a height, that its top cannot be difcerned by the light of the flambeaux. In another large empty vault, which our guide told us was the cathedral in the primitive times, are two large pillars, which fupport an arch hewn out of a rock; and near them an ancient baptiftry.

Every curious traveller, who is defirous of reaping a proper advantage from his travels through Italy, fhould not omit fpending fome days in obferving the country round Puzzuolo, Cuma, &c. In the road leading from the fuburbs of Chiaia to the *Grotto del Monte di Paufilypo*, on an eminence to the left, is a garden, now in the poffeffion of Paolo Ruffo, where are the ruins of an ancient maufoleum. It was originally in the form of a pyramid, but the lower part, which is all now remaining, refembles a large oven; but a guide will be neceffary to find the way, which, toward the cave of Paufilypo, is fo narrow, and runs along fuch a high precipice, that it is dangerous to perfons fubject to fwimmings in the head. This piece of antiquity is faid to be the tomb of the poet Virgil, but without any foundation for fuch a conjecture. In the wall, within, are ten fmall niches or cavities, intended for the reception of urns.

In going by water from Naples to Puzzuolo, not far from cape Paufilypo, you pafs by a dome, hewn out of a rock, fuppofed to be the remains of a temple of Venus, though vulgarly, for what reafon I know not, called *la Scuola di Virgilio*.

Formerly, in going from Naples to Puzzuolo, it was neceffary to crofs mount Paufilypus, which was
famous

Grotto of PAUSILYPO.

famous for its delightful prospect; but at present that trouble is saved by a broad subterraneous road hewn through the mountain in a straight line. The entrance at each end is near a hundred feet high; but toward the middle, much lower. On each side of the mountain, near the middle, two large vent-holes for air and light, are cut through the roof of this grotto. The light, however, is not sufficient, and the dust very troublesome. The bottom of it was, in the time of Pedro de Toledo, viceroy of Naples, paved with broad stones like the city, and is cleaned several times a year, when it is pretty free from dust. The breadth is between eighteen and twenty feet, so that two carriages may conveniently pass one another. The length of this subterraneous passage is about three hundred and forty-four *cannæ*, or something above half an Italian mile. Near the middle of the passage, on the left, is a small chapel or oratory hewn out of the rock, in which a lamp is kept constantly burning. The vulgar ascribe this grotto to Virgil, whom they will have to have been a magician. The Neapolitan writers in general pretend, that it was the work of one Cocceius. Seneca, in his fifty-seventh letter, complains greatly of its dust and obscurity. Possibly, the cutting of a road through the mountain might not at first be thought of; but the large quantity of stones that were, from time to time, hewn out of it to supply the buildings of Naples and Puzzuolo, might occasion such deep evacuations on both sides, that at last, for the benefit of travellers, they determined to penetrate through the intermediate space, and open a passage through the bowels of the mountain. That this passage is the effect of human industry, is evident from the traces of chissels and other tools. The earthquakes which have made such havock in these parts, have hitherto spared this useful work.

At coming out of the grotto of Pausilypo, the road turns on the right-hand, and brings you into a delightful

delightful country, decorated with vineyards, through which you pafs to the *Lago d'Agnano*, of a circular figure, and about an Italian mile in circumference. In fome parts of it, about high-water, is a ftrong ebullition; and, on approaching near it, the motion of the water is perceptible, and poffibly proceeds from the violent afcent of the effluvia, but without the leaft degree of heat. On this lake ftand the fudatories of St. Germano, confifting of fome apartments built of ftone, where the heat and fulphureous vapour arifing from the earth, eafily caufe a profufe fweat.

Within lefs than a hundred paces of thefe falubrious fudatories, is a fmall natural cavity, known by the name of *Grotta del Cane*, or, *the Dog's Grotto*; a dog being the animal commonly pitched upon, to fhew the furprifing effect of the vapour in this cavity.

It is about twelve feet in length, five broad, fix high, and twenty paces diftant from the lake of Agnano. The ground at the top and on the fides, is of a dufky green colour; and the vapour afcending in it, is condenfed into very clear drops, unlefs, as this effect is not always conftant, thefe rather proceed from the rain-water collected from the hill above it.

This grotto is continually open, having no door to it. On the way to it is a hut where dogs are kept purpofely, to fhew ftrangers the effects of this cave. The owner of the dog, going into the cavern, holds the creature forcibly down to the ground, when, in a minute and a half, or two minutes time, he is feized with violent convulfions, which continue for a minute and a half longer, till at laft he lies quite motionlefs. The man indeed, during the operation, is almoft on his knees, but keeps his head up as high as poffible, that the vapours, in their afcent, may not affect him. The dog, having lain between two and three minutes, in all appearance dead, is thrown into an adjacent lake, where, in half a minute, he fhews fome figns of life, and continues giddy for about a minute

minute after he is taken out, and reels in walking: of a sudden recovers, and leaps on his master with the utmost joy and fondness. It must however be observed, that if any creature be too long in the grotto, it dies irrecoverably; and that some animals can endure it much longer than others.

Properly speaking, it is not the water, nor any particular quality in the lake of Agnano, that recovers the dog when seemingly dead, but the fresh air, in which alone, though much slower, the animal is found to come to himself. In this case, the water has the same effect as on a person in a swoon, by invigorating the respiration, the entire suppression of which would otherwise be followed by certain death. The effluvia which float copiously near the bottom of the grotto, and never rise higher than ten inches, become mortal, probably by their subtilty stopping the circulation of the blood; and this is also evident from the dissection of a frog which died in this cavern, not the least air being perceivable in its lungs.

On the same account, and for want of dense air, or from a stagnation of it, a lighted torch immediately goes out, when lowered from the upper part of the grotto to within ten inches of the bottom; and not only the flame is extinguished, but even the snuff; and the smoke, being pressed by the dense air above, is observed to make its way out at the mouth of the grotto forward, not in a perpendicular, but horizontal direction, at the distance of about ten inches from the bottom. To this rarefaction of the air it is owing, that a loaded piece, when placed at the bottom of this grotto, will not go off, nor will the powder take fire; which last is, however, effected when a quantity of powder is set on fire by means of a train laid on a narrow board, whereby the vapour at the bottom is driven out of the grotto.

About three Italian miles from the extremity of the main land, lies the island of Caprea, sufficiently
noted

noted for the diffolute life of Tiberius in his infamous retreat.

On the right, nearer to Puzzuolo, lies Monte Secco, on which are only a few small shrubs, and a kind of broom. The summit of this mountain, which was anciently in the form of a cone, is now sunk into a concave oval, whose conjugate, or shortest diameter, is about 1000 feet, and its transverse, or longest, 1246. It is generally known by the name of *Solfatara*.

A lover of natural curiosities must be highly delighted here, as he may see Vesuvius in miniature, without any apparent danger or trouble. Though Vesuvius is two German miles distant from Solfatara, these two volcanos have a communication with each other; it being observed, that the smoke, heat, and force of the subterraneous fire are less violent in Salfatara when Vesuvius rages, and affords a vent to the sulphureous vapours; whereas, on the other hand, the heat of the former increases when the latter is at rest.

On the surface of this mountain are several fissures or cracks emitting smoke; in proportion as they are extended, the heat is increased, so that at last it becomes insupportable. A sword, or other piece of iron, being held over one of these spiracles, a sweetish kind of fluid drops from it; but a piece of paper is not the least moistened, though confined for a long time over one of the chasms, but becomes very dry and stiff. The stones near these holes and cracks seem to be in continual motion; and small stones, dropped into these holes, are ejected to the height of twelve feet, and sometimes thrown on one side, like the more ponderous masses from Vesuvius. In some places the sand, by the force of the vapours, springs up and down near the spiracles, like the sparkling or cyder or champaigne.

The stones near these apertures are covered with a yellow substance, resembling the yolk of an egg boiled

boiled hard, with a white efflorescence or bloom upon it, which they say is the sal ammoniac.

At the time I visited Solfatara, some workmen were employed on a vein of a greyish kind of ashes, intermixed with whitish sulphureous stones, several feet in thickness. These ashes exactly resemble those ejected by mount Vesuvius in extraordinary eruptions, and which have been known to cover the streets of Naples five or six inches deep. They also, beside sulphur, extract vitriol, of a sapphire colour, better than that of Rome, and also the best kind of alum. The large leaden kettles, used in this operation, are not heated by a culinary fire, but by the natural heat issuing thro' the holes in the ground over which the vessels are placed. Beside these, this district yields excellent gypsum, and of the earth itself they make vases and cups, which are drank out of, and reckoned very beneficial in several disorders. The hot vapour, issuing through these apertures, is said to be of great use in pains of the eyes, ears, limbs, and stomach; the head-ach, bilious fevers, and sterility.

In this valley was formerly a boiling lake of black water, the ebullition in which sometimes rose upward of ten feet high: but nothing of this is now to be seen, nor is there any rivulet on the surface of the ground in all this plain. There are, indeed, subterranean rivers, one of which directs its course toward Puzzuolo. The soil hereabout is so hollow, that it is dangerous riding over it. On a spot near the place where the sulphureous stones are dug, I caused a hole to be made a foot and a half deep, and a stone, weighing about fifteen or twenty pounds, to be thrown into it; upon which a rumbling noise was immediately perceived under the ground, like that of thunder, or the discharge of cannon at a distance; and from the long continuance of the sound, and its various repercussions, it was natural to conclude, that it was reflected through a great many caverns. In several places, by only stamping on the ground

with

with the foot, the effect was exactly like that of striking against a vault. The sulphureous effluvia of Solfatara frequently reach as far as Naples, and tarnish the marble and silver utensils.

The ancients, misled by poetical fables, were of opinion that the giants were confined in the abyss, under the Solfatara, and that the effluvia from the earth was owing to their eructations. Even Dio himself says, that these giants often appeared, both by day and night, before some dreadful eruption of mount Vesuvius. Nor has Christianity itself banished these chimeras; a thousand idle stories are told of spirits frequently appearing on the borders of this mountain, and uttering doleful lamentations: whence the vulgar conclude, that these spiracles extend either to hell, or, at least, to purgatory. Nor are the Capuchin monks, of a neighbouring convent, wanting in their endeavours to propagate such ridiculous tales. Their church is built on the spot where St. Januarius is said to have been beheaded. A great heat is continually perceived in this structure, and principally issues from some holes before the high altar. Here is an elegant marble bust, supposed to represent St. Januarius, and said to be the work of a Pagan artist, from the mere description of that saint, given him by the devout women who gathered up his blood. This bust serves as an original for all sculptors and painters in their statues or portraits of St. Januarius.

Puzzoli is eight Italian miles from Naples, and derives its Latin name, *Puteoli*, either from a sulphureous vapour, or the great number of *putei* or pits made here, by carrying on the sulphur works, and digging for sand, which was here anciently found under water, and very good for buildings.

The situation of the city is on a declivity, and the many beautiful stones thrown up by the sea on the shore, are a sufficient proof of its former wealth and splen-

splendor. Many of them are, indeed, of a blue or red colour; but others are verde antico, porphyry, &c. and seem to have been used in mosaic works; among them are also frequently found agate, cornelian, amethyst, jasper, onyx, beryl, lapis lazuli, and the like; and many of them cameos and intaglios. This city has suffered very much from the devastations of war, inundations, and earthquakes, especially from the latter, in the year 1538.

[Mr. Sharpe gives us a ludicrous tradition relating to this place, as follows:——" I am not to tell you that St. Januarius is the patron of Naples, their guardian saint. There is a famous statue of him at Puzzoli, which the Saracens, in one of their expeditions to this kingdom, wantonly defaced, by breaking off his nose, which one of them carried away in his pocket. Upon this, storms arose, and continued blowing so violently that they could never put to sea; till providentially some of them thought it was owing to the resentment of the image, who would not be appeased so long as his nose was in their possession: upon which they threw it into the sea; and fine weather immediately succeeding, they sailed prosperously to their havens. In the mean while, the artists endeavoured to repair the image with a new nose; but neither art nor force could fasten one on: at length, some fishermen took up the original nose in their nets; but disregarding it, because they did not know what it was, they flung it again into the sea; nevertheless, the nose continuing to offer itself to their nets in whatever place they fished, they began to conceive it must be something supernatural. One of them, more cunning than the others, suggested it might be the nose of the saint; upon which they applied it to the statue, to examine whether it fitted, and immediately, without any cement, it united so exactly, as hardly to leave any appearance of a scar; in which state we now see it."——]

Puzzoli

Puzzoli has a very commodious harbour, and in it fourteen piers, rifing above the furface of the water, which were, in the time of the Romans, joined together by arches. The pillars are built with large blocks of that fpecies of ftone called *piperno*, faced with brick-work; and the interftices are filled up with a very hard mortar, made with Puzzoli fand.

We now return back acrofs the country, to Loretto, on the coaft of the Adriatic. In the way between Rome and Loretto, lies the city of Spoleto, fituated on the acclivity of a mountain: it is a town of mean appearance, but, like others of the lower clafs in Italy, contains many romantic infcriptions concerning its antiquity, and other trifling occurrences which have happened there.

Loretto is famous throughout the whole Chriftian world, for the *Cafa Santa*, or houfe in which the Virgin Mary is faid to have dwelt at Nazareth. It is pretended to have been carried by angels through the air, in the month of May 1291, out of Galilee to Terfato in Dalmatia; and from thence four years and a half afterward to Italy: in which country, about midnight, on the 10th of December 1294, it was firft fet down in a wood, in the territory of Recanati, about a thoufand paces from the fea. If we will believe Turfellini, all the trees, on the arrival of this facred manfion, bowed with the profoundeft reverence, and continued in that pofture till they gradually withered. But this pious wood, through the irreverence of the inhabitants, was rooted up in 1575, in order to improve the land.

A rich and devout lady, called Laureta, being at that time the owner of the place, the holy houfe was from her called the houfe of Laureta. This holy manfion did not, however, continue long in this place, the barbarities committed by banditti, who infefted the road leading thither, deterred pilgrims from reforting to it to pay their devotions; fo that, at the end of eight months, the angels again took it up, up, and depofited it on a hill, about a thoufand paces nearer to Racanati. This place belonged to two brothers, who at firft received this invaluable prefent with the greateft joy; but the profits arifing from the refort of fo many pilgrims, and the rich offerings they brought to the holy houfe, raifed fuch feuds betwixt them, as terminated in a duel, in which both were killed on the fpot. To prevent the like misfortunes for the future, the holy Virgin again directed the angels to remove her houfe a bow-fhot further up the country, to an eminence, about two thoufand geometrical paces from the fea, and is the place where it now ftands. This happened a few months after it had been placed on the eftate of thofe contentious brothers. And it is believed, as undoubted fact, that the *Cafa Santa* had, within a year after its arrival in Italy from Dalmatia, changed its place three times in the diftrict of Recanati.

The Roman Catholic writers are at a lofs for an anfwer to the objection, that the *Cafa Santa* had been near two hundred years in Italy, before any author of that country mentioned it. But what fufficiently contradicts the account of the Italian monks, are thofe given by St. Vincent and other writers, with regard to the Virgin's houfe, which they affirm was ftill ftanding at Nazareth, when, according to the computation of the inhabitants of Recanati, it had been long famous among them. However, after the time of pope Pius II. authors make more frequent mention of the Madonna of Loretto, to whom his holinefs in perfon offered a golden cup, in purfuance of a vow, with an infcription on it fuitable to the occafion. This offering, and the omnipotence afcribed to the Virgin Mary by his holinefs, had not the defired effect; for he died that very year at Ancona, and even of the fame complication of diforders, againft which he had recourfe to her affiftance.

With regard to the dimenfions of the *Cafa Santa,* Terfellina fays it is about forty feet long, almoft twenty

twenty broad, and about twenty-five feet in height; but by a more accurate survey and menfuration, the houfe is actually forty-three palmi wanting two inches long in the infide, eighteen palmi four inches broad, and twenty-fix palmi in height. Hence it appears, that the length is thirty-one feet three quarters, the breadth thirteen feet three inches, and the height eighteen feet nine inches, Englifh meafure, reckoning a palmi and a half equal to thirteen inches. In the center, where the roof clofes, it is five palmi higher than at the fides. Formerly the roof was made of timber only; but left the great number of lights continually burning there fhould happen to fet it on fire, pope Clement VII. erected an arched roof; and to prevent any damage to the houfe, by making this alteration, and at the fame time to ftrengthen its foundation, it was ftrongly compacted with rafters, planks, and cords, and fufpended by machines and pullies, till the walls were carried high enough to be joined with thofe of the old ftructure. They alfo took an opportunity of making an alteration in the doors; for there being only one entrance on the north fide, which was the front, it was inconvenient, on account of the prodigious concourfe of people who vifited this holy manfion; and therefore it was thought advifable to wall up this entrance, and make three others, two for the people, and a third for the clergy, and thofe they pleafed to introduce into the moft facred part of the chapel. Thefe breaks, however, were not begun without previous faftings, prayers, and other ceremonies, performed by the pope's order. It is pretended that the architect Nerucio, who undertook the repairing of this houfe, beginning his work before the proper preparations were performed, was feized with a fudden indifpofition, which almoft coft him his life. The window on the weft fide, oppofite to the image of the Virgin Mary, was alfo at the fame time enlarged, and fecured with bars of iron gilt. The beams, tiles, and other materials, that

that were taken away in making these repairs, are deposited under the floor of the *Casa Santa*, that they might not be carried to other places, and exposed as reliques, to the prejudice of Loretto. With this view, people are also persuaded to believe, that there are numberless instances of persons, who, by presuming to carry away clandestinely, the least bit of stone or mortar, belonging to this sacred house, have brought upon themselves diseases, and numberless other misfortunes: nor could they ever rest, till they had restored what they had unjustly taken from the *Casa Santa*. The people must therefore think it no small favour to kiss the walls of this holy house. This edifice is manifestly built of bricks, of an unequal size; though the popish writers will have it, that it is a kind of unknown stone. On the cieling is painted the assumption of the Virgin Mary; but almost defaced by the smoke of such a number of lamps continually burning in this house.

On the top of *Casa Santa* is a small tower, which the Romans cannot deny to be the work of Christians; because it doth not seem in the least probable, that the Virgin Mary had such an ornament on her mean habitation. The two small bells in the tower, are only rung in violent storms of thunder and lightning, in confidence that their sound only will disperse any tempest, and prevent its ill effects.

In the *Casa Santa* is a small place, which may be esteemed the Holy of Holies. It is separated from the other part by a silver balustrade, and has a gate of the same metal. This is said to be the spot where the holy Virgin was sitting when the angel Gabriel appeared to her. The silver balustrade was the gift of cardinal Portocarrero, and the gate of Magalotti. The window through which the angel came into the house, is shewn on the west side the holy mansion.

The image of the Virgin is of cedar, five palmi in height; and the divine infant, which is of the same wood, on her right arm, not quite two palmi. She

She holds in her left-hand a globe, and two fingers of her right hand are extended, as if giving her benediction. The faces of both these images are covered with a kind of silver varnish; but so tarnished with the continual smoke of the lamps, that the holy Virgin wants only a thicker upper-lip to make her a compleat negro. The garment of the holy infant is of a flame colour; but that of his mother azure, with which she is so modestly dressed, that nothing of the statue is seen except the face, and the tip of the toes. The mantle hanging down her shoulders is of the same colour, and disseminated with stars of gold; her hair is parted, some hanging on her shoulders, and some down her back. On her head is a triple crown of gold, adorned with pearls and diamonds; and a smaller one of the same kind, is placed on the infant Jesus. Both were the gift of Lewis XIII. of France, and are valued at seventy-five thousand scudi or crowns.

The gold chains, rings, and jewels, wherewith this image is loaded, I will pass over, as they are so often varied and changed; several being frequently deposited in the treasury to make room for new ones. Her apparel is not always the same, being often varied; during the seven days of passion-week, she is dressed in black, and every day furnished with a fresh suit. A great deal of ceremony is used in dressing and undressing the image; bowing with the most profound reverence, whilst the spectators petition the statue with loud invocations, the noise of which increases as the priests proceed in undressing the image; fancying, perhaps, that their cries and ejaculations must sooner reach the heart of a naked virgin, than when she is dressed. The sculptor has taken care that the modesty of the priests should not be offended at the sight of a female statue naked, by adding a proper drapery. The chief ornaments with which this image is generally decorated, are 1. A jewel set in gold, consisting of thirteen rubies, sixty-six emeralds, three

hundred

LORETTO.

hundred and forty-one diamonds: it was an offering of Anne, princefs of Neuburg, and confort to Charles II. king of Spain. 2. A gold crucifix, fet with feveral large and beautiful emeralds, the gift of cardinal Paolo Sfondrata. 3. Two large pearls fet in gold, hanging on the divine infant's head; prefented by a princefs of Darmftadt. 4. A crucifix fet with diamonds, given by cardinal Marefcotto. 5 and 6. Two other crucifixes, fet with rubies and diamonds, offered by the cardinals Barberini and Corfi. 7. The collar and badge of the Golden Fleece, fet with large topazes, fapphires, rubies, and emeralds; the gift of Catherine, wife of Gabriel Bethlen Gabor, prince of Tranfylvania. 8. A large golden heart, fufpended on a gold chain, fet with rubies and diamonds; offered by Maximilian I. elector of Bavaria. 9. A clufter of diamonds, rubies, and emeralds, fet in gold, on which is a pelican feeding her young ones with her blood, reprefented by a very lirge and beautiful ruby at her breaft; an offering of the dutchefs of Ucceda. 10. A large emerald, fet round with diamonds and rubies, which hangs on one fide of the infant's hands; the gift of the dutchefs de Salviati. 11. Three admirable emeralds fet in gold, and furrounded by diamonds and other emeralds; prefented by Violanta Beatrix, a princefs of the houfe of Bavaria, and widow of Ferdinand, hereditary prince of Florence. The niche in which the image is placed, is adorned with feventy one large Bohemian topazes, the offering of the cavalier Capra.

On the right fide is a gold ftatue of an angel, profufely decorated with diamonds and other jewels; one of his knees is inclined, as offering a golden heart, fet with large diamonds, terminating in a flame, which glitters with rubies and pearls, with a lamp continually burning over it. This piece, faid to have coft fifty thoufand ducats, was offered by Maria Beatrix Eleanora, of the houfe of Efte, queen of king James II. of England, that by the interceffion of the Virgin she might have a son. Accordingly, soon after, as is said, her desires were accomplished in a son, the pretender to the British crown.

On the left side of the statue of the Virgin, is an angel of silver in the above-mentioned posture, offering a golden heart, crowned with glittering pearls, emeralds, and diamonds, and like the former, terminating in a flame. This was the gift of Laura Martinozzia, widow of Alphonso IV. duke of Modena, and mother of the above-mentioned queen of England.

On the right-hand of the Virgin, is a statue of an angel, weighing three hundred and fifty-one pounds. He is represented, offering, on a cushion of the same metal, an infant of gold, which weighs twenty-four pounds. This was a present from Lewis XIII. of France, given pursuant to a vow at the birth of the dauphin, who was afterward Lewis XIV. Beside this, there are many other images of children, both in gold and silver; also several other valuable votive pieces: but to enumerate them all, would tire the reader's patience.

The robe in which this image was dressed, when brought from Dalmatia to Italy, is made of red camblet, and kept in a casket of glass. The cup, out of which both the Virgin and her infant are said to have eaten and drank, is shaped like a porringer, or shallow bowl. It is made of earth, and glazed, but now set in silver. This vessel is not only kissed, but rosaries, agni Dei, crucifixes, and paper caps, with the Virgin of Loretto painted on them, are rubbed against it, from a firm persuasion, that they become a specific remedy against the head ach and other diseases. An ague is said to have been perfectly cured, by only drinking a little cold water out of this vessel: even the oil and wax of the lamps and candles burning before the image, are not without their medicinal and anodyne qualities. Beside the above dish, here are several other pieces of furniture belonging to the holy Virgin, but very mean. Under the image is the hearth, or fire-place, where she used to dress her victuals, and is now called *Sacrosanctus Caminus*.

Before the holy Virgin, seventeen golden lamps are continually burning. Among the thirty-seven silver lamps, burning in the other part of the *Casa Santa*, several weigh fifty, eighty, a hundred; and four of them a hundred and twenty-eight pounds. For supplying all these lamps with oil, legacies have been left, and annual pensions appropriated by the persons who offered them. The altar stands in the middle of the party-wall, which separates the *Sanctum Sanctorum* from the other part of the chapel. It is insulated, and does not intercept the full view of the image of the Virgin, which stands high and forward in the sanctuary of the chapel behind the altar. The Roman Catholics pretend, that this altar was made by the apostles themselves, and brought hither from Galilee, with the holy house. On it is a quadrangular stone, upon which St. Peter is said to have celebrated the first mass. The rich *Palliotto*, embellished with jasper, *lapis lazuli* and agate, was an offering of Cosmo II. great duke of Tuscany.

Over the window, through which the angel Gabriel entered the house at the annunciation, is a picture of the crucifixion, pretended to have been brought hither by the apostles, and said to have been executed by St. Luke.

The present pavement of the *Casa Santa* consists of square pieces of white and red marble. The walls seem formerly to have been plaistered with mortar, part of which, here and there, with the portrait of the Virgin, and a group of angels painted on it, is still remaining.

The outside of the *Casa Santa*, notwithstanding the mean appearance of the walls within, is splendidly decorated with the most costly marble, so contrived, as to serve as a case for it, a small interval being left between the marble and the brick walls of the holy manſion. This is partly to be aſcribed to the veneration entertained for theſe ſacred materials, and partly to an apprehenſion, that they would not admit this new unhallowed marble in contact with them, but repel them with ſuch violence, as by the ſhock to endanger the lives of the workmen; which, if we will believe tradition, formerly happened to ſome fooliſh builders, who were deſirous of ſtrengthening theſe ſacred walls by ſome new additions.

This marble ſtructure, which incloſes the *Caſa Santa*, was begun by pope Leo X. in 1514, and though not quite finiſhed, conſecrated in 1538 by pope Paul III. It was at laſt compleated in 1579, and pope Gregory XIII. had the honour of putting the finiſhing hand to this ſplendid ſtructure. It ſtands in the middle of a fine ſpacious church, which preſerves it from the injuries of wind and weather. The pilgrims commonly perform their firſt proceſſion by going round the holy houſe on their knees, though they are under no particular injunction to do this; but left to the dictates of their devotional zeal to make this kneeling circuit as often as they pleaſe. It is about fifty feet in length, thirty in breadth, and the ſame in height; and the materials employed are all of the whiteſt Carrara marble. The two longer ſides are each embelliſhed with ſix Corinthian pillars of variegated marble; and the two ſhorter, with four each. In the inter-columniations are bas-reliefs, repreſenting the moſt remarkable incidents in the life of the Virgin; between theſe ten ſtatues of the prophets, and above them the ten ſibyls. Among the prophets, on the ſouth ſide, David with the head of Goliah at his feet, is particularly admired for its curious workmanſhip; and on the north ſide is a groupe repreſenting the eſpouſals of the Virgin, and a boy playing with a dog; while his mother, with a child in her arms, beholds him with a countenance full of the utmoſt maternal tenderneſs, the expreſſion of which is truly admirable. It was deſigned and begun

gun by Contucci, but finifhed by Rafaelle du Monte Lupone and Tribulo, which laft artift alfo performed the famous ftatue, reprefenting a man breaking a ftick. On the eaft fide, in a bas-relief, exhibiting the extraordinary conveyance of the *Cafa Santa*, through the air, is a peafant driving his afs, the expreffion of which cannot be viewed without pleafure.

No perfon is admitted with a fword, or other weapon, which muft be delivered to an ecclefiaftic, who fits over againft the door of the fanctuary, and alfo receives the little pecuniary gratuities made for the benefit of the church. A fcudi is fufficient for a company of two or three perfons to give, and the like fum is required for feeing the treafury. But it is quite otherwife with regard to the prefents offered by pilgrims, which may be eafily imagined to amount annually to many thoufand ducats.

The extraordinary, and almoft divine worfhip paid by Roman Catholics to the Virgin Mary, is very well known: and fince the veneration for reliques has, in the laft century, been carried to an exorbitant pitch, it may be eafily concluded, what a continual refort of people muft be to a houfe where the Virgin Mary was born, brought up, efpoufed, and lived after marriage; in which alfo our Saviour's incarnation was revealed to her, where fhe was overfhadowed by the Holy Ghoft, and laftly, where our Saviour himfelf paffed a great part of his life. From this laft circumftance, fome Roman Catholics, when afked why this relique preferably to any other memorial of the evangelical hiftory, efpecially the holy fepulchre, was brought away from the infidels by the miniftry of angels and removed into Europe? anfwer, that among other reafons it arofe from that natural fondnefs our Saviour, like other men, always retained for a place where, in his youthful days, he had paffed fo many agreeable hours.

The

The number of pilgrims who visited this holy house, is said, formerly, for several years successively, to have amounted to two hundred thousand. But the Protestant doctrine, since the reformation, has given a severe blow to the sale of indulgencies; and even the zeal of those who still adhere to the Roman church, is greatly abated with regard to tiresome pilgrimages: so that, at present, the number of pilgrims who annually repair hither for the sake of devotion, seldom exceeds forty or fifty thousand. Not many years since, nine thousand pilgrims were at Loretto at one time; and it may easily be conceived, what confusion such a number of people must occasion in this little town. Some come a-foot, others ride on asses or horses. The female pilgrims, whose circumstances enable them to be at the expence, generally chuse to come to Loretto in carriages; and, as large companies frequently travel together, many diverting incidents often happen on the road. As soon as they reach the paved way leading down a hill into the suburbs, they begin singing some hymn, which continues till they enter the church. But if the company be too large, the ceremony of going on their knees round the *Casa Santa* is omitted, and they must make use of some other method to shew their devotion. The poor pilgrims are received into an hospital, where they are provided with beds, as also bread and wine, every morning and evening, for three days. The greatest concourse at Loretto, is from the beginning of May till the middle of July; great numbers are also to be seen in September, it having been revealed to Paulus à Sylva in a vision, that the Virgin Mary was born on the eighth day of that month.

The large church, which entirely covers the *Casa Santa*, is built of Istrian stone, which very much resembles that of Tivoli stone, used at Rome. The iron grates before the several chapels in the church, were forged out of the fetters of four thousand Christians, who, by the naval victory of Lepanto, in the

time

LORETTO. 155

time of pope Pius V. in 1571, were released from Turkish slavery. Several confessionals are placed up and down in the church, with superscriptions over them, indicating in what language strangers may confess, and receive absolution. Above twenty Jesuits attend constantly as confessors, and among these a person of any European nation, may find one at least, who understands his native language.

The many masses founded here for ever, beside others that are well paid for, and said daily on particular occasions, enable the *Casa Santa* to maintain eighty chaplains, who with the canons, beneficiaries and ecclesiastics, visiting Loretto out of devotion, constantly perform this essential part of the Romish religion. The number of the masses daily said in the *Casa Santa*, and in the great church which surrounds it, amount to a hundred and twenty-three; and in the whole year, to forty-four thousand eight hundred and ninety-five.

The eunuchs also who belong to the choir of the holy chapel say masses here; and, on such occasions, carry their testicles about them in a small box: concluding, by mathematical calculation, that $\frac{99}{100}$ and $\frac{1}{100}$ are always equal to an integer. This practice is seldom heard of at Rome; but in the upper parts of Italy is very common.

The walls of the church of Loretto were formerly hung with a multitude of pictures and votive pieces; some of wood, some brass, and others of wax; but the number of these beginning to obscure the church, and not adding greatly to its elegance, it was decreed, in the year 1673, to remove the major part of them, and apply the silver and gold to better uses. In the church near the *Casa Santa*, is still a picture of a priest offering his entrails to the Virgin Mary. The occasion of this picture, according to the inscription under it, is as follows. The priest was by birth a Dalmatian, lived in the beginning of the sixth century, and entertained a high veneration for the *Madonna di Loretto*.

Loretto. It was his misfortune to be taken prisoner by the Turks, and solicited to embrace the Mahometan and abjure the Christian religion; but he not only rejected their proposals, and opposed their menaces, but also never ceased to call upon the name of Christ, and the holy Virgin. Being asked the reason for such continual invocations, he answered, that these names were imprinted on his heart, and therefore it was not in his power to forbear. Upon their threatening to tear his heart and bowels out of his body, if he did not desist from his invocations, and renounce Christ and Mary, he replied, the first was in their power; but the latter impossible for them to perform. Upon this the Turks immediately put their threats in execution; but the priest, in the midst of his torture, persisted in calling on the Virgin Mary, promising, at the same time, a pilgrimage to Loretto. They therefore put his heart and the entrails into his hands, telling him by way of sarcasm, that he might now perform his vow, and carry his offering to Loretto. But, to their astonishment, the martyr rose immediately, and with his heart and entrails in his hands, proceeded on his journey, and arrived at Loretto, where he shewed his mangled body; and after offering his heart and entrails, relating the whole affair, and receiving the holy sacrament, he expired.

The Jesuit Terfellina adds, that these entrails hung a long time in the church, as a memorial of the miracle; but decaying by length of time, they were taken away, and their place supplied by a representation of them cut in wood. Pope Paul III. however, ordered the latter to be removed, the vulgar beginning to render more homage to them, than even to the Virgin Mary herself.

It is not improbable, that many silver tablets and votive pieces, which make but little show, are melted down, and sent to the mint to be coined; as also, that the superfluous jewels, not employed in ornaments, are converted into money, and applied to better uses: especially

especially if they have been the offerings of persons long since dead, or other circumstances render any further inquiry improbable. This I know, that foreign jewellers find their accounts greatly in visiting the convents of Italy, and have purchased many rich jewels for small sums of ready money, which the Monks are very fond of, secrecy being strictly enjoined the purchasers at the same time.

In the *Sala del Tresoro*, on a stone in the pavement, is the date 1626, cut as a memorial of a thief, who, in that year, found means to convey himself into this place; but by a particular miracle, the pavement, as they say, opening under him, he sunk down to his waist, so that being unable to stir, he was easily taken, and suffered the punishment he deserved. Others tell this story with additional circumstances; but the true design of the whole is, to deter others from making any future attempts on this valuable treasury.

The inhabitants of Loretto, notwithstanding their boasts of the extraordinary and visible protection of the Virgin Mary, especially with regard to this sacred treasure, do not think it advisable to put it to the trial; for not only the window of the *Sala del Tresoro* is secured with a strong iron gate, but even the city itself also fortified; which, according to an inscription on one of the bastions, was done in the year 1521, under the pontificate of Leo X. These fortifications may prove a sufficient security to the town against any sudden attack of pirates; but are otherwise of little importance; for, in many places, the houses serve instead of walls.

Loretto is commonly without a garrison, so that it is surprising the Turks have not made greater efforts than they have hitherto done, in order to possess themselves of the precious booty deposited here. The Roman Catholics indeed allege, that in all the attempts which the Turks have hitherto made against Loretto, they have been driven off, either by an extraordinary

traordinary miracle, or are seized with a supernatural panic. But the true reason why the Turks do not make a formal attempt on this place, may arise from the great shallowness of the Adriatic in these parts; whereby the approach of large ships to that shore is rendered entirely impracticable: beside, Loretto lying only three Italian miles from the sea, and in an open country, no descent can be made with such secrecy and expedition as not to alarm the whole country. And no sooner is a Turkish squadron known to be at sea, than a strong garrison is immediately sent hither from the neighbouring country.

The annual revenue of the *Casa Santa*, from lands and other settled funds and stipends, is by themselves allowed to amount to near thirty thousand scudi, exclusive of the presents and offerings of devotees, which, and from the resort of so many thousand votaries, must be very considerable.

The trade of Loretto, beside the inns, public houses, and lodgings of strangers, consists chiefly in making medals, crucifixes, images of the Virgin Mary, painted paper caps, ribbands, and rosaries, which are bought up by strangers, as amulets for the head-ach, fits, and other diseases.

Loretto is about a mile in circumference, and has a fine prospect toward the sea, and a beautiful valley finely planted with trees. The suburb extending to Monte Reale, is finely built. In clear weather, about sun-rising, the mountains of Croatia, though a hundred and fifty miles from Loretto, are discernable.

Foreigners resorting hither, in such crowds, occasion a great consumption of provisions at Loretto; and tho' your host is sure to exact upon you as much as possible, yet the entertainment cannot be complained of. The inhabitants are very courteous; and at the post-houses between Rome to Bologna, you have much more polite usage than in those between Florence and Rome. Their frequent converse with strangers, doubtless, serves to polish their manners.

The

ANCONA.

The roads in the country about Loretto, as well as the town itself, swarm with beggars, who, in spring, strew flowers before strangers, and throw some into the carriages, in order to obtain their charities.

The distance between Loretto and Ancona, is fifteen Italian miles, the road lying through a most agreeable plain, interfected by the rivers Mufone and Afpido. The number of streams and rivers that have their source in the east-side of the Apennines, is greater than can be found in any other chain of mountains of the same extent.

Ancona is but a mean place, and stands on hilly and uneven ground, and it has its name from its shape, being built in an angle like that of the elbow.

The stature and complexion of the inhabitants of Ancona, especially the fair sex, are greatly superior to the rest of the inhabitants of Italy, so that they seem to be another people. The same may be observed of the inhabitants of Senigallia, Fano, and Pefaro as far as Remini. If it be true, that the polite and beautiful youths reforting to the univerfities, added to the grand retinue of a court, contribute to render Leipsick, Hall, and Drefden, the nurferies of fine men: the superior beauty of the female fex at Fano, Ancona, &c. may, with equal justice, be attributed to the great number of strangers and pilgrims, continually travelling through those cities.

The eastern part of Italy is pleafanter and more fertile than the generality of places lying on the west side; especially if you include the coast between Genoa and Leghorn.

The whole Adriatic sea abounds with testaceous and most other kinds of fish. A singular species of the former is the Ballani, or Ballari, found alive in large stones. The shell of this fish is rough and of an oblong figure, somewhat refembling a date, and are thence called Dattili del Mare. They are generally found on the shallows near Comero, or Aonaro, ten miles from Ancona.

Rimini,

Rimini, or Araminium, was formerly a confiderable city, but now greatly decayed, efpecially fince the fatal blow it received by an earthquake in the year 1671. It is, however, ftill remarkable for feveral pieces of its ancient fplendour. Without the town, toward Pefaro, is a triumphal arch, the front of which is decorated with two beautiful Corinthian pillars, and two bufts.

A few Italian miles from Rimini, you pafs a bridge over the river Cufa, which, by Clementivi Giacomo Villani, and other learned men, has been taken for the ancient Rubicon. Two miles on this fide Sefenatico, the road croffes the river Fiumefino; and fcarce fixty paces before you crofs the Pifatello, which likewife empties itfelf into the Fiumefino. However fmall and fhallow the Piffatela may appear in dry weather, it is the ancient Rubicon, fo celebrated in Roman hiftory, for being the limit which divided the Italian provinces from Cifalpine Gaul. Whence the hoftile views of Julius Cæfar, on his paffing this river with his army, could be no longer concealed.

After paffing Rimini, the face of the country is vifibly changed for the worfe; efpecially between Cervia and Ravenna, where the foil is remarkably barren, the parts on the fea-coaft being covered with fands, and the more inland country, full of moraffes, fens, and the like.

Ravenna, ridiculoufly fuppofed to have been founded by Efau, was very famous, not only during the flourifhing ftate of ancient Rome, but a confiderable time afterward; being the feat of the Exarch, or the emperor's viceroy in Italy. But, at prefent, it hardly contains fifteen thoufand inhabitants; a fum fo difproportionate to the number of convents, of which are no lefs than twenty-four in the city, that it muft fenfibly feel the weight of this ufelefs load.

Among other antiquities in this city are the remains of the walls belonging to the palace of Theodoric, king of the Oftrogoths; the upper part of it is decorated tated with pillars, and in the lower part is a very large porphyry coffin, in which the remains of that king were depofited. The Rotunda is fituated without the city, on the right hand in paffing out through the Porta Cibo. It has at prefent the appearance of an old ruined cupola or chapel; is fixteen common paces in diameter, and its pavement, except in the midft of fummer, generally under water. It is faid to have been built in 526, by Amalafunta, daughter to king Theodoric. The moft remarkable part of it is the roof, in the form of an inverted difh, and confifts of one fingle ftone, which, not many years ago, was fplit by the lightning. It is as hard as flint, and faid to have been brought hither from Egypt. It is four geometrical feet in thicknefs, one hundred and fourteen in circumference, and thirty-one feet two inches in diameter, according to an account of it, written on vellum, and kept on the altar of the chapel. It is not eafy to fay, in what manner fo enormous a mafs, which weighs near one hundred tons, could have been raifed to the top of this ftructure, efpecially as the modern machines were then unknown: but, whoever has feen the ftupendous obelifks at Rome, will be the lefs furprifed at this. Round the circumference of this ftone, on the top of the Rotunda, were formerly the ftatues of the twelve apoftles, their names being ftill on the pedeftals, which project a little way beyond the roof.

On the right hand, without the Porta Cibo, are the remains of the towers of the old caftle. On the left, where the fea formerly wafhed the city walls (as is evident from the iron rings ftill remaining, and which were ufed in faftening fhips) are at prefent feveral fields well cultivated; Ravenna now lying three Italian miles from the fea. As Mifenum was the ancient port for the Roman fleet in the Mediterranean, to intimidate the inhabitants of Gaul, Spain, Mauritania, Africa, Egypt, Sardinia, and Sicily; fo the harbour of Ravenna was ufed to awe the provinces of Epirus, Macedonia, Achaia, Proponris, Pontus, Crete, and Cyprus;

Cyprus; as is evident from Vegetius, lib. iv. and Suetonius in the Life of Auguſtus.

From Ravenna to Bologna is five ſtages, and the road lies through Faenza, Imola, and St. Nicola. Part of this road, eſpecially in wet weather, is very dangerous, running along the banks of the river L'Amoni; but when you are paſſed this, you enter a moſt beautiful road, extending through pleaſant groves, walks, and elegant vineyards.

Bologna, with regard to its extent, the number of its nobility and other inhabitants, and the importance of its trade, is doubtleſs next to Rome, the moſt opulent and beautiful city in the eccleſiaſtical ſtate. The number of its inhabitants amount to between eighty and ninety thouſand; but the whole diſtrict, which includes three hundred and eight cities, towns, and villages, contains three hundred and eight thouſand ſouls.

The inhabitants are reckoned very facetious, and famous for their ſatirical raillery: notwithſtanding which, they behave with the utmoſt politeneſs to ſtrangers, and appear to be excellent mechanics, and very induſtrious. The great quantity and valuable quality of their ſilk, is productive of a large trade; and the ſmall river Reno, a branch of which runs through the city, is very convenient for the ſilk mills, in which a ſingle wheel turns four or five thouſand ſmall cylinders with ſurpriſing velocity; and, if the ſilk be good and ſtrong, does more work than ſo many thouſand hands. The damaſks, ſattins, taffaties, and velvets of Bologna, are in great repute. The inhabitants likewiſe deal largely in hemp and flax, great quantities of the former being exported to Venice for ſails and cordage. The wine and oil produced in this neighbourhood, ſupply the adjacent provinces; and the wine from the vineyards of Bologna is ſo ſtrong, that it is generally diluted with one fourth part of water; except that appointed for the ſacrament, which is genuine, and may be purchaſed at the convents.

The

The country round Bologna produces vaft quantities of honey and wax, great part of which is exported, and all kind of provifions are in great plenty and exceeding good. Here are the beft inns in the whole tour of Italy, efpecially the St. Marco and il Pelegrino. Fowls of all kinds are very large, and their flefh delicious. The Bologna cervallat and other kinds of faufages, and dried tongues are famous not only throughout Europe, but are often fent to the Eaft and Weft Indies.

The nuns of this city are very ingenious in making artificial flowers, of filver, filk, muflin, enamel and ifinglafs. The fineft flowers are indeed, at firft, intended only for prefents, but there are abundance of them in the fhops, where ftrangers may purchafe them at a very reafonable price. They alfo imitate all kinds of fruit, fo exactly in wax, that the moft curious eye can hardly diftinguifh them from the products of nature.

Formerly the little dogs of Bologna breed, were a very confiderable advantage to that city; but at prefent, that foible is fo far exploded, that even at Bologna itfelf, the breed is fo fcarce, that one of tolerable beauty is valued at four or five guineas. Some pretend that the method for checking the growth of thefe animals, is to rub their legs, and the fpine of their backs with fpirit of wine, as foon as they are whelpt, and frequently repeating the operations.

The ladies of Bologna, efpecially thofe of rank, drefs entirely after the French mode; but thofe of the middle clafs generally wear a black gown, and over their heads a filk veil of the fame colour; but generally enjoy more liberty than in any other part of Italy. The number of blind people in this city is remarkable; but I have never been able to procure any fatisfactory account of the caufe. Numbers of people alfo are feen walking the ftreets with fpectacles on, who are fo far from labouring under any defect of fight, that their eyes wander about without fo much as looking through the glaffes. This is a Spanish custom, and supposed to indicate a remarkable gravity; and hence several ecclesiastics affect it.

[Mr. Sharpe informs us, he came to Bologna in "Rogation week, when all the communities of the city, walk several days in form, every man with a wax taper in his hand, and every community with a crucifix, or dying saviour. During the procession, both through the church and streets, there is an accompanyment of martial music, and tolling of bells. There was such an extraordinary succession of crucifixes, that I was much tired with the sameness of the objects; but at last, the appearance of a Madona, which closed the procession, brought me relief. She was painted, as are many others in Europe, by St. Luke, and is much reverenced here, for the number of miracles she has wrought in favour of the Bolonese. This ceremony would provoke some protestants, and furnishes all, with strong arguments against catholic tenets and practices: for, during the appearance of the several figures of Christ, the people were so indifferent, that I observed some of them stood with their hats on; but, upon the exhibition of the blessed Virgin, they not only prostrated themselves on their knees, but, in answer to three bows made by the picture, they, in the attitude of kneeling, bent their heads to the ground three times. At the church door, there was a kind of Litany pronounced, to the praise of the blessed Virgin, where the response of the people, for several minutes together, was, *ora pro nobis*. A moderate catholic may refine, and plead, that the picture is not an object of worship, but a mere *memento* of the Virgin; yet, a man who travels through popish countries, will always believe the picture itself is honoured; and a protestant may naturally ask, how it happens, that one Madona has more fame, and more power than another, if it be only a picture to remind us of the original? I could write you a letter every week on the single subject of vulgar religious prejudices, were I to enumerate all that I hear: but, I cannot forbear telling you, that

the

the common people of Bologna believe, that if the Madona was not carried in this procession, she, the picture, would defcend from her ftation, and walk through the ftreets.

At Rome, there is a fociety, who advance money to the poor, upon depofiting a pawn, without intereft. This defign appears ufeful; but I had not an opportunity of learning whether it be abufed, as moft other good intentions are. I fhould not have mentioned it, but that there is a like inftitution at Bologna, with this remarkable ancient infcription over the gate of the building, where the bufinefs is tranfacted. *This inftitution was, &c. &c. in order to put an end to the ufury practifed by the Jews.* The truth is, that in thofe times, the Jews were the only factors, or money lenders, in Europe, and it is no wonder, that what was a Jewifh practice, fhould be held in fuch deteftation by Chriftians; but, with the times, we fee the modes of religion totally alter, and good bifhops now, make no fcruple to receive five per cent. if they can get it honeftly. A few days fince, I beftowed a minute's penfive contemplation on the monument of Galileo. I could not but reflect with forrow, and fome indignation, that the priefts of the fame church, treated him as a blafphemer, for afferting the Copernican fyftem, who now treat the Hutchinfonians as fanatics, for doubting it. I am not to tell you, that poor Galileo remained in the prifons of the inquifitions many years, fuffering extream hardfhips in his old age there, and was not fet at liberty till he retracted his doctrine.

At Bologna, as at Florence, the nobles are numerous and poor; indeed, for the fame reafon; that is to fay, becaufe all the children are noble, and, becaufe it is a fafhion to divide their eftates almoft equally amongft them: this cuftom had a very good effect, when it was honourable to be engaged in commerce, as was the cafe, when the trade of Europe was in a manner carried on by the nobles of Florence, Venice,

Venice, and Lombardy: every fon, by this article, improved his fortune, and enriched his country. But the difcovery of the paffage to the Indies, by the Cape of Good Hope, putting an end to this monopoly, and to the exorbitant gains attending it, commerce, by degrees, became contemptible, as it grew lefs profitable; and the greater part of the nobility, finding no refources beyond their pitiful incomes, became wretched. I have been credibly informed, that a noble at Florence, with five hundred pounds a year, is reputed to be in pretty good circumftances."—]

The country between Bologna and Modena is delightful and fertile, abounding efpecially in vineyards. The horned cattle of this country are very large, and moftly of a white colour. Here, fix or eight oxen are put to a carriage, with a great number of bells hanging about them, the ringing of which is not at all difagreeable.

Not far from Bologna the triumviri, M. Lepidus, M. Antonius, and C. Octavius, formed that confederacy which afterward proved fo bloody in its confequences to the Roman republic. Plutarch, in his life of Cicero, c. 67. and in that of Antony, c. 24. fays, that this interview happened on a little ifland; to which Dio, lib. 24. adds, that the ifland was formed by a fmall river, (namely, the Rhenus) running near Bologna. However, no river in the neighbourhood of this city, forms an ifland which correfponds with the defcription given by that hiftorian, which muft only be underftood of a place for the greateft part furrounded with water.

Modena is an ancient city, of which we find frequent mention made in the Roman hiftory. When Decius Brutus was befieged here, Hirtius made ufe of Pigeons (which he had trained up by hunger for fuch a fervice) as meffengers to give the befieged notice of his defigns, and to receive the like intelligence from Brutus on their return. In memory of this contrivance, pigeons are even to this day trained
up

MODENA.

up at Modena to carry letters from the city to a place appointed, and bring back anfwers to them. What advantage thefe winged meffengers were of to the city of Leyden when hard preffed by the Spaniards, is fufficiently known from the hiftory of the fixteenth century.

The city of Modena is faid to contain thirty-five thoufand inhabitants; which computation, to me, feems much too high, and not at all credible. Little or no handicraft trade and traffic is feen ftirring here; and though great numbers of mafks (in making of which Modena is faid to excel) are annually exported to Venice and other places, fo inconfiderable an article of commerce, can contribute but little to the profperity of the city.

Two Italian miles from Saffuolo, in the Modenefe, is a chafm in the earth, called la Salfa, which emits fmoke, flame, afhes and ftones, of a fulphureous fmell, and throws many of them to the height of forty ells. Thefe eruptions generally happen in fpring and autumn, and are fometimes attended with rumbling noifes and explofions. The mountain on which this cleft appears, is rendered entirely barren by thefe continual ejections. During its eruptions, the Petroleum wells at Saffo, and Monte Gibbio, become quite foul and thick. Paolo Boccone, in his *Mufea di Fifica & di Efperienze*, which was publifhed at Venice in quarto, in 1697, remarks, that la Salfa agrees not only in its effects, but alfo to the time of its eruptions, with mount Ætna in Sicily, and that this agreement was particularly obfervable on the 10th, 11th, and 12th of May, 1693.

The road between Modena and Parma is part of the Via Æmiliæ, and very pleafant. It lies through gardens and fine walks, and is planted on both fides with white mulberry trees, interwoven with vines. The whole plain confifts of plantations and inclofures, every where furnifhed with rows of vines and fruit trees, fo that a more delightful profpect cannot be conceived.

M 4.   Five

Five miles from Reggio is a long bridge, over the river Lenza, which is the boundary between Modena and Parma.

Parma is a populous and large city, consisting of broad regular streets, and many fine houses; which, according to the custom of the Italians, are called palaces. The river Parma divides it into two parts, which are connected to one another by three stone bridges. Its circumference is four Italian miles, and the citadel very much resembles that of Antwerp. The number of the inhabitants are computed to be between forty-five and fifty thousand.

The large theatre, famous throughout all Europe, was built by Rainutius I. in the year 1618. The parterre or pit, is sixty-five common paces in length, and the stage sixty-two. Before the theatre, on each side, is an equestrian statue representing one of the ancient dukes, and several other statues on the sides of the pit; in the latter are twelve rows of seats, rising gradually behind one another, such as were common in the old Roman amphitheatres; and over these is a double gallery. It is, indeed, said, that this amphitheatre will conveniently hold betwixt eight and nine thousand spectators; but this a single glance of the eye is sufficient to contradict. The greatest singularity is the construction of this edifice; for a word spoken ever so low on the stage, is distinctly heard all over the pit, consequently the singers and other actors, are saved a good deal of trouble; and it is also remarkable, that no confused reduplication or echo happens, be the voice raised ever so high. It is said, that when Lewis XIV. intended to build an opera-house in the palace of the Thuilleries at Paris, he sent the celebrated architect Vigarani to Parma, in order to find out the cause of the extraordinary echo in this theatre; but to no purpose.

As the illumination of the large theatre at Parma, is very expensive, a smaller has been erected for common use, in a contiguous saloon, which has a pit large
enough

enough to contain two thousand spectators. On its sides are three rows of seats, and opposite to the front of the stage eight more, rising one above another like an amphitheatre, and over these three galleries.

The duke's library is in a large hall, and makes a very grand appearance, the books being all in French binding, and the shelves on which they are placed, supported by elegant pillars. There are not above seventeen or eighteen thousand volumes in this library; and the only method taken to preserve them from worms and moths, is to carefully beat them at certain times. The manuscripts are all by themselves, and in the same binding. The printed books are mostly in folio, particularly those of history; few or no small pieces being to be met with in this collection.

The yearly revenues of the duke of Parma are computed at between five and six hundred thousand crowns. It is said the salt works alone, all charges deducted, produce above fifty thousand crowns. These salt works are carried on at Salso, four and twenty Italian miles from Parma, where there are twelve pits of natural brine, two hundred ells deep: the water of these being boiled in large cauldrons or coppers, evaporates till all the aqueous particles are separated; after which it is mixed with blood of animals, beginning to putrefy, and all boiled together about an hour, and carefully skimmed. By this process, a pure and white salt is obtained.

In divers parts of the Parmasan territories, Petroleum is gathered: sometimes without water, and sometimes floating on the surface of the water.

The Parmasan cheese, so famous in most parts of Europe, owes its goodness to the excellent pastures near Placentia; where the meadows, during the whole summer, may be watered at pleasure, by means of small sluices, which convey water from the Po: beside, the water of that river is impregnated with a slimy substance, which proves a very good manure to the grounds they overflow. The cows here yield
such

such a large quantity of milk, that, in a good season, a person possessed of fifty cows, can make a rich cheese of one hundred weight every day.

The distance from Parma to Placentia, is about thirty-three Italian miles; and about five miles from the former, is a ferry over the river Taro; and a little farther on the left, lies Castello Guelfo, still kept in repair. Not far from the latter is the Castello Gebellino; both these castles retain their names from the two factions by which Germany and Italy were for so long a time rendered a scene of slaughter and confusion.

Borgo St. Domino, a post-stage, is the residence of a bishop; but at the same time a very mean place. Its neighbourhood abounds with truffles. The whole road is very good and delightful, like that between Faenza and Bologna; running in a direct line betwixt fine level walks, where the inclosures on each side, are planted with rows of fruit trees, intermixed with vines; especially the parts about Reggio and Placentia, which are so excellently cultivated, as to appear like one entire orchard or garden. In so fine a country, it may be readily supposed, that the clergy have not omitted to procure themselves fat benefices, and liberal endowments: and I have been assured, that of the twenty-eight thousand inhabitants of the city of Placentia, two thousand are monks, nuns, and other ecclesiastics.

The castle of Placentia is but meanly fortified; nor is the city in a condition of making any tolerable defence. The distance of the Po from Placentia, is between five and six hundred paces; and from the top of one of the city towers, is a most charming prospect of the whole neighbouring country, justly called Piacenza, or Placentia, pleasantness. The principal street, called Stradone, is twenty-five common paces broad, and three thousand feet long, extended in a straight line; but the houses in general cannot be commended for their beauty.

In

CREMONA. 171

In the principality of Placentia are several salt works, and large quantities of vitriol are made and refined there. Near the Appenine mountains are some iron forges, and they have also begun to smelt copper.

The distance between Placentia and Cremona is eighteen Italian miles, through a very fertile country; but the road less pleasant, and not kept in so good repair, as the Via Æmiliæ, leading to Placentia. Cremona is an university, founded by the emperor Sigismund; but at present in a very declining condition; and the fortification of the city of little importance.

Cremona is forty Italian miles distant from Mantua, and about half way between these two cities is a neat but small town, called Bozzolo, defended by a castle, being the capital place of a small principality of the same name. Three miles from thence near St. Martino di Marcana we crossed the Oglio, a middling river. In winter after great rains, the road between Cremona and Mantua is almost impassable from the deepness of the soil: when we travelled this way, though the weather had for a long time been very dry, it was but indifferent. This inconveniency is richly compensated by the fertility of the neighbouring country, and the exuberant productions of the fields and meadows, cannot be sufficiently admired; the trees, which are planted in rows, being covered with vines, which twine themselves round them. The great numbers of nightingales frequenting this spot of land, by their warblings add new charms to the delightful scene.

Mantua lies in a lake or morass, caused by the overflowing of the Mincio. This morass, on the side toward Cremona, is not above two or three hundred paces wide, but on the opposite side extends itself near an Italian mile. The course of the river Mincio lies through this city, which is fortified with a citadel; but more indebted to nature than art for its strength. The vapours from the stagnant putrid wa-

ters

ters about this city during the summer, render it so unhealthful, that none stay in Mantua but such as cannot avoid it. The number of parish churches in this city amount to eighteen; beside which there are forty convents; doubtless too many for a place, which, exclusive of the imperial garrison, has not above ten thousand Christian inhabitants. The number of Jews amount to four or five thousand, which have a particular Ghetto or quarter, the gate of which is shut every evening. They have four or five synagogues here; the principal is well built, and has a skylight in the roof.

No court being kept here since the last war, this place is much decayed in its trade, which was once considerable; and the silk manufacture alone, brought large sums into the country, which in ancient times was in a flourishing condition. The museum founded here by the duke, rendered this city very famous in the last century; but they have been dispersed by the ignorance of the soldiers, when this city was taken by the imperialists on the 18th of July 1630. Some apartments of the palace are still worth seeing.

Mantua is an episcopal see, dependent on the pope. Julio Romano was the architect of the cathedral, who also painted the cieling and the tribuna.

The distance between Mantua and Verona is three post-stages, or twenty-four Italian miles. Ten miles from the latter lies Villa Franca, where are still remaining the walls of a spacious old castle. On the left the mountains of Trent, covered with snow, begin to appear: the road is stony, and the soil poor; but the rows of white mulberry-trees, intermixed with vines, give the country a delightful aspect.

Verona has been celebrated for its beauty, though it will not bear comparison with most of the large cities in the lower parts of Italy. The streets are generally narrow, crooked, and dirty; and the houses but meanly built. In short, Verona, with the pleasant country round it, appears more beautiful when

viewed

VERONA.

viewed from the neighbouring eminences, than it is really found on entering it. The fortifications are of little importance, though it has three caftles; namely, il Caftello Veccuno, St. Pietro, and St. Felice. The fecond is faid to have been anciently a temple of Diana; from the top of this fortrefs is an elegant profpect of the city. The river Adige divides Verona into two parts, nearly equal, but have communication with each other by means of four ftone bridges. All thefe ftructures are well built; but il Ponte Nuovo deferves a particular notice, on account of the fine profpect from it, of the river and the country, terminated by the hill, on which ftands Caftello St. Felice. The number of its inhabitants, at prefent, is faid to amount to between forty-eight and fifty thoufand; whereas, about a hundred years ago, they exceeded feventy thoufand. The beft ftreet in the city is called the Curfo, where, at the conclufion of the carnival diverfions, great numbers of the common people run foot-races. Formerly common proftitutes were permitted to run for the prize, but that cuftom has been abolifhed, and a horfe-race exhibited in its ftead, on the laft Sunday in Lent; the prize is a piece of gold, or fome other rich ftuff.

The largeft area in this city is the Piazza d'Armi, where the two ufual fairs in April and Autumn are kept. In the center is a marble ftatue reprefenting the republic of Venice, Verona having, for fome centuries, been under that jurifdiction. The family of the Scaligers (from whom the learned Julius Cæfar Scaliger would fain derive his pedigree) were formerly lords of Verona; one of whom, for his better fecurity, and at the fame time to awe the city, not only erected the Caftello Vecchio, at the end of the Curfo, but alfo built a bridge over the Adige, which is ftill in good condition, and deferves particular notice, on account of the breadth of its arches: the diftance between the piers of the firft arch being feventy feet, that of the fecond eighty-two, and of the third one

hundred

hundred and forty: the whole length of the bridge is three hundred and forty-eight feet. In the castle is, at present, a small garrison, together with a governor.

The principal magistrates, by whom the Venetians govern this province, are the Podesta and Capitaneo, or general. All civil affairs are under the direction of the former, and the military under that of the latter. Both these continue no longer in office than sixteen months. A handsome house was begun for the general, but is still unfinished.

Antiquarians meet with a most valuable piece of antiquity at Verona, which gives a clearer idea of the theatrical performances of the ancient Romans, than any other extant; namely, the celebrated amphitheatre: which, through a succession of so many centuries, has, by the commendable care and attention of the inhabitants, been preserved in such excellent repair, that it is far preferable to that of Vespasian at Rome, though considerably less. This noble structure, according to some, was built in the reign of Augustus; but there is little probability that such a sumptuous edifice should be erected so early in a province of Italy, when the capital of the empire could not boast of any thing equal to it before the reign of Vespasian. To this may be added, the silence of Pliny the elder, whose accuracy in the enumeration of the most celebrated edifices and artists of his time, particularly of those relating to his native place, would not have suffered him to omit a structure of this nature. Another argument is, that during the first century, there was no such amphitheatre at Verona; for Pliny the younger, who lived at the close of Trajan's reign, does not mention it, though he is so particular in relating the shews, plays, and sports of gladiators, exhibited at Verona, by his friend Maximus, in memory of his deceased wife. On the other hand, this amphitheatre must have been erected about that time, the structure exhibiting evident marks of the
flourishing

flourishing state, both of architecture and sculpture, and consequently of the Roman empire itself.

According to Maffei's mensuration, the longest diameter of the amphitheatre of Verona, from the first arch of the principal entrance to the opposite arch, is four hundred and fifty Veronese feet; the greatest breadth three hundred and sixty; the length of the area within the walls, according to his computation, two hundred and eighteen feet, six inches; the breadth one hundred and twenty-nine; and the outward circuit of the whole edifice, one thousand two hundred and ninety feet. The Verona foot is exactly one third more than a Roman palmi, used in architecture. Its present height is, indeed, but eighty-eight feet; but, from evident marks on the walls, it appears to have been at first above one hundred and ten. The lowest row of seats is, as it were, buried in dirt and rubbish; but, if we include this, the number of the rows of steps or seats, rising one above another to the highest gallery, amount to forty-five. This method of building of amphitheatres was the most convenient for holding a great number of spectators, in such a manner, that the nearest row did not intercept the view of the Arena, from those who sat at the greatest distance. If we allow a foot and a half for each person, the amphitheatre at Verona would contain twenty-two thousand one hundred and eighty-four spectators. The internal area of the Colyfæum at Rome, does not greatly excel this; and, according to Fontana, the length of that edifice is but five hundred and sixty-four Verona feet, its breadth four hundred and sixty-seven; the internal area is two hundred and seventy-three feet in length, and one hundred and seventy-three in breadth; and the circuit of the whole building, one thousand five hundred and sixty-six Verona feet. Consequently, according to this computation, the Colyfæum contained at most but thirty or thirty-four thousand persons sitting. Though none of the seats are now remaining, the amphitheatre of Verona

is

is much more perfect, and has no holes or chasms in the wall.

The present edifice is not meerly the ancient structure, but owes its good condition to repairs, many of which are the works of the moderns. The new stones may be easily distinguished from the ancient work, which is much neater. The height of the seats is not the same in all, but generally a foot and five inches, and their common breadth two feet two inches. Near the twenty-sixth row, reckoning from the bottom, there is one so narrow, as is scarce sufficient for a seat; and for this reason appears not to be the work of antiquity, but of the moderns who repaired it. The ancient seats were of red marble, but the modern repairs of a red brittle stone. The stone seats being very cold, they were, for the greater conveniency of the spectators, covered with boards, and some for persons of rank with cushions. Hence it appears, that an amphitheatre built of stone might receive some damage by fire. There are in this amphitheatre separate flights of steps, by which the spectators ascended from the vaults below. The apertures from these steps, into the rows of seats, on account of the multitudes of people crouding, and, as it were, pouring through them to see the spectacles, are by Macrobius, Saturn. lib. vi. cap. iv. called *vomitoria*; the number of which in this amphitheatre are sixty-four, being disposed in four rows.

With regard to the outside of this amphitheatre, it contained seventy-two arched entrances; and the keystone of each arch being numbered, every class of people knew where to go in and come out of the amphitheatre, and no confusion or disturbance could arise. These arches are, for the most part, eleven feet eight inches wide, and eighteen feet high. The lower part of the pillars are buried about four feet under the present surface of the ground, as appears by the ancient main entrance, where the earth has been cleared away. The balustrade over the entrance

trance is a modern work. Two galleries over the lower arches reprefent, as it were, the fecond and third ftories. No pedeftals have been found, either in this amphitheatre, or in that at Rome mentioned above; from whence we may conclude, that it was not ornamented with ftatues, in any other part, except over the grand entrance; and if on any particular folemnity, ftatues were placed in thefe amphitheatres, they muft have been but fmall, and remained but a fhort time. Thefe moveable ftatues may probably be the figures feen on fome ancient medals, that reprefent amphitheatres. Few or no fragments of ftatues have, indeed, been dug up near this amphitheatre. The ftones of the ancient part of this ftructure are not cemented together, but faftened with iron cramps and braces.

It is no wonder fuch a ftately theatre fhould be built at Verona, preferable to other cities; for hiftorians agree, that it was very large and populous during the times of the ancient Romans; but whether this amphitheatre, like that at Rome, could be laid under water, cannot be determined, as the river Adige is fome feet lower than its area, and there are no traces of aqueducts near it. On the other hand, fome arches are fhewn in the water below St. Pietro, fuppofed to be the remains of a Naumachia, which was not fupplied from the river Adige, as the river did not flow in ancient times through the city; but from the eminences of Montorio and Avefa, from whence it was conveyed to Verona by leaden pipes. Both thefe places are about two Italian miles from the city, and the leaden pipes, which are ftill kept in repair, are laid over a bridge, and furnifh feveral private houfes with frefh water.

On the left hand of the road leading from Verona to Caftello Vecchio, the ancient courfe of the Adige, before it was carried into the city, is ftill vifible.

Near the city is a fine plain, called Campus Martius, where the mufters and military exercifes of the people are performed. Since the year 1712, when the booths of the annual fairs, held till then in the Piazza d'Armi, were burnt down, they have, for the greater fecurity and conveniency, been removed to the Campus Martius, and there very prettily difpofed. The principal commodities exported from this city to other countries, are medicinal plants, gathered on Monte Baldo, olives, (thofe efpecially from this neighbourhood being accounted excellent) oil, fome wine, linen, woollen, and filk manufactures. The neighbouring parts are, indeed, at prefent, no lefs plentifully provided with the fame commodities; but a greater vent might be opened for them at Venice.

The annual revenue of the bifhopric of Verona amounts to between four and five thoufand crowns.

The beft wines at prefent produced in the neighbourhood of this city, are two forts of white, one of which is called Garganico Bianco, and the other Vino Santo. The latter, in my opinion, is the beft; and in flavour refembles the old Hungarian wines.

They have from hence to Venice, a very commodious water-carriage for goods; and the paffage thither, in a bark, takes up no more than three days and a half: but the coming back is more troublefome, the barge being drawn by oxen, and cannot be performed in lefs than eight days.

In the Olivetan church, or Madonna in Organo, was formerly a wooden afs, within the belly of which, as fome bigotted people believed, the remains of the afs on which our Saviour made his public entry into Jerufalem were depofited. The ftory of this afs. and its travels through feveral countries, till at laft it died in the neighbourhood of Verona, where it was kept with the greateft veneration, are related by Miffon; but intermixed with fuch farcaftical reflections, as will not be much relifhed by Roman catholics: the Veronefe in particular refent his expofing their fondnefs for the reliques of the Jewifh afs, as it had laid them open to the ridicule of a nick-name. And it is

doubtlefs

doubtlefs owing to the farcaftical remarks of Miffon, and the fneering enquiries of ftrangers and travellers after the reliques of this afs, together with the fuperftitious abufes it occafioned among the common people, that the áfs has not appeared in any public proceffion thefe eight years paft. The Veronefe even conceal it from the public view, and almoft venture to deny the whole affair: fo that it is not eafy for a ftranger to procure a fight of it. For my own part, I fhould not have been greatly difappointed if I had not feen it: but by a meer accident I happened to walk into a chapel belonging to St. Benedict's church, where I had an opportunity of taking a full view of this famous afs. It ftands behind the wooden altar-piece which reprefents St. Benedict, and may be opened like a door. The afs itfelf is a good piece of fculpture, done fome centuries ago, by a devout monk of this convent. The image of our Saviour, fitting upon it, which is alfo of wood, has a book in the left hand, and the right extended as if giving the benediction.

The women of Verona are well fhaped, and of a healthy complexion, which may doubtlefs be attributed to the goodnefs of the air. The breezes from the neighbouring mountains refrefh this city every evening during the hotteft part of fummer. The orange-trees muft not be expofed to the open air in the winter, yet the climate produces all kinds of fruits and vegetables in perfection. The country about Verona produces peaches, melons, figs, ftrawberries, truffles, very large artichokes, afparagus, chefnuts, apples, pears, plums, grapes, olives, and divers forts of herbs.

Betwixt Verona and Vicenza is the diftrict of Bolco; and not far from Veftene Nuova are found all forts of petrified fifh, of the falt-water kind: the foil is a fort of white loam. Thefe fifh are in general well preferved; their bones are entire and frequently their fcales.

The distance between Verona and Vicenza is thirty Italian miles. The road lies through a stony but fertile and pleasant country.

Vicenza contains a great many elegant buildings, and the tops of several of them ornamented with statues; particularly those in the area, or piazza, before the council-house. Had it fountains, it would be a Piazza di Novona in miniature. After this city fell under the Venetian yoke, they erected here, as in other conquered cities, the arms of St. Mark on a lofty pillar, which are a winged lion. On another pillar of the same kind stands the image of our Saviour. The city of Vicenza is of no great extent; however, there are in it fifty-seven churches, convents, and hospitals; the cathedral affords nothing worth a traveller's notice.

This country produces plenty of excellent wine, particularly that of Vicenza is highly celebrated, as it may be drank during the pains of the gout without the least inconvenience.

The inhabitants are accused of being more addicted to revenge than other Italians; whence they are commonly called *gli assassini Vicentini*, " the assassins " of Vicenza." Whether this character be just, or not, I shall not pretend to determine; but this I know, that travellers, especially Germans, who are generally too hot, and ready on the least occasion to use the cudgel, should take particular care, in every part of Italy, to avoid quarreling, especially with the postilions and others of the lower class; in many of whom revenge is so predominant a passion, that they have been known to follow a traveller, privately, six or eight stages, in order to watch an opportunity of gratifying it by an assassination.

Open violence is indeed little to be apprehended from them; upon which account the more care is necessary, and the danger the greater; cowards being always cruel.

Murder

Murder in Italy is confidered in a very different light from what it is in other countries. When a robbery has been committed, either in the ftreets, or market-place, affiftance is always ready to purfue the offender; but the affaffin flies unmolefted into a church, or convent, where, to the honour of the clergy be it fpoken, the villain receives all poffible affiftance for making his efcape from the hands of the civil magiftrate. I remember, that a poftilion who drove me, was treacheroufly ftabbed at the pofthoufe of Piftoia; and though the fact was committed in the prefence of more than ten perfons, not one of them ftirred to apprehend the murderer.

Vicenza is eighteen Italian miles from Padua; and the road lies through a beautiful and level country. Paffengers may alfo go by water from one place to the other, upon the river Bachiglioni and Medoace minor; but this paffage is tedious, being no lefs than fixty Italian miles.

The city of Padua boafts of being the fource from which the republic of Venice derived its origin and profperity. But it is now fome centuries fince Padua has been under the dominion of the Venetians, and is at prefent fo much declined from its former ftate, that it hardly contains forty thoufand inhabitants.

The univerfity founded here by the emperor Frederic II. to injure that of Bologna, has not at prefent above four or five hundred ftudents. This change was in a great meafure owing to the unbridled licentioufnefs of the fcholars, which was carried to fuch a pitch of infolence, that no perfon, after dufk, could, without danger of his life, walk the ftreets; and it is ftill the fafeft method not to be out in the night at Padua.

If a proteftant traveller dies here, he is, without any difficulty, buried either in a church or convent, provided he has taken care to get himfelf matriculated in the univerfity.

The Franciscan church, dedicated to St. Antonio di Padua, is one of the most remarkable in the city.

The high veneration of the inhabitants of Padua for St. Anthony, is so very extraordinary and universal, that even beggars ask alms in the only name of St. Anthony. What can be more shocking than the following words on one of their votive tables, *Exaudit S. Antonius quos non exaudit Deus.* " St. Anthony hears " those whom God himself does not hear."

The chapel of this saint is almost covered with votive pieces, and pictures, representing the favours obtained by his intercession. On one side are shewn two wax tapers of the thickness of a man's body, and fixed in an iron frame, said to have been offered by a Turk, with the intent of blowing up the whole chapel by means of explosive ingredients concealed in them; but it seems St. Anthony prevented this misfortune by rising from his coffin, and ordering them to be put out. A fragrant odour is said to be constantly emitted from his remains, through a crevice behind the altar. The tongue of this saint is kept in a glass shrine in the sacristy with the greatest veneration, and prayers are frequently offered up to it. The number of silver candlesticks, crucifixes, gold chalices, pixes, and other utensils belonging to this chapel is prodigious, and the value immense.

Among the civil edifices of Padua, il Palazzo della Raggione, or the town-house, is esteemed the principal, though the great hall doth not deserve the praise common fame hath bestowed upon it. The plan is rhomboidal, a hundred and twenty-four common paces in length, and forty-three in breadth. The roof is lofty, strengthened with iron bars, and covered with lead. On the cieling, Giotto and some of his disciples have allegorically represented the influences of the sun in the twelve signs of the zodiac; but this apartment has not a proper light for fine paintings, nor are they kept in proper order.

PADUA.

The Paduans are firmly perfuaded, that the bones found in a leaden cheft, in St. Juftina's church, in the year 1413, are actually thofe of Titus Livy, and accordingly were brought with great folemnity to the council-houfe, at the requeft of Xiccone Polentoni, chancellor of Padua, and indeed the reftorer of learning in Italy.

The air round Padua is efteemed very healthful, though few cities have fo many apothecaries, in proportion to the number of inhabitants. Vipers are not fo good one year as another; thofe taken in the neighbourhood of Rome, are counted the beft, and on that account, great quantities are fent from thence to Venice, as an ingredient in the *theriaca Andromachi*, or Venice treacle. As venomous animals have their poifon more powerful and efficacious in warm climates and dry foils, confequently thofe about Padua, a cool and moift country, muft be inferior in virtue to thofe of Rome.

The territory of Padua is fubject to ftorms, particularly thofe from the fea-coaft are extreamly violent.

For the honour of the mufes, and the better inftruction of youths in the univerfity, houfes for the *donne libre*, or *donne del mondo*, are publicly tolerated at Padua. Thefe ladies have their refpective dwellings appointed them, where they live together in a kind of fociety, and offer their fervice to the public. And that fo laudable an inftitution may not be liable to any objection, it is the particular province of fome phyficians to make frequent, and ftrict enquiry among thefe *donne*, left any bad confequences enfue to fuch young people as converfe with them. There are two of thefe public temples of Venus in the city of Padua: and what is fomething fingular, one of them joins to the convent of the Eremitical fathers, and the other to a nunnery of St. Blaze.

The Jews have alfo a particular quarter allotted in the city, and are not fuffered to refide in any other part.

Any traveller defirous of improvement, cannot think his time loft in making an excurfion into the country, to the fouth of Padua. The village of Abano, in Latin *Aponum*, about four Italian miles and a half from that city, is much frequented in fummer, on account of the warm baths in its neighbourhood.

If Pliny, by the Fonta Patavini, means the baths of Abano, not one of them at prefent emits any fmell, as he has obferved of them; yet they contain three forts of water, of very different qualities. Some of the fprings yield great quantities of fulphur, and have particular rooms for bathing; where, by means of fteps, you defcend to any depth required. Others again are boiling hot; from which the water iffues in fuch quantity, as to drive a mill at the diftance only of twenty paces from the fource, and ftill continues hot at that diftance.

The wooden pipes, by which the water is conveyed to thefe baths, are incruftated with a white lapideous fubftance, not eafily feparated from the wood. The exact impreffions of the veins and knots of which, on this concretion, give it the perfect refemblance of petrified wood.

A fudatory, or fweating-place, has been erected here, the effect of which is produced by the fteam of the water. Some of the fprings, which are lukewarm, are faid to be impregnated with lead; and others, from their reddifh fediment, and other indications, feem to be ferruginous. Here is alfo a Bagno di Fango, or muddy bath, where arthritic diforders have been cured by the external application of the warm fediment.

The diftance betwixt Padua and Venice, is reckoned twenty-five Italian miles; and the paffage by water is performed in eight hours. The barques or barges made ufe of for this purpofe, are commodioufly fitted up, being adorned with windows, fculpture and painting. A barge of this kind, called *brucello*, or *burchiello*, may be hired for a fingle perfon, or a whole company together, for a Louis d'or at the moft. We went

went as far as the Lagune, or flats, on a canal, and the river Brenta, which, by means of four sluices, is rendered so commodious. that the boats may be drawn along by horses. This passage is pleasant, on account of the prospects which every where delight the eye.

Five Italian miles from Venice are the shallows, on which, at low water, you may almost every where touch the bottom with a pole. On the south side of Venice, the sea is of a greater depth, particularly in certain places; but vessels of any considerable burden cannot come up to the city on any side, which is no small security to it from invasions. On the side toward the Terra Firma, all imaginable care is taken to prevent the shallow parts from becoming dry land; by which means the city would be deprived of its advantageous situation.

The city is defended from the violence of the waves by several small islands. It must be owned, that the great number of islands dispersed in the sea, with the churches and other magnificent buildings towering above the water, give the city a very magnificent appearance at a distance: and the canals, which in most parts of the city run close to the houses, excite an admiration in strangers, as the sight is very uncommon. But, excepting the piazza of St. Mark, and a few other places, Venice may be said, without injustice, to have nothing beautiful or grand, when compared with many other cities in Italy. Il Canale Maggiore, or the great canal, is very beautiful, on account of its breadth, and has some grand houses on its banks; but the others are crooked and narrow, and in summer time emit a bad smell, from the great quantity of filth daily running into them. The tide ebbs and flows here about every six hours; but it is not sufficient to cleanse the small canals.

The gondolas glide very swiftly on these canals, but afford a gloomy spectacle; being painted black, and trimmed with black cloth, or serge. They will not carry above four or five perfons; and as it is impoffible to ftand upright in one of thefe gondolas, it has the appearance of going into a hearfe covered with black. The fare of a gondolier is feven or eight livres a day, except on Holy Thurfday, when they raife their price. The noble Venetians themfelves are obliged to paint and trim their gondolas with black, in order to prevent an ambitious emulation among them, in excelling one another in the fplendor of thefe naval equipages. The lady of a noble Venetian, for the firft or fecond year after her marriage, is indulged with greater freedom in this refpect. And foreigners may purchafe what gondolas they pleafe; but few tarry long enough in this city to make ufe of this indulgence. So that the only perfons here who diftinguifh themfelves by fplendid gondolas, are the foreign minifters; who make their entries in thefe vehicles, decorated with the fineft painting, gilding, and fculpture. The canals interfect the whole city; but by means of fmall bridges, of which there are above five hundred, you may go a great way by land. Moft of the houfes that front the water, have back-doors to the ftreets, by which they have a communication, by the bridges, with one another. The ftreets are very narrow, and after rain very flippery; but particular care ought to be taken in croffing thofe bridges, the fteps and pavement being of the fame white ftone as the ftreets.

The city of Venice, according to fome, ftands on fixty iflands; but others increafe the number to feventy-two. Indeed, if all the fpots which have fucceffively appeared above the water in the Lagune, are to be counted iflands, the number will ftill be greater. It is probable that fome parts of the city were originally iflands, fo as to require no art or labour to make them more compact. Perhaps the whole foundation was formerly a Terra Firma, as it would otherwife be difficult to conceive how fprings of frefh water fhould be found here. The number of thefe

VENICE.

these amount to near two hundred; but many are so indifferent, that the principal families preserve rainwater in cisterns, or are supplied with water from the Brenta.

The circumference of the city of Venice is about six Italian miles, and takes up about two hours to make the circuit of it in a gondola. The inhabitants are supposed to be about two hundred thousand, including those of the islands of Murano, la Guideca, and those who live on board the barges.

Among the diversions of this city, the carnival is generally counted the chief; but I question whether an impartial judge would be of that opinion.

Young persons, indeed, who delight only in debauchery, and licentiousness, may here tire themselves, if not satiate their desires; but these diversions, as well as others, practised on festivals, especially on Ascension day, are of such a nature, that those who find any real pleasure in them, must have abandoned all regard to virtue.

The courtesans who offer their favours here, are absolutely lost to all sense of modesty and common decency; and the greatest part of them have for their debaucheries and villainous practices, been driven out of the neighbouring dominions, and often bear on their backs, the marks of the punishment they have suffered by the hands of the common hangmen.

The Italians are very fond of masquerades, and generally appear in masques during the whole time of the carnival, except from the preceding Friday to the Shrove-Tuesday, the last day of that jovial season.

A stranger is soon tired of their *ridottos*; and, as the purses of most travellers will not permit them to game high, it would be imprudent to venture too far in this diversion, especially as the cards are different from what he has been accustomed to. A noble Venetian always holds the bank in the ridotto room, and close by every banker, sit two ladies in masques,

who

who are allowed to put him in mind of any miſtakes he may chance to commit to his difadvantage.

The grand fcene of all the follies exhibited during the carnival, is in the Piazza di St. Marco, where mountebanks, buffoons, and others who live by preying on the vulgar and innocent, erect their ſtages and booths, to exhibit their ſhews. But the moſt ridiculous of all are the old women and men, who fit on a table, and are confulted like oracles, concerning future events and the fuccefs of enterprizes. Thefe fortune-tellers, in order to deliver their oracular anfwers, in fuch a concourfe of people, with the greater fecurity and fecrecy, make ufe of a long fpeaking-trumpet, the fmall end of which the confultors apply to their mouths, and convey their enquiries by a whifper, while the conjurer lays his ear to the other aperture, and inverts the trumpet to refolve the propofer's queſtions. It is diverting to fee fimple girls, whofe looks and behaviour betray a great deal of fear and confufion, coming up to thefe fortune-tellers, to enquire the fates of their amours. Thefe impoſtors, in order to gain the greater credit, place fome paltry globes, and other aſtronomical inſtruments, on a table before them.

In the piazza round St. Mark's fquare, are feveral coffee-houfes, chiefly frequented by foreigners. Formerly the company might fit down, and converfe together at their eafe; but that cuſtom has been prohibited, and no benches or chairs allowed: a difcovery having been made, that the fon of Balognos, the imperial envoy, had taken the opportunity of a carnival to difcourfe with feveral of the Venetian nobility in mafques.

The ufe of mafques is allowed, not only in carnival time, but alfo on feveral other occafions; as on the four public feaſts of the republic, at the *regatta* or rowing-matches, and other diverfions in honour of foreign princes; at the nuptials of one of the nobles;

on

VENICE.

on the election of procurators of St. Mark, and of Patricians, and also when they enter upon their office; at the public entry of ambassadors, the patriarch, or *premicerio*, and the like. The Venetian ladies are impatient for these occasions, and their husbands equally watchful to preserve the honour of the marriage bed. Nor is it adviseable to commence any intrigue with these bewitching syrens, there having been instances of its being attended with the most fatal consequences.

On the last Thursday of the carnival, when licentiousness is carried to its greatest pitch, bulls are baited in several streets, particularly in St. Mark's square. These Feste de' Tori may also be seen every Friday morning near the shambles.

The Italian plays in general, are wretched performances; and even those of Venice not much better. As the whole design of the actors is to raise a laugh among the audience, they use all kind of grimaces, and even postures offensive to modesty.

If a traveller cannot contrive to be at Venice in carnival time, the best way is to order his route so as to be there about Ascension-day; and if one of the two must be omitted, I would advise it should be the carnival: for the Ascension festival has all the diversions of the carnival, as masquerades and operas, without any ridottos, or the dissolute revellings of the latter: which are sufficiently compensated by the delightfulness of the season, the annual fair, and the solemnity of the doge's marriage with the sea. This fair begins on the Sunday before Ascension-day, and lasts till Whitsunday; during which time, St. Mark's square is filled with stalls, forming several streets, and all kinds of goods are exposed to sale at the shops in the narrow streets called Le Mercerie, contiguous to that square.

On Ascension-eve the vespers are very magnificently performed, and the miraculous blood of our Saviour, and other precious reliques kept in St. Mark's treasury, exposed to public view in the cathedral.

On

On Afcenfion-day about ten in the morning, after a fignal given by firing of guns, and ringing of bells, the doge, or when he happens to be indifpofed, the vice-doge, who is always one of the fix confeglieri, goes on board the Bucentaur, and being accompanied by feveral thoufand barques, gondolas, and gallies finely decorated, and the fplendid yachts of ambaffadors, is rowed about two hundred paces out to fea, between the iflands of St. Erafmo, and il Lido di Malamocco. In the mean time the patriarch (who that morning, according to an ancient cuftom, in commemoration of the fimple diet of the clergy in former days, is treated in the Olivetan convent, on the ifland of St. Helena, with chefnuts and water) together with feveral of the clergy, come on board the Bucentaur, and prefent the doge and figniora with curious nofegays, which on their return they offer to their acquaintance. The doge is faluted, both at his arrival and on his return, by the cannon of a fort on the Lido, and with the fmall arms of the foldiers, drawn up along the fhore of the Lido; together with the guns from the caftle on the ifland of Rafmo, or Erafmo. Both iflands are only two Italian miles from the city; and from an eminence on the Lido, is a diftant view of this grand proceffion ; and the vaft number of gallies which almoft cover the furface of the water, make a fplendid appearance.

In the mean time fome hymns are fung on board the Bucentaur, by the band of mufic belonging to the church of St. Mark, and particular prayers appointed for the occafion are faid, till the doge has paffed the two forts of Lido and St. Erafmo ; and then he proceeds a little toward the Lido fhore, with the ftern of his barge turned to the open fea. Here the patriarch pours out fome water which has been confecrated with particular prayers, and is faid to have the virtue of allaying ftorms and the raging waves. After this the doge drops a gold ring into the fea, through a hole near his feat, at the fame time repeating thefe
words,

words, *Despousamus te mare, in signum veri perpetuique dominii.* " We espouse thee, O sea, in token of our " real and perpetual dominion over thee." The ring is of gold, but plain and without any stones, so as hardly to be worth more than three or four dollars. This ceremony is said to have been first instituted by pope Alexander III. in acknowlegement for the assistance granted by the Venetians: for under the doge Sebastiano Ziani, in the year 1177, they not only defeated, in a sea-fight, but also took prisoner Otto, son to the emperor Frederic I. The truth of the whole story is, however, dubious.

The doge, in his return, goes ashore on the island of Lido, where he hears mass performed by the patriarch, in the church of St. Nicholas. In the evening the principal members of the council, and all who accompanied the doge in the Bucentaur, are entertained at the ducal palace. The dessert, representing gondolas, castles, and other figures, is exposed all day to public view.

The sculpture on the new Bucentaur represents the Pagan deities of the sea, nymphs, rivers, sea-animals, and shells, &c. The gilding, which is finely executed, cost between ten and twelve thousand silver ducats. But it must be confessed, that the finest yacht belonging to the king of Great Britain, makes a more splendid appearance, though it cost a much less sum than the former.

There are three officers on board the Bucentaur, under the title of admirals; the first called admiral of the arsenal, the second, admiral of the Porto del Lido, and the third, admiral of del Porto di Malamocco. The first who commands in the vessel, has a most ridiculous oath imposed upon him; namely, that he will bring the doge safely back to the city, in spite of storms and tempests. He is not, indeed, in any great danger of forfeiting his oath: for, if a brisk gale happens to blow, the solemnity is postponed till the ensuing Sunday. This caution proceeds from an exceffive care for the doge and the fignora; and, at the fame time, ferves to detain ftrangers here, who refort from the Terra Firma, by which means more money is fpent in this city.

[The dominions of Venice confift of thofe in Italy, of a confiderable part of Dalmatia, of four towns in Greece, and of the iflands of Corfu, Pachfu, Antipachfu, Santa Maura, Curzolari, Val di Compare, Cephalonia, and Zante.

The Venetian territories in Italy contain the duchy of Venice, the Paduanefe, the peninfula of Rovigo, the Veronefe, the territories of Vicenza and Brefcia, the diftricts of Bergamo, Cremafco, and the Marca Trevigiana, with part of the country of Friuli. They extend eaft and weft from the river Adda, which flows from the lake of Como, and reach in one continued line to the duchy of Carniola; where the curve they form along the Adriatic fea is fomewhat interrupted by the Auftrian dominions, after which they extend from north to fouth along the coaft of the fame fea, and terminate at the province of Iftria. Thus the Venetian territories are bounded on the north by Trent, Tirol, and the country of the Grifons; on the eaft by Carniola and the gulph of Venice; on the fouth by the fame gulph, Romania, and the duchy of Mantua; and on the weft by the dutchy of Milan: extending about a hundred and eighty miles in length, and in fome parts an hundred in breadth.]

The doge of Venice is faid to be " a king with re-
" gard to his robes, a fenator in the council-houfe,
" a prifoner in the city, and a private man out of it."
Neither his fons nor brothers are permitted to enjoy any great offices in the city, nor to accept of embaffies without the fenate's confent; of a fief from a foreign prince; nor a benefice from the pope. Even the doge himfelf is not permitted to marry the fifter or relation of a prince without the permiffion of the grand council. After his deceafe, his adminiftration is ftrictly examined, and frequent opportunities offer of laying a
heavy

VENICE.

heavy fine on his heirs, for his mal-adminiftration. Even during his life-time he is fubject to the decrees of the ftate-inquifition; the prefident of which has the privilege of vifiting at all times, his moft fecret clofets, fearching his bed and all his writings, without his daring to fhew the leaft refentment. In affairs of ftate he has not the leaft prerogative; nor can he leave the city without the confent of the fenate; and during his ftay on the Terra Firma, he is confidered only as a private nobleman.

The yearly revenue of his office amounts to about twelve thoufand dollars, or four thoufand pounds fterling, which is fpent in defraying the expences of four entertainments he is obliged to give every year. He does not dare to take the fmalleft prefent from any foreign prince; nor can he refign his dignity, though he may be depofed. Even inftances are to be found of feveral doges, who have been executed according to their different fentences; and fome punifhed with the lofs of their eyes.

It is furprifing that under the above circumftances, the dignity of a doge of Venice fhould be fo eagerly fought after; but it muft be remembered, that the human heart is captivated with external pomp and fplendor; and the ftate and retinue of the doge on all occafions, is very fplendid. He is prefident in all councils; and in the great council he has two votes. All the courts rife when he approaches, when on the contrary, he never rifes from his feat, nor takes off his cap, or corno, except at the elevation of the hoft at mafs, before a prince of royal blood, or a cardinal, to whom he always gives the right hand. His name is alfo ftamped on the coin of the republic; all public letters and credentials are directed to the doge, and anfwered in his name. He has likewife the nomination of the canons and primicerio, or dean of St. Mark's church. He prefents to the lower offices of the palace, and creates knights, with feveral other confiderable privileges.

VOL. V.   O   In

In order as much as possible to prevent all intrigues in the election of a doge, it is conducted in the following manner: after the funeral of the late doge, the whole grand council is assembled, except those under thirty years of age, who are excluded. A number of balls equal to the number of persons present, which generally amounts to above a thousand, are put into a vessel, thirty of which are gilt with gold, and the rest with silver. Every one of the nobles according to his seniority draw a ball, and those who draw the golden balls, withdraw into a private room to continue the election; but in drawing the golden balls, left two or three persons of the same family, should be appointed electors, all the relations of that nobleman who has drawn a gilt ball, are obliged to withdraw; and for every person who retires on this account, a silver ball is taken out of the vessel that none may remain. After this the thirty electors, who have drawn the golden balls, draw a second time out of another vessel, in which there are twenty-one silver and nine golden balls. The nine who draw these golden balls, choose forty other electors, all of different families, but are allowed to name themselves of the number; and as all these nine cannot choose an equal number of electors, each of the persons who draw first has the privilege of choosing five, and each of the remaining, four new electors. These forty electors draw from a vessel in which are twenty-eight silvered and twelve golden balls; and those who draw the latter, choose twelve other electors, of whom the senior nominates three, and each of the remaining eleven, two; so that the whole number is twenty-five. These, again, by drawing gold and silver balls are reduced to nine, each of which nominates five persons, who are likewise reduced by lot to eleven. Lastly, these eleven nominate forty-one electors, the eight senior naming four each, and the others three. Each of these, whose number amounts to forty-one, as in the foregoing elections confirmed by the great council, are locked up in a

particular

particular apartment of the ducal palace, where they are confined till they have chosen a doge. In the mean time they are treated in the same manner as the cardinals in the conclave; but the time of their confinement here is not so long; for the preliminary elections, with the nomination of the last forty-one electors, are generally dispatched in two days, and the election of a doge commonly in about seven or eight more. The person elected doge must have twenty-five votes out of the forty-one in his favour.

When a person is chosen, he is not permitted to decline the office. In the year 1688, an instance of this happened, when Andreas Contareni, on making some difficulty of accepting the dignity, was threatened with banishment and confiscation of goods, unless he immediately took upon him the office.

All the nobility, amounting to about sixteen hundred, have a seat in the great council. The senate, or Pregadi, consists of about two hundred and fifty members, and is the chief assembly; having the power of making war, peace, and foreign alliances; together with the disposal of all offices both by sea and land. The senate also appoints ambassadors, fixes the standard of the coin, imposes duties and taxes for the service of the state. These two assemblies, namely, the great council and the senate, meet on Sundays and holidays in the palace, in the forenoon during summer, and in the afternoon in winter. The votes are not collected with a becoming decency and regularity for such an august assembly; the charity-boys, or Bollottini, making a great bustle in running about to distribute the balls, or to put them again into the boxes, called *bossoli*, which are painted on one side green, and on the other white. In putting the hand into the balloting box, the person who sits next cannot distinguish on which side the partition the ball is put. The balloting being ended, the drawers, of which there are two also of different colours in each box, are taken out, and the number of votes carefully computed. The balls in the white drawer are for the affirmative, and thofe in the green for the negative.

In order to fee the great council and fenate fitting, you muft pay fomething at the door, and alfo leave your fword; the nobles themfelves not daring, on pain of death, to enter the fenate-houfe armed while the council fits. The lower gates of the palace are locked, and fome of the procurators of St. Mark, from their *logietta* or little gallery, at St. Mark's tower, keep a watch, and give notice of the leaft appearance of any difturbance.

The doge, with his fix *configlieri*, called *la figniora* and *il configlietto*, and a few others, fit on a feat raifed above the reft. The great number of members renders it neceffary to tranfact feveral weighty affairs by committees.

The third council is called *il Pien Collegio*, and confifts of the doge and his fix counfellors. In this council letters and inftruments relating to the ftate are read, ambaffadors admitted to audience, and other affairs of importance are tranfacted.

Il Configlio di Dieci, confifts of ten counfellors, the doge and his fix *configlieri*. This court decides all criminal cafes, without appeal; and is much dreaded for its feverity, as its power extends itfelf even to the doge himfelf, and is called *Exellfo*, or the high council.

The procurators of St. Mark formerly had only the care of the building of the epifcopal church; but in time, wills, guardianfhips, and making a proper provifion for the poor, fell under their jurifdiction: and what renders the office ftill more confiderable is, that it is for life. The number of thefe procurators is at prefent only nine; but when the ftate is diftreffed for money thefe offices may be purchafed.

The tribunal called the ftate inquifition, confifts of three prefidents, who are very attentive to every thing that has a tendency to difturb the public tranquillity;

quillity; so that every prudent person should be very careful in talking on state affairs. The very nobility themselves are forbid to hold any conversation with ambassadors, or foreign ministers; for they often violate this order at ridottos and balls, having then an opportunity of wearing masques.

For the greater security of the state, heads of leopards and lions are carved on the wall of the ducal palace, with their mouths open, to receive information, by billets, of any plot or treason against the state, or public tranquillity. Behind these mouths are boxes placed to receive these billets, of which the inquisitors alone have the keys. It is left to the discretion of the inquisitors to determine how far such intelligence may be relied on.

Il Tribunale della S. Inquisizione, or the holy inquisition, which the pope at last obliged the republic to receive after a long opposition, consists of the apostolic nuncio, the patriarch, the inquisitor and three senators, as *assistenti* or lay-assessors, nominated by the republic. The power of this court, so formidable in other countries, is here under great restrictions; and all affairs of moment are previously made known to the state by the three assessors. Whatever relates to Jews, Greeks, witchcraft, and the like, is not cognizable by the inquisition; their vigilance being confined meerly to heresy and the abuse of the sacraments. Consequently, protestants are permitted the peaceable exercise of their religion in private.

The Lutherans belonging to the German factory maintain a preacher of their own, who wears a lay habit, and stiles himself counsellor to the duke of Saxe-Meinungen. This the republic connives at; and protestants, on their part, omit singing psalms in their meetings. They formerly used to bury their dead in the Lido, but a few years ago the German house has purchased of the monks of St. Christopher a piece of ground for that purpose. Such as are scrupulous about kneeling in the streets to the host, need be under no apprehenfions at Venice, where, on account of the narrownefs of the paffages, and the great numbers of canals, the Eucharift is carried to the fick without any proceffion.

Here is a particular college inftituted for the regulation of drefs; but their jurifdiction does not extend to ftrangers, nor to the ladies of noblemen, during the two firft years after their marriage, who are then called noviziate: they are, however, only indulged in wearing a pearl-necklace, a gold fringe round the bottom of their gowns, and giving their gondoliers, or bargemen, ribbons to wear in their hats or caps. But here, as well as in other countries, the drefs of the women is connived at; efpecially the courtefans, who readily find patrons, under whofe protection they trefpafs againft this fumptuary law with impunity. Inftances, however, are not wanting of their being fined.

The piazzo di St. Marco, or St. Mark's palace, is the greateft ornament of the city, and hath the form of a parallelogram, the fide, which is two hundred and forty paces in length, and feventy-five in breadth, extending itfelf to the fouth along by the ducal palace to the canal. The moft confiderable part of the area is between the church of St. Marco, and St. Geminiani, which is fix hundred and eighty feet in length, two hundred and feventy common paces in breadth, but not uniform; being, near St. Mark's church, a hundred and twenty-fix common paces exclufive of the colonade; but nearer St. Geminiano, it is only eighty-nine paces broad. The moft confiderable buildings, befide the ducal palace and the two above-mentioned churches, are called Procurati, where part of the procurators of St. Mark refide.

Between the two galleries of the Broglio, near the fide of the canal, are two large pillars of agate, brought hither from Conftantinople in the year 1192, when the Venetians made themfelves mafters of that city, under the command of Sebaftiano Ziani, their doge. They were three in number, but one of them in un-

lading

lading fell into the canal, and funk fo deep in the mud that it could never be found. Nicolo Barattiero of Lombardy erected the two remaining pillars, after they had lain years on the ground. On the pillar that ftands next the ducal palace is a brafs lion with his head toward the eaft, as an emblem of the republic's dominion over feveral places in the Levant. On the other pillar is a marble ftatue of St. Theodore, or as fome fay, St. George, holding his fhield in his right-hand, which muft either proceed from a miftake of the fculptor, or perhaps it was copied from an intaglio. The Venetians indeed fay, it was done defignedly, to exprefs the juftice of the republic, which only acts on the defenfive, but not on the offenfive.

Between thefe two pillars all malefactors are executed; nor would a noble Venetian pafs between them on any terms, becaufe when the doge Murrano Falier, who in the year 1354, was beheaded for treafon againft the ftate, came to Venice after his election, he was obliged to land between thefe two pillars, the water being very high in the oppofite canal. An armed galley is always kept in readinefs on any fudden exigency.

The Zecca, or mint, lies behind the Procuratu Nove, and at the entrance ftands the ftatues of two lions in a ftern pofition; one was done by Titiano Afpetti, and the other by Girolamo Campagna.

From the Italian word *zeccha*, the zecchino or gold coin derives its name, which paffes for a lira more than a German ducat, though both are equal in weight. This coin is over valued in order to prevent the exportation of the zecchins, or at leaft to induce ftrangers to fend them back to the Venetian dominions. One of the fmalleft pieces of money at Venice, is called gazzetta; and as the literary news-papers at Venice, on a fingle leaf, fo early as the fixteenth century, were fold for a gazzetta apiece, all kinds of news-papers were from thence called gazzette, or gazettes.

In the apartment over the mint, are feveral fine pieces of painting by Palma, Tintoretto, Marco Titiano, Diano, and others.

The great arsenal is situated in another part of the city, and the gratuities and perquisites paid for seeing it, amount to between thirty and forty lires. Sometimes those who preside over the arsenal are very suspicious, and not long since, they walled up two windows of the Franciscan convent, facing the tower, having been informed that two Frenchmen had, by the help of a telescope, taken from thence an exact view of the arsenal. The different accounts given by travellers of these affairs, depend in a great measure on the temper of the person who attends them. One of our company asked our guide, if while we were viewing them, one might minute some things down, which was readily granted. This famous armory is two and a half Italian miles in circuit, and surrounded with water, and twelve towers. Facing the main entrance is a small marble lion, erected under the gateway. Every one that goes in, is obliged to leave his sword, which is returned at his coming out. The edifice is divided into four large halls, two on the ground floor, and two on the upper story. The arms are ranged along the walks or galleries, embellished with the armour and trophies of Scardenbeg, Mocenigo, Franciscus Morofini, Ziani, Giustiani, Castrani, and other warriors. Over the trophies of Morofini, hang four red hats, to shew that he had been four times commander in chief. In his left hand he holds a blue cap, which the pope sent him. Here are the helmet of Attila, the iron head-piece worn by Calleonius's horse, and several arms taken from the Turks.

In the cellar is a large vessel, filled with wine four times a day, and every workman in the arsenal, though there are a thousand or more, may drink as often, and as much as he pleases. The wine is drawn out by cocks, and supposed not to be extraordinary good; being generally mixed with two thirds of water. On the island, on which the arsenal stands, is a fine spring of water.

The

The republic hath in all fifty gallies, five and twenty are at sea, and the rest almost ready to quit the harbour. They have likewise twenty-four men of war on the stocks. For each ship and galley, a particular place is built, where they lie unrigged, and unmasted, under cover, and can be kept there without receiving any damage, between fifty and sixty years. From these kind of sheds, they are also launched into the deep canals, of which they have three in the arsenal. Beside the abovementioned twenty-five gallies, in the Venetian arsenal lie, always ready rigged, four galeasses, and the like number of bomb-galliots: and two galeasses are continually kept at sea. A galeass is a large sort of galley, with a low deck, having three masts with sails, and between thirty and fifty oars to each side, and six or seven rowers to every oar. These sit under a deck, on which are guns. Toward the head of this vessel are three tiers of guns, the uppermost consisting of ten pounders, and the other two of four and twenty pounders. Toward the stern, it has two tiers, each consisting of eighteen pounders. The whole number of guns is commonly forty cannon and six culverines. A galeass carries twelve hundred men, the rowers included.

Formerly such a vessel had orders not to strike to twenty-five Turkish galleys; and the captain, who is always a nobleman, was sworn to observe the order: but the case is now altered, and the Turkish navy has of late become more formidable.

A galley is much flatter bottomed than a galeass, and has but two masts, namely, a foremast and mainmast; with only twenty-five or thirty oars on a side, and five or six galley slaves to every oar. It generally carries no more than five guns, the largest of which is placed at the head, and carries a ball weighing between thirty and thirty-four pounds. These vessels go fast, but are not fit for bad weather, and consequently they seldom go far from shore. The Venetians pretend that their gallies exceed all others, as being double-timbered.

timbered. The galliots are smaller than the gallies, and are principally used for transports. Of these fifty are always ready rigged in the arsenal, together with four advice-boats, of which last, the like number are continually out at sea.

The sailors in the Venetian fleet, are mostly natives of Italy. The republic accustom their subjects but very little to military exercises, being sensible that the people, by reason of their severe oppression, have no great liking to their superiors; and thus the government deprives them of all means, whereby they might be enabled to shake off that yoke, which they bear with such reluctance. Their wars with the Ottoman Porte are usually carried on by troops which they hire from the German princes.

The bridge called Ponte Rialto, is intirely of marble, and consists of a single arch, ninety feet wide*, from the base of one pier to the other. It was built by the architect Antonio dal Ponte, stands on twelve thousand piles of elm, and cost the republic two hundred and fifty thousand ducats. Its breadth a-top is thirty-seven common paces, and divided by two rows of shops, into three streets, the middle street of which is the broadest. At each end, are fifty-six steps of ascent to it. The great canal over which this bridge is built, is narrower here than in any other place, and only forty paces over. It is thirteen hundred paces in length, and along its banks, are the best houses in all the city.

Close to the Rialto are the exchange and the bank. The latter belongs to the state, and pays no interest for money lodged here; the merchants depositing it, partly for security, and partly for the greater facility of transferring and remitting it in trade.

The roofs of the houses in Venice are flat, and covered with tiles. The flooring in most of the apart-

---

* The centre arch of Blackfriars Bridge at London, is said to be two feet wider than this celebrated bridge.

The Famous BRIDGE of RIALTO.

ments, is a kind of red plaifter, made of pulverized marble and brick, mixed up with oil, and is both beautiful and lafting.

Among the curious collections of pictures at Venice, thofe are to be preferred, which, fome years ago, were purchafed by the field marfhal count Sculemburg, if it might be conjectured that they were to remain any confiderable time in this city. Some pieces by Caftiglione, deferved particular notice, together with the laft fiege, and the new fortifications of Corfu, which is not only painted on a picture, but curioufly modelled in wood. Corfu is not only a bulwark to the Venetians, againft the attack of foreign enemies, but likewife very advantageous on the account of its falt-works, which, with thofe of the ifland of Chiofa, an ifland and city, not lying far from the influx of the Brenta Nuova, and twenty miles diftant from Venice, yield an annual revenue of upward of five millions of livres. There is now a garrifon of four thoufand men, conftantly kept in the caftle of Corfu; and fince count Sculemburg caufed feveral new fortifications to be added to it, may juftly be looked upon as one of the ftrongeft places in Europe.

The ifland of Murano, but a fmall mile diftant from Venice, is governed by its own magiftrate, and faid to contain eighteen thoufand inhabitants.

The beautiful looking-glaffes, and other elegant glafs-work, made in this ifland, have fpread its reputation into foreign countries; yet this trade is very much decayed, other nations having improved themfelves greatly, and difcovered an art of making glafs, which far furpaffes that of Venice, for largenefs. The Murano looking-glaffes are only blown, whereas in other places, they are caft and ground.

The Venetian clergy are in no great repute, either for learning or morals. The nuns do not obferve the ftricteft difcipline, neither are thofe of noble families kept under a proper reftriction: for as they do not voluntarily enter into this reclufe way of life out of a

principle

principle of devotion, but are perfuaded to take this galling yoke upon themfelves againft their inclination, for the conveniency of their families; they do every thing in their power to make it fupportable. The nuns of St. Lorenzo threatened to fet the convent on fire, rather than fubmit to be brought under a greater reftraint. The nuns, on account of their diftinguifhed rank, bear the title of *excellenza*. The vulgar at Venice, as in other places, are fuperftitious; but perfons of quality are often known to run into the other extream, and not give themfelves any concern about religion. Their fkill in politics has given them a clear infight of the indignity and detriment accruing by fubmitting to the ecclefiaftical power, and encouraged them to affert feveral privileges and liberties, of which other nations have fuffered themfelves to be deprived by the encroachments of the pope. In order to fupport and perpetuate this liberty, and at the fame time prevent difturbances, every perfon who embraces an ecclefiaftical life, is excluded from the great council, and from having any fhare in the government.

The patriarch, who is at the head of the clergy, ftiles himfelf *Divina miferatione Patriarcha Venetiarum*, without the addition ufed by the bifhops of other nations, *& laneta Sedes Apoftolicæ gratia*. He is primate of Dalmatia, metropolitan of the archbifhops of Candia, and Corfu, and alfo of the bifhops of Chrozza and Tercello. The council chooses him out of the nobility, and the pope confirms the nomination. His power and dignity are but very inconfiderable, and even at Venice itfelf, does not extend to the dean and chapter of St. Mark, who bear the title of Primicerio.

The number of churches, convents, and hofpitals at Venice, are a hundred and fourfcore.

In the ftreets, near many of thefe religious edifices, are fet up white ftones, infcribed with the word *Sacrum*, or *Il Sacrato*, to know how far the privileges of every fuch foundation extends.

[From

VENICE.

[From the description given by Mr. Sharpe, of Venice, we have extracted the following particulars.——" Venice, with a few alterations, might appear much more magnificent than it now is: the windows, instead of sashes, are still, as in the other parts of Italy, made of small panes of glass, inclosed in lead, which is exceedingly paltry; and what is still worse, they are covered with iron grates, exactly resembling those of our prisons, which makes a dreadful gloomy view of the fronts of their palaces. These grates were formerly called *gelosias*, but I question whether they still retain that name; for never was so entire a revolution effected in the manners of a nation, as in this instance of jealousy. In ancient days, wives were immured in Italy, and husbands were jealous: now, no women on earth are under so little restraint, and the word jealousy is become obsolete. The shutters of their houses are plain deal boards, tacked together without the least form or decoration, and not painted like ours in England; so that when a palace is shut up, it very much resembles a bridewell, or an hospital for lunatics. They likewise lay on the roofs of their houses such heavy clumsy tiles, that they very much offend the eye. House-rent is remarkably cheap for so large and so trading a city. A house of seventy pounds a year, I should have guessed at near two hundred, and so of others I enquired after.

The republic is extreamly rigid in what regards the quarantine; and indeed, as they border upon those confines where the plague so frequently breaks out, they cannot be too watchful. There is not the least connivance ever practised; all letters, to whomsoever directed, are first opened by the officers, and then smoaked before they are delivered. Were Mr.— to have handed over a news-paper to me, and we had been detected in the action, I must inevitably have performed quarantine in the Lazaretto, a certain number of weeks. A few years since, a boy got on board

board one of the veffels performing quarantine, and ftole fome tobacco; he was purfued into Venice, and fhot dead in the ftreets. There are many cuftom-houfe officers in their boats, watching the quarantine night and day, who would certainly kill the firft man who fhould attempt to efcape on fhore, before the expiration of the quarantine.——

The theatres are not now open; but when they are, all the world goes thither, particularly in the feafon of the carnival, where the barcaroles (gondaliers) make fo great a figure, that it is faid of them, what our Bickerftaff faid of the trunk-maker in the Tatler, that what they cenfure or applaud, is generally condemned or approved by the public: in fhort, that it is the barcaroles who decide the fate of an opera or play. Thefe barcaroles are certainly fuch a body of fober men as in England we have no inftance of amongft the lower clafs of people: in mafking-time, however, they indulge the tafte of gaming, and doubtlefs often play with the nobles their mafters; but the brownnefs and coarfenefs of their hands betray their occupation: befide that, it is impoffible for them to forbear making their boafts, or their complaints, of good and bad fortune, when their dialect and deportment never fail to difcover them.

The number, as well as the character of this people, renders their body very refpectable: when one confiders, that in all the great families, every gentleman keeps a diftinct gondola rowed by two men, except fome few who have but one rower, it will be readily conceived that the number of barcaroles muft be very confiderable. They are exceedingly proud of their ftation, and with fome reafon; for their profeffion leads them into the company of the greateft men of the ftate; and it is the fafhion to converfe with them, to hear their wit and humour, and applaud all they fay: befide, the pay of a barcarole is about eighteen pence Englifh, with liveries and little perquifites, which, in fo cheap a country, is a plentiful

tiful income to a sober man : accordingly, it is notorious, that all of them can afford to marry, and do marry.

The manner of rowing a gondola, standing and looking forward, may be seen in every view of Venice, and this manner is absolutely necessary for the guidance of a boat in these narrow canals; but it is curious to observe how dexterous they are by use; for it is very rare that they touch, much less endanger oversetting, though they are, every instant, within half an inch of each other. One cannot be an hour on these canals without seeing several of the barcaroles shifting themselves; for it is a custom amongst them, to have always a dry shirt ready to put on, the moment after they have landed their fare; and they would expect to die, if by any accident they were under the necessity of suffering a damp shirt to dry on their bodies. On the other hand, it is curious to observe how little they dread damp sheets through all Italy, at least in summer; and the people at inns are so little apprised of an objection to damp sheets, that when you beg they would hang them before the fire, they do not understand you, and desire you will feel how wet they are; being prepossessed, that you mean they have not been washed : in fact, unless you have servants who will dry them for you, it is in vain to expect it should be done.

Gallantry is so epidemical in this city, that few of the ladies escape the contagion. No woman can go into a public place, but in the company of a gentleman, called here a *cavaliere servente*, and in other parts of Italy, a *cicesbeo*. This cavaliere is always the same person; and she not only is attached to him, but to him singly; for no other woman joins the company, but it is usual for them to sit alone in the box, at the opera or play-house, where they must be, in a manner, by themselves, as the theatres are so very dark, that the spectators can hardly be said to be in company with one another. After the opera, the lady and her *cavaliere servente* retire to her casine, where they have a *tete-a-tete* for an hour or two, and then her visitors join them for the rest of the evening or night: for on some festival or jolly days, they spend the whole night, and take mass in their way home. You must know a casine is nothing more than a small room, generally at or near St. Mark's-Place, hired for the most part by the year, and sacred to the lady and her cavaliere; for the husband never approaches it. On the other hand, the husband has his revenge; for he never fails to be the *cavaliere servente* of some other woman. There are many examples where the cavaliere, and not the husband, is the object; where the cavaliere is taken immediately into service, and for whose sake the marriage is a pretext and screen.

So many opportunities must, therefore, render this republic a second Cyprus, where all are votaries to Venus, unless it please heaven to pour down more grace amongst them, than falls to the share of other nations in this degenerate age: but the detractors deny that the husbands believe in this partial favour, and assert, they have very little fondness for their children, compared with the parents of other kingdoms: they are the children of the republic, say they, but not so certainly the children of their reputed fathers: the girls, therefore, are early sent to convents, where they remain till they marry or die, and are visited by their fathers and mothers seldom or never; if they marry, they at once burst out from a secluded life, and a narrow education, into the scene of licentiousness I have just described. ———

This is the picture of Venetian amours in the present age; but charity would lead one to hope the colours are laid on too strong: politicians, however, pretend to give an easy solution of this licentiousness amongst the ladies: they tell you, that, in former times, the courtezans were a useful class of citizens, whose arms were always open to the wealthy, whether they were young or old; that now they have no such character among them, and the stews that are connived at, receive only the very dregs of the people. Every diffolute man of fortune is, therefore, in a manner, driven into the practice of either keeping a mistress, or becoming a *cavaliere servente*: the former method is more expensive, and less honourable; the latter, consequently, the more prevalent.

The bank of the Rialto is a very small office, and the whole business is transacted by a few clerks, who sit in a small room like an open booth, which faces the exchange. The business of the bank may be aptly compared to that of a banker in England, where merchants deposit a large sum of money, and draw upon the shop for their disbursements.———

We have this day seen a wedding of two of the greatest families in Venice: I say families; for all matches are rather alliances of families, than attachments of the parties married. These marriages are generally public, and the relations are desirous to have as many assistants and witnesses at church as they can collect: it is usual upon this occasion to send an invitation to foreigners. All the women who are admitted, have likewise a formal invitation; but no gentleman is denied entrance. The ladies, who are the acquaintance of the parties, appear as gawdy as their sumptuary laws will suffer them; but these laws oblige them to wear black; so that their laced ruffles and head-dress, with their diamonds, are the chief ornament; and, to say the truth, though their diamonds are numerous, they appear to great disadvantage, by being ill-set in a large quantity of silver. The number of the well-dressed ladies was only fifteen; the rest of the women in the church were of low rank. The bride alone was dressed in white, with a long train; the bridegroom in the usual black dress of a Venetian noble, not unlike one of our counsellors in England with a judge's wig. She was led up toward

toward the altar by a Venetian noble, where she kneeled, with her husband on her right-hand. They both continued on their knees till the ceremony was finished, which, with the mass, was above half an hour. She was then handed out of the church by the same noble; and, as is the custom, she curtsied and paid her compliments, *en passant*, to all her's and her husband's friends. Upon this occasion there are epithalamiums printed, and made presents of to certain spectators and acquaintance. It must happen now and then, that a rich Venetian has no son; in which case, a daughter may be a great fortune; but, in general, a young lady with six or seven thousand pounds, is esteemed a good fortune; for the ambition of the noble families is to unite, as much as possible, their riches with their name. The ladies here, as also at Turin and Milan, are generally very fair: the men are not so handsome, but I think remarkably tall. Look at any class amongst them, the nobles for example, and you will find very few short men amongst them."——

Mr. Sharpe farther remarks,——" Venice, from its system of policy, opens the doors of her nobles to very few strangers. No country in the world adheres more rigidly to her ancient laws and customs than this republic. Amongst others, there is one ordinance that not only prohibits the nobles themselves from holding the least intercourse with foreign ministers; but it is so very severe, that should even one of their servants pass the threshold of an ambassador, he would infallibly be sent to prison. The law renders the life of a foreign minister exceedingly dull and unsocial; beside that, it stops the channel through which young gentlemen on their travels would naturally find access to the best company. I believe the origin of this law at Venice, had its rise from a frivolous narrow conceit of preventing plots against the state; but, in a sumptuary view, it may be useful, as it suppresses that emulation in luxury, which

which the visits betwixt their nobles and the foreign ministers would naturally produce.

The nobles are said to be above fifteen hundred in number, and it will therefore be readily supposed, that far the greater part of them are poor; as all the sons are noble, and they have no means of adding to their patrimony, but by attaining magistracies and offices in the government, which are not lucrative, compared with English employments. By an antient act of the senate, a noble must not be concerned in any article of commerce, though it is whispered that many of them have clandestine partnerships. The sons too being all nobles, they divide their estates more equally than in monarchical kingdoms, where the eldest son only, in order to support the honour of the family with the more splendor, enjoys the title and estate. It is true, that in Venice, the eldest has some benefit from his primogeniture; but, for the reasons I have mentioned, that benefit is not very considerable. It is the ambition of every noble to marry one daughter to a noble; on which account he sends the others to convents, that he may be better enabled to give her a fortune, and provide handsomely for his sons. There are four convents in Venice, to which four hospitals are annexed, that give names to the convents. They are of a very singular institution in one article, being open to a certain number of poor young women, who are thoroughly instructed in both vocal and instrumental music. They exhibit in their churches, on particular days of the week, and some festivals, and are much frequented, as the performance is finer than one expects in any other place than a theatre. The condition upon which they accept their education, is to remain in the convent until such time as their talents shall induce some one to marry them. This happens very rarely, so that they generally sing on till their voices are lost, and their names are almost forgotten. The founders of this charity had, as it appears, too exalted an opinion of the power of music; for, however beautiful the girls may be, they trust only to their melody, being intercepted from the sight of the audience, by a black gauze hung over the rails of the gallery in which they perform: it is transparent enough to shew the figures of women, but not in the least their features and complexion.———

The poor people live very well in the city of Venice, which, however, may, in a great measure, be ascribed to their ignorance of gin and brandy. They love gaming, and are, consequently, often needy; but the government connives at it, and are rather pleased to have them so: as for those who, by sickness, or other accidents, are reduced to poverty, there is an abundance of charitable foundations; however, the swarms of beggars are surprisingly great. The trade of begging, in all catholic countries, will necessarily prosper, so long as that species of charity, which is bestowed on beggars, continues to be inculcated by their preachers and confessors, as the most perfect of all moral duties.

I must take notice of some disadvantages this city labours under. The water here is such an invitation to gnats, that no stranger to this place will conceive the torments we suffered every day and night from these insects; and it must be granted that the canals, at low water, are often, in the summer, very offensive, perhaps unwholsome. The bread is indifferent, and the wine, as through all Italy to this city, very bad. As they live in the midst of salt water, all the water they drink, except what is brought from the Brenta, is collected from the rain which falls on their houses: to this end they dig a well, which, at a certain depth, they surround with a wall of terras, made very compact, that the salt water in the canals may not transude into the well: then they lay a bed of sand, through which the water filters into the well, as they imagine, in the most perfect state of the purest water: however, as every housekeeper thinks
his

VENICE.

his well better finished than that of his neighbour, one may conclude that some of them are porous, and do admit more or less salt water into them. The frequency of diarrhæas is another argument, that the water they drink is purgative; but perhaps one of the greatest inconveniencies of these wells is, that they do not contain water enough for a family, in case of long droughts, which frequently happen in Italy.

All pleadings at the bar must be in the Venetian dialect, which is unpleasant to the ear of a foreigner; and though none but an Italian should dare to criticise on the stile and taste of an Italian, yet a foreigner may venture to pronounce, that the Venetian dialect is a corrupt Italian, as they have letters in their alphabet which most of the natives of this town can never learn to utter; and are therefore obliged to drop entirely, or to substitute others in their place. For example, in all words where the letter *g* is introduced, this observation takes place; for, instead of pronouncing it in the words, *Giudice, Giulio, Giovanne,* and a thousand others, they say, *Dudice, Dulio, Diovanne,* &c. and in the words *Mangiare, Ragione,* they drop it almost entirely, and say *Maniare, Raione,* &c. Then again the Tuscans, and indeed the Italians of almost every other state, pronounce the *ci* and *ce,* as we should by putting an *h* betwixt the initial and final letters, as in the words *chirp* and *chefs*; but a Venetian has not the power of expressing those words, otherwise than *firp* and *fefs*.

If this stricture on their language be a little too bold, I may venture at least to take some freedoms with the indecorum of their bar. I shall not enter into the particulars of the extraordinary forms of their narrators, their interruptors, &c. a noisy, uncivilized manner of pleading; but shall only describe, if I am able, the agitation and fury of the pleaders, more like that of a demoniac, than of a man endeavouring, by sound reason, to convince the judges and the audience of the justice of his client's cause. Every advocate mounts into a small pulpit, a little elevated above the audience, where he opens his harangue with some gentleness, but does not long contain himself within those limits; his voice soon cracks, and what is very remarkable, the beginning of most sentences (whilst he is under any agitation, or seeming enthusiasm, in pleading) is at a pitch above his natural voice, so as to occasion a wonderful discord: then, if he means to be very emphatical, he strikes the pulpit with his hands five or six times together, as quick as thought, stamping at the same time, so as to make the great room resound with this species of oratory. At length, in the fury of his argument, he descends from the pulpit, runs about pleading on the floor, returns in a violent passion back again to the pulpit, thwacks it with his hands more than at first, and continues in this rage, running up and down the pulpit several times, till he has finished his harangue. They seem to be in a continual danger of dropping their wigs from their heads, and I am told it sometimes happens. The audience smile now and then at this extraordinary behaviour; but were a counsellor to plead in this manner at Westminster, his friends would certainly send for a Bedlam doctor. I take it for granted there may be some few who speak with more dignity; but the advocates I saw were all men of eminence in their profession; and believe me, when I assure you, that the account I have here given of the usage of the bar, is exact and simple, though it may seem to favour of extravagance."—]

In travelling from Venice to Vienna, the shortest road is through Padua, where you agree with a vetturino, who for carriage and diet generally charges from twelve to fourteen ducats for every passenger; but as few remarkable objects present themselves in that road, to satisfy the curiosity of a traveller, our company determined to take the way of Trieste and
Fiume,

Fiume, two places now famous for commerce, and from thence to take a view of the natural curiosities in the duchy of Carniola. Those who are fearful of committing themselves to the mercy of the sea, may perform the journey by first going in a bark to Fosette, and from thence in a chaise to Palma. Being arrived at Monte Falcone, a bark may be easily hired to Trieste.

The mildness of the season encouraged us to take the shortest way, by going from Venice to Trieste by sea, and accordingly we provided ourselves with certificates of health, which are distributed gratis, at a large edifice opposite the salt-office.

Trieste is beautifully situated on the declivity of a hill, about which the vineyards form a semicircle. The town is but small, and the fort, which stands on an eminence, is surrounded with ditches; but otherwise in a very defenceless condition, and garrisoned only with forty-five men. They are at present erecting some new fortifications on both sides of the narrow passage leading into the inner harbour. The natives of Trieste are accused of being lazy and proud, never applying themselves to any useful employment, and of being of such an envious disposition, as to molest strangers to the utmost of their power.

About a German mile from Trieste is the castle of Servulo, situated on a high mountain, from whence there is an inchanting prospect. Near it is the mouth or entrance of a famous cavern, in which the lapideous exudations have formed, on the top and sides, several large pillars, and a variety of figures of white and blue colours. This cavern is very spacious, and at the entrance into it, being on the side of a mountain, upward of thirty stone steps are cut in the acclivity, for the conveniency of those who are fond of the curiosities of nature. In a rock, just under the castle of St. Servulo, is another cave, to the entrance of which you pass over a draw-bridge. The inhabitants of the country, in troublesome times, used to lodge their goods and effects in this cavern; and by drawing up the bridge effectually secure them from the enemy.

Fiume is situated in a valley near the sea; and noted for good wine, figs, and other fruits.

Adlsberg, or, in the Sclavonian language, *Calle Poſtoina*, is seven German miles distant from Fiume. After ascending about half way up the acclivity near Adlsberg, by the mill, you arrive at a large cavern, divided into several spacious passages. The sparry decorations of the roof appear like isicles, and wonderfully delight the eye. The sides likewise are covered with the same natural exudations, to which the imagination of the curious spectator frequently gives various forms, never intended by nature; so that it is no wonder to hear some people pretend that they have seen the heads of horses, dragons, tygers, and other monstrous appearances. If a person's curiosity will lead him so far, he may rove about two German miles in the subterraneous passages of this cavern.

About a German mile farther, towards the north-west, are also several remarkable caverns; in one of which, great part of the castle of Lueg, belonging to count Cobentzl, stands as under a roof. In the Sclavonian language this castle is called Jamma, which signifies a hole or cave.

About three quarters of a league from Adisberg, is the remarkable subterraneous passage, called St. Mary Magdalen's Cave, to which there is no going but on horseback. The stones and bushes are exceeding troublesome; but even this fatigue is amply rewarded by the satisfaction a curious person enjoys, in seeing such an extraordinary cavern. It is not, indeed, equal to that of Adlsberg in height, but in several other particulars, far surpasses it; and I must confess, is the finest I ever saw. You first descend into a kind of hole, where the earth seems to be fallen in, for ten paces before you arrive at the entrance,

trance, which appears like a chasm in a rock, caused by an earthquake. Here the torches are lighted to conduct travellers, the cave being extreamly dark, and divided into several apartments or halls. The vast number of pillars, formed by nature, in this wonderful cavern, give it a very magnificent appearance, being exceeding beautiful, as white as snow, and almost transparent. The bottom is of the same materials, so that a person may imagine he is walking among the ruins of some stately palace, surrounded by magnificent pillars and columns, some entire, and others mutilated.

At Planina, those who are curious take horse, in order to visit Cirknitz, about a German mile from it. This is but a small village, and of itself not worth seeing; but the lake, which lies about half a league from it, is very famous, and has been the subject of the disquisitions of many naturalists.

It is a common proverb, that in the Cirknitzersee a person may sow, reap, hunt, and fish, within the space of one year; but this circumstance is not peculiar to the lake, but common to every other spot overflowed with water in the winter and spring; but what is really wonderful, is the ebbing and flowing of this lake. The former happens in a long drought, whether it be summer or winter; and the last year the water was absorbed twice entirely: the first time in the summer, and the second in the winter following. The lake generally continues to ebb for five and twenty days; the water, during that time, running off by holes or cavities, which are eighteen in number, resembling so many whirlpools. The cavities do not absorb an equal quantity of water in the same time; for that called Ramine empties itself in five days, and in five days more the Vodonos becomes dry: five days after this, the Reschatto is evacuated; and at the end of five days more the Koten pool is empty: and lastly, at the end of the succeeding five days the Levische is dried up. The water,

during

during that time, is also abforbed by the other thirteen holes or whirlpools; so that in twenty-five days the lake is entirely dry. After a fortnight's settled drought in summer, the lake is observed again to ebb; but if it happens to rain for two or three days, it fills again. Instances have been known of its being dried up three times in a year.

Any peasant may purchase the liberty of fishing in this lake for three siebenzehner, or one and fifty crutzers, in which part of this lake he pleases, and as often as he will, till the waters begin to fall; but on the return of the water, this licence must be again purchased. Some of the pools or cavities, which have but few fish in them, are given to peasants to be cleared; and when the water begins a bell is rung at Cirknitz, on which all haste to the place of this gleaning, as it is called, from which only a few holes are exempted. What fish is not consumed while fresh, is dried by the fire. Above one hundred peasants take the advantage of this fishery, and the men and women run promiscuously to the pools, quite naked, notwithstanding both the magistrates and clergy have used their joint endeavours to suppress this indecent custom; which gives occasion to a great deal of laughter and indecent language among strangers who happen to be present. Beside, such sights are strong temptations to recluses; and though the women of the lower class in this country cannot boast of their beauty, yet they are not disagreeable to those who never see any of the sex beside.

Notwithstanding every part of the lake is absolutely dried up, and nothing remains alive in it except the spawn and young fry in Narte and Piauze, and the fish in the river Jesser; yet, on the return of the water, as great a number of fish are seen in it as before. The fish that return with the water are of a very large size, particularly jacks, weighing from fifty to seventy pounds each; a convincing proof

that

CIRKNITZERSEE.

that the reservoir which supplies this lake with water is well stocked with fish.

When great quantities of rain fall, three of the cavities, namely, Koten, Jenslenza, and Tressetz, eject water to the height of two or three fathoms. If the rain continues, and especially if attended with claps of thunder, the water issues out of all the holes through which it was absorbed, those of Velka and Mala Karlousa alone excepted, and the whole lake is again filled with water in twenty-four, nay, sometimes in eighteen hours. Some of the holes or cavities only eject, but never absorb water; while others both eject and absorb, during the ebb or flow of the lake. Nor do fish rise with the water through all the holes, owing possibly to the narrowness of the syphons through which the water flows. Sometimes even live ducks, with grass and small fish in their stomachs, have emerged from these cavities; a sufficient proof that there must be a large lake under the Cirknitzersee. The water in the latter sometimes rises suddenly five or six feet above the usual height.

On one side of the lake, considerably above the surface of the water, is a rock, in which are two holes at some distance from each other; through both which the water issues, during a thunder shower, with great noise and impetuosity. When this happens in the autumn, a great number of ducks are ejected; these fowls are fat, of a black colour, blind, and almost destitute of feathers; but in about a fortnight, are full-fledged, recover their sight, and fly away. Each of these apertures is about six feet diameter, and eject, during these storms, a constant column of water of the same dimensions.

This lake has three pleasant islands, beside a peninsula. Its greatest extent is a large German mile, or two leagues, and one league in breadth. The inhabitants call it Zerknishu Jessen; the former denoting a small church, and the latter water. The greatest depth, exclusive of the cavities and holes, is is about four fathoms. Strabo calls it *lugeam paladem*, either from the town of Lueg, not far from it, or from its deep and cavernous bed.

Being desirous of viewing the imperial quickfilver mines of Idra, I determined to take the shortest road from Planina, which lies through Loidsch; but was obliged to go by the way of Upper Laubach, a town situated about two German miles from Planina.

Virgin quickfilver, or *minera mercurii*, is that prepared entirely by nature, and is found in the ore of these mines in globules or little drops, and sometimes flows like the milk from a cow; so that in six hours a single person has been known to gather above six and thirty pounds of this virgin mercury, of great use in making the *noctuluca mercurialis*, or lucid barometers, which being shaken in the dark, in a perpendicular direction, emit light; but brighter when the mercury falls, than when it rises.

Virgin mercury may be known by the following experiment. Let an amalgama be made of mercury and gold, put it over the fire to evaporate, and if it be virgin mercury, it will carry all the gold away with it, which common mercury will not.

Every common miner receives weekly, in money and provisions, about a guilder and a half, or 3 s. 6 d. sterling; but the health of many of them is extreamly impaired, being often affected with nervous disorders, violent tremblings, and sudden convulsive motions in their heads and legs. The quickfilver infinuates itself surprisingly into the bodies of many of those workmen. The same pernicious effects have been felt by goldsmiths, who cannot gild without using quickfilver; on which account it is also safest to work in the open air. Those who silver lookingglasses at Venice, are very subject to paralytic disorders. On the other hand, there are instances of persons labouring under venereal distempers, who have been cured by working in the quickfilver mines.

The

The penetrative fubtilty of mercury is lefs furprifing, as it appears from accurate obfervations, that a little globule of quickfilver, not exceeding a coriander feed in magnitude, may, by only preffing it between the finger and thumb, be divided into twenty-feven millions of fmall particles, all retaining their argentine luftre and globular form, as may be feen through a microfcope.

There is a confiderable demand for quickfilver at Venice, where it is ufed in filvering looking-glaffes, and fome of it is fent to Rome and Naples.

From Laubach to Gratz in Stiria, are ten ftages: the third, namely, from St. Ofwald to Franze, is very craggy; and on the road is a ftone infcribed with thefe words, *Fines Carnioliæ*, marking the limits between the duchy of Carniola and the country of Cilley. About twenty paces on this fide of it is a fine fquare pyramid on a bafis of black marble; and on the top an eagle, with his wings expanded, and looking toward Carniola. In his claws are a globe and fcepter; on each fide of it is a fulfome infcription in Latin.

Two ftages from Gratz, in the way to Vienna, on the right-hand of Retelftein, is a cave, out of which are continually dug large bones, called *Unicornu Foffile*, not unlike thofe of Canftein. The entrance into this cave is very fpacious, and under a rock. Thefe bones may be conjectured to have belonged to fome wild beafts, which, at the time of the deluge, or fome other extraordinary inundation, had fheltered themfelves in this cavern.

Laxemburg, formerly known by the name of Lachfendorf, is generally the fpring-refidence of the imperial court. A large plain in the neighbourhood, is very commodious for hunting the heron, a diverfion of which the late emperor Charles VI. was very fond: but the palace is not worth feeing, either with regard to architecture or furniture.

From Neuftadt, almoft to Luxemburg, is a vaft and barren plain: and I muft confefs that all Stiria, and that part of Auftria bordering on it, did not anfwer the idea I had before formed of them, either in point of beauty or fertility. But from Luxemburg to Vienna is a charming country, and the road leading over Vinerberg, a fmall hill, but affording an excellent profpect, is delightfully planted with rows of trees.

[As we are going to enter the city of Vienna, the capital of the whole German empire, and the refidence of the emperor, it will be a proper place here to add a few words of general defcription, of the vaft collective body which compofes that celebrated empire; without defcending to minute particulars.

Germany, which is called by the French Allemagne, and by the natives themfelves Deutfchland, is bounded by France, the Netherlands, and the German Sea on the weft; by South Jutland and the Baltic on the north; by Polifh Pruffia, Poland, and Hungary on the eaft; and by the Gulph of Venice, the dominions of the ftate of Venice and Swifferland on the fouth; extending from 45° 4′ to 54° 40′ north latitude, and from 6° to 19° 45′ eaft longitude: accordingly its greateft extent from north to fouth is fix hundred and forty Englifh miles in length, and five hundred and fifty in breadth.

Germany is divided into ten circles, in order to promote and maintain the public welfare; for the more juft divifion and collection of the aids granted by the empire, either in men or money; and for preventing and remedying the diforders in the taxes, coinage, &c. The circles have, however, no particular regulation with refpect to precedence, but are very differently ranked in the ordinances and acts of the empire. Thefe are the Auftrian, the Burgundian, the Electoral Rhenifh, the Franconian, the Swabian, the Upper Rhenifh, the Lower Rhenifh,

Weft-

GERMANY.

Westphalian, the Upper and Lower Saxon. But this division of the circles is imperfect, in not including all the dominions of the German empire; for Bohemia, Moravia, the Lusatias, and the Silesias, are not comprized within them; nor was a sufficient regard paid to the situation of the countries.

With respect to religion, the circles are divided into those that are entirely Popish, as the Austrian and Burgundian; into such as are wholly Protestant, which are those of Upper and Lower Saxony; and into the mixed, to which all the others belong.

The emperor's title runs thus, "F. by the grace of God elected a Roman emperor, and at all times augmenter of the empire of Germany." Next follow the titles of the hereditary imperial dominions. The states of the empire give the emperor the title of most illustrious, most powerful, and most invincible Roman emperor; but the last is omitted by the electors.

The prerogatives of the emperor consist partly in his being looked upon by all other crowned heads and states in Europe as the first European potentate, and consequently has precedence given him and his ambassadors. With respect to the German empire, he is its supreme head, and as such enjoys many privileges. Yet his power in the administration of the German empire is limited, as well by the capitulation of the election, the other laws of the empire, by treaties, as by the customs of the empire. Those privileges which he has the right of exercising without the advice of the states, are called his *reservata*; but his greatest power does not consist in these, which are far from being repugnant to the liberties of the states of the empire.

His rights, with respect to ecclesiastical affairs, consist in little more than confirming ecclesiastical elections, and sending commissaries to the elections of archbishops, bishops, and abbots, that they may be performed

performed in due order; but the commiffary is never perfonally prefent at thefe elections.

With refpect to temporal affairs, the emperor has the right of beftowing perfonal dignities; as for inftance, the creating of noblemen, as lords, barons, counts, who enjoy the dignity of princes, and of knights and gentry, as alfo that of raifing countries and territories to a higher rank; of beftowing coats of arms, as alfo the enlarging, improving, and altering them. He has the power of eftablifhing univerfities, and enabling them to confer academical degrees; of granting a right of holding fairs and markets, and of erecting any place into a fanctuary. He has likewife the power of beftowing letters of refpite, of fecuring a debtor againft his creditor, and of conferring majority on minors. He can put children who are born out of wedlock upon the footing of fuch as are legitimate; can confirm the contracts and ftipulations of the members of the empire; and fo far remit the oaths extorted from them, that they may commence an action at law againft another, on account of the very thing for which the oath was adminiftered.

The emperor, however, has no right, without the confent of the collective ftates of the empire, to put one of thofe ftates under the ban; to exclude a ftate of the empire from a feat and voice in its colleges; to interfere in the laws of the empire; to conclude treaties in affairs relating to the empire; to involve it in a war; to raife levies; or to conclude a peace in which the empire is concerned; to appoint taxes in it; to regulate the coinage; to build forts in the empire; or to determine religious difputes.

The fucceffor in the adminiftration is frequently chofen by the electors during the life of the emperor, and the perfon fo chofen, is ftiled king of the Romans. He is elected and crowned in the very fame manner as the emperor; and though he has properly no kingdom,

dom, is actually a crowned head; is saluted with the title of majesty, and enjoys the title of perpetual augmenter of the empire, and king of Germany. He bears a spread eagle with one head, in his arms, and takes precedence before all other kings of Christendom.

With respect to the emperor's court and chancery, he has for his assistants the arch-offices of the empire, which are filled by electors.

Of the nine electors, three are spiritual, and the rest temporal. Of the former is the elector of Mentz, who is arch-chancellor of the holy Roman empire, and director of the electoral college. The elector of Treves, who is the second spiritual elector, is the arch-chancellor of the holy Roman empire in Gaul and the kingdom of Arles; but this is at present no more than a mere title. He has the first voice at the election of a king of the Romans, and consequently precedes the elector of Cologn. The elector of Cologn is arch-chancellor of the holy Roman empire in Italy, and has a second voice at the election of a king of the Romans.

The temporal electors are the following: the king of Bohemia, the elector of Bavaria, the elector of Saxony, the elector of Brandenburg, the elector Palatine, and the elector of Hanover. The king and elector of Bohemia is arch-cup-bearer of the holy Roman empire. His other prerogatives are, his preceding all other temporal electors, walking in procession immediately after the emperor, followed by the empress, and the electors of Mentz and Cologn; and in the electoral college he has a third voice. The elector of Bavaria is arch-sewer of the holy Roman empire. The elector of Saxony is arch-marshal of the holy Roman empire. At the diets, and on other solemn occasions, he carries the sword of state before the emperor, and at the coronation rides into a heap of oats, and fills a silver measure with them. The elector of Brandenburg is arch-chamber-

chamberlain of the empire, and carries the fcepter before the emperor, and prefents him with water in a filver bafon, for him to wafh his hands. The elector Palatine has the office of arch-treafurer, and throughout all Germany is protector of the order of St. John; he can alfo raife nobles and gentlemen to the degree of counts. The elector of Bavaria being put under the ban of the empire, and the Palatine obtaining the office of arch-fewer, the elector of Brunfwic Lunenburg alfo obtained the office of arch-treafurer, a title which he ftill bears, till another fuitable office be found him. He enjoys the alternate fucceffion of the bifhopric of Ofnaburg, with fome other rights and privileges; and his electoral jurifdiction extends both to the territories of Hanover and Zell. Indeed, the emperor Leopold raifed the illuftrious houfe of Hanover, on account of the extraordinary fervices both he and the empire had received from it, to the electoral dignity, fo early as the year 1692; but thofe electors obtained neither a feat nor a voice in the electoral college till the year 1708.

After thefe follow in rank the princes of the empire, who are partly fpiritual and partly temporal; partly old, and partly new, or firft raifed to that dignity fince the reign of Ferdinand II. The fpiritual princes are either archbifhops, bifhops, or princely abbots; and to them likewife belong the Teutonic mafters, together with the mafterfhip of the order of St. John. Among the temporal princes is an archduke, and the reft are either dukes, palfgraves, margraves, landgraves, burgraves, princes, or princely counts.

The diet of the empire is an affembly of the emperor, and of all the ftates, or their envoys and plenipotentiaries, in order to confult and take refolutions in fuch affairs as concern the whole German empire. The diet is fummoned by the emperor, who, after confulting with the electors, appoints the time and

place

VIENNA.

place where it shall meet, which must be within the German dominions. The emperor either assists at it in person, or has a principal commissary, who is generally an old imperial aulic counsellor, and a person of learning raised to the dignity of a baron.

The respective states may either appear themselves, or by their envoys; or charge another state, or its envoys, with their voice.

The states of the empire, in their consultations, divide into three colleges, the electoral, the princely, and the college of the imperial cities: each of the two first, which are called the higher colleges of the empire, has a principal and bye-chamber of its own; but all the three colleges meet to hear the imperial proposals, and at the exchanging of the conclusions of both the higher colleges against the imperial cities, in the hall of correlatives.]

The city of Vienna is not of itself very large; consisting only of twelve hundred and thirty-two houses; and a walk round the ramparts may be performed in little more than an hour. The number of its inhabitants, from exact computations, amounts to fifty thousand: but the suburbs, which extend between five and six hundred common paces from the fortifications, occupy a large space of ground; so that it would take four hours to ride round the line thrown up against the malecontents of Hungary in 1704, though this, on both sides, only extends to Leopoldstadt. If therefore the whole suburbs be included under the name of Vienna, the number of inhabitants will amount to between three hundred and three hundred and fifty thousand; of which the burials are annually about seven thousand. The streets in the city are very narrow and crooked. The imperial court has the privilege of quartering soldiers in the second story of each citizen's house; and as this is a great diminution of the proprietor's rents, beside the narrowness of the fronts, the citizens endeavour to make themselves amends by the height of the build-

buildings; so that the houses in Vienna are from six to seven stories high: one of these, in the square, called Ilof, has on one side seven stories, and on the other eight.

There are in Paris more magnificent houses than at Vienna, but the courts before them, and the gates, which are generally shut, greatly diminish their appearance. The palaces in Vienna are indeed generally hid, as it were, in narrow streets; but in stateliness and extent, they very far surpass those at Paris, especially if the grand structures in the suburbs are included.

A person of quality and fortune, who is fond of gaming, may here indulge that disposition to the full, and is sure of being received in all assemblies. But it is necessary, previously, to weigh the state of your purse, before you engage too far, as gaming is here carried to a very great height.

Beside the assemblies of the first nobility, here are many others, consisting of such persons as are not admitted into those of the best quality; for Vienna swarms with upstart noblemen, or with persons who give themselves out for such, though really they have no claim to nobility. As soon as a man becomes master of a fortune, his head is turned with the thoughts of a patent of nobility, and few set out with less than the title of a baron.

Among those who live most agreeably at Vienna, are the proctors or attornies of the imperial court of justice, some of whom acquire annually upward of ten thousand guilders, each equal to two shillings and four pence. Most citizens employ such an agent or attorney at the rate of twenty-four, to thirty guilders a year, for managing any processes; a nobleman thirty-six guilders. The Protestants are allowed the public exercise of their religion at the houses of the Swedish, Danish, and Dutch ambassadors; but they must take care not to meet a procession of the host, unless they think proper to pay the usual adoration.

The

VIENNA.

The imperial park, or paddock, called Prater, an iſland in the Danube, is much frequented in the ſpring for its pleaſant airy walks   The *Au-Garten* is open all the year, where the walks, hedges, and groves are ſo pleaſant, that it is generally frequented by perſons of diſtinction. Beſide the imperial riding-houſe, thoſe of the princes Schwartzenberg, Lichten-ſtein, Dietrickſtein, count Staremberg, and eſpecially that of count Paar in Aliter-ſtreet, are well worth ſeeing.

The trade of Vienna is little anſwerable to its largeneſs and convenient ſituation. This is partly owing to the heavy duties on moſt commodities brought hither, particularly thoſe on wine, oxen, and other proviſions coming out of Hungary. The eaſt-country company pay three per cent. for all they import, which has cauſed them to raiſe their prices conſiderably.

[Lady Montagu affords us the following entertaining particulars relating to this famous city.——

" We travelled by water from Ratiſbon, a journey perfectly agreeable, down the Danube, in one of thoſe little veſſels, that they, very properly, call wooden houſes, having in them all the conveniencies of a palace, ſtoves in the chambers, kitchens, &c. They are rowed by twelve men each, and move with ſuch an incredible ſwiftneſs, that in the ſame day you have the pleaſure of a vaſt variety of proſpects: and within the ſpace of a few hours, you have the pleaſure of ſeeing a populous city, adorned with magnificent palaces, and the moſt romantic ſolitudes, which appear diſtant from the commerce of mankind, the banks of the Danube being charmingly diverſified with woods, rocks, mountains covered with vines, fields of corn, large cities, and ruins of antient caſtles. I ſaw the great towns of Paſſau and Lintz, famous for the retreat of the imperial court, when Vienna was beſieged. This town, which has the honour of being the emperor's reſidence, did not at all anſwer my expectation, nor ideas of it, being much less than I expected to find it: the streets are very close, and so narrow, one cannot observe the fine fronts of the palaces, though many of them very well deserve observation, being truly magnificent. They are built of fine white stone, and are excessive high. For as the town is too little for the number of the people, who desire to live in it, the builders seem to have projected to repair that misfortune, by clapping one town on the top of another, most of the houses being of five, and some of them of six stories. You may easily imagine that, the streets being so narrow, the rooms are extreamly dark, and what is an inconveniency much more intolerable in my opinion, there is no house has so few as five or six families in it. The apartments of the greatest ladies, and even of the ministers of state, are divided, but by a partition, from that of a taylor or shoe-maker; and I know no body that has above two floors in any house, one for their own use, and one higher for their servants. Those that have houses of their own, let out the rest of them to whoever will take them, and thus the great stairs (which are all of stone) are as common and as dirty as the street. 'Tis true, when you have once travelled through them, nothing can be more surprisingly magnificent than the apartments. They are commonly a suite of eight or ten large rooms, all inlaid, the doors and windows richly carved and gilt, and the furniture such as is seldom seen in the palaces of sovereign princes in other countries. Their apartments are adorned with hangings of the finest tapestry of Brussels, prodigious large looking-glasses in silver frames, fine japan tables, beds, chairs, canopies, and window-curtains of the richest Genoa damask or velvet, almost covered with gold-lace or embroidery. All this is made gay by pictures and vast jars of japan China, and large lustres of rock crystal. I have already had the honour of being invited to dinner by several of the first people

of

of quality, and I muſt do them the juſtice to ſay, the good taſte and magnificence of their tables very well anſwer to that of their furniture. I have been more than once entertained with fifty diſhes of meat, all ſerved in ſilver, and well dreſſed; the deſſert proportionable, ſerved in the fineſt china. But the variety and richneſs of their wines, is what appears the moſt ſurpriſing. The conſtant way is, to lay a liſt of their names upon the plates of their gueſts along with the napkins, and I have counted ſeveral times, to the number of eighteen different ſorts, all exquiſite in their kinds.——I muſt own, I never ſaw a place ſo perfectly delightful as the Fauxbourg of Vienna. It is very large, and almoſt wholly compoſed of delicious palaces. If the emperor found it proper to permit the gates of the town to be laid open, that the Fauxbourgs might be joined to it, he would have one of the largeſt and beſt built cities in Europe.——

I have ſo far wandered from the diſcipline of the church of England, as to have been laſt Sunday at the opera, which was performed in the garden of the Favorita; and I was ſo much pleaſed with it, I have not yet repented my ſeeing it. Nothing of that kind ever was more magnificent; and I can eaſily believe, what I am told, that the decorations and habits coſt the emperor thirty thouſand pounds ſterling. The ſtage was built over a very large canal, and at the beginning of the ſecond act, divided into two parts, diſcovering the water, on which there immediately came, from different parts, two fleets of little gilded veſſels, that gave the repreſentation of a naval fight. It is not eaſy to imagine the beauty of this ſcene, which I took particular notice of. But all the reſt were perfectly fine in their kind. The ſtory of the opera is the enchantment of Alcina, which gives opportunities for great variety of machines and changes of the ſcenes, which are performed with a ſurpriſing ſwiftneſs. The theatre is ſo large that it is hard to carry the eye to the end of it, and the habits in the utmost magnificence, to the number of one hundred and eight. No house could hold such large decorations; but the ladies all sitting in the open air, exposes them to great inconveniencies: there is but one canopy for the imperial family; and the first night it was represented, a shower of rain happening, the opera was broke off, and the company crouded away in such confusion, that I was almost squeezed to death.——But if their operas are thus delightful, their comedies are, in as high a degree, ridiculous. They have but one play-house, where I had the curiosity to go to a German comedy, and was very glad it happened to be the story of Amphitrion. As that subject has been already handled by a Latin, French, and English poet, I was curious to see what an Austrian author would make of it. I understand enough of that language to comprehend the greatest part of it; and beside, I took with me a lady that had the goodness to explain to me every word. The way is to take a box, which holds four, for yourself and company. The fixed price is a gold ducat. I thought the house very low and dark; but I confess, the comedy admirably recompensed that defect. I never laughed so much in my life. It begun with Jupiter's falling in love out of a peep-hole in the clouds, and ended with the birth of Hercules. But what was most pleasant was the use Jupiter made of his metamorphosis; for you no sooner saw him under the figure of Amphitrion, but instead of flying to Alcmena, with the raptures Mr. Dryden puts into his mouth, he sends for Amphitrion's taylor, and cheats him of a laced coat, and his banker of a bag of money, a Jew of a diamond ring, and bespeaks a great supper in his name; and the greatest part of the comedy turns upon poor Amphitrion's being tormented by these people for their debts. Mercury uses Sosia in the same manner. But I could not easily pardon the liberty the poet has taken of larding his play with, not only indecent expressions, preffions, but fuch grofs words, as I do not think our mob would fuffer from a mountebank. Befide, the two Sofia's very fairly let down their breeches in the direct view of the boxes, which were full of people of the firft rank that feemed very well pleafed with their entertainment, and affured me this was a celebrated piece. I fhall conclude my letter with this remarkable relation, very well worthy the ferious confideration of Mr. Collier.

In order to go to court, continues lady Montagu, I was fqueezed up in a gown, and adorned with a gorget, and the other implements thereunto belonging, a drefs very inconvenient, but which certainly fhews the neck and fhape to great advantage. I cannot forbear giving you fome defcription of the fafhions here, which are more monftrous, and contrary to all common fenfe and reafon, than it is poffible for you to imagine. They build certain fabrics of gaufe on their heads, about a yard high, confifting of three or four ftories, fortified with numberlefs yards of heavy ribbon. The foundation of this ftructure is a thing they call a *bourlé*, which is exactly of the fame fhape and kind, but about four times as big as thofe rolls our prudent milk-maids make ufe of to fix their pails upon. This machine they cover with their own hair, which they mix with a great deal of falfe, it being a particular beauty to have their heads too large to go into a moderate tub. Their hair is prodigioufly powdered to conceal the mixture, and fet out with three or four rows of bodkins (wonderfully large) that ftick out two or three inches from their hair, made of diamonds, pearls, red, green and yellow ftones; that it certainly requires as much art and experience to carry the load upright, as to dance upon May-day with the garland. Their whalebone petticoats outdo ours by feveral yards circumference, and cover fome acres of ground. You may eafily fuppofe how this extraordinary drefs fets off and improves the natural uglinefs, with which God Almighty

Almighty has been pleafed to endow them, generally fpeaking. Even the lovely emprefs herfelf is obliged to comply, in fome degree, with thefe abfurd fafhions, which they would not quit for all the world. I had a private audience (according to ceremony) of half an hour, and then all the other ladies were permitted to come and make their court.—When the ladies were come in, fhe fat down to *quinze*. I could not play at a game I had never feen before, and fhe ordered me a feat at her right-hand, and had the goodnefs to talk to me very much, with that grace fo natural to her. I expected every moment, when the men were to come in to pay their court; but this drawing-room is very different from that of England; no man enters it but the grand mafter, who comes in to advertife the emprefs of the approach of the emperor. His imperial majefty did me the honour of fpeaking to me in a very obliging manner; but he never fpeaks to any of the other ladies, and the whole paffes with a gravity and air of ceremony that has fomething very formal in it.——I had an audience next day of the emprefsmother, a princefs of great virtue and goodnefs, but who piques herfelf too much on a violent devotion. She is perpetually performing extraordinary acts of penance, without having ever done any thing to deferve them. She fuffers her maids of honour to go in colours; but fhe herfelf never quits her mourning; and fure nothing can be more difmal than the mourning here, even for a brother. There is not the leaft bit of linen to be feen; all black crape inftead of it. The neck, ears, and fide of the face are covered with a plaited piece of the fame ftuff, and the face that peeps out in the midft of it, looks as if it were pilloried. The widows wear, over and above, a crape forehead-cloth; and in this folemn weed, go to all the public places of diverfion without fcruple.—

Her ladyfhip farther remarks, that " the two fects that divide our whole nation of petticoats, are utterly unknown

unknown in this place. Here are neither coquettes nor prudes. No woman dares appear coquette enough to encourage two lovers at a time. And I have not seen any such prudes, as to pretend fidelity to their husbands, who are certainly the best natured set of people in the world; and look upon their wives' gallants as favourably, as men do upon their deputies, that take the troublesome part of their business off their hands. They have not however the less to do on that account; for they are generally deputies in another place themselves; in one word, it is the established custom for every lady to have two husbands, one that bears the name, and another that performs the duties. And the engagements are so well known, that it would be a downright affront, and publicly resented, if you invited a woman of quality to dinner, without, at the same time, inviting her two attendants of lover and husband, between whom she sits in state with great gravity. The sub-marriages generally last twenty years together, and the lady often commands the poor lover's estate, even to the utter ruin of his family. These connexions, indeed, are as seldom begun by any real passion, as other matches; for a man makes but an ill figure that is not in some commerce of this nature, and a woman looks out for a lover as soon as she is married, as part of her equipage, without which she could not be genteel: and the first article of the treaty is establishing the pension, which remains to the lady, in case the gallant should prove inconstant. This chargeable point of honour, I look upon as the real foundation of so many wonderful instances of constancy. I really know several women of the first quality, whose pensions are as well known as their annual rents, and yet no body esteems them the less; on the contrary, their discretion would be called in question if they should be suspected to be mistresses for nothing. A great part of their emulation consists in trying who shall

get

get most; and having no intrigue at all is so far a disgrace, that I will assure you, a lady who is very much my friend here, told me but yesterday, how much I was obliged to her for justifying my conduct in a conversation relating to me; where it was publicly asserted, that I could not possibly have common sense, since I had been in town above a fortnight, and had made no steps toward commencing an amour. My friend pleaded for me that my stay was uncertain, and she believed that was the cause of my seeming stupidity, and this was all she could find to say in my justification. But one of the pleasantest adventures I ever met in my life, was last night, and it will give you a just idea, in what a delicate manner the belles passions are managed in this country. I was at the assembly of the countess of ———, and the young count of ——— leading me down stairs, asked me how long I was to stay at Vienna; I made answer that my stay depended on the emperor, and it was not in my power to determine it. Well, madam, said he, whether your time here is to be longer or shorter, I think you ought to pass it agreeably, and to that end you must engage in a little affair of the heart.— My heart, answered I gravely enough, does not engage very easily, and I have no design of parting with it. I see, madam, said he sighing, by the ill nature of that answer, I am not to hope for it, which is a great mortification to me that am charmed with you. But, however, I am still devoted to your service, and since I am not worthy of entertaining you myself, do me the honour of letting me know, whom you like best amongst us, and I will engage to manage the affair entirely to your satisfaction. You may judge in what manner I should have received this compliment in my own country; but I was well enough acquainted with the way of this, to know that he really intended me an obligation, and I thanked him with a very grave curtsey, for his zeal to serve me, and only assured him I had no occasion to make use of it.———

It

It is not from Austria that one can write with vivacity, and I am already infected with the phlegm of the country. Even their amours and their quarrels are carried on with a surprising temper, and they are never lively, but upon points of ceremony. There, I own, they shew all their passions; and it is not long since two coaches meeting in a narrow street at night, the ladies in them not being able to adjust the ceremonial of which should go back, sat there with equal gallantry till two in the morning: they were both so fully determined to die upon the spot rather than yield, in a point of that importance, that the street would never have been cleared till their deaths, if the emperor had not sent his guards to part them; and even then they refused to stir, till the expedient could be found out, of taking them both out in chairs, exactly in the same moment. After the ladies were agreed, it was with some difficulty that the pass was decided between the two coachmen, no less tenacious of their rank than the ladies. This passion is so omnipotent in the breasts of the women, that even their husbands never die, but they are ready to break their hearts, because that fatal hour puts an end to their rank, no widows having any place at Vienna. The men are not much less touched with this point of honour, and they do not only scorn to marry, but even to make love to any woman of a family not as illustrious as their own; and the pedigree is much more considered by them, than either the complexion or features of their mistresses. Happy are the shes that can number amongst their ancestors, counts of the empire; they have neither occasion for beauty, money, nor good conduct to get them husbands. It is true, as to money, it is seldom any advantage to the man they marry; the laws of Austria confine the woman's portion to two thousand florins, (about two hundred pounds English) and whatever they have beside, remains in their own possession and disposal.

Thus

Thus here are many ladies much richer than their husbands, who are however obliged to allow them pin-money agreeable to their quality; and I attribute to this considerable branch of prerogative, the liberty that they take upon other occasions.

If I should undertake to tell you all the particulars in which the manners here differ from ours, I must write a whole quire of the dullest stuff that ever was read, or printed without being read. Their dress agrees with the French or English in no one article, but wearing petticoats. They have many fashions peculiar to themselves; they think it indecent for a widow ever to wear green or rose colour, but all the other gayest colours at her own discretion. The assemblies here are the only regular diversion, the operas being always at court, and commonly on some particular occasions. Whenever they have a mind to display the magnificence of their apartments, or oblige a friend by complimenting them on the day of their saint, they declare, that on such a day the assembly shall be at their house in honour of the feast of the count or countess——such a one. These days are called days of Gala, and all the friends or relations of the lady, whose saint it is, are obliged to appear in their best cloaths and all their jewels. The mistress of the house takes no particular notice of any body, nor returns any body's visit; and whoever pleases, may go, without the formality of being presented. The company are entertained with ice in several forms, winter and summer; afterward they divide into several parties of ombre, piquett, or conversation, all games of hazard being forbid.

I saw the other day the Gala for count Altheim, the emperor's favourite; and never in my life saw so many fine cloaths ill fancied. They embroider the richest gold stuffs, and provided they can make their cloaths expensive enough, that is all the taste they shew in them. On other days the general dress is a scarf, and what you please under it.

But

VIENNA.

But now I am fpeaking of Vienna, I am fure you expect I fhould fay fomething of the convents; they are of all forts and fizes, but I am beſt pleafed with that of St. Lawrence, where the eafe and neatnefs they feem to live with, appears to me much more edifying than thofe ſtricter orders, where perpetual pennance and naſtineffes muſt breed difcontent and wretchednefs. The nuns are all of quality. I think there are to the number of fifty. They have each of them, a little cell perfectly clean, the walls of which are covered with pictures, more or lefs fine, according to their quality. A long white ſtone gallery runs by all of them, furnifhed with the pictures of exemplary fiſters; the chapel is extreamly neat and richly adorned. But I could not forbear laughing at their fhewing me a wooden head of our Saviour, which they affured me, fpoke, during the fiege of Vienna; and, as a proof of it, bid me remark his mouth, which had been open ever fince.

Nothing can be more becoming than the drefs of thefe nuns. It is a white robe, the fleeves of which are turned up with fine white callico, and their headdrefs the fame, excepting a fmall veil of black crape that falls behind. They have a lower fort of ferving nuns, that wait on them as their chamber-maids. They receive all vifits of women, and play at ombre in their chambers with permiffion of their abbefs, which is very eafy to be obtained. The grate is not one of the moſt rigid; it is not very hard to put a head through; and I do not doubt but a man, a little more flender than ordinary, might fqueeze in his whole perfon. The young count of Salamis came to the grate, while I was there, and the abbefs gave him her hand to kifs. But I was furprized to find here, the only beautiful young woman I have feen at Vienna, and not only beautiful but genteel, witty and agreeable, of a great family, and who had been the admiration of the town. I could not forbear fhewing my furprize at feeing a nun like her. She made a

thoufand

thousand obliging compliments, and desired me to come often. It will be an infinite pleasure to me, said she, sighing, but I avoid, with the greatest care, seeing any of my former acquaintance, and whenever they come to our convent, I lock myself in my cell. I observed tears come into her eyes, which touched me extreamly, and I began to talk to her in that strain of tender pity she inspired me with; but she would not own to me, that she is not perfectly happy. I have since endeavoured to learn the real cause of her retirement, without being able to get any other account, but that every body was surprised at it, and nobody guessed the reason. I have been several times to see her; but it gives me too much melancholy to see so agreeable a young creature buried alive. I am not surprised that nuns have so often inspired violent passions; the pity one naturally feels for them, when they seem worthy of another destiny, making an easy way for yet more tender sentiments. I never in my life had so little charity for the Roman catholic religion, as since I see the misery it occasions; so many poor unhappy women! and then the gross superstition of the common people, who are some or other of them, day and night, offering bits of candle to the wooden figures, that are set up almost in every street. The processions I see very often are a pageantry, as offensive and apparently contradictory to common sense, as the pagods of China. God knows whether it be the womanly spirit of contradiction that works in me, but there never, before, was such zeal against popery in the heart of, &c.]

The country about Vienna produces good pasture; and they begin to purchase cows from Switzerland, to stock some noblemen's estates in these parts. The hill, called Callenberg, affords a very beautiful prospect of the city of Vienna, and the places in its neighbourhood.

Baden, situated near Vienna, is as much frequented for its warm baths as for assemblies, and other diversions.

fions. Both fexes bathe here without diſtinction, in the fame bath, and at the fame time. The bathing frocks are made to cover the whole body: the womens have their heads elegantly dreſt, and leads are faſtened to the bottom of their petticoats to keep them down. The baths are chiefly recommended to patients in rheumatic pains, or lameneſs; pains in the joints, or other arthritic diſorders; barren women reſort hither and find relief.

Baden is three miles from Vienna. Before the cathedral is a fine monument dedicated to the holy Trinity. Thoſe kind of pillars are very ornamental to a city, and though ſeldom ſeen in other Roman catholic countries, are frequently found in the Auſtrian territories.

The imperial court generally refides in ſummer at the Favorita, in the ſuburbs of Wieden. This is indeed a more commodious palace than the imperial caſtle, the reſidence of the court during winter: but neither the building nor gardens are of a magnificence ſuitable to ſo great a prince. In hot and dry weather, the duſt raiſed by the horſes and carriages, between Vienna and the Favorita, would be ſcarcely ſupportable, were it not that a cart laden with water, by continually paſſing and re-paſſing, lays the duſt, by means of a leather pipe, ſo contrived as to ſprinkle the whole road with a gentle ſhower.

The fine weather and delightful ſeaſon induced me to make an excurſion into the neighbouring parts of Hungary, and ſhall communicate the following ſhort account of my journey. The diſtance from Vienna to Preſburg, is reckoned ten German miles, but in a poſt chaiſe is performed in ſeven or eight hours.

[Hungary, the antient Pannonia, received its preſent name from the Hungarians, a race of the Huns, a Scythian or Tartar nation, who in the ninth century took poſſeſſion of the country: but the Hungarians themſelves call it Magyar Orſzag: the Sclavonians give

give it the name of Wergierſka; by the Germans it is called Ungern, and Hungerland; and by the Italians Ungharia.

The name of Hungary is uſed both in a limited and extenſive ſenſe. In the former, this country is bounded on the ſouth by Servia and the river Drave, which ſeparates it from Sclavonia; on the eaſt by Walachia and Tranſylvania; on the north by the Carpathian mountains, which ſeparate it from Poland; and on the weſt by Moravia, Auſtria, and Stiria. But in its more extenſive ſenſe it comprehends Sclavonia, Dalmatia, Boſnia, Servia, and Tranſylvania, lying between the forty-fourth degree forty minutes, and the forty-ninth degree north latitude, and between the ſixteenth and twenty-fifth degree, fifty minutes eaſt longitude from London.]

The city of Preſburg lies on a plain. Its buildings are very mean, and its fortifications conſiſt only of a walk and ditch. The ſuburbs are chiefly on an eminence, and the caſtle on a hill; it is ſquare, and adorned with four towers. In the lower ſuburbs is a hill, famous on account of its being the place where the king of Hungary goes on horſeback, and brandiſhes his ſword toward the four cardinal points, to ſignify, that he is determined to protect his country againſt his enemies on every ſide.

The exchequer of Hungary is kept at Preſburg, but is under a kind of ſubordination to that of Vienna.

The ſeven royal free mine towns are Cremnitz, Konigſberg, Schemnitz, Neuſohl, Buggantz, Dullen and Libeton. Theſe mines are the ſupport of ſeveral thouſands, and the expence of working all of them amounts yearly to above a million of guilders.

Tokay is ſituated about thirty Hungarian, or ſixty German miles from Schemnitz, and is well known through all Europe for the excellency of its wine; but thoſe are miſtaken who affirm that the tract of land on which this wine grows is very ſmall, and produces yearly ſcarce a thouſand hogſheads; for all acquainted

with

with the country muft know, that the fpot of land which yields this generous liquor, is called in the Hungarian dialect, *hefy allya*, " the country under the " hills;" it contains above feven miles in circumference, and is interfperfed with feveral towns of equal or better fituation than Tokay itfelf. If all the wafte ground in this tract of land was cultivated, no part of Europe would be without Tokay wine, as it is not a proper liquor for common drinking. If a perfon purchafes a large quantity of Tokay wine, it is proper to carry it away in carriages drawn by Hungarian oxen, which will turn to very good account. The chief place for intelligence in thefe affairs is Cafchau.

Tokay lies in a fine country, and is pleafantly fituated; the mountains here not being fo fteep and craggy as about Crenitz and Schemnitz. That the air of a country abounding with hills and valleys is more falutary to the human body than that of a level country, is very evident, both from obfervation and hiftory.

The drefs of the women in the mine towns is not difagreeable; their fhifts are trimmed with ribbons, while others hang from their head-drefs down their backs; but the peafants and clowns are but meanly cloathed. The men are particularly fond of a furred cloak; and the women generally wear boots, and fome a long furred garment. Their fhifts are coarfe, and faftened round their waifts with a girdle. Their head-drefs is of linen, with two lappets hanging down behind. Blue is the moft ufual colour worn here by both fexes. There is fomething very manly in their drefs; and it muft be allowed that the cloaths of the Hungarian gentry are very becoming. The common people in Upper Hungary, fpeak very little of the true Hungarian language, but polite perfons in large towns fpeak Latin, German, or Sclavonian. The Latin fpoke by the vulgar is very indifferent, of which the huffars afford a fufficient fpecimen.

Six or seven thousand of the inhabitants of Schemnitz, which constitute two thirds of the city, are lutherans; but the magistrates are always Roman catholics. At Cremnitz, the magistracy is shared between the two religions, but no protestant is capable of any office in the imperial mines.

In Upper Hungary the protestants are very numerous, especially in the country; but in some places they are forcibly driven to the Romish churches like sheep.

Buda lies about twelve Hungarian miles from Schemnitz; and on the left hand of this road, is the town of Carpen, together with the mountain of the same name, so famous for being the supposed rendezvous of witches.

They divide the distance between Vienna and Prague, into twenty-one stages and a half, but there is beside the post road another, leading through Snoim, Iglaw, and Dzaslau, which is four miles shorter.

Bohemia is well peopled, and abounds in towns and villages. The state of Bohemia have been at the expence of above twenty-four thousand guilders for a correct map of that kingdom, which was at last executed by that famous engineer, John Christopher Muller.

Prague has broader streets but fewer stately palaces than Vienna. The bridge over the Molda, exceeds in length those of Ratisbon and Dresden; being seven hundred and forty-two paces long; and the breadth of it fourteen common paces: so that there is room for three carriages to pass a-breast. It is supported by sixteen pillars, and the sides are adorned with twenty-eight statues of saints. The crucifix, and the statue of St. Nepomuc are of brass; but the rest are all of stone. St. Nepomuc, who was thrown over this bridge by order of king Wenceslaus, for refusing to reveal what the queen had divulged to him at confession, is now become the patron of bridges, and by his
superior

superior merit, greatly leſſened the intereſt of all the other ſaints among the Bohemians.

In old Prague the jeſuits have one of the largeſt colleges belonging to their order, except thoſe of Liſbon and Goa. Two hundred and ten fathers of that order commonly reſide here. It is called Collegium Clementinium, from the church of St. Clement adjoining to it. In the tower of the Clementine college is an obſervatory, from which there is an elegant proſpect over the city. On the top of it is Atlas holding a large and curiouſly contrived armillary ſphere. In the church near the Trinhofe is the monument of Tycho Brahe, who has rendered his name immortal by his chemical proceſſes, and aſtronomical obſervations.

They ſhew here the apartment in the office belonging to the Bohemian ſecretary of ſtate, from which, in the year 1618, baron Slavata, great chancellor of the kingdom of Bohemia, baron Martinitz, grand marſhal, together with M. Platter, ſecretary of ſtate, were thrown headlong from a window, for warmly eſpouſing the intereſt of the houſe of Auſtria, contrary to the ſentiments of the majority. This apartment ſerves at preſent for the aſſembly of the ſtates. Theſe three noblemen had the good fortune of being received by a dunghill at the foot of the wall, and what is really ſurpriſing, they did not receive the leaſt hurt, notwithſtanding the window out of which they were thrown was twenty-eight ells or ſix ſtories from the ground; and ſecretary Platter is ſaid on this occaſion to have made a needleſs apology to the other two for his rudeneſs in falling upon them. I went down into the caſtle Moat to take a view of the place where they fell, and under a window which looks toward the city, I found in the bottom of the ditch overgrown with buſhes, a pedeſtal on which ſtands a quadrangular pyramid, terminating in a globe, and on that a crucifix. It was erected in memory of the eſcape of William Slavata, baron of Culm and Koſchemberg, who

who was thrown from the above window on the 23d of May 1618.

About four and twenty feet from this spot, under a window on the other side of the apartment near a common sewer, in a filthy situation, stands a triangular pyramid, inscribed on two of its sides with the words Jesus and Maria; and on the third an inscription to perpetuate the same accident.

In the treasury at Loretto is shewn a golden triangle set with a variety of rubies, on which is enameled the image of the virgin Mary; as crowned by the holy Trinity. This was the joint offering of Slavata, Martinitz and Platter, as a memorial of their wonderful preservation which they chiefly attributed to the virgin Mary.

The white tower is a state prison for persons of rank in Bohemia. Formerly in one of the rooms was a sort of iron machine in the shape of a woman, which, when any delinquent was brought near it, would embrace him with its arms, and squeeze him to death: some are of opinion, this machine has been removed to St. Peter's church, where the upper consistory is held, and particularly used for the execution of ecclesiastical criminals.

On the ratschin or castle-hill is the palace belonging to count Czernini, which in magnitude is indeed inferior to Wallenstein house on the lower side of the hill; but, with regard to the magnificence of the structure, and richness of the furniture, has few equals in the world. It has been almost a hundred years in building, and the grand hall is not yet finished. In a church opposite to this palace the Capuchins have erected a *casa santa* exactly resembling that at Loretto; the walls within like those of the original, are black and smoaky; but in some of the bas-reliefs on the outside a very great difference is perceived, those of the capuchin Casa Santa being only of Stucco, and those of Loretto of marble. The former are also greatly inferior to the latter in the beauty and delicacy of the work-

workmanship. The treasure amassed in this chapel is prodigious, amounting to several tons of gold.

In Prague are a hundred churches, and almost as many convents. The city is not very populous, in proportion to its extent; for the whole number of its inhabitants does not exceed one hundred and twenty thousand; fifty thousand of which are Jews, and seventy thousand Christians. The trade of this city is inconsiderable, the Moldaw not being navigable.

[Lady Montague writes thus from Prague.—" The kingdom of Bohemia is the most desert of any I have seen in Germany. The villages are so poor, and the post-houses so miserable, that clean straw and fair water are blessings not always to be met with, and better accommodation not to be hoped for. Though I carried my own bed with me, I could not sometimes find a place to set it up in; and I rather chose to travel all night, as cold as it is, wrapped up in my furs, than go into the common stoves, which are filled with a mixture of all sorts of ill scents.

This town was once the royal seat of the Bohemian king, and is still the capital of the kingdom. There are yet some remains of its former splendour, being one of the largest towns in Germany, but, for the most part, old built and thinly inhabited, which makes the houses very cheap. Those people of quality who cannot easily bear the expence of Vienna, chuse to reside here, where they have assemblies, music, and all other diversions, (those of a court excepted) at very moderate rates; all things being here in great abundance, especially the best wild fowl I ever tasted. I have already been visited by some of the most considerable ladies, whose relations I know at Vienna. They are dressed after the fashions there, in the manner that the people at Exeter imitate those of London; that is, their imitation is more excessive than the original. It is not easy to describe what extraordinary figures they make. The person is so much lost between head-dress and petticoat, that they have as much occasion to write upon their backs, " This is a woman," for the information of travellers, as ever sign-post painter had to write, " This is " a bear."]

The distance between Prague and Dresden is sixteen German Miles.

Dresden has been long famous for its royal palaces, straight and uniform streets, beautiful situation, and splendid court; but with regard to the number of houses and inhabitants, is inferior to several cities in Germany. The houses in the suburbs and city are computed at about two thousand five hundred, and the inhabitants of Old and New Dresden are said not to exceed forty thousand, above five thousand of which at present are papists. But in this computation the garrison is not included.

The place which affords the greatest entertainment to a curious stranger, is the Green-Room, or Museum. This collection was begun by the elector, and placed in a green room, which name it still retains. Several apartments are, indeed, at present, green; but the disposition is now greatly altered, and the number of curiosities so far increased, that the Museum consists of seven rooms and a cabinet. The fee for seeing this Museum is generally discharged with four or five guilders, given to the attendant who opens the doors.

The palace is magnificently furnished, and the drawing-rooms particularly are worth seeing.

In the year 1711, a beautiful edifice, designed for a green-house, was begun in the Zwinger garden; but as another place appeared more convenient for that purpose, it was converted into an inestimable repository of medals, natural curiosities, antiquities, minerals, petrifactions, rare animals, insects, shells, amber of various kinds. In this structure is also a library, together with an anatomy room, in which are

a cola collection of all inftruments relating to furgery, chemiftry, metallurgy, geometry, aftronomy, mathematics, mechanics, and botany.

The royal Gardens are adorned with above fifteen hundred ftatues; the modern pieces, which are of white marble, are difpofed in various parts; but the antiques depofited in a palace erected in the center of the garden.

The arfenal is faid to contain arms for a hundred thoufand men, together with fifteen hundred brafs cannon; among which the field-pieces are the fmalleft. Here are two large mortars, called Romulus and Remus, fent hither as a prefent from the elector of Brandenburg, which throw bombs of five hundred pounds.

The Japanefe palace, near the white gate in old Drefden, was formerly a feat of count Fleming's; but purchafed by his majefty for a hundred thoufand dollars, by which the count got twenty thoufand dollars. The quantity of porcelain, both foreign and made here, is immenfe. The veffels for culinary ufes only are valued at a million of dollars. In one of the upper ftories are forty-eight vafes of blue and white China, which the king of Poland purchafed of the king of Pruffia for a whole regiment of dragoons. One room is full of porcelain, faid to be painted by Raphael. The red porcelain made here, that ftrikes fires, is now ordered to be antiquated, in order to enhance its value. But the whole procefs of making it is defcribed in writing, and depofited in fome fecret place. The manufactory of common porcelain is carried on near Drefden; but the moft valuable fpecies is made at the caftle of Meiffen. Botticher, the firft inventor of the porcelain, died in the year 1719. A ftate-bed, together with fome chairs formed out of beautiful feathers of different colours, and which coft thirty thoufand dollars, are to be feen in the Japanefe palace.

The Turkifh garden and palace are in Plau-ftreet. The firft floor of this palace is decorated with great variety of pieces of painting, reprefenting the ceremonies

monies in the Turkish Seraglio, together with the baths and audience-room; a prospect of St. Sophia's church, and several habits worn by the Turks in general, especially those worn by the great officers of state.

At the king's country seat, at Neustadt-Oftra, are fourteen tame stags, which draw a carriage, and one is broke for the saddle. They set out briskly, but are apt to flag very soon. There is also a white stag; and one with two brandished horns growing on the right side of his head, together with some Indian stags.

[Lady Montague describes the city of Dresden as " the neatest I have seen in Germany; most of the houses are new built; the elector's palace is very handsome, and his repository full of curiosities of different kinds, with a collection of medals very much esteemed.——The Saxon ladies resemble the Austrian, no more than the Chinese do those of London; they are very genteelly dressed after the English and French modes, and have, generally, pretty faces, but they are the most determined *minaudieres* in the whole world. They would think it a mortal sin against good breeding, if they either spoke or moved in a natural manner. They all affect a little soft lisp, and a pretty *pitty pat* step; which female frailties ought, however, to be forgiven them in favour of their civility and good nature to strangers, which I have a great deal of reason to praise."]

Not far from Dresden, in the road to Plauen, is a mill for cutting and polishing jasper. Near this mill some cart-loads of Saxon jasper are still to be seen; but the work is now discontinued, and the mill used in polishing looking-glasses. In the first story they are ground, and in the second polished. The water puts thirty-eight of these machines in motion, and two or three of the smaller glasses are placed under several of them. The whole management requires but a few hands, and is far better contrived than the looking-glass manufacture at Paris. John Mechior Dillinger,

KONIGSTEIN.

Dillinger, who, by several works in the royal Museum, has rendered his name immortal, is one of the most ingenious artists of this city. He had even young children by five wives. When the Czar, Peter the Great, was at Dresden, in the year 1712, he chose to lodge at Dillinger's house, with whose contrivances he was so delighted, that he ordered a model of his house to be made in wood, and sent into Russia, as a perfect specimen of a commodious dwelling.

The Dresden, or rather Meissen porcelain, is famous all over Europe; and produces a very advantageous trade. Wood and timber is another considerable article carried on at Grimma. A great quantity of paper is also made in Saxony, particularly at Dresden, Zwickam, Pforta, Freyberg, Kirchberg, Tannenberg, and Luntzenau; and exported by means of the Elbe. Liebenwirda, Dippoldiswolda, Waldenburg, and Wurtren, carry on a considerable trade in earthen ware; but this, as well as other branches, might be improved, were not all the vessels on the Elbe obliged to pay toll at two and thirty places between Perna and Hamburg. Musea, Torgaw, Wurtzen, Eulinburg, and Merseburg, are remarkable for excellent beer.

They have several linen manufactures in many towns of Saxony; and an advantageous trade is carried on with Hamburg in canvas and sail-cloth, and the returns from thence are drugs, wine, butter, herrings, and dried fish.

Fort Konigstein is so remarkable for its uncommon situation, that I could not deny myself the pleasure of visiting it. Pirna lies about a German mile from Pillnitz, and in it is the castle of Sonnenstein, used as a prison for persons of distinction, but neither remarkable for architecture or fortifications.

The distance from Pirna to Konigstein is a long German mile, and without a written order from the governor at Dresden no person is admitted into this castle. It is situated on a rock, cut so steep that it

appears

appears quite perpendicular; and the fort in many places has projections, or baftions, which command the fide of the rock. The afcent toward Drefden is the leaft difficult; but well fortified and defended with three batteries of cannon. Wood and other luggage are drawn up to the fort by the help of cranes. The garrifon confifts of a hundred and fifty men only; but, on the firft alarm from the governor, the villages are obliged to furnifh fome hundreds more. Konigftein is always furnifhed with provifions for twenty-fix years; and on the top is a fine meadow, a wood, and feveral gardens, in which are thirty-eight different kinds of fruit and foreft trees. It requires half an hour to walk round the ramparts, and travellers are always fhewn the place from whence a fhoemaker of Drefden, when a child, fell down the rock, without receiving any hurt. The fortrefs is furnifhed with five cifterns, or fmall refervoirs for preferving rain or fnow water, and in them feveral kinds of fifh, for the governor's ufe. The water ufed by the garrifon is drawn up by a wheel from a well, whofe depth is nine hundred Drefden ells. Forty years were fpent in finking this well before a fufficient quantity of water could be obtained. I obferved, that when a pitcher of water was poured down the well, it was exactly five and forty feconds before it reached the furface of the water. It is always kept clean and in good repair, for which purpofe general Kyaw, though no water drinker, contrived a machine for letting workmen down to the bottom of the well. But this is not the only monument he has left behind him; a large cafk was finifhed at Konigftein, in the year 1725, by his direction, fixteen ells in length, and its diameter at the bung twelve, and at the ends eleven ells. It confifts of a hundred and fifty-feven ftaves, eight inches thick, and the two heads of fifty-four pieces. Each head weighs feventy-feven hundred and feventy pounds. The cafk is at prefent filled with good Meiffen wine, amounting to upward of fix thoufand
quintals,

quintals, which coſt above forty thouſand dollars (or 6000 l. ſterl.) reckoning the quart of wine only at four Groſchen, or 3 d. ½ d Engliſh money. Before this caſk was conſtructed, the Heidelberg tun was reckoned the largeſt in the world; but according to the common computation, this of Konigſtein contains ſix hundred and forty-nine hogſheads more than that of Heidelberg.

The top of the caſk is railed round, and affords a room for fifteen or twenty perſons. Here alſo is a variety of welcome-cups, which are offered to thoſe who are fond of ſuch honours. The vault where the Konigſtein caſk is depoſited, as in a temple of Bacchus, is contiguous to the church.

Leipſick, is famous both on account of its trade, and noble univerſity. The civility of the inhabitants, the ſplendor of its buildings, and the charming gardens with which it is ſurrounded, render it far ſuperior to many capital places.

In the univerſity library are a great number of Greek and Ruſſian books; and more manuſcripts of Malabar, written on the leaves of palm trees, than in any library in Europe. In a particular apartment is a repreſentation of the two ſolar ſyſtems of Tycho and Copernicus, with all the viſible ſtars. Each of theſe armillary ſpheres are ten feet in diameter. The maker of them was Mr. Semler, miniſter of St. Ulrich's in this city.

The exchange is a beautiful ſtructure, and the cieling of the great hall elegantly painted. The Appel gardens are planted with a variety of yew trees, and ornamented with ſtatues, water-works and canals, and in one of the latter a Bucentaurus. In a ſtructure near theſe gardens is a manufacture of velvet, and of gold and ſilver tiſſue.

The diſtance between Leipſick and Halle is five German miles. It was originally only a village, called Dobreſol, or as the peaſants ſtill pronounce it Dicbreſala, brefala, which fignifies good falt, there being rich falt fprings at Halle.

Being defirous of acquiring fome further knowlege in metals, I determined to go from Halle to Eifliben, where, before the war, the copper works were in fuch condition, that above thirty fmelting houfes were erected in the country between Mansfelt and Eifliben. Thefe generally produced above a thoufand tons of copper in a year, and every hundred weight of copper contained ten or twelve ounces of filver.

Eifliben is the native place of Luther, and among other reliques of that famous reformer, his wooden bedftead is fhewn here. In the confiftorial chamber at Eifliben, is a print of Luther, faid to have been wonderfully preferved in a fire, that happened at Artern; but if the fire at that place fpared Luther's picture, it fhewed no refpect to the houfe at Eifliben, where he was born, which was totally confumed. However, that the memory of it might not be buried in oblivion, a fchool has been built on the fpot, and over the door is placed a buft of Luther. Above the chamber door ftands a ftatue of him, holding a crucifix in his hand.

Weimer is diftant from Iena about two German miles, fituated in a pleafant country, and in a valley near the Ilme. With regard to the palace of Wilhemfburg, only the Corps de Logis, and one of the wings are finifhed; but when compleated will make a noble appearance. The old caftle near it, before which is a wooden bridge, is called the Red Palace. The duke's library has been much augmented with the choiceft books that could be procured. The cabinet of medals, among which is the moft valuable collection of Saxon coins, was purchafed of count Haugwits, grand marfhal to the elector of Saxony.

The diftance between Weimar and Erfurt is three German miles. The whole piece of land between Iena and Gotha is fo pleafant, and fo finely cultivated;

that if all Thuringen was equal to this part, it might juftly be reckoned among the fineft provinces in Germany. A more delightful and convenient fituation can hardly be found in the empire, than that of Erfurt, and the great number of fteeples in that city give it a grand appearance. The river Gora flows in rivulets through moft of its ftreets. The number of houfes do not exceed twelve thoufand.

A thoufand men are in the garrifon of Erfurt, confifting of five hundred of the troops of the elector of Mentz, and a battalion of Imperialifts. In the road to Gotha is a fort called Cyriacfburg. The citadel of Erfurt or Peterfberg is fortified in the modern manner.

On a bridge over the Gera is a ftone, marked with a wheel, faid to be the center of the city, near which is fhewn the houfe of the famous Dr. Fauftus. Gotha is three German miles from Erfurt; the city lies in a valley, but the duke's palace ftands on an eminence. It was anciently called Grimmenftein, which name, after the troublefome times, under duke John Frederick, was changed to Friedenftein.

The mufeum at Gotha contains feveral remarkable curiofities; particularly feveral onyxes of divers kinds, wrought into various figures, and fet in feveral pieces of work, to the value of fixty thoufand dollars.

Befide the ducal palace, Frederickfthal for entertainments and affemblies is worth feeing.

The diftance between Gotha and Garnftadt is three German miles. The latter is fituated in a level and fruitful country. Near it the river Gera turns a mill or machine for grinding of corn; and is at prefent farmed for two thoufand guilders a year.

The road from Ilmenaw to Schluffingen lies through part of the foreft of Thuringen. No grain, except oats, grows here; but this is compenfated by the great plenty of wood. Here are many iron works, and the vaft quantities of wood prove of the utmoft
advantage

advantage in smelting the ore. Several sulphur mines are also found here, and in different parts glass-houses are erected. At Mannebach are slate quarries which prove of considerable advantage to the country. In the slates are often found impressions of fish and plants.

The distance between Coburg and Bamberg is six German miles; the road runs through a pleasant valley, watered by the Itch. It will be necessary first to make some observations on the margraviate of Bareith, before I proceed to describe the difficult road over the mountains.

The margraviate of Bareith particularly abounds with marble of various colours, beyond any other province of Germany. From Schwarzenbach in the forest, or near Preseck, is dug a grey sort of marble, with yellow spots, which shine like metal. In the parts about Ilof in Voigtlande, they have a red, black, and grey sort: some pieces of the last are variegated with red spots like drops of blood. Green marble is dug at Naila, yellow at Sheitberg, and various kinds at Lichtenberg near Heerwagen, as also at Gold-Cronach.

In the city of Bareith there is nothing remarkable enough to attract a traveller's notice. The hermitage not far from hence, built by the late marcgrave, has beautiful grottos, and excellent marble sculptures.

The road from Bareith over Hollfeld to Bamberg is mountainous and stony, though not near so bad as that over Streitberg to Erlang. The lovers of petrefactions may, in all these parts, find a great variety of such curiosities.

The city of Bamberg, which was formerly called Babenberg or Pfaffenberg, lies in a delightful and fertile country. The clergy seem to have been good judges of the fruitful spots in a country; for we seldom meet with a religious foundation which is not possessed of some of the best land in the whole province where it stands. Bamberg abounds in all sorts

NURENBERG.

of garden vegetables, fruit, grain, and wine; but especially in liquorice, which is exported to moſt parts of Europe.

Under the juriſdiction of the republic of Nurenberg, beſide the capital, are four other towns, namely, Altdorf, Herſbruck, Lauff, and Graffenberg in the upper palatinate, and alſo above five hundred villages. In the city of Nurenberg are a hundred and twenty eight capital ſtreets, and four hundred ſmaller; and it is adorned with twelve large, and a hundred and thirty-three ſmall fountains, beſide a hundred and ſeventeen wells. This city alſo contains ſixteen churches, and forty-four religious houſes; twelve bridges, ten market places, three hundred and ſixty-five towers on the city-walls, twenty-one thouſand houſes, and twenty-five thouſand families. You cannot eaſily walk round it in leſs than three hours. I will not, however, pretend to aſſert that this computation is abſolutely true, eſpecially with regard to the number of villages, houſes, and inhabitants. The Regnitz, which runs through this city, drives about a hundred and ſixty mills in the territory of Nurenberg. It is the opinion of ſome that Nurenberg is the centre both of Germany and Europe.

Of what importance the trade carried on by the Nurenbergers in former times was to Italy, appears both from the privileges the German houſe ſtill enjoys, and the reſpectful letter ſent by the doge and ſenate of Venice to Nurenberg, when the former was under very great difficulties in the year 1509. The trade indeed is at preſent greatly below its former flouriſhing condition, and continually decreaſing from that carried on by three other towns, namely Erlang, Schwobach, and Furth; one third of the laſt belongs to the city of Nurenberg, another to the Marcgrave of Anſpuck, and the other to the chapter of the cathedral of Bamberg. But notwithſtanding all this, Nurenberg is ſtill famous for its manufactures, which are exported to all parts of the known world: and

VOL. V.   S   though

though the toys called Nurenberg ware seem of little importance, the annual profit arising from them amounts to a hundred thousand dollars: and in the year 1728, the Nurenberg company sold as many toys in Constantinople only, as came to more than seventeen thousand guilders.

The council of this city has always two presidents, who continue in their office four weeks only, when they are succeeded by four others. It consists of twenty-four burgomasters, eight elders, who, like the former, are of the Patrician order, and eight masters of companies; but the last are only summoned when any extraordinary deliberations are on the carpet.

Nurenberg has, for many centuries, had the honour of keeping the most valuable part of the imperial crown jewels, together with the reliques belonging to them. The jewels are deposited in a separate apartment, and the whole shewn only to princes and counts of ancient families.

Some time since, a society was formed at Nurenberg, under the name of the Pegnitz academy, with a view of improving and refining the German language and poetry. Their scheme was not the best concerted, so that at present, though the Pegnitz society still subsists, they have made so small a progress in the undertaking, that they seldom meet.

The best performers in vocal music generally hold their meetings on festivals, and perform even in private houses for a small fee. Music flourishes greatly in Nurenberg.

Conversation with the fair sex is under much greater restraint in Nurenberg, than in most other large cities; a stranger is hardly permitted to see them in their private assemblies; and even the natives of the place, unless particular friends, are not admitted.

It is now some years since a good porcelain manufactory has been established in this city.

Those

Those who delight in mechanic arts and manufactures, may here abundantly gratify their curiosity. It is now some centuries since the Nurenberg artists have been classed among the best in Germany; and, indeed, to exhibit the merits of this city, in promoting and improving useful knowlege of all kinds, would afford matter for a large volume.

[From lady Montagu we derive the following remarks relating to this city.——" I have, says she, already passed a large part of Germany, have seen all that is remarkable in Cologn, Frankfort, Wurtsburg, and this place. It is impossible not to observe the difference between the free towns, and those under the government of absolute princes, as all the little sovereigns of Germany are. In the first there appears an air of commerce and plenty. The streets are well built, and full of people, neatly and plainly dressed. The shops are loaded with merchandize, and the commonalty are clean and chearful. In the other you see a sort of shabby finery, a number of dirty people of quality tawdered out; narrow nasty streets out of repair, wretchedly thin of inhabitants, and above half of the common sort asking alms. I cannot help fancying one, under the figure of a clean Dutch citizen's wife, and the other like a poor town lady of pleasure, painted, and ribboned out in her head-dress, with tarnished silver-laced shoes, a ragged under-petticoat, a miserable mixture of vice and poverty.——They have sumptuary laws in this town, which distinguish their rank by their dress, prevent the excess which ruins so many other cities, and has a more agreeable effect to the eye of a stranger, than our fashions. I need not be ashamed to own, that I wish these laws were in force in other parts of the world. When one considers impartially, the merit of a rich suit of cloaths in most places, the respect and the smiles of favour it procures, not to speak of the envy and the sighs it occasions (which is very often the principal charm to the wearer) one is forced to confefs, that there is need of an uncommon underftanding to refift the temptation of pleafing friends, and mortifying rivals; and that it is natural to young people to fall into a folly, which betrays them to that want of money, which is the fource of a thoufand bafeneffes. What numbers of men have begun the world with generous inclinations, that have afterward been the inftruments of bringing mifery on a whole people, being led by a vain expence into debts that they could clear no other way, but by the forfeiture of their honour, and which they never could have contracted, if the refpect the multitude pays to habits, was fixed by law, only to a particular colour, or cut of plain cloth. Thefe reflections draw after them others that are too melancholy. I will make hafte to put them out of your head by the farce of relics, with which I have been entertained in all Romifh churches.

The Lutherans are not quite free from thefe follies. I have feen here, in the principal church, a large piece of the crofs fet in jewels, and the point of the fpear, which, they told me very gravely, was the fame that pierced the fide of our Saviour. But I was particularly diverted in a little Roman Catholic church which is permitted here, where the profeffors of that religion are not very rich, and confequently cannot adorn their images in fo rich a manner as their neighbours: for not to be quite deftitute of all finery, they have dreffed up an image of our Saviour over the altar, in a fair full-bottomed wig, very well powdered. I imagine I fee your ladyfhip ftare at this article, of which you very much doubt the veracity: but, upon my word, I have not yet made ufe of the privilege of a traveller."] ·

The diftance between Nurenberg and Ratifbon is twelve German miles, the laft eight miles of which is very craggy and uneven. A mile on this fide of Ratifbon we croffed the Naab, and a little beyond it afcended a fteep hill, from which we had a fine prof-

RATISBON.

pect over the vaſt plain on which Ratiſbon is ſituated. This free imperial city contains five different ſtates within its circuit, viz. the cathedral of Ratiſbon, the imperial abby of St. Emmeran, the lower minſter, the upper minſter, and the city itſelf. This ſee is immediately ſubject to the pope, without acknowleging any metropolitan. In the cathedral are buried ſeveral biſhops of Ratiſbon; and on the right-hand, in the cathedral, a wooden crucifix as big as life, the hair of which the credulous vulgar believe continues growing.

The city of Ratiſbon has a good library belonging to it in the council-houſe, but contains more books in the civil than municipal law.

The bridge over the Danube was begun in 1135, and compleated in eleven years. It conſiſts of free ſtone, reſting on piles of oak, driven to a conſiderable depth in the bed of the river. The length of this bridge is four hundred and ſeventy common paces, or a thouſand and ninety-one feet; and conſiſts of fifteen arches. It is commonly ſaid of the three principal bridges in Germany, that Dreſden bridge is the fineſt, that of Prague the longeſt, and that of Ratiſbon the ſtrongeſt. The juriſdiction of the city of Ratiſbon reaches no further than the end of the bridge; and the town of Amhoff, on the other ſide of the river, belongs to the elector of Bavaria.

The envoys at Ratiſbon, as repreſentatives of electors, have very lofty ideas of their office and dignity, and aſſume ſuch ſtate, that when the widow of duke Frederic Henry of Saxe-Zeitz, a princeſs of the houſe of Holſtein Wickfenburg, came to pay a viſit to the cardinal of Saxe-Zeitz her brother-in-law, her highneſs could but very ſeldom appear in public, becauſe the ladies of the electoral envoys took the precedency of her. The electoral envoys were alſo for taking the right-hand of a Bavarian prince, and likewiſe of a prince of the houſe of Wittenberg. If ſovereign princes of Germany attend at the diet themſelves, they

they sit in the college, above all the envoys of princes; but the envoys of Austria, Burgundy, and Saltsburg have, by prescription, exempted themselves from this rule, and always maintained the precedency, so that the Holstein envoys never assist at the college when a session is held.

The envoys indeed regulate their conduct by the instructions of their respective courts: however, cases may happen, in which favour may be shewn to a party, even contrary to such instructions; namely, when it is agreed with other envoys to acquiesce in the majority of voices, from which the envoys are not often willing to dissent. Several envoys from princes of the empire are directed to conform to the vote of the Austrian envoy.

From the great number of representatives, and their different talents, it is easy to imagine that a proper secrecy in the diet is not always observed. The secretaries are indeed neither admitted into the next rooms, nor at the conferences of the evangelic body; yet the transactions in both are soon known.

It is a question with some, whether the continual sitting of a diet be advantageous or not to the emperor and the empire: for my own part, I cannot see why it may not be answered in the affirmative. The emperor's minister is always maintaining, that the advantages are wholly on the side of the Germanic body, and that the charges of the diet to the house of Austria amount to upward of a hundred thousand dollars a year. But it is evident, that it is no less for the emperor's advantage, as otherwise he must, on every occasion, be obliged, at a very great expence, to send an envoy to every court, of whose assistance he may, on any emergency, stand in need: beside, it would be hardly possible for the small states of Germany to defend themselves against the great and potent houses. Perhaps one or two of the most powerful states might find their account in the dissolution of the diet, but the general good of the Germanic

manic body would inevitably suffer by it; and the consequence would be no other than absolute anarchy.

Foreigners can never be at a loss for amusements at Ratisbon, as they have free access to the canonese's daily assemblies, and a great variety of entertainments. Those gentlemen, who are fond of gaming, will also meet with persons here ready to gratify their disposition; for it is not unknown how far an immoderate passion for this diversion has carried some Ratisbon ladies. As the states of the empire, who send envoys to the diet are very numerous, and as every court sends fresh instructions to its respective envoys when any new affair comes on the tapis, the envoys, amidst so many vacations or adjournments of the diet, cannot be said to have a very fatiguing employment.

[Lady Montagu's account of Ratisbon cannot but prove agreeable. She says that—" All the nobility of this place are envoys from different states. Here are a great number of them, and they might pass their time agreeably enough, if they were less delicate on the point of ceremony. But instead of joining in the design, of making the town as pleasant to one another as they can, and improving their little societies, they amuse themselves no other way, than with perpetual quarrels, which they take care to eternize, by leaving them to their successors: and an envoy to Ratisbon receives, regularly, half a dozen quarrels among the perquisites of his employment. You may be sure the ladies are not wanting, on their side, in cherishing and improving these important piques, which divide the town almost into as many parties as there are families. They chuse rather to suffer the mortification of sitting almost alone on their assembly nights, than to recede one jot from their pretensions. I have not been here above a week, and yet I have heard from almost every one of them, the whole history of their wrongs, and dreadful complaints of the injustice of their neighbours;

bours; in hopes to draw me to their party. But I think it very prudent to remain neuter, though if I was to stay amongst them, there would be no possibility of continuing so, their quarrels running so high, that they will not be civil to those that visit their adversaries. The foundation of these everlasting disputes, turns entirely upon rank, place, and the title of excellency, which they all pretend to, and what is very hard, will give it to no body. For my part, I could not forbear advising them (for the public good) to give the title of excellency to every body, which would include the receiving it from every body; but the very mention of such a dishonourable peace was received with indignation. And indeed I began to think myself ill-natured, to offer to take from them, in a town where there are so few diversions, so entertaining an amusement. I know that my peaceable disposition already gives me a very ill figure, and that it is publicly whispered as a piece of impertinent pride in me, that I have hitherto been saucily civil to every body, as if I thought no body good enough to quarrel with. I should be obliged to change my behaviour, if I did not intend to pursue my journey in a few days. I have been to see the churches here, and had the permission of touching the relics, which was never suffered in places where I was not known. I had, by this privilege, the opportunity of making an observation, which I doubt not might have been made in all the other churches, that the emeralds and rubies which they shew round their relics and images, are most of them false; though they tell you that many of the crosses and madonas, set round with these stones, have been the gifts of emperors and other great princes. I do not doubt indeed but they were at first jewels of value; but the good fathers have found it convenient to apply them to other uses, and the people are just as well satisfied with bits of glass amongst these relics. They shewed me a prodigious claw set in gold,

which

which they called the claw of a griffin; and I could not forbear asking the reverend priest that shewed it, whether the griffin was a saint? The question almost put him beside his gravity; but he answered, they only kept it as a curiosity. I was very much scandalized at a large silver image of the Trinity, where the Father is represented under the figure of a decrepid old man, with a beard down to his knees, and triple crown on his head, holding in his arms the Son, fixed on the cross, and the Holy Ghost, in the shape of a dove, hovering over him."]

There is an odd custom which prevails at the peasants weddings in the villages about Ratisbon. When the bridesman, at the conclusion of the ceremony, attends the bridegroom from the altar to the pew, he pulls him by the hairs, and gives a box on the ear, to remind him of the exhortation of the priest, with regard to the duty he owes to his wife, and make him remember the marriage contract.

The distance between Ratisbon and Ingolstadt is five post stages, and the road lies all the way through a fine plain. Ingolstadt is remarkable for the beauty of its buildings, its strait broad streets, and, among Roman Catholics, for the university founded there.

Neuburg, the capital of the dutchy of the same name, is a league and a half from Ingolstadt. It is a handsome town, pleasantly situated, and contains the ducal palace, particularly remarkable for a fine hall.

Two miles from Donawerth lie Hochstadt and Blenheim; places which will never be forgotten, on account of the victory obtained in 1704, by the confederates over the united armies of the French and Bavarians. But the field of battle is destitute of any monument whatever.

Several medals were struck on this occasion; but the noblest monument which ever any general could boast of, was erected at the public expence, to the duke of Marlborough; namely, Blenheim house, six English

English miles from Oxford; which is said to have cost the English nation upward of a million sterling.

Krailsheim is a Post town of Anspach, and remarkable on account of the dean's library. The country of Anspach is fertile, where, by erecting more manufactories, the Zaubel wool might be employed to very great advantage, being extremely fine and soft, and of it are made hats and stockings. This wool grows on a small sort of sheep, which are shorn twice a year, and also yean every spring and autumn. They often bring two lambs at a time, but these are apt to degenerate. Their flesh is fatter, and better tasted than that of another kind bred here, called Flemish sheep, which yield a long coarse wool; but at the same time are more hardy than the Zaubel sort; the latter being so tender, that they are never left in the open air during the night. There is, indeed, no venturing with safety, any flocks in the fields all night, on account of the great number of wolves which harbour in the neighbouring woods. Though several of these animals have been destroyed, yet they are not suffered to be entirely extirpated, that the great men of the country may not be deprived of the pleasure of wolf hunting.

The imperial city of Heilbrunn derives its name from an excellent spring, which by means of seven conduits supplies it with water: but at present it is not used medicinally, though it still retains its character for extraordinary purity. The emperor Charles V. attributed his recovery from a fit of illness, in the year 1547, to the use of this spring: this event is commemorated by a monument on the house belonging to the prelates of Scopthal, but at present occupied by the post-master.

Formerly the women of Heilbrunn, by way of mourning, wore on their heads a sort of horn, made of black cloth, about a span in length. I not only observed such a figure engraved on a pillar in the church,

church, but a few years ago I met with some old women here, who still retained this fashion. This custom may easily be deduced from the Germans of the most remote antiquity, an erect horn denoting joy, as an inverted one was the emblem of sorrow.

The city of Heidelberg is very delightfully situated on the Neckar; and, as the palace stands on an eminence, the prospect from it over the valley toward Schwetzingen cannot be exceeded. This palace was almost entirely destroyed by the French, in the year 1693; and indeed, with such outrageous barbarity, that even the electoral burying place was not spared, but the bodies, half decayed, thrown about the streets, some of the inhabitants having concealed themselves in the old ruinous tombs. The Palace consists of several bui'dings joined together, some of which are in a good taste, and of beautiful sculpture. To the disgust conceived by the present elector against this city, because they would not give him an absolute grant of the church of the Holy Ghost, is owing, that little furniture is to be seen in this palace, beside some old and capital family pictures; and that he removed his court to Manheim and Schwezingen; the latter of which is too small for that purpose, and except a beautiful orangery, has nothing to recommend it.

The famous Heidelberg tun was repaired in the year 1727, and beautified with a variety of ornaments. At present it is full of wine, and is said to contain two hundred and four tons: on the top it is flat, and railed round, so that several persons may dine and walk about on it. This huge cask was first made in the year 1664, by order of the elector Charles Lewis; and some idea may be formed of its bulk from the iron hoops round it, which are 110 hundred weight.

The electoral territories on the Lower Rhine, namely Juliers, Bergue, and Ravenstein, yield an annual revenue of nine hundred thousand guilders;
and

and the like sum accrues from the provinces of the Upper Rhine, exclusive of the large produce arising from the management of the ecclesiastical lands; and the taxes in the provinces, both of the Upper and Lower Rhine, are nearly equal, and amount annually to a million of guilders: and the remaining revenues are expended in paying the troops, and for other exigencies of state.

About two leagues from Heidelberg, the Bergstrasse or mountain road begins, and extends as far as Darmstadt; but the last part of this Road is from Heidelberg to Bensheim, the length of which is eight leagues. The top of the continued chain of hills and mountains on the right-hand, is covered with woods, and more toward the plain with vineyards. The level road is planted with rows of walnut-trees, and on both sides are very fruitful fields and meadows. Some writers call the mountain road the Priest's-seat; as the Popish Clergy have always had the sagacity to pitch on the best spots to reside on; however, in several places of the Palatinate, this selfishness of the clergy has not had the intended effect, and they have been obliged to content themselves with what they could get.

Manheim lies about four leagues from Weinheim, and at the same distance from Heidelberg. It is situated in a low valley, and is one of the most beautiful cities in all Germany. All the streets are constructed in straight lines intersecting one another at right angles; so that there are streets or vistos at each corner but symmetry, uniformity, and proportion, have not been duly observed in the houses.

The unwholesomness of the air, and badness of the water, are great detriments to this place; but these inconveniencies have been in some measure redressed, by conveying water from the Neckar. Persons of distinction, however, have their water from Heidelberg, both for drinking and culinary uses; which

water

water was formerly fold at Manheim for a croutzer per quart.

The elector palatine claims a privilege from an ancient patent granted by the emperor, of the property of the Rhine; and therefore ftiles himfelf hereditary governor of the Rhine. He alfo affumes the title of *Dominus Rheni & Nicri*, or lord of the Rhine and Neckar; and as fuch allows no Wittemberg boats or other veffels to come higher than Hilbron upon that river. There are now at Manheim fome pretty yachts and other veffels belonging to the elector. He alfo appoints an admiral of the palatinate, which poft was lately held by the Duterfen.

The fource of the Rhine is in the country of the Grifons, and is divided into Upper, Lower, and Middle Rhine; the latter iffues from the mountain of St. Maria, the Upper has its fource in the mountains of Crifpalt, and the lower Rhine is formed by the mountains of Adula, near the Vogelberg, and rifes originally from the ice hills or mountains, which are above a German mile over.

They dig copper and iron near the Marine, befide great quantities of filver; and from the fand gather gold duft. The gathering of gold is one of the royalties belonging to the elector palatine.

Franckfort lies three German miles from Darmftadt. The road between thefe two cities is for the moft part fandy.

The fairs held at Franckfort are famous all over Europe; and fome dealers, who are competent judges, have affured me, that ten million of dollars would hardly purchafe the merchandife in the warehoufes, and thofe expofed to fale in the fair. Franckfort fairs exceed thofe of Leipfick, though the latter, by reafon of the fmallnefs of the town, make a greater appearance. The yearly revenue of the city of Frankfort is computed at fix hundred thoufand guilders.

Among

Among the curiosities of this city, the chief, worth a stranger's notice, is the *azure bulla*, or golden bull. It is kept in the town-house in a tortoise-shell box, set with mother of pearl, and lined with yellow velvet. The book itself is very much soiled, but an ample description of it is to be found in Thulemacius.

The bridge over the Maine, from Franckfort to Sachsenhausen, is four hundred and fifty common paces in length.

The hasel-tree in Mr. Haffel's garden in this city, mentioned by the Franckfort chronicles above two hundred years ago, is worth observation. The lower part of the trunk measures seven Franckfort ells in circumference; its height is equal to the houses near it; and it bears nuts every year. The shells of the nuts it produces are very thick, but have the same flavour with others. The emperor Leopold dined twice under this tree. The soil of the garden must be particularly favourable to hasel-trees; for though the adjacent ground yields only common shrubs, four hasel trees, planted within these fifteen years, are above twenty feet high already. These recruits are substituted as the above-mentioned old tree begins to decay.

Though I did not visit Mentz in this tour, yet as I formerly had an opportunity of viewing this city, I am unwilling entirely to omit it, as a traveller may find here many particulars worthy his notice. The high street is strait, wide, and well built; being adorned with a beautiful fountain, near which is a sumptuous palace, built by two brothers of the name of Dalberg.

The elector's palace contains nothing remarkable; but the Favorita is a modern edifice, and for its situation, the prospect over the Rhine and Maine, the architecture, and the disposition of the gardens, which are adorned with pyramids, statues, cascades, and other water-works, is a most elegant and delightful place.

From

From Manheim I vifited Landau, five German miles from the former. It is fituated in a low plain, and the morafs before the German or Manheim gate, is a good defence. On the other fide, namely, without the French gate, are very ftrong out-works, excellently contrived for the defence of each other. Landau, at the beginning of this century, was three times taken on this fide; in the fourth and laft fiege, however, the French made the greateft efforts on the fide of the Manheim gate. This fortification was planned by Vauban; and round it are feven baftions, which confift of two ftories, and a platform on the top, fo that they form three batteries. In order to defend any breaches that may happen to be made, every baftion has alfo its counter-guard.

In my journey between Landau and Luneville, I met with nothing remarkable. The roads are bad as far as Weiffenburg, where you enter on the caufeway. This town is fituated in a fpacious valley, but its fortifications are old and ruinous. Hagenau is larger and better fortified, but its buildings are irregular. The parts about Saverne are very pleafant, being planted with rows of trees; and as the cardinal de Rohan often refides here in his new palace, he has cut feveral avenues through the woods, both for his own diverfion, and that of ftrangers who delight in hunting. A little beyond Saverne we afcended a fteep mountain, at the top of which is an infcription in the rock, importing that this road, which before was impracticable for carriages, was thoroughly compleated in the year 1616, after a good deal of trouble.

Before the year 1702, Luneville was a mean place; but the French, at the beginning of this century, thinking it neceffary to garrifon Nancy, the late duke of Lorrain, in order to remove all fufpicion that the emperor might entertain of his partiality, withdrew to Luneville, and there built a palace, at which he
refided

resided every summer: but about thirteen years ago, great part of this edifice was destroyed by fire, which, however, in a short time rose, like the phœnix, more beautiful from its ashes.

Popery is the predominant, and indeed the only religion tolerated in the dominions of the duke of Lorrain; and such care is taken to support it, that whatever subject of Lorrain is convicted of turning Protestant, though chargeable of no other crime, is condemned to death.

The distance between Luneville and Nancy is about five leagues, and the post-horses are changed at St. Nicolas, a small town much frequented by pilgrims, on account of some reliques of St. Nicolas, bishop of St. Mire.

Nancy is situated in a fine plain, about half a league from the river Meortie, and consists of the old and new city. In the latter, the streets are broad, straight, and well built. The roofs of the houses, according to the customs of this country, are so flat, that you may walk upon them. In the old city, the oblong area, or broad street before the palace, makes a good appearance. The fortifications were demolished to gratify the French, and nothing now remains of them but the walls and some bastions. This city was restored to the duke of Lorrain, in this defenceless state, at the treaty of Ryswick, on condition that the duke shall not fortify Nancy, nor any other place, without the consent of the French king.

TRAVELS
THROUGH
FRANCE,
BY
SACHEVEREL STEVENS, Gent.

Interspersed with the Remarks of later Travellers.

BEFORE we enter France with Mr. Stevens, it will be proper to premise a few words of general description of that large and famous kingdom.

France obtained its present name from the Franks, who in the fifth century passed out of Germany into Gaul, and made themselves masters of the whole country, from the Rhine to the mouth of the Loire. This kingdom is bounded by the British channel, and the Netherlands, toward the north; on the east by Germany, Swisserland, and Italy; on the south by the Mediterranean sea, and Spain, from which it is separated by the Pyrenean mountains; and on the west by the Atlantic ocean: extending from 43° to 51° of north latitude, and from 4° west to 7° east longitude. Did not the province of Bretagne extend itself above an hundred miles farther into the ocean than any other part of the kingdom, it would be nearly of a square form, and the breadth and length almost equal, that is, about five hundred and forty miles; but allowing for the hills and valleys, with the winding of the roads, it would in a traveller's account be above six hundred miles over either way.

The air of this country is mild and wholesome, particularly the interior parts of the kingdom. The winters,

winters, however, in the northern provinces are cold, and last four or five months. Indeed the cold is in that season generally much severer there than in England; for we being surrounded by the sea are less subject to continued frosts, and are beside better provided with firing. They have, however, the advantage of clear settled weather, and are but little troubled with those fogs, which are so disagreeable in Great Britain and other countries. The summers in France are hotter than with us.

France, with respect to its situation, has the advantage of every kingdom in Europe, the seas which border upon it affording the inhabitants an easy communication with the rest of the world; the northern shores being washed by the British channel, the western coast by the Atlantic ocean, and the south by the Mediterranean. Hence no country can be better situated for the advancement of trade and navigation.

The chief mountains of France are the Alps toward Italy, the Pyrenees, which border on Spain, and those of the Cevennes and Auvergne. It is extremely well watered with navigable rivers, the chief of which are the Loire, the Rhone, the Garonne, and the Seine. Of these the Loire is the largest.

The country of France is in general fertile, yet has many barren tracts and mountains. In some parts it produces plenty, and in all of them a sufficiency of the necessaries of life. In plentiful years it yields more corn than is necessary for the subsistence of the inhabitants; but a bad harvest is generally succeeded by a scarcity: and in war-time there has been often a great dearth of grain, which is the more felt in this country as bread is the principal food of the inhabitants.

This kingdom enjoys great plenty of wine, which is produced in all its provinces. Among the several French wines, that of Champagne is reckoned the best, it being a good stomachic, racy, and in taste and flavour exquisite, with an agreeable tartness. That

of

of Burgundy, the beſt of which is produced about Beaume, has a fine colour, and a pleaſant taſte. The wines of Angers and Orleans are alſo delicate, but a little heady. In Poiƈtou is produced a white wine that reſembles Rheniſh. The neighbourhood of Bourdeaux and the lower parts of Gaſcony produce excellent wines. Pontac grows in Guienne. Muſcadel and Frontiniac are the delicious products of Languedoc. Between Valence and St. Valliere, along the banks of the Rhone, is produced a very agreeable, but roughiſh red wine that has a taſte not unlike that of bilberries; it is named hermitage, and is eſteemed for its wholeſomeneſs.

The territories for oil of olives are Provence and Languedoc. Theſe and other provinces produce ſaffron, and the northern parts in particular have large orchards, and make great quantities of cyder, which is there the common drink of the inhabitants. Bourdeaux exports great quantities of prunes, and capers are principally produced in the country about Toulon. Flax and hemp thrive in ſeveral parts of the kingdom; but linſeed is produced only in the north. Moſt of the provinces abound in wool, and ſilk is cultivated with great induſtry, eſpecially in Languedoc, Provence, Lionnois, and Dauphiné; and, during all the time in which the inhabitants attend on the ſilk-worms, public prayers are offered up for the proſperity of thoſe uſeful inſects.

France alſo produces horned cattle, ſheep, and hogs; but they are neither ſo numerous, nor in general ſo fat and fleſhy as thoſe of Great Britain.

The title of the king is Lewis XV. by the grace of God king of France and Navarre. The title of ſire or lord, is given him by his ſubjects, as a mark of his unlimited power; and foreigners ſtile him the Moſt Chriſtian king, or his Moſt Chriſtian majeſty; but the king's ſubjects are not to make uſe of it. Since the year 1359, when Hubert count Dauphin of Viennois, united his country to the crown of France,

France, the king's eldest son, and presumptive heir to the crown, has been stiled Dauphin.

According to French writers their king never dies, but as soon as his eyes are closed, the next prince of the blood succeeds to the throne, and is instantly invested with the supreme authority: but where the king is a minor, that is, before he has entered the fourteenth year of his age, the administration of the government is entrusted to a regent, usually the queen-mother, or a prince of the blood, according to the determination of the parliament of Paris; in which the rest of the kingdom generally acquiesce. But if the deceased king has appointed a regent by his will, that is seldom disputed. By a law termed the salique law, the crown of France can never be enjoyed by a woman.

When a new king enters into his fourteenth year, he goes in great state to the parliament of Paris, attended by the princes of the blood, the peers, and general officers of state. This assembly is generally called his bed of justice, and here he is declared to be of age; yet the regent frequently procures himself to be constituted prime minister, and under that title still continues to govern the kingdom till his majesty thinks fit to take the reins of government into his own hands.]

I arrived at Bologne, says Mr. Stevens, on the 15th of September 1738, but to my no small mortification, we were obliged to anchor at least half a league from the shore, till the next morning, when the tide being low, we had no opportunity of reaching the harbour: a boat from the town approached the ship, and though we were then not above a mile from the shore, asked a crown each person to carry us to land, which unreasonable demand was refused; but another boat made toward us, and for one shilling each carried us to Bologne, where we were slightly searched.

The inhabitants, efpecially the women, as I paffed along the ftreets to my inn, feemed to make a grotefque appearance. Inftead of a cloak, they wore a piece of black cloth, which covered their head and fhoulders, and fome had it hanging down to the waift: the people in general wore wooden fhoes.

This city is the capital of the Boulonnois, and is fituated at the mouth of the river Liane, which forms the harbour. It has delightful public walks, which, as the town is feated on a hill, affords an agreeable profpect of the fea. The cathedral church is dedicated to the virgin Mary, and has a fine ftatue of her, to which the inhabitants pay the profoundeft adoration: it is of folid filver, and placed in a fmall chapel behind the choir, finely ornamented with a great number of filver lamps. There are alfo feveral convents for the reception of perfons of both fexes, moft agreeably fituated, and adorned with paintings; but the city is very indifferently built. In the afternoon I reached Montreuil, a ftrong fortified town, fituated on a hill; but the private buildings are very indifferent.

[Dr. Smollet writes thus from Bologne.—" The cuftom-houfe officers at Bologne, though as alert, are rather more civil than thofe on your fide of the water. I brought no plate along with me, but a dozen and a half of fpoons, and a dozen tea-fpoons: the firft being found in one of our portmanteaus, when they were examined at the bureau, coft me feventeen livres *entreé:* the others being luckily in my fervant's pocket, efcaped duty free. All wrought filver imported into France, pays at the rate of fo much per mark: therefore thofe who have any quantity of plate, will do well to leave it behind them, unlefs they can confide in the dexterity of the fhip-mafters; fome of whom will undertake to land it, without the ceremony of examination. The ordonnances of France are fo unfavourable to ftrangers, that they oblige them to pay at the rate of five per cent. for all the

the bed and table linen which they bring into the kingdom, even though it has been used. When my trunks arrived in a ship from the river Thames, I underwent this ordeal: but what gives me more vexation, my books have been stopped at the bureau; and will be sent to Amiens at my expence, to be examined by the *chambre syndicale*; lest they should contain something prejudicial to the state, or to the religion of the country. This is a species of oppression which one would not expect to meet with in France, which piques itself on its politeness and hospitality: but the truth is, I know no country in which strangers are worse treated, with respect to their essential concerns. If a foreigner dies in France, the king seizes all his effects, even though his heir should be upon the spot; and this tyranny is called the *droit d'aubaine*, founded at first upon the supposition, that all the estate of foreigners residing in France was acquired in that kingdom, and that, therefore, it would be unjust to convey it to another country. If an English protestant goes to France for the benefit of his health, attended by his wife, or his son, or both, and dies with effects in the house to the amount of a thousand guineas, the king seizes the whole, the family is left destitute, and the body of the deceased is denied christian burial. The Swiss, by capitulation, are exempted from this despotism, and so are the Scots, in consequence of an ancient alliance between the two nations. The same *droit d'aubaine* is exacted by some of the princes in Germany: but it is a great discouragement to commerce, and prejudices every country where it is exercised, to ten times the value of what it brings into the coffers of the sovereign."—

The Doctor makes the following sarcastical remarks on the people here. — " The inhabitants of Bologne may be divided into three classes; the noblesse or gentry, the burghers, and the canaille. I do not mention the clergy, and the people belonging to the law. The noblesse are vain, proud, poor, and slothful.
Very

Very few of them have above six thousand livres a year, which may amount to about two hundred and fifty pounds sterling; and many of them have not half this revenue. The nobless have not the common sense to reside at their houses in the country, where, by farming their own grounds, they might live at a small expence, and improve their estates at the same time. They allow their country-houses to go to decay, and their gardens and fields to waste; and reside in dark holes in the Upper Town of Bologne, without light, air, or convenience. There they starve within doors, that they may have wherewithal to purchase fine cloaths, and appear dressed once a day in the church, or on the rampart. They have no education, no taste for reading, no housewifery, nor indeed any earthly occupation, but that of dressing their hair, and adorning their bodies. They hate walking, and would never go abroad, if they were not stimulated by the vanity of being seen. I ought to except indeed those who turn devotees, and spend the greatest part of their time with the priest, either at church, or in their own houses. Other amusements they have none in this place, except private parties of card-playing, which are far from being expensive. Nothing can be more parsimonious than the œconomy of these people: they live upon soupe and bouillé, fish and sallad: they never think of giving dinners, or entertaining their friends; they even save the expence of coffee and tea, though both are very cheap at Bologne. They presume that every person drinks coffee at home, immediately after dinner, which is always over by one o'clock; and, in lieu of tea in the afternoon, they treat with a glass of sherbet, or capillaire. In a word, I know not a more insignificant set of mortals than the nobless of Bologne; helpless in themselves, and useless to the community; without dignity, sense, or sentiment; contemptible from pride, and ridiculous from vanity. They pretend to be jealous of their rank, and will entertain

entertain no correspondence with the merchants, whom they term plebeians. They likewise keep at a great distance from strangers, on pretence of a delicacy in the article of punctilio: but, as I am informed, this statelinefs is in a great measure affected, in order to conceal their poverty, which would appear to greater disadvantage, if they admitted of a more familiar communication. Considering the vivacity of the French people, one would imagine they could not possibly lead such an insipid life, altogether unanimated by society, or diversion. True it is, the only profane diversions of this place are a puppet-show and a mountebank; but then their religion affords a perpetual comedy. Their high masses, their feasts, their processions, their pilgrimages, confessions, images, tapers, robes, incense, benedictions, spectacles, representations, and innumerable ceremonies, which revolve almost incessantly, furnish a variety of entertainment from one end of the year to the other. If superstition implies fear, never was a word more misapplied than it is to the mummery of the religion of Rome. The people are so far from being impressed with awe and religious terror by this sort of machinery, that it amuses their imaginations in the most agreeable manner, and keeps them always in good humour. A Roman catholic longs as impatiently for the festival of St. Suaire, or St. Croix, or St. Veronique, as a school-boy in England for the representation of punch and the devil; and there is generally as much laughing at one farce as at the other. Even when the descent from the cross is acted, in the holy week, with all the circumstances that ought naturally to inspire the gravest sentiments, if you cast your eyes among the multitude that croud the place, you will not discover one melancholy face: all is prattling, tittering, or laughing; and ten to one but you perceive a number of them employed in hissing the female who personates the virgin Mary.—
The

The bourjeois of this place seem to live at their ease, probably in consequence of their trade with the English. Their houses consist of the ground-floor, one story above, and garrets. In those which are well furnished, you see pier glasses and marble slabs; but the chairs are either paultry things, made with straw-bottoms, which cost about a shilling a-piece, or old-fashioned, high-backed seats of needle-work, stuffed very clumsy and incommodious. The tables are square fir boards, that stand on edge in a corner, except when they are used, and then they are set upon cross legs that open and shut occasionally. The king of France dines off a board of this kind. Here is plenty of table-linen however. The poorest tradesman in Bologne has a napkin on every cover, and silver forks with four prongs, which are used with the right hand, there being very little occasion for knives; for the meat is boiled or roasted to rags. The French beds are so high, that sometimes one is obliged to mount them by the help of steps; and this is also the case in Flanders. They very seldom use feather-beds; but they lie upon a *paillasse*, or bag of straw, over which are laid two, and sometimes three matrasses. Their testers are high and old-fashioned, and their curtains generally of thin bays, red, or green, laced with taudry yellow, in imitation of gold. In some houses, however, one meets with furniture of stamped linen; but there is no such thing as a carpet to be seen, and the floors are in a very dirty condition. They have not even the implements of cleanliness in this country. If there is no cleanliness among these, much less shall we find delicacy, which is the cleanliness of the mind. Indeed they are utter strangers to what we call common decency; and I could mention some high-flavoured instances, at which even a native of Edinburgh would stop his nose. There are certain mortifying views of human nature, which undoubtedly ought to be concealed as much as possible, in order to prevent giving offence: and

and nothing can be more abfurd, than to plead the difference of cuftom in different countries, in defence of thofe ufages which cannot fail of giving difguft to the organs and fenfes of all mankind. Will cuftom exempt from the imputation of grofs indecency a French lady, who shifts her froufy fmock in prefence of a male vifitant, and talks to him of her *lavement*, her *medicine*, and her *bidet*? An Italian fignora makes no fcruple of telling you, fhe is fuch a day to begin a courfe of phyfic for the pox. The celebrated reformer of the Italian comedy introduces a child befouling itfelf on the ftage, OE, NO TI SENTI? BISOGNA DESFASSARLO, *(fa cenno che fentefi mal odore.)* I have known a lady handed to the houfe of office by her admirer, who ftood at the door, and entertained her with *bons mots* all the time fhe was within. But I fhould be glad to know whether it is poffible for a fine lady to fpeak and act in this manner, without exciting ideas to her own difadvantage in the mind of every man who has any imagination left, and enjoys the entire ufe of his fenfes, howfoever fhe may be authorifed by the cuftoms of her country? There is nothing fo vile or repugnant to nature, but you may plead prefcription for it, in the cuftoms of fome nation or other. A Parifian likes mortified flefh: a native of Legiboli will not tafte his fifh till it is quite putrefied: the civilized inhabitants of Kamfchatka get drunk with the urine of their guefts, whom they have already intoxicated: the Nova Zemblians make merry on train-oil: the Groenlanders eat in the fame difh with their dogs: the Caffres, at the Cape of Good Hope, pifs upon thofe whom they delight to honour, and feaft upon a fheep's inteftines as the greateft dainty that can be prefented. A true bred Frenchman dips his fingers, imbrowned with fnuff, into his plate filled with ragout: between every three mouthfuls, he produces his fnuff-box, and takes a frefh pinch, with the moft graceful gefticulations; then he produces his handkerchief,

kerchief, which may be termed the flag of abomination, and, in the use of both, scatters his favours among those who have the happiness to sit near him. It must be owned, however, that a Frenchman will not drink out of a tankard, in which, perhaps, a dozen of filthy mouths have slabbered, as is the custom in England. Here every individual has his own gobelet, which stands before him, and he helps himself occasionally with wine or water, or both, which likewise stand upon the table. But I know no custom more beastly than that of using water-glasses, in which polite company spirt and squirt, and spue the filthy scourings of their gums under the eyes of each other. I knew a lover cured of his passion, by seeing this nasty cascade discharged from the mouth of his mistress.

The common people here, as in all countries where they live poorly and dirtily, are hard-featured, and of very brown, or rather tawny complexions. As they seldom eat meat, their juices are destitute of that animal oil which gives a plumpness and smoothness to the skin, and defends those fine capillaries from the injuries of the weather, which would otherwise coalesce, or be shrunk up, so as to impede the circulation on the external surface of the body. As for the dirt, it undoubtedly blocks up the pores of the skin, and disorders the perspiration; consequently must contribute to the scurvy, itch, and other cutaneous distempers."]

The road for great part of the way to Abbeville is extreamly delightful, it extending several miles thro' an avenue of fine spreading trees. The last-mentioned city is seated on the river Somme, and appears to be strongly fortified. There are three draw-bridges over broad and deep moats before you can enter the town. Here is a large manufacture of woollen stuffs, and several churches and convents, in some of which are tolerable paintings. But though it is a handsome

well-

well-built town, our accommodations were very indifferent, and the wine exceeding bad.

Between Abbeville and Beauvais is a fine open champaign country, extreamly fertile, and abounding with hares, that frifk and play by the fide of the road, which is for the moſt part paved. This city is one of the beſt I had ſeen in France: I reckoned up twelve churches, chiefly in the Gothic taſte; one of them, called St. Peter's, is a noble building, and the choir is moſt beautifully and richly ornamented. The market-place is ſpacious and neat, and the town enjoys a fine ſituation on the river, amidſt ſeveral pleaſant villages, country-houſes, and delightful vineyards, that form on the whole a moſt agreeable proſpect.

I by this time was become fully ſenſible of the badneſs of the inns in general on this road, and of the impoſing diſpoſition of the people, who are ready to take all advantages of ſtrangers, but more eſpecially of the Engliſh, whom they imagine to be made of money.

From Beauvais I proceeded through a pleaſant road to St. Dennis, which has a moſt magnificent cathedral, where the royal family of France are interred, and a famous collection of curioſities; but being deſirous to reach Paris, I did not ſtay to ſee them. The road to Paris, which is about ſix miles diſtant, is broad and well paved, with a row of fine ſpreading trees on each ſide, forming an agreeable viſta.

I arrived at Paris on the 25d of September, at about four in the afternoon, entering through the gate of St. Dennis, which reſembles an ancient triumphal arch, and is beautifully adorned with baſſo relievos, repreſenting the victories of Lewis XIV. It ſeems to be full ſixty feet high, and almoſt as broad. At this gate your chaiſe will be ſtopped by officers, who will want to ſearch your baggage, and
have

have it in their power to give you a great deal of trouble; but by making them a prefent of half a crown, and ordering your fervants to treat them with extraordinary complaifance, they will give you but little interruption.

On paffing through the above gate you enter the Rue St. Dennis, which is long, and almoft as broad as Fleet-ftreet; the houfes are high, and make a good appearance, and the ftreet is well paved; but at night is only lighted by lanthorns hung upon cords in the middle of the ftreet, with a fmall candle burning in each. As I did not underftand French, I on my firft arrival boarded and lodged in a private family on reafonable terms, where I had a mafter to inftruct me, and made a refolution not to vifit any of my countrymen, till I had made a fufficient progrefs in the language.

The firft place I went to fee was the royal hofpital of the invalids, in the quarter called St. Germain's, where the Englifh generally refide. This celebrated hofpital was founded by Lewis XIV. and is fituated near the river Seine, almoft oppofite to the Tuilleries, or royal gardens. It is built of ftone, and confifts of five handfome quadrangles, in which 7000 difabled foldiers are faid to be lodged, and decently maintained after the manner of the Chelfea penfioners. The middle fquare is very grand, and almoft as large as all the other four. They are furrounded with piazzas and galleries; on the walls are painted fome of the battles of Lewis XIV. and in the principal apartments are feveral valuable pictures. The new church adjoining to it is efteemed the fineft piece of architecture in all Paris. The front is ftately, and adorned with columns and pilafters of the Doric and Corinthian orders; the dome is finely painted, and round it on the infide are fix chapels, in each of which is the ftatue of a faint of white marble.

I next vifited the chapel of St. Sulpice, and it happening to be a feftival of that faint, it was richly

hung

hung and illuminated with a multitude of lamps and wax candles: the high altar, which is generally covered, was expofed to public view, moſt ſplendidly decorated with precious ſtones: near it ſtood a ſilver ſtatue of the virgin Mary as big as the life. The windows of this church are finely painted.

From hence I went to the cathedral of Notre Dame, a magnificent Gothic ſtructure, that very much reſembles Weſtminſter abbey. It is ſupported by above a hundred lofty pillars, and againſt one of them is built the repreſentation of a rock, upon which is a caſtle, with the ſtatue of St. Chriſtopher of a gigantic ſize. The high altar is compoſed of fine Egyptian marble, and near it is an image of the virgin Mary, with Chriſt lying dead on her knees: this is allowed to be a maſter-piece. On one ſide is the ſtatue of Lewis XIII. and on the other that of his ſon Lewis XIV. both in a poſture of adoration. There are alſo ſeveral large figures of angels, ſaid to be of ſilver. At the weſt end of this ſtructure are two towers, and in the middle ſtands a ſpire, which appears too ſmall for ſo noble an edifice. The front is adorned with the ſtatues of ſeveral of the kings of France.

At a ſmall diſtance is the hoſpital called the Hotel Dieu, or the houſe of God, in which patients are attended with the greateſt care and tenderneſs by nuns, who diſcharge the office of nurſes. To the honour of this hoſpital, all manner of patients are admitted, without regard to country, religion, or diſeaſe, and no ſecurity is required for their burial in caſe of death; nor are thoſe who labour under any incurable diſeaſe ever diſcharged and ſuffered to periſh in the ſtreets.

In St. Anthony's ſtreet is a church belonging to the jeſuits, that has a very magnificent altar: on one ſide of it ſtands a large ſilver image of an angel, with its arm extended, and holding in its hand a golden caſe in the ſhape of a heart; on the other ſide ſtands another angel in the ſame poſition: but what is moſt extraordinary, within theſe golden hearts are the real ones

ones of Lewis XIII. and XIV. This church is a neat and elegant modern ſtructure.

The palace of the Tuilleries adjoins to the Louvre, near the river ſide: the gardens are large and finely laid out. They are viſited by the quality, and all who wear a black bag and a ſword are permitted to walk here, though all their other apparel may not be worth a crown. Here is a fine terrace-walk of a conſiderable length, from whence you have a proſpect of a part of the town, the river Seine, and the adjacent country. Here are alſo ſeveral baſons, fountains and fine ſtatues. The palace is a magnificent ſtructure, and ſtands ſo near the Louvre, that a ſtranger may eaſily miſtake them for one place: this was doubtleſs the original intention of the builder, and had it been finiſhed, it would have formed the largeſt, and perhaps the moſt beautiful ſtructure in the univerſe.

Though the city hath ſeveral bridges, yet only three of them are worth notice. The Pont Neuf, or new bridge, is a very fine one, adorned with an equeſtrial ſtatue of Henry IV. on a very handſome pedeſtal, which at the corners have ſome braſs ſtatues. This bridge is compoſed of twelve arches, and on each ſide is a foot-path, on which are ſeveral ſtalls or ſmall ſhops; but in the evening they are obliged to be taken down. This bridge affords a fine proſpect of the Louvre, Notre Dame, and all that part of the town; and near the end of it toward the Louvre, is the curious fountain of the Samaritan, ſo called from the ſtatues of our Saviour and the Samaritan woman placed upon it. Except Weſtminſter-bridge, to which this is certainly inferior, I think this is the nobleſt bridge I ever ſaw.

The water of the river Seine generally looks green and dirty, which is not to be wondered at, as it is commonly filled with covered barges full of waſherwomen cleaning their linen: yet it is carried in pails through the ſtreets, and ſold as milk is in London. I cannot here help remarking, that the French wo-

men

men are the worst laundresses in Europe: they wash their linen in cold water in the river, and as to ironing and plaiting, they have not the least notion of it. There are here indeed some English women, who will finish them pretty neatly, but not so white as in England, which may in a good measure be owing to the water.

Pont Royal is a handsome stone bridge of five arches, built by Lewis XIV. almost opposite to the Tuilleries.

The last bridge worthy of notice is Pont St. Michael, on which are several houses and handsome shops.

The palace of Luxemburg was built by Mary de Medicis, and is a noble edifice, chiefly of the Tuscan order, situated in a part of the town called the University. The great gallery is worthy the attention of the traveller, and among the rest are several curious paintings by Paul Rubens, containing the most remarkable transactions of the life of that queen. The other apartments are also richly furnished, and adorned with a fine collection of valuable paintings. The gardens of this palace are elegantly laid out, and ornamented with fountains. They are daily visited by the nobility and others, like those of the Tuilleries; but more especially on Sundays, when several thousands of all ranks make their appearance there. It is here the custom for the gentlemen and ladies of the first quality, though richly dressed, to sit down to discourse on the grass.

I had not been long at Paris before I had an opportunity of being a melancholy spectator at the execution of a person broke upon the wheel, as it is commonly called. The unhappy criminal was convicted for shooting at a person with an intent to kill him; he wounded the man terribly in the face, and though he survived, the rigour of the sentence was not moderated. The execution was at the Greve, a sort of square, in which stands the town-house. In the middle of this square a scaffold was erected; and at half an hour after four the prisoner was brought to it in a cart, attended by the city guard walking two and two, and a priest accompanying the dying man. On the scaffold was erected a large cross, exactly in the form of that commonly represented for St. Andrew's. The executioner and his assistants placed the prisoner on it, in such a manner, that his arms and legs were extended agreeably to the form of the cross, and strongly tied down. Under each arm, leg, &c. was cut a knotch in the wood, as a mark where the executioner might with greater facility, break the bone. He held in his hand an iron bar, not unlike an iron crow, and in the first place broke his arms, then in a moment after both his thighs. It was dreadful to see the poor wretch writhe his body with agony, and to observe the distortions of his face. It was a considerable time before he expired, and it would have been longer, had not the executioner given him what is called the *coup de grace*, or merciful stroke, on his stomach; which at once put an end to his misery. They then took the dead body from the cross, and put it on a wheel, fixed to a long pole, where he was exposed for some time; and this part of the ceremony occasions the common expression of being broke upon the wheel, though it is performed on a cross.

Some time after, I took the advantage of a fine day, in order to visit the palace of Versailles, which is twelve miles from Paris. There are several ways of going this short journey; but the most agreeable passage is, in my opinion, in the galliot, a small barge, which sets out every morning from the Pont Royal, and lands you at Seve, from whence you have a delightful walk to Versailles, through an avenue consisting of three rows of trees, that extend a mile and a half, quite up to the palace.

At the extremity of the vista you come to a large parade, on each side of which are the king's stables;

these are noble structures, that might be mistaken for palaces; they contain a great number of fine horses, but the best are English hunters, of which his majesty is extreamly fond. Having passed the parade, you enter through the gate of the iron palisade, into the first court, which is flanked by four pavillions; but these buildings make no extraordinary figure, and fell far short of my expectations. From hence you pass through the gate of another palisade, into the second court, which is smaller, but has more grand and pompous buildings. The third court, to which you ascend by five steps, is terminated by a very noble edifice. Here is a fine portico, with three large doors neatly gilt, by which you enter the hall; which is supported by marble columns, and adorned with statues. The grand stair-case is very wide; it is of the most beautiful marble, and is finely decorated with painting and sculpture. Oppofite the wings and front of this court, are valuable busts, and in the centre stands a fountain adorned with gilt statues: the front of the palace next the garden is extreamly noble, and makes you ample amends for your disappointment, at your first entrance into it from Paris. It is entirely of stone, and of a prodigious length; which has this difadvantage, that if it be viewed at some distance in the gardens, it appears much too low for the length.

The principal rooms are the following: the hall of plenty, and that where stands the billiard-table, in which are some excellent paintings by the greatest masters. The hall of Venus is very beautiful, and, beside the other curiosities, has an ancient statue of a Roman consul finely executed. The hall of Mercury, is adorned with paintings by Titian, and other eminent hands; and in that of Mars, is a fine painting of the family of Darius at the feet of Alexander the Great, by Le Brun: in this piece the passions are beautifully expressed. The grand gallery is 222 feet long, and 30 broad: the cieling which is arched, is lofty and

and finely painted by Le Brun, with allegorical figures, reprefenting the hiftory of Lewis XIV. from the peace of the Pirenees, to that of Nimeguen, in nine large compartments and eighteen fmall ones. This magnificent gallery is adorned with eight antique ftatues, and many valuable bufts, vafes, and tables of porphyry and alabafter. On the fide fronting the garden, it has feventeen lofty windows; and the oppofite fide is wainfcotted with looking-glafs, which has a moft pleafing effect. The whole is finely ornamented with gilding, as are moft of the other apartments. The furniture is, however, now much foiled, and with refpect to neatnefs and cleanlinefs is far inferior to that in the ftate-rooms in the palaces of Kenfington, Hampton-Court, and Windfor. The apartments of the king and queen are finely painted; and in his majefty's bed-chamber are fome excellent pictures: his bed is of crimfon velvet, richly embroidered with gold, which is called the winter furniture, for in fummer they put on thinner and lighter. The bed ftands in a fmall alcove, and before it is a gilt baluftrade. The cabinet of rarities is of an octogonal figure, and contains a furprizing collection of curiofities in agate, cryftal, jewels, medals and other antiquities, with feveral paintings by the greateft mafters. The chapel is a very noble ftructure; the architecture is of the Corinthian order, and the infide is adorned with a variety of ftatues, baffo relievos, and paintings.

The gardens afford new fcenes of aftonifhment. In the firft walk, as you advance directly from the terrace along the front of the palace, you come to two bafons; and in the midft of each the water is thrown up in the form of a wheat-fheaf, to the height of about thirty feet. The borders of thefe bafons are adorned with feveral groupes of brazen figures, reprefenting river gods, and nymphs. At the corners of this terrace, are two other marble bafons, where the fountains form two fine fheets of water, and upon the borders are feveral figures of animals made of brafs.

Below thefe fountains is a very noble one, adorned with the ftatues of Latona, Apollo, and Diana. There are here many other fountains and cafcades, the beauty of which exceeds all defcription: but what is moft admired is the grand canal 1600 yards long, and 64 broad, with a large octagon bafon at each end, and interfected in the middle by another canal about 260 yards in length. Here the court fometimes take the diverfion of failing in yachts and galleys. The labyrinth is a fine grove with two ftatues at the entrance; the one of Æfop, and the other of Cupid holding a clue of thread in his hand, intimating the neceffity of fuch a guide to prevent his being loft in the intricate windings of the place. At each turning you meet with a fountain adorned with fine fhells, in which is reprefented in a lively manner, one of Æfop's fables, and the fubject is expreffed in four lines of French verfes in golden letters, on a plate of bronze painted black.

The orangery or green-houfe is a noble piece of architecture, confifting of feveral galleries, the largeft of which is 400 feet long, and 30 broad, and all of them are adorned with columns of the Tufcan order. Before this green-houfe is a fine parterre, with a fountain in the middle of it, which throws the water 40 feet high, and the whole parterre is decorated with ftatues, vafes, and other ornaments.

The Trianon, or fummer-houfe, is fituated at the entrance of a wood. Its front is adorned by a beautiful periftyle of marble columns. At the extremity of the wings of the building are two pavilions, and on the top a fine baluftrade. His majefty's apartments are richly furnifhed, and adorned with exquifite paintings: the gallery is very noble, and affords a better profpect of the gardens, than even the great gallery of the palace. It has private gardens prettily laid out, that contain a great variety of the moft beautiful flowers; and moft of the bafons and fountains have marble borders. It is furrounded with

pleafant

pleasant groves, in some of which are fine cascades, especially in that of Laocoon.

The menagerie resembles a common farm-house. It stands in the centre of seven little courts, where are kept the wild beasts, and all sorts of fowl: but on entering it, you are agreeably surprised at the elegant appearance of the apartments: in one of them is a rich settee bed or couch, for his majesty, and the cieling is covered with looking-glass.

One great advantage, which all people enjoy at Versailles is, that they have constantly free access into the gardens, provided they are equipped with a bag-wig and a sword.

Some time after I made an excursion from Paris to the palace of St. Germain's, which is about four leagues distant from that city, and situated on a high hill, at the foot of which runs the Seine: on the other side is a large forest, and adjoining to the house, a park which has some vistas leading from the palace. It was formerly a hunting seat: the garden and magnificent terrace were laid out, and formed under the direction of Lewis XIV. who also enlarged the building, on account of his having received his first breath in that palace: here also king James II. resided, and spent the remainder of his days in meditating on his own imprudence. The palace is much out of repair, and chiefly inhabited by English, Scotch, and Irish families, the adherents of that misguided prince. It has something the appearance of a castle; and is surrounded with a fine gallery, that affords a view of all the adjacent country. Indeed, had Lewis XIV. bestowed but half the expence on this place, as he did on Versailles, it would have been probably the most delightful palace in the universe.

I had not yet met with any place in France, so agreeable and pleasant as the town of St. Germain; which is very populous, and the air being esteemed the best of any about Paris, great numbers resort thither for the benefit of their healths.

About a league from hence, is the small village of Marli, situated near the banks of the Seine, where is a palace said to have been built by Lewis XIV. but this structure is not answerable to the magnificence of the gardens, which are extreamly fine, and the fountains and cascades exceed some of those at Versailles. Here is the machine that fills the grand reservoir, from which the innumerable water-works at Versailles and Marli are supplied.

On my return to Paris, I visited the palace where the duke of Orlean resides. This is a noble building, but the outside is not comparable to the beauty of the apartments, which are richly furnished, and kept in neater order than the palaces generally are: here are abundance of excellent paintings executed by the greatest masters. The gardens are public, and as much frequented as the Tuilleries and Luxemburg; but are greatly inferior to both.

Not far from thence stands the college of the Sorbonne, the most celebrated in France: it was originally a mean structure, but was rebuilt by cardinal Richlieu, and contains apartments for thirty doctors. The church is a fine edifice, adorned with plaisters of the Corinthian order, and several statues of saints and angels: the inside of the dome is elegantly painted, and in the middle of the choir is the tomb of that cardinal in a reclining posture, supported by religion, with several emblematical figures of the sciences at his feet.

The houses of Paris are generally very high, consisting of six or seven stories; and sometimes seven or eight different families live in one house. In some streets inhabited by the nobility there is scarce a house to be seen; they being built with a wall before them. At the grand gate generally stands a Swiss porter, with large whiskers; and sometimes I have seen two or three lusty footmen embroidering a waistcoat, working the wrist-bands of a shirt, or knitting stockings, though dressed and powdered out like men of quality.

The

The square of Vendome, or of Lewis the Great, is large and handsome, of an octagonal form, and the houses are regularly built. In the center is an equestrian statue of Lewis XIV. in brass, standing on a marble pedestal; which has this inscription, *Viro immortali*; or, *To the immortal man:* other inscriptions form an elogium on his virtues and exploits.

The generality of the streets are narrow, and have no foot-ways on each side with posts, for the safety of the passengers, as our streets have in London; one cannot therefore walk in them without danger; for the hackney coachmen commonly drive very fast, which, from the crouds caused by the narrowness of the streets, occasions many accidents. The hackney coaches are far genteeler, and easier than ours, and more in number; but regulated much in the same manner. There is also a vehicle used here called a vignerett, made after the manner of our common chairs, but more clumsy: it is placed upon two small wheels, and has two shafts like a cart, in which is a person who draws it like a horse; and if the passenger has a servant, he goes in the rear, pushing it forward.

[Dr. Smollet observes from Paris,——" Nothing gives me such chagrin, as the necessity I am under to hire a *valet de place*, as my own servant does not speak the language. You cannot conceive with what eagerness and dexterity those rascally valets exert themselves in pillaging strangers. There is always one ready in waiting on your arrival, who begins by assisting your own servant to unload your baggage, and interests himself in your affairs with such artful officiousness, that you will find it difficult to shake him off, even though you are determined beforehand against hiring any such domestic. He produces recommendations from his former masters, and the people of the house vouch for his honesty. The truth is, those fellows are very handy, useful, and obliging; and so far honest, that they will not steal in the usual way. You may safely trust one of them to bring you a hundred loui'dores from your banker; but they fleece you without mercy in every other article of expence. They lay all your tradesmen under contribution; your taylor, barber, mantua-maker, milliner, perfumer, shoemaker, mercer, jeweller, hatter, traiteur, and wine-merchant: even the bourgeois who owns your coach pays him twenty sols per day. His wages amount to twice as much, so that I imagine the fellow that serves me, makes above ten shillings a day, beside his victuals, which, by the bye, he has no right to demand. Living at Paris, to the best of my recollection, is very near twice as dear as it was fifteen years ago; and, indeed, this is the case in London; a circumstance that must be undoubtedly owing to an increase of taxes; for I do not find that in the articles of eating and drinking, the French people are more luxurious than they were heretofore. All manner of butchers meat and poultry are extreamly good in this place. The beef is excellent. The wine, which is generally drank, is a very thin kind of Burgundy. I can by no means relish their cookery; but one breakfasts deliciously upon their *petit pains* and their *patés* of butter, which last is exquisite.

The common people, and even the bourjeois of Paris, live at this season (October) chiefly on bread and grapes, which is undoubtedly very wholesome fare. If the same simplicity of diet prevailed in England, we should certainly undersel the French at all foreign markets: for they are very slothful with all their vivacity; and the great number of their holidays not only encourages this lazy disposition, but actually robs them of one half of what their labour would otherwise produce: so that, if our common people were not so expensive in their living, that is, in their eating and drinking, labour might be afforded cheaper in England than in France. There are three young lusty hussies, nieces or daughters of a blacksmith

smith, that lives juft oppofite to my windows, who do nothing from morning till night. They eat grapes and bread from feven till nine. From nine till twelve they drefs their hair, and are all the afternoon gaping at the window to view paffengers. I do not perceive that they give themfelves the trouble either to make their beds, or clean their apartment. The fame fpirit of idlenefs and diffipation I have obferved in every part of France, and among every clafs of people.

Every object feems to have fhrunk in its dimenfions fince I was laft in Paris. The Louvre, the palais-royal, the bridges, and the river Seine, by no means anfwer the ideas I had formed of them from my former obfervation. When the memory is not very correct, the imagination always betrays her into fuch extravagancies. When I firft revifited my own country, after an abfence of fourteen years, I found every thing diminifhed in the fame manner, and I could fcarce believe my own eyes."———

"After all, it is in England only, where we muft look for chearful apartments, gay furniture, neatnefs and convenience. There is a ftrange incongruity in the French genius. With all their volatility, prattle, and fondnefs for *bons mots*, they delight in a fpecies of drawling, melancholy church mufic. Their moft favourite dramatic pieces are almoft without incident; and the dialogue of their comedies confifts of moral, infipid apophthegms, entirely deftitute of wit or repartee. , I know what I hazard by this opinion among the implicit admirers of Lully, Racine, and Moliere.

I do not talk of the bufts, the ftatues, and pictures which abound at Verfailles, and other places in and about Paris, particularly the great collection of capital pieces in the Palais-royal, belonging to the duke of Orleans. I have neither capacity nor inclination to give a critique on thefe *chef d'oeuvres*, which indeed would take up a whole volume. I have feen this great magazine of painting three times with aftonifhment; but I fhould have been better pleafed, if there had not been half the number: one is bewildered

dered in such a profusion, as not to know where to begin, and hurried away before there is time to consider one piece with any sort of deliberation. Beside, the rooms are all dark, and a great many of the pictures hang in a bad light. As for Trianon, Marli, and Choiffi, they are no more than pigeon-houses, in respect to palaces; and, notwithstanding the extravagant eulogiums which you have heard of the French king's houses, I will venture to affirm, that the king of England is better, I mean more comfortably lodged. I ought, however, to except Fountainbleau, which I have not seen.

The city of Paris is said to be five leagues, or fifteen miles, in circumference; and if it is really so, it must be much more populous than London; for the streets are very narrow, and the houses very high, with a different family on every floor. But I have measured the best plans of these two royal cities, and am certain that Paris does not take up near so much ground as London and Westminster occupy: and I suspect the number of its inhabitants is also exaggerated by those who say it amounts to eight hundred thousand, that is two hundred thousand more than are contained within the bills of mortality. The hotels of the French noblesse, at Paris, take up a great deal of room, with their court-yards and gardens; and so do their convents and churches. It must be owned, indeed, that their streets are wonderfully crouded with people and carriages."

The doctor remarks, that—" the French begin to imitate the English, but only in such particulars as render them worthy of imitation. When I was last at Paris, no person of any condition, male or female, appeared but in full dress, even when obliged to come out early in the morning; but at present I see a number of frocks and scratches in a morning in the streets of this metropolis. They have set up a *petite poste*, on the plan of our penny-post, with some improvements; and I am told, there is a scheme on foot for supplying every house with water, by leaden pipes, from the river Seine. They have even adopted our practice of the cold bath, which is taken very conveniently, in wooden houses, erected on the side of the river, the water of which is let in and out occasionally, by cocks fixed in the sides of the bath. There are different rooms for the different sexes; the accommodations are good, and the expence is a trifle. The tapestry of the Gobelins is brought to an amazing degree of perfection; and I am surprised that this furniture is not more in fashion among the great, who alone are able to purchase it. It would be a most elegant and magnificent ornament, which would always nobly distinguish their apartments from those of an inferior rank; for in this they would run no risque of being rivalled by the bourgeois. At the village of Chaillot, in the neighbourhood of Paris, they make beautiful carpets and screen-work; and this is the more extraordinary, as there are hardly any carpets used in this kingdom. In almost all the lodging-houses, the floors are of brick, and have no other kind of cleaning, than that of being sprinkled with water, and swept once a day. These brick-floors, the stone-stairs, the want of wainscotting in the rooms, and the thick party-walls of stone, are, however, good preservatives against fire, which seldom does any damage in this city. Instead of wainscotting, the walls are covered with tapestry or damask. The beds in general are very good, and well ornamented, with testers and curtains.

Fifteen years ago the river Seine, within a mile of Paris, was as solitary as if it had run through a desart. At present the banks of it are adorned with a number of elegant houses and plantations, as far as Marli."———

" In the character of the French, considered as a people, there are undoubtedly many circumstances

truly

truly ridiculous. You know the fashionable people, who go a hunting, are equipped with their jack boots, bag-wigs, swords and pistols: but I saw the other day a scene still more grotesque. On the road to Choisli, a *fiacre*, or hackney-coach, stopped, and out came five or six men, armed with musquets, who took post, each behind a separate tree. I asked our servant who they were, imagining they might be archers, or footpads of justice, in pursuit of some malefactor. But guess my surprize, when the fellow told me, they were gentlemen *à la chasse*. They were in fact come out from Paris, in this equipage, to take the diversion of hare-hunting; that is, of shooting from behind a tree at the hares that chanced to pass. Indeed, if they had nothing more in view, but to destroy the game, this is a very effectual method; for the hares are in such plenty in this neighbourhood, that I have seen a dozen together in the same field. I think this way of hunting, in a coach or chariot, might be properly adopted at London, in favour of those aldermen of the city, who are too unwieldy to follow the hounds on horseback."——

Mr. Thicknesse gives the following general view of Paris.—" It is certainly much inferior to London in size and beauty, yet almost every street furnishes either a church a convent, or something worthy of attention. The place Victoire, is a small circus, and in the center thereof is a fine statue of Lewis XIV.; indeed neither this circus, nor any of the squares in Paris, are equal in size or beauty to the smallest that adorn the environs of the city of London. The Luxembourg and Tuilleries gardens are indeed very fine, as gardens, but not so pleasing as St. James's and Hyde Park. Every thing in Paris has been so often, and so much better described, than it is in my power to do, that it would be absurd in me to attempt giving you an exact description of any thing; nor have I seen a quarter part of what a stranger is told he must see. The manufacture at the Go-
bclins

belins is one thing, however, that gave me great delight; and what added to it was, that I found the principal conductor to be an Englishman, whose apartments, ornamented with this work, and his own ingenious pencil, contributed greatly to the pleasure I received: indeed the sister arts seem to dwell with him, and his musical family, in that royal palace; and the execution of this inimitable art of painting in worsteds to such a degree of perfection, is well worthy of the sanction of a king of France. I must now mention a beauty which Paris has, that London has not; Paris being walled in, the ramparts more than half round the whole city, are nobly adorned with four rows of stately trees, in the center of which is a broad road for coaches, and on each side very fine shady walks. Upon these ramparts are to be seen, every fine evening, many of the people of fashion in their coaches, which are often gaudy, but oftener truly elegant, and painted in a most exquisite manner; not with arms, crests, or initial letters, but with a variety of pastoral scenes. On the margin of these walls are a great number of coffee-houses, and places of public entertainment, where are exhibited a variety of amusements, something in the way of Bartholomew Fair; but you may imagine better executed, by a people whose characteristic it is, to laugh and be merry. The coffee-houses, &c. are decorated with a great deal of eye-trap, and in most of them are harlots and musicians; and there the bourgeois, with their wives and children, enjoy a little fresh air, and the view of the adjacent country, which is to be seen in great variety from the different parts of these ramparts. The English are apt to think the French are very poor, but if fine houses, expensive furniture, superb equipapes, and a great number of servants, are proofs to the contrary, it is not so. There are certainly more coaches in Paris than in London, and, I believe, more inhabitants; but certainly London is more than one third larger.

The river Seine makes but a poor figure at Paris, when put in competition with the Thames; but when the great diſtance it is from the main ocean is conſidered, and the many leagues its fantaſtic courſe takes to diſembogue itſelf, it muſt be conſidered as a wonderful and noble river. The banks are hard and firm on each ſide, and are adorned with a great number of houſes, and ſome villages. Two leagues from Paris, upon the banks of this river, is St. Cloud, where the duke of Orleans has a noble ſeat, and where, under his protection, the porcelain manufacture is carried on, and brought to an exquiſite degree of perfection. From this ſeat you have a fine view of Paris, the Bois de Bolloigne, and the beautiful line of beauty (according to Mr. Hogarth) that the river Seine exhibits. Greenwich Park is not ſo crouded on holidays, as the duke of Orleans park is every Sunday during the ſummer; but none of the French nobility ſhut up themſelves and their houſes as the Engliſh do. In the many years I have lived in, and near London, I could never ſee lord Burlington's gardens, though I had frequently a ticket. In France, the appearance of a gentleman, and particularly a ſtranger, is a ticket to go any where, and ought to be a ſufficient tie to every one not to abuſe the confidence repoſed in him. Scribbling upon the windows, and the like, is not common in France; I do not recollect that I have once ſeen any writing upon the windows of the public inns, but what was done by the hand of an Engliſhman."

Dr. Smollet's remarks concerning the French ladies are as follows.—" I ſhall not pretend to deſcribe the particulars of a French lady's dreſs. Theſe you are much better acquainted with than I can pretend to be: but this I will be bold to affirm, that France is the general reſervoir from which all the abſurdities of falſe taſte, luxury, and extravagance, have overflowed the different kingdoms and ſtates of Europe. The ſprings that fill this reſervoir are no other than vanity and ignorance. It would be superfluous to attempt proving, from the nature of things, from the firſt principles and uſe of dreſs, as well as from the confideration of natural beauty, and the practice of the ancients, who certainly underſtood it as well as the connoiſſeurs of theſe days, that nothing can be more inconvenient, and contemptible, than the faſhion of modern drapery. I ſhall only mention one particular of dreſs eſſential to the faſhion in this country, which ſeems to me to carry human affectation to the very fartheſt verge of folly and extravagance; that is, the manner in which the faces of the ladies are primed and painted. When the Indian chiefs were in England, every body ridiculed their prepoſterous method of painting their cheeks and eye-lids; but this ridicule was wrong placed. Thoſe critics ought to have confidered, that the Indians do not uſe paint to make themſelves agreeable; but in order to be the more terrible to their enemies. It is generally ſuppoſed, I think, that the ladies make uſe of fard and vermillion for very different purpoſes; namely, to help a bad or faded complexion, to heighten the graces, or conceal the defects of nature, as well as the ravages of time. I ſhall not enquire at preſent whether it is juſt and honeſt to impoſe in this manner on mankind: if it is not honeſt, it may be allowed to be artful and politic, and ſhews, at leaſt, a defire of being agreeable. But to lay it on as the faſhion in France preſcribes to all the ladies of condition, who indeed cannot appear without this badge of diſtinction, is to difguiſe themſelves in ſuch a manner, as to render them odious and deteſtable to every ſpectator, who has the leaſt reliſh left for nature and propriety. As for the fard or white with which their necks and ſhoulders are plaiſtered, it may be in ſome meaſure excuſable, as their ſkins are naturally brown, or ſallow; but the rouge, which is daubed on their faces, from the chin up to the eyes, without the least art or dexterity, not only destroys all distinction of features, but renders the aspect really frightful, or at best conveys nothing but ideas of disgust and aversion. You know, that without this horrible masque, no married lady is admitted at court, or in any polite assembly; and that it is a mark of distinction which no bourgeois dare assume. Ladies of fashion only have the privilege of exposing themselves in these ungracious colours. As their faces are concealed under a false complexion, so their heads are covered with a vast load of false hair, which is frizzled on the forehead, so as exactly to resemble the wooly heads of the Guinea negroes. As to the natural hue of it, this is a matter of no consequence, for powder makes every head of hair of the same colour; and no woman appears in this country, from the moment she rises till night, without being compleatly whitened. Powder or meal was first used in Europe by the Poles to conceal their scald heads; but the present fashion of using it, as well as the modish method of dressing the hair, must have been borrowed from the Hottentots, who grease their wooly heads with mutton suet, and then paste it over with the powder called *buchu*. In like manner, the hair of our fine ladies is frizzled into the appearof negroes wool, and stiffened with an abominable paste of hog's grease, tallow, and white powder. On the whole, when I see one of these fine creatures sailing along, in her taudry robes of silk and gauze, frilled and flounced, and furbelowed, with her false locks, her false jewels, her paint, her patches, and perfumes; I cannot help looking upon her as the vilest piece of sophistication that art ever produced."——

[Mr. Thicknesse, however, accuses the Doctor of colouring his picture too high:——" The account I give, says he, and that of Mr. Smollet's, of the great disregard to cleanliness among the French nation

tion in general, is to be underftood, however, not to belong to their perfons, but their houfes, cookery, &c. The ladies of France, in particular, are very attentive to cleanlinefs about their own perfons. The various kinds of wafhing chairs, biddets, &c. that are expofed to fale at almoft every fhop in Paris, plainly fhew, that partial bathing is as much in practice in modern France, as general bathing was in old Rome: even the female fervants and common people are much cleaner about the heels in particular, than they are in England.

There are certainly a great number of fine women in France; and a man who cannot fee and feel the influence of their beauty, in fpite of the fingularity of the paint, pomatum and powder, fo much complained of; I more than fufpect, can look upon a beautiful woman in England with a philofophical indifference.

I am afraid we have a great many pretty women in England, who never wet their fkin, but when they wafh their hands and face; and I often think of a witty faying of l—d C—d's upon this fubject; it is too well known to be repeated; but I am well fatisfied it does not hold good in this kingdom. I muft, however, own, the quantity of rouge put on by the ladies here, is very fingular, and to outdo what nature ever did, very abfurd: the truth is, it fteals upon them by degrees, their eyes become habituated to it, and they do not fee it in the fame manner that every one elfe does. Add to this, it is a mark of diftinction; and I am perfuaded, if it was not in England a mark of another kind, it would prevail as much there as it does here; but if the ladies of France would leave off fnuff, they would captivate men of all nations, as well as their own: however, I know fome ladies of high rank who ufe no paint; in deep mourning none do. I cannot account for it, but this kingdom abounds more with human deformity, than any part of the world I have ever feen; and

I now muſt remind you to be particularly careful how you walk in the ſtreets of Paris, the narrowneſs of which, the great number of coaches, carts, cabrioleᴛs, and various kinds of voitures, together with the multitude of people crouding through every ſtreet, render walking in Paris very dangerous: ſcarce a day paſſes that terrible accidents do not happen from the brutality of coachmen, carmen, and the like; and though I have been particularly cautious and careful, I have had ſome narrow eſcapes.—Paris is not informed of accidents, robberies, murders; and the like, by daily papers, as we are in London; and, perhaps, this is one reaſon why people are leſs upon their guard. Beſide the accidents that happen in broad day-light, there are a great many murders committed at Paris in the night. There is a place in Paris where the bodies of murdered perſons, or ſuch who have been thrown out of the windows, are expoſed, in order to be owned; and this place is ſeldom without the body of ſome murdered or drowned perſon: theſe murders, however, I preſume, are not committed in cool blood, but rather rencounters that happen at houſes of ill fame. The common people in England decide their quarrels generally at handy-cuffs; but in France every barber wears a ſword, and almoſt every man knows how to uſe one; and this, in ſome meaſure, accounts for the frequency of murders in Paris.

A ſtranger, whoſe attention in the ſtreets is moſt likely to be employed in looking about him, ought not to walk in Paris till that curioſity is abated, for it certainly is not ſafe even to the citizens themſelves.

To an Engliſhman it ſeems very ſtrange to go into an inn and make a bargain for his bed, his ſupper, his horſes and ſervants, before he eats or ſleeps; yet this is common in France, and for a ſtranger even neceſſary: for though you will meet with no kind of civil reception at the inns upon the road in France, as with us, at your entrance, you will meet with an exorbitant bill (without this precaution) at your departure. Therefore when you come into an inn, where you intend to stay all night, or to dine, ask the price of your room and bed, and order a supper or dinner at thirty, forty, fifty, or sixty sols per head; you will then be well served with, perhaps, many dishes, any one of which, had you ordered in particular, would have been charged treble. There are certainly many disagreeable circumstances arise in travelling in France, that do not so frequently attend traveling in England; but then it is in England alone that these inconveniencies do not arise: however, a man that can have good bread, good wine, and an hard egg, with clean sheets, and shelter over his head, has a great many comforts that many of his betters are without. Certainly the Castle of Marlborough is not to be found in every town in France. A man with a small purse, a bad constitution, and of a peevish temper, cannot travel from one side of this kingdom to the other, without meeting with a great variety of circumstances that will ruffle his mind; and so he would if he sat at home in his own chimney corner. It is not, however, what we meet with at sea-port towns, at auberges on the road, or the company that in general frequent such towns and such houses, that are to characterize a nation. I have seen a sailor put a quid of tobacco out of his mouth to sun it for a second regale, and another steal it, and put it reeking hot into his own; and a man that keeps such company, without ever seeing better, might with truth say, that Englishmen are the foulest feeders in the universe. At elegant tables in France, to every cover is set a large deep glass, three parts full of water, wherein the bowl of your wine glass is inverted, to keep it cool and clean; for as often as you drink it is again immersed in the water-glass: and should you either dip your fingers after dinner, or wash your mouth in this (though your own water-glass) glafs) it would be deemed the height of ill-breeding. The eafy addrefs of people of fafhion in France, is very captivating. Nothing is fo difagreeable as a low-bred Frenchman; no man is more agreeable than a well-bred Frenchman: a low-bred Englifhman fhocks you with his vulgarity; a low-bred Frenchman fickens you with his impertinence."—]

I left Paris, continues Mr. Stevens, on the 24th of April 1739, and having paffed through feveral towns and villages, which had the appearance of great poverty, met with nothing remarkable till I came to Fontainbleau, a fmall town about forty miles from Paris. The palace is in a fituation inexpreffibly romantic, in the midft of a vaft and wild foreft, great part of which is rocky and mountainous: the palace contains what is called the old caftle, which, together with the new palace, forms an extraordinary but very irregular groupe of buildings. The front of the great gate of the draw-bridge is fupported by large marble pillars, and embellifhed with fome fine ftatues: round the court are feveral turrets and galleries: from thence you afcend to the court of fountains, which is adorned with a great number of marble and brafs ftatues, and a fine bafon, with beautiful images fpouting water. Several other large buildings adjoin to this; but the whole, as hath been already obferved, is irregular and confufed. The apartments are grand and magnificent, and the furniture rich: the gallery of the ftags is noble, and runs quite along the orangery; the paintings are beautiful, and reprefent all the royal palaces, and fome other fine feats in France. In another gallery Henry IV. is drawn with his nobles, all in hunting-dreffes; the portraits of feveral kings, queens, and princes of the blood royal, are in another apartment. In the gallery of Ulyffes, the hiftory of that hero is beautifully painted; it is likewife adorned with feveral of the fabulous ftories in Ovid's Metamorphofis; and in another apartment are painted the battles of Henry IV.

The

The queen's gallery is very fine, and has several pictures reprefenting the victories of the French monarchs; and in moft of her majefty's apartments, the cielings are finely painted and gilt. The gardens feem well laid out, and are adorned with a number of ftatues and water-works: the orangery in particular is very beautiful: in the middle is a large bafon with brafs ftatues; a beautiful figure of Diana holds a ftag by his horns, and is furrounded by four hounds. From the pine garden you have a moft delightful profpect of the palace; and in the middle is the reprefentation of a liquid rock, from which iffues a prodigious quantity of water; and the grottos, parterres, and cafcades feem to be numberlefs.

On our leaving Fontainbleau, the next place of confequence at which we arrived was Challons, a large town in Burgundy, pleafantly fituated on the river Soane, encompaffed with a wall. It has a ftrong caftle, and a large ancient cathedral. From thence we proceeded to Lyons in a coche-d'eau, a large boat not unlike one of our company's barges: it has windows on each fide, and within is very coɴvenient. It is towed along by horfes, which, when the banks are good, go on a full trot. The paffage is extreamly pleafant, and you are all the way entertained with the moft charming profpects. At fome diftance on the right-hand, are lofty mountains, the fides of which are covered with vineyards; and on the left you furvey fertile plains of a great extent: thus thefe agreeable fcenes, fomewhat diverfified, continue till you arrive at Lyons. When you enter this city by water, you perceive two large rocks on each fide of you, with the ruins of fome ancient caftles on their fummits, that have a romantic appearance.

Lyons is a place of great antiquity, the capital of the Lyonois, and the fecond city of France. It is fituated on the Rhone and the Soane, which at the end of the town unite and form one river. No inland town can be better fituated for commerce, from its having two such fine navigable rivers, and its being nearly the center of Europe. From the top of the church of Notre Dame you have a prospect of the whole city and the adjacent country, and I could plainly discern the Alps, though more than sixty miles distant; their tops appearing like large white clouds, occasioned by their being covered with snow, though it was now May, and the weather excessive hot. There is here a very strong ancient castle, cut out of a large rock, that makes an antique appearance, and is used for a state prison. There is also a fine stone bridge of twenty arches across the Rhone, and three bridges over the Soane; it is observable of these rivers, that the water of one is perfectly green, and the other as transparent as crystal. The abbey of Notre Dame d'Assnai is much admired for its antiquity, some imagining it to be the Athæneum, the celebrated college built by the emperor Caligula; and near it are the remains of an ancient temple, built in honour of the emperor Augustus. Among the modern structures, the cathedral of St. John is remarkable, for a most curious clock that shews the course of the stars, according to Ptolemy's system, the motion of the sun and moon, their rising and setting, as also the length of the days and nights, with the increase and decrease of the moon. It has a most remarkable dial wound up but once in seventy years, on which there is a perpetual almanack: on the top of the clock is a brazen cock, which crows and claps his wings twice every hour; somewhat lower is the image of the Virgin Mary, in a sitting posture: when the clock strikes a little door opens, and an angel coming out, goes to the Virgin, and immediately the Holy Ghost descends in the form of a dove; but soon ascends again, and the angel returns. The clock is very ancient, but esteemed a curious piece of workmanship. The church is large, and remarkable for its decent plainness within;

there

there being no statues, images, or even pictures allowed of.

The square of Lewis the great is very beautiful; two sides of it are magnificently built. At a small distance from one side passes the Rhone, and on the opposite side the Soane: there are some fine walks, with rows of trees on each side, much frequented in the evening by great numbers of people; from whence, as it is situated in the lowest part of the city, there is a most beautiful prospect of houses, gardens, churches, and convents, rising in a due gradation above each other. In the middle stands an equestrian statue of Lewis XIV. and two other fine marble figures, representing the above rivers. Near this place is the grand hospital La Charité, which is a prodigious pile of building; this, with the Hotel Dieu, and the town-house, are well worth seeing.

[Dr. Smollet writes thus from Lyons.——" The country, from the forest of Fontainbleau to the Lyonnois, through which we passed, is rather agreeable than fertile, being part of Champagne and the dutchy of Burgundy, watered by three pleasant pastoral rivers, the Seine, the Yonne, and the Soane. The flat country is laid out chiefly for corn; but produces more rye than wheat. Almost all the ground seems to be ploughed up, so that there is little or nothing lying fallow. There are very few inclosures, scarce any meadow-ground, and, so far as I could observe, a great scarcity of cattle. We sometimes found it very difficult to procure half a pint of milk for our tea. In Burgundy I saw a peasant ploughing the ground with a jack-ass, a lean cow, and a he-goat, yoked together. It is generally observed, that a great number of black cattle are bred and fed on the mountains of Burgundy, which are the highest lands in France; but I saw very few. The peasants in France are so wretchedly poor, and so much oppressed by their landlords, that they cannot afford to inclofe their grounds, to give a proper refpite to their lands, or to ftock their farms with a fufficient number of black cattle to produce the neceffary manure, without which agriculture can never be carried to any degree of perfection. Indeed, whatever efforts a few individuals may make, for the benefit of their own eftates, hufbandry in France will never be generally improved, until the farmer is free and independent.

From the frequency of towns and villages, I fhould imagine this country is very populous; yet, it muft be owned, that the towns are in general thinly inhabited. I faw a good number of country feats and plantations near the banks of the rivers, on each fide; and a great many convents, fweetly fituated, on rifing grounds, where the air is moft pure, and the profpect moft agreeable. It is furprifing to fee how happy the founders of thofe religious houfes have been in their choice of fituations, all the world over.

In paffing through this country I was very much ftruck with the fight of large ripe clufters of grapes entwined with the briars and thorns of common hedges on the way-fide. The mountains of Burgundy are covered with vines from the bottom to the top, and feem to be raifed by nature on purpofe to extend the furface, and to expofe it the more advantageoufly to the rays of the fun. The vandange was but juft begun, and the people were employed in gathering the grapes; but I faw no figns of feftivity among them. Perhaps their joy was a little damped by the bad profpect of their harveft; for they complained that the weather had been fo unfavourable as to hinder the grapes from ripening. I thought, indeed, there was fomething uncomfortable in feeing the vintage thus retarded till the beginning of winter: for, in fome parts, I found the weather extreamly cold, particularly at a place called Maifon-neuve, where we lay; there was a hard froft, and in the morning the pools were covered with a thick cruft

of

of ice. The highways seem to be perfectly safe. We did not find that any robberies were ever committed, although we did not see one of the marechausse from Paris to Lyons. You know the marechausse are a body of troopers well mounted, maintained in France as safe-guards to the public roads. It is a reproach upon England, that some such patrol is not appointed for the protection of travellers."———

Lyons is a great, populous, and flourishing city; but I am surprized to find it is counted a healthy place, and that the air of it is esteemed favourable to pulmonic disorders. It is situated on the confluence of two large rivers, from which there must be a great evaporation, as well as from the low marshy grounds which these rivers often overflow. This must render the air moist, frouzy, and even putrid, if it was not well ventilated by winds from the mountains of Swisserland; and in the latter end of autumn, it must be subject to fogs."———]

On my leaving Lyons, I proceeded by water to Vienne, the capital of Dauphiny, which is situated on the Rhone, at the bottom of very high mountains. Here are to be seen the ruins of an amphitheatre, several palaces, and two famous castles, built on the summit of one of these mountains. Here is also a fine cathedral dedicated to St. Maurice.

My next stage was to Valence, an episcopal city on the banks of the Rhone. It is neat and well-built, and has several good convents. From thence we proceeded to St. Esprit, which is remarkable for its stone bridge of twenty-six arches over the Rhone, esteemed the finest in all France: but the passage under it is thought very hazardous, on account of the rapidity of the stream. There is here a beautiful and strong citadel, built on a rock by the river side.

On the 15th of May I arrived at Avignon, a city in Provence subject to the pope, as is the whole district belonging to it. His legate resides here, and

has

has a very fine palace, in which he keeps his court, and is attended like a fovereign prince by his guards. This palace is fituated on a large rock, and has a noble and extenfive profpect of the beautiful meandrings of the Rhone, with the fine country all around. I vifited the apartments, which are hung with crimfon velvet, bordered with gold lace. The city has feven gates, and is encompaffed with a very ftrong wall. The churches and convents are exceeding grand, and appeared more magnificent than any I had yet feen. In the church of Notre Dame are the tombs of two popes, who refided here during the fchifm in the church, while their antagonifts continued at Rome.

From this city I fet out for Aix, the road to which lies through a moft beautiful country. You pafs over feveral downs covered with lavender, thyme, rofemary, and other aromatic herbs; and through vallies intermixed with vineyards, and groves of olive and almond-trees. Aix, the capital of Provence, was founded by Caius Sextus a Roman conful: the air is efteemed the beft in France, and being fituated in a beautiful plain, that on one fide abounds with vineyards, orange, olive, fig, and almond-trees, and on the other is terminated at a fmall diftance by very high mountains; thefe advantages induce abundance of foreigners to dwell there, and it is feldom without fome Englifh families. The town is well built, and the ftreets are large and well laid out; the public walk is very beautiful, and has fome refemblance to the Mall in St. James's Park. There are four fine fountains continually playing, at proper diftances. The trees on each fide form a moft agreeable fhelter from the heat of the fun; and behind them are two rows of well-built houfes, fo that it is the moft pleafant ftreet I ever faw; whence in the fummer evenings it is full of good company, who are very civil and polite.

The

The metropolitan church, dedicated to St. Saviour, is an ancient fine building: in a little cell in this church, they tell you, Mary Magdalen died, after having lived there several years. A small glimmering light is kept continually burning in it, and you are permitted to look through an iron grate; but no stranger has the liberty of going in: the place has a solemn melancholy appearance. They likewise pretend that she was buried at St. Beaume, a few leagues from hence.

The road from Aix to Marseilles is as charming as can be imagined: at a small distance before you arrive at this last city, you see some hundreds of gentlemen's seats, dispersed for two or three miles round the city.

Marseilles is a fine large city, situated on the Mediterranean sea; and at the entrance of the port, are two strong forts opposite to each other, so that no ship can come into the harbour without their permission. This city is said to have been built 700 years before the birth of Christ, and from its advantageous situation, it enjoys a prodigious trade, and is extreamly populous. The haven for the reception of ships is very fine and safe, and here are kept the gallies filled with slaves. The town is situated at the bottom of a hill, and is the most regularly built of any town I have seen in France; but the streets are kept very dirty, which renders the place excessively offensive, especially in the summer season. It has a good quay, on the side of which are handsome houses, and before them a fine pavement, which forms an agreeable walk for the inhabitants in the cool of the evening, during the summer season, when the heat is intolerable. Near the quay is a row of small shops or huts, kept by slaves, who sell old cloaths, toys, knives, &c. I have frequently seen seven or eight of them chained together, and working in the public streets like horses; the sight of these wretches, with the rattling of their chains, seem very odd to
English-

Englishmen, unaccustomed to behold such miserable objects. The church of Notre Dame is neat; it was formerly, according to some, the temple of Pallas, or according to others, of Diana. It has a fine silver statue of the Virgin Mary, above five feet high, wearing on her head a rich crown. The church of St. Saviour was anciently a temple of Apollo, and is worthy of observation; as is also the abbey of St. Victor, at the foot of the citadel.

From this city I set out in a felucca for Italy, and as I am now taking leave of France, it will be proper to give some account of the manners of the people. The French then appear to be the most lively, and the gayest people upon earth, which is in a great measure owing to the purity of the air, and the happy situation of the country. On a first acquaintance with them they are loquacious, free and open. Their nobility are the politest in Europe; but their civility is attended with very little real sincerity; they are fond of shew, and delight in making a figure for a few months at the capital; though, for the rest of the year, they are obliged to live but meanly at their country seats. The women are very free in their behaviour, and have a graceful easy air peculiar to themselves; they are extremely talkative, and of an insinuating disposition; they seem naturally coquets, and given to intrigue; but rob themselves of all their native charms by paint, and smearing their cheeks with red. The common people are the poorest, and at the same time, the merriest in the world. They seem very devout in their churches, except on feast-days, when they are generally too much taken up in admiring the music and ornaments of the church.

France abounds in mineral springs, and quarries of excellent marble, and has mines of iron, copper, and lead. The vineyards of this country produce excellent wine; and the olive-tree thriving to perfection in the south of France, particularly in Provence,

vence, the oil is by some preferred to that of Spain and Italy; and the management of the silk-worm makes a principal part of the employment of many thousands of the inhabitants.

[Mr. Thicknesse gives the following hints of information, which will not be useless to persons travelling to France; and which will be a proper conclusion to our account of that kingdom and people.
——" As the post-houses furnish you only with horses and drivers, it will be necessary to hire a chaise upon your arrival at Calais: and M. Dessin will provide one for you to Paris for three louis-d'ors; but for a long tour, you will do well to purchase one; and there will be no difficulty in meeting with a tolerably good chaise for twenty guineas. The post-master general has the direction of all the post-horses in France; the posts are farmed under him for the use of the king; and ordonnances are published from time to time, which regulate the number of horses to be taken, and the prices to be paid for them.

The French post-chaises have only two wheels; and when one person is in them, must have two horses; and if two people, they must have three.

When the carriage has four wheels, there must be four horses and two drivers; but in case there should be three persons in it, you are charged at the rate of five horses; and if four persons, you must have six. If a person extra is in the carriage, or a servant behind, you are obliged to pay at the rate of one horse (25 sols) for every such person. It will sometimes happen, when several chaises have gone the same road before you, that the post-houses cannot supply you with all the horses you require, and rather than wait for the return of wearied horses, you go on to the next stage without your full number; yet in that case you are obliged to pay for the whole number prescribed in the ordonnance. The price of each horse is 25 sols for each post, and 5 sols is the pay fixed by the ordonnance for each driver; though

no

no person gives them less than ten, unless they misbehave. There are a few *postes royales*, viz. at Paris, Versailles, and Lyons, and at all other places whereever the king is, and during the time the court is held there; at these posts you always pay double; both at entering and going out.

From Calais to Paris is thirty-two posts, and the last is a royal one, which makes it at the rate of thirty-three; but to make it more familiar, I give you an example of the expences of going post from Calais to Paris.

For one person, 2 horses (50 sols) and driver (10 sols) 33 posts, at 3 livres per post - - - 99
Hire of a chaise 3 louis-d'ors, or - - - - 72
                            ———
                            171 livres, or *l. s. d.*
                                             7   9   7½

For 2 persons 3 horses (75 sols) and driver (10 sols) at 4 livres 10 sols per post - - -
                            liv. sols.
                             140   5
Hire of a chaise - -   72
                            ———
                            212 5 or *l. s. d.*
                                         9   5   8½

But in case you should bring over an English chaise, having four wheels, the expences would increase, viz.

For two persons (if only one in a carriage with four wheels, it is the same) 4 horses (5 livres) 2 drivers (1 livre) at 6 livres per post, 198 livres, or - -
                            l. s. d.
                             7 13   1½
Rating the use of the chaise at -   -   3   3
                                        ———
                                        10 16   1½

This

This difference, occasioned by four wheels, which appears but trifling in this instance, will, however, in going from Calais to Marseilles, arise to a considerable sum, as will readily appear, when you consider that the distance is about one hundred and forty posts, including the royal posts; and therefore two persons in the chaise must have one hundred and forty additional horses, and as many drivers; but if you should be alone, you will have the same number of drivers, and double that number of horses extraordinary to pay for.

As to your servant, you will find him of greater service on horseback, than he can be in the carriage; and if you have a two wheel chaise, the expence is the same; but you must provide him with a saddle and strong boots, and when he is mounted, the horse, without guiding, will carry him to the next post; and before the chaise arrives, the fresh horses will be ready, and waiting in the highway. By this means you will not be delayed more than three minutes, and can go two or three posts in a day farther; you will also be relieved from the importunity of common beggars, which is not the least inconvenience in this country, where they are in great numbers, and more troublesome, than in England."]

AN ACCOUNT OF THE KINGDOMS OF SPAIN AND PORTUGAL:

Collected from the Remarks of the Reverend Mr. CLARKE, Chaplain to the Earl of Bristol when Ambassador extraordinary at Madrid in 1760, and from other Writers.

OF all the countries in Europe, none are less visited by strangers, the maritime towns excepted, than those of Spain and Portugal; which is partly owing to their situation out of the road to other countries; and partly to the pride and bigotry of the inhabitants, their ignorance of the arts and manufactures; and these countries containing few monuments of antiquity.

In Spain, the want of that general education and knowlege, which is so universally diffused throughout this island, renders the progress of all enquiry very slow and difficult: the reserved temper and genius of the Spaniards make it still more embarrassed; but the caution they use, and the suspicions they entertain with regard to heretics, especially priests, are generally sufficient to damp the most industrious and inquisitive researcher. Add to this that invincible obstacle to all free enquiry in catholic countries, the inquisition, and then it is apprehended that the reader

will

will not wonder, that he finds so little entertainment and information in the following particulars.

Spain, including Portugal, is the most western part of all the continent of Europe, and is a large peninsula encompassed on every side by the sea, except on that part which joins to France, from which it is separated by a continued range of mountains called the Pyrenees; on the east and south it is bounded by the Mediterranean, the streights of Gibraltar, and the Atlantic ocean; on the west by that ocean, and by Portugal, which extends along the coast a considerable distance; on the north by that part of the Atlantic ocean called the Bay of Biscay, and also by the Pyrenean mountains; extending between 36° and 44° north latitude, and between 10° west and 30° east longitude, that is, thirteen degrees from east to west, and eighteen from north to south. The whole circuit of Spain, in a continued direction from town to town, and from port to port, exclusive of the windings of the creeks and bays, amount to about six hundred leagues, or eighteen hundred miles, including Portugal, which was anciently a part of Spain.

In most of the provinces the air is pure and dry, but in June, July, and August, the days are extreamly hot, especially in the middle of the country; yet in the night a traveller shivers with cold. Toward the north, and in the mountainous parts, the air is, as usual, cooler than in the south, and near the sea it contracts a moisture. It seldom rains, and the winter frosts are never so severe as to bind up the ground. The want of temperature in the heat, and the coolness of the night, is the reason that seed lies a long time in the ground before it shoots up; sometimes indeed a cool breeze, by the Spaniards called a gallego, issues from the mountains of Galicia; and this, without great precaution, occasions violent, and sometimes fatal colds.

Among the many mountains in Spain, the Pyrenees are the most remarkable. These separate Spain from France,

France, and extend from the Mediterranean to the Atlantic ocean, which is about two hundred and twelve miles, and in some places are above an hundred miles in breadth. Over these mountains there are only five passages out of Spain into France, and even these are narrow; one of them leads from St. Sebastian's in Guipuscoa, to St. Jean de Luz; the second from Maya in Navarre to Annoa; the third from Taraffa in Navarre to Pie de Port; the fourth through the county of Comminges in Arragon; and the fifth leads from Catalonia to Languedoc.

The kingdom of Spain consists of main land and islands. The main land is divided into fourteen provinces, some of which are reckoned to belong to the crown of Castile, and others to Arragon: the former are Old and New Castile, Biscay, Leon, Asturia, Galicia, Estremadura, Andalusia, Granada, Murcia, and Navarre; the latter includes only Arragon, Catalonia, and Valencia, with the islands in the Mediterranean.

The foreign possessions of the crown of Spain in Africa, are the towns of Ceuta, Oran, and Masalquiver, on the coast of Barbary; in Asia, the islands of St. Lazarus, the Philippines, and Ladrones; the greatest part of the main land of South America; and in North America, Mexico, New Mexico, California, the island of Cuba, part of Hispaniola, Porto Rico, &c.

This monarchy was limited by its Cortes, or parliament, composed of representatives sent from the cities and towns; each of which, according to the old Gothic plan, sent procurators, or deputies, chosen by and out of the aldermen of their respective cities. No act could pass in this parliament by majority of voices; it required the unanimous assent of all the members. All its acts were afterward carried to the king to be confirmed. This Cortes has rarely been called since the year 1647, when they gave Philip IV. the *millones*, or general excise, and will probably never be assembled any more, as their power is great, and they can call ministers so severely to an account.

The

The laft meeting of it was in May 1713, when it affembled to receive the renunciation of Philip V. to his rights upon the crown of France. This affembly was antiently the keeper of the revenues of the crown. But Charles V. and his minifters laid them afide, becaufe they could get no money from them: and having obtained a grant of the fale of the bull of the crufado from the pope, they found they could get money without the help of a Cortes, and fo took their leave of an affembly which few princes or minifters are fond of feeing.

Now this Cortes is laid afide, Spain is no longer a mixed monarchy, but entirely abfolute; the whole government being folely in the hands of the king and his minifters, and the councils, which are altogether at their devotion. This change from mixed to abfolute monarchy was occafioned by the timidity of the commons of Caftile, who having in their laft ftruggle for expiring freedom, fupported for fome time a war againft the crown, on a fingle defeat deferted the noble caufe of liberty in the moft abject manner. This war began in the year 1520, and lafted only two years: at which time Charles V. carried his point with a high hand, and told the Cortes, he would always have the fupplies granted firft, and then he would pafs the bills they petitioned for, and not before; to which they timidly fubmitted.

Their kings, according to the laws of Spain, are declared of age, or out of their minority, on the completion of their fourteenth year. In regulating the fucceffion, after the death of Charles II. a medium was obferved between the falic law, and the ufage of Caftile; namely, that any male heir, howfoever diftant, fhould inherit before a female, who was to have no right but after the extinction of every male branch.

The laws of Spain are compounded chiefly of the Roman civil law, the royal edicts, and probably certain provincial cuftoms. Where they thought the

Roman law was not sufficiently extensive, they have made large additions of their own. These are called the *Leyes de Partidas*; and form at present a system of modern Spanish law, which have been published by Berni and Catala in six volumes octavo. The name *Partidas* comes from the division of them into chapters. As to what we call common law in England, the Spaniards have no such thing; their provincial customs have some resemblance to it, but their laws are *Leges Scriptæ*. Much, however, of the feudal and Gothic constitutions still remain: thus the grandees have still their vassals, and very extensive powers over their persons. Their great court of civil law is divided into the two chanceries of Valladolid and Granada, which include the whole kingdom. All other causes go before the respective courts to which they belong, whether civil, criminal, or commercial, which are as follow:

1. The royal or supreme council of Castile. This and the following council are frequently assembled as one, to determine appeals made from the chanceries of Valladolid and Granada: and sometimes affairs of the police are referred to them by the king.

2. The second hall of government. The determinations of these are not final, but the ultimate appeal lies to the following court.

3. The hall of the *mil y quinientos*. So called, because the parties must first deposit here one thousand five hundred doblas, (about 223 l.) before the appeal can be lodged, which is not a large sum, considering law-expences. This is nothing else but a committee of the supream council.

4. The hall of justice. This is a court for matters purely litigious, and is a part of the supream council.

5. The hall of the province. This is a court of matters chiefly relating to the police.

6. The fiscal: the office of the attorney general for the royal council.

7. The

7. The hall of the *alcaydes de la cafa y Corte*. This hall was inftituted by Alphonzo X. to fuperintend the lodgings for the court, and to provide them. As every houfe in the kingdom was fubject to this inconvenience, the landlords of houfes made a compofition with the crown to get rid of this grievance.

8. The fupreme council of war. This determines all caufes relating to the army; except what belongs to the council of the Indies.

9. Council of the inquifition. This confifts of an inquifitor-general; of five councellors, whereof one muft always be a Dominican; of a procurator; two fecretaries of the chamber; two fecretaries of the council; an Alguazil-mayor; a receiver; two reporters; two qualificators, and counfellors; and a legion of familiars, or fpies. Of this we fhall treat more particularly prefently.

As the Spanifh church certainly remained pure, uncorrupted, and unpapiftical till toward the eighth century; fo from that period downward, paganifm artfully, and by almoft imperceptible infinuations, gradually ftole in, wearing that mafk or vizor, which we now call popery. Whatever triumphs Chriftianity may formerly have gained over the Gentile worfhip, paganifm, in all catholic countries, is now entirely revenged; fhe triumphed in her turn from the moment fhe eftablifhed herfelf in the form of popery. Concealed under this drapery, fhe prefides in the very tabernacle and fanctuary of Chriftians, and is worfhipped fitting between the horns of the altar. When you enter a Roman catholic, apoftolic, papiftical, Chriftian temple, at your firft view you fee that all is Pagan. The late Dr. Middleton hath very learnedly, elegantly, and effectually proved this point to demonftration. The refemblance is fo ftriking between the ufe of the ancient thura, and the modern incenfe; their *afpergillum*, *lavacrum*, &c. and the prefent holy water; the bleffing of horfes, and the ancient benediction of cattle; the fame profufion of lamps and wax-lights; between the ancient *votivæ tabulæ*,

tabulæ, ἀναθήματα, and the modern votive lamps, offerings, and pictures: the multitude of shrines, crosses, and altars in the churches, roads, hills, and high places; and particularly of images, which will naturally bring to mind that satirical joke of Petronius, who said he never walked the streets, but he could much more easily meet with a god than a man.

The absurdity of their reliques is beyond measure ridiculous: such as the thigh of St. Lawrence, with the skin burnt, and marked with the prongs, which he was turned with on the grid-iron. There are said to be the heads of two thousand martyred virgins in the convent of our lady of Atoche near Madrid, where the British standards, taken at the battle of Almanza, still remain.

The crusade against the followers of Waldo (a merchant of Lyons) or the Albigenses, in 1160, gave birth probably to the Inquisition. Pope Gregory IX. first devised that horrid tribunal, but Innocent IV. was the first, who had abilities and courage sufficient to bring it to a due maturity, and gave it a just establishment. The form of it, and the number of its members, differ greatly in different countries. In Spain it was established chiefly by cardinal Ximenes, who knew perfectly well what political use could be made of it. The Spaniards still support it, not so much with an intention to burn Jews or heretics, as they do in Portugal; but to enjoy the benefit of one religion: the want of such uniformity being, they apprehend, a great inconvenience to other states. Monf. Voltaire indeed is of another opinion; he tells us, that if there was but one religion in England, the government would soon become despotic; if there were two, they would cut each others throats; but as there are so many religions amongst us, things go on very quietly. Such a tribunal, shocking as it is to humanity, has nothing but false political ends to plead in its excuse: and where nature and religion must be sacrificed, such a policy is only worthy of a Machiavel, a Ximenes, or an emperor of Japan. The

principles,

principles of toleration are founded in nature, reason, humanity, justice, and true policy. If in a well civilized state the majority are of one religious persuasion, the most that you can lawfully do is, to lay those who are dissentient, under such restrictions, as shall prevent their disturbing, or subverting the civil or religious harmony of the state. This is all that appears to be allowable; and of this nature are the laws in England and Ireland against the papists. But when you come to molest innocent subjects, to take from them their possessions, to expose them to tortures and cruel deaths, or drive them to seek settlements in other countries; you then exceed your power, play the part of a Syracusan tyrant, and it becomes persecution; like the expulsion of the Moors, or the revocation of the edict of Nantz.

Spain has 8 archbishops, and 46 bishoprics.

The supream office of this Holy Tribunal, as they call it, is at Madrid; but there are also inferior holy tribunals, or inquisitionary offices, placed in the great cities almost all over Spain. This holy office used antiently to acknowlege only the power of the pope above it, and bad defiance to all other controul. It raised itself far above the authority of their kings, who were often bridled, humbled, and even punished by it. It then was truly formidable, when supported by the united force of papal and royal authority. Their *auto de fes*, or solemn acts of faith, used to be exhibited commonly when their princes came of age, or at their accession.

In the year 1724, there was printed in London, *The Trials and Sufferings of Mr.* Isaac Martin, *who was put into the Inquisition in Spain for the sake of the Protestant Religion*. The account he gives is as follows.

" In the beginning of Lent, in the year 1714, I arrived at Malaga with my wife and four children.

Landing my goods at the custom-house to be searched, a large Bible, and other books of devotion that I had, were found and seized. I asked what was the reason, and was told, that they must be examined, to see if there was nothing written against the holy faith of the church of Rome. Knowing that there were no books of controversy, I thought I should have them again. I went several times to the clergy to get them, and asked advice of the consul, and other gentlemen, how I should do to get them. They telling me it was in vain to trouble myself, for I should never get them, I gave over going to the clergy, and lost my books.

I had not been above two or three months at Malaga, but I was accused, in the bishop's court, of being a Jew, and that my name was Isaac, and that of one of my children, Abraham. I, hearing of it, acquainted the consul, who bid me not to mind it; that the Irish papists had given that information; and bid me keep no correspondence with them, for they were a scandalous sort of people.

During four years, that I was at Malaga, I and my family were much tormented by the clergy and others, persuading us to change our religion; and especially by an Irish priest, who made it his business to go from house to house to gain converts, as he called them. Finding that I could not be at rest, I resolved to dispose of what I had, and to retire to England, where I might serve God, in the exercise of my religion, in peace and quietness, without being tormented to change it. I had no sooner given out that I would dispose of what I had and retire, but there was a great noise that I was to be taken up by the Inquisition; which I could not believe: but, some days after, I found, to my sorrow, that it was true.

About nine o'clock at night, being a late hour in those countries, people knocked at my door, I asked them what they would have? They said, they wanted to come in. I desired them to come the next morning,

ing, for I did not open my doors at such an hour. They answered, they would break them open; which, accordingly they did, being about fifteen priests, familiars, a commissioner, and others belonging to the Inquisition, in arms. I asked them what they wanted? They told me, they wanted the master of the house; to which I replied, I am the man, what do you want with me? who are you all? They answered, we belong to the Inquisition; take your cloak and come along with us. I was surprised at this, and said, pray, gentlemen, stay a little, that I may give notice to my consul; for I am an Englishman, and the Inquisition has nothing to do with me. But they answered, your consul has nothing to do in this case. Come, let us see if you have no arms about you. Where are your beads? I said, I am an English protestant; we carry no private arms, nor make use of beads. When they had searched me, and taken my watch, money, and other things that I had in my pockets, they carried me to the bishop's prison, and put me in a dungeon, with a pair of fetters on; forbidding the prisoners, upon pain of excommunication, to have any conversation with me, for I was a heretic, and a very dangerous man against the holy faith.

My wife and children fell a crying, to see so many men in arms carrying me away: but she was forced to go and cry in the neighbourhood, for they turned her and her children out of doors, and kept the house to themselves five days, till they had taken every thing away: and then they returned her the key to go into her house again, where she found nothing but the bare walls.

Four days after I had been in the dungeon, my fetters were taken off, and I was examined by the commissioner of the Inquisition, who had taken me up. He asked me, whether I had any effects beside what was found in my house? And whether any body owed me any money? which he bid me tell him, and

said

said I must go to the Inquisition at Granada. I begged of him to let me be examined at Malaga, and to tell me what I was taken up for; he told me I should hear that at Granada. Then I desired him, for God's sake, to let me see my wife and children before I went; but he told me it could not be done. The next morning, having two pair of fetters on, I was mounted upon a mule, and so led out of town, the people crying out after me, *Go to Granada to be burnt; you are a Jew; you are an English heretic*; huzzaing and making scoff at me. Thus was I conducted out of Malaga, without having the liberty to see my family, or any room to believe that I should ever see them any more.

The mule that I was upon was loaded, and my fetters being very troublesome to me, and hurting the mule's neck, she threw me, and pitching upon a point of a rock, I almost broke my back; insomuch that I could not get up again without help. That day we came to a place called Velez-Malaga, where I had the good fortune to meet with an English merchant, a very worthy gentleman, and a good friend of mine, who was very sorry to see me in this dismal condition. He sent for a surgeon to dress my back, which was very much bruised, and told me that he would do me any service that he could. I told him what had happened to me, and as he lived at Malaga, desired him to assist my family, and to charge my wife from me, not to change her religion; but to take care of the children, and if she found that I was a lost man, to retire to England. I desired him to present my service to all the protestants that were at Malaga, and to desire the consul to write to Madrid to our envoy, that he might know what had happened to me, and might demand me at the court of Madrid, as being an English protestant, over whom the Inquisition had no power. My friend told me that he would do what I desired of him, and that he believed they had given out that I was a Jew, only for a pretence to take me up, in order to make me change my religion.

I asked

I asked of the carrier, that had me in custody, whether we could not get a coach or chaise to go to Granada, for my back pained me very much upon the mule: but he told me, that a horse could hardly go the road; that he was sorry for my pain; but, dead or alive, I must go to Granada with him, and be there at such a time; for so were his orders, and he must obey them. The next morning, mules being ready, my friend gave me some money, and some provisions for the road. Then, embracing one another with tears in our eyes, we parted.

It is seventy-two miles from Malaga to Granada. We were three days on our journey, and I suffered very much from the fall I had received; but the trouble of mind that I was in was greater.

When I arrived at Granada, the carrier made me stay in an inn, till such time as it was almost dark; for they put no body in the Inquisition by day-light. He asked me if I would not write to my wife, which I did; but could perceive, by his discourse, that the letter was to go to the Inquisition, and my wife never received it. When night came, I was carried to the holy office of the Inquisition, as they call it. The first thing the gaol-keeper did, was to take off my fetters, which eased me very much; then I was led up one pair of stairs along some galleries, where coming to a door, the gaol-keeper opened it, and then opening a grated door, led me into a dungeon, where he remained with me till such times as the under gaol-keeper fetched a lamp, and the things that the carrier had brought, which was an old bed, a few old cast-off cloaths, and a box full of books. I desired the gaol-keeper to let me have some of them to read; but he nailed the box up, and told me, that they must go to the lords of the holy office, and that there were no books allowed there. I was very sorry to see them, for there happened to be two, which were books of controversy.

After the gaol-keeper had searched me, and took the money that my friend had given me, he took

a pen

a pen and ink, and writ down what the carrier brought, and asked me what the buttons of my roquelau were made of, and the buttons of my coat; I told him some were gold, and some were silver. He bid me count them exactly, both great ones and small ones, took my rings off my fingers, and an exact account of every rag that I had, and writ them all down, as if I was making my will; then told me that I was in a holy place, and that there was nothing lost there, that I should have them all again when I went out. After that he asked me if I had no private arms, nor no money hid about me? telling me that I must declare it upon pain of two hundred lashes, if I did not; to which I answered, I was an Englishman, and that we never carried private arms about us. Then he asked me, what religion I was of? I told him I was a protestant. What! Then you are no Christian! said he. Yes, I am, though you do not reckon me so, said I. But he answered, You are not right Christians, you are heretics; and after having asked my name, and several frivolous questions, to which I answered, he began thus.

You must observe a great silence here, as if you were dead; you must not speak, nor whistle, nor sing, nor make any noise that can be heard; and if you hear any body cry, or make a noise, you must be still, and say nothing, upon pain of two hundred lashes I told him, I could not be always upon the bed, and asked, whether I might not have the liberty to walk? He told me I might, but softly.

Then he asked me, if I would have any thing to eat or drink? I desired him to give me a little wine, which he did, with some bread, and half a dozen wall-nuts; bidding me make my bed, and put out my lamp, and he would call upon me in the morning. Then bolting the door, he left me to myself, in a dismal apartment, and full of sorrow.

After I had prayed to God, to give me patience in my troubles, and to deliver me from the cruel hands

into

into which I was fallen; I went to bed; but had little reſt that night, for I found it very cold; the floor being bricked, and the walls between two and three feet thick: ſo that though I was up one pair of ſtairs, I was as if I had been in a cellar, it being froſty weather at that time. Night being over, I perceived day-light through a hole, about a foot long, and five inches broad. But, the walls being ſo thick, there was but little came in. The hole was juſt by the cieling; ſo that I could ſee nothing but the ſky. A little while after, came the gaol-keeper, to light my lamp; he opened the cloſe door, and through the grated one, lighted it, and bid me dreſs myſelf; for I muſt go for ſome proviſions, and muſt light my fire, and dreſs my dinner.

 Sometime after, he came and took me down ſtairs with him to a turn, ſuch as they have in convents; where a man at the other ſide, whom you cannot ſee, turns in your allowance. They gave me half a pound of mutton, (their pounds are but ſixteen ounces, and at Malaga they are thirty-two) about two pound of bread, ſome kidney-beans, ſome raiſins, and about a pint of wine, and two pound of charcoal. I had a little earthen ſtove to light my fire in; a pipkin to boil my victuals; ſome earthen plates, and pitchers to hold water; a baſon; a broom to ſweep my dungeon; three baſkets, one for bread, meat and greens; another for charcoal; and the other to ſweep my dirt in; and a wooden ſpoon: but I had no knife nor fork, no table, and nothing to ſit upon, but ſome boards that were faſtened in the wall, upon which my bed was placed. The gaol-keeper ſhewed me how I muſt manage my allowance; he parted my meat in three parts, and told me it muſt ſerve me three days, and then I ſhould have more. Then he ſhewed me how to light my fire, and told me that I muſt be ingenious, and learn to dreſs my victuals nice, and to make the meat favoury. I thanked him very kindly for ſhewing me, and away he went.

I thought

I thought it very hard to be reduced to such short allowance, having before lived in plenty. I dressed the third part of my meat, with some kidney-beans, as well as I could; and though I was in great pain from the fall I had received, I eat my meat, and could have eaten more if I had it. That done, I went to bed. In the afternoon, the gaol-keeper came to see me. I told him I had a great pain in my back. He told me, I should have a doctor, which I had the next morning; who ordered me to be blooded, which was done accordingly. He gave me some oil to anoint my back; but I could not anoint it myself, so that I made no use of it, but to burn. The doctor was two or three times with me: and I kept my bed three or four days; during which time they brought me my victuals ready dressed; but it was three months before the pain of my back was quite gone.

That day sevennight, that I was put into the Inquisition, the gaol-keeper bid me to get myself clean, for I must go to audience. I, not knowing what he meant, desired him to repeat what he had said; and so he did. The word audience surprising me, I asked him who I must go before? He replied, You must go before the lords of the holy tribunal, to be examined. I told him it was very well; and desired him to send for a barber to shave me. But he answered, there were no barbers allowed but three times a year. I went along with him, and he would hardly allow me to take my perriwig on my head. Coming into a room, I found two men, one sitting between two crucifixes, and the other at his left hand, with pen, ink and paper before him. He was the secretary, and a young man. My lord was an old man, of about sixty years of age, looked like a lean jesuit, and was the chief of the three lords inquisitors. He bid me sit down upon a little stool that was there on purpose, which fronted him; so that there was a table between him and me, and a crucifix in the

middle

middle of it that fronted me. And thus he began to speak to me with a great deal of gravity, and I heard him with a heavy heart, and a very uneasy mind.

Inquisitor. What was you brought here for? How came you here? Can you speak Spanish? *Martin.* My lord, I don't know what I was brought here for. I can speak Spanish, but not so well as English or French. If you please to send for an Irish, or a French priest, I should be glad; for I am afraid that I have not Spanish enough to answer your lordship in some things that you may demand of me. *Inq.* I find you speak Spanish enough. What have you done? What is your name? What countryman are you? What religion are you of? *Mart.* My lord, I don't know what I have done. My name is Isaac Martin. I am an Englishman, and a protestant. *Inq.* Will you take an oath that you will answer the truth to what shall be demanded of you? *Mart.* Yes, my Lord, I will. *Inq.* Well, put your hand upon that crucifix, and swear by the cross. *Mart.* My lord, we swear upon scripture. *Inq.* It is no matter for scripture; put your hand upon the cross. [I put my hand upon the cross, and thus he begun.] You must tell me what your father and mother's names were, and what their fathers and mother's names were, what brothers and sisters they had, and what brothers and sisters you have, where they were born, and what business they followed, or follow? [To which I answered to the best of my knowlege; too long to be here inserted.] You say you are an Englishman. We have great belief in them; they are generally people that speak the truth; I hope you will. *Mart.* My lord, I don't know that I have done any thing that I should be afraid of. Your lordship has given me my oath; and if you had not, I should have told the truth. *Inq.* It is very well, Isaac. [Then he begins to ask about my wife's relations, as he had about mine; and what name my wife and children had; to which I answered directly.]

Where

Where was you born, Isaac, and in what parish? *Mart.* My lord, I and my family were all born at London, but in different parishes. *Inq.* Are you a scholar? Have you studied Latin? *Mart.* No, my lord, I have had but a common education. *Inq.* What do you call a common education in your country? You have been at school; what did you learn there? *Mart.* My lord, I learn'd to read, to write, and to cast accompts; that is what we call a common education. *Inq.* What sect are you of? For in England you have several religions, as you call them. *Mart.* My lord, there are different opinions in England, in matters of religion. I am of that which is called the church of England; and so were my father and mother. *Inq.* Was you baptized? *Mart.* Yes, my lord, I hope I am a Christian. *Inq.* How are you baptiz'd in England? *Mart.* We are baptiz'd in the name of the Father, and of the Son, and of the Holy Ghost. *Inq.* Do you take the sacrament in your religion? *Mart.* Yes, my lord. *Inq.* How do you take it? *Mart.* My lord, we take bread and wine, as our Saviour gave to his apostles. *Inq.* Do you confess your sins to your clergy, as we do in the church of Rome? *Mart.* No, my lord, we confess them only to God Almighty. *Inq.* Do you know the Lord's prayer, the Belief, and the Ten commandments? *Mart.* Yes, my lord, and will give you an account of my religion, if you please, and prove to you, that I am a Christian, though I have been called a Jew, and a heretic. *Inq.* What do you believe in your religion? *Mart.* My lord, we believe the same creed that you have. *Inq.* Have you any bishops in your religion? Have you been confirmed? *Mart.* My lord, we have archbishops, and bishops; but I don't remember whether I have been confirm'd. *Inq.* Isaac, you have been brought up in the dark, it is a pity; but you may enlighten yourself if you will. *Mart.* My lord, I hope I have light enough to save myself, if I live according to it. [His discourse being very long, and I very

I very much troubled in mind, the tears came into my eyes; which he perceiving, spoke thus to me, very smoothly.] *Inq.* Don't cry, nor don't be afraid; there is no body put to death here, nor no harm done to any body; I hope your case is not so bad but it may be remedied. You are among Christians, and not among Turks. *Mart.* My lord, I know very well that I am amongst Christians; and that the laws of Christ are merciful: but I have been used as if I had committed murder. *Inq.* Well, have patience, you shall have justice done you; you must think of what you have done, or said, during the time that you lived at Malaga, and confess it; for that is the only way to get out of your troubles. But let us continue our examination. To be sure, you was not brought here for nothing, was you? *Mart.* My lord, I don't know what I was brought here for. *Inq.* You must think of that, and you must tell me how old you are; and, from as far as you can remember, the life that you have led, what company you have kept, what business you have followed, what countries you have travelled in, and what languages you can speak? *Mart.* I have been a traveller this many years, and have made several trading voyages; sometimes in one country, and sometimes in another; and can't remember how long I have lived in every place, but I will tell you as well as I can. *Inq.* It is very well, Isaac, tell the truth. [After I had told him, to the best of my knowlege, he said,] It is very well, Isaac; you have been a great traveller; you have been wild in your time. *Mart.* Yes, my lord, too wild; for if I had stayed at home, as I ought to have done, I should not be in this misery as I am. *Inq.* In your religion, do you believe in the virgin Mary, the mother of God, and in the saints? Don't you worship them? *Mart.* My lord, we believe that the virgin Mary is the mother of Jesus Christ carnally; and believe she and the saints are happy; but we don't worship them. *Inq.* What! Don't you worship the mother of God, and the saints, that are always praying for us? *Mart.* No, my lord, we worship only one God in three persons, and nothing else. *Inq.* [He speaks to the secretary.] It is pity that he has been brought up in heresy; he talketh pretty well. [Then he makes a long discourse to me, representing to me,] What a pity it is, that England has left the true faith, and has embraced heresy; that formerly produced a great many saints; but now it produced nothing but schisms and heresies: that our bishops and clergymen were a strange sort of people, to marry as they did; [and thus he ran on a long while: to which I answered,] That I believed England produced as many good men as ever it did; [but he bid me hold my tongue; and told me,] I knew nothing of those affairs; bid me think of what I had done, or said, during my living at Malaga, that I should have time to think of it, and to think upon what he had told; bid me go to my dungeon, and he would send for me another time. [To which I said:] *Mart.* My lord, I hope that your lordship will consider that I have a family; and I beg that your lordship will dispatch me as soon as possible. *Inq.* I will do all that I can to dispatch you; go and think upon what you have done or said; I hope your case is not very bad, and can be remedied, if you think upon what I have said to you. [It was a long audience, for it lasted an hour and a half.]

When I came to my dungeon, I reflected upon what had happened to me during my living at Malaga, and upon what my lord had said to me. I found by his discourse that he was very well informed what countryman I was, what family I had, what their names were, what religion I was of, where I had travelled, and what languages I could speak. As the gaol-keeper came mornings and nights to light my lamp, I desired him to tell me what he thought of my case, and how I must behave myself at audience. I made as much a friend of him as I could, in order to

learn

learn something of the ways practised in the Inquisition. But they are sworn to keep them secret; so that I could not learn much of him. He told me, that I was there for the good of my soul; that the lords of the Inquisition were very merciful; that I must not be afraid; that there was no body put to death there, nor no harm done to any body: that the lords of the Inquisition demanded only a true confession; that he believed my case was but a small matter, that I could remedy easily; and advised me, as a friend, not to contradict them, let them say what they pleased, for they were holy, just men.

I thanked him for his advice; but found that my lord and he were both liars, in telling me that I had no occasion to fear; and that there was no harm done to any body there; for I knew, that in the holy office of the Inquisition (as they call them) they torture people; they whip them; they send them to the gallies; and they burn them alive, without any body's daring to find fault, though it should happen to their own relations; upon pain of being put there themselves, if the Inquisition should hear of it: for they pretend to be as infallible as the pope in their way of justice; and that whatever they do is just; and the king himself has nothing to do with them; for they are above him, and he himself subject to the Inquisition.

A week after, I was called to audience, and coming into the room, my lord began thus: Well, Isaac, how do you? Do you remember what you have done or said whilst you lived at Malaga? Have you reflected upon what I said to you? *Mart.* Yes, my lord; but I can't remember every thing that has happened in four years time. *Inq.* Well, let us hear what you have remembered. *Mart.* My lord, during my living at Malaga, I was attacked and insulted several times about my religion. I hope your lordship allows, that an honest man ought to defend his religion. *Inq.* Yes, Isaac, he may defend it.

Mart. My lord, it is what I have done, and the same liberty have the Spaniards in my country; for if a bishop should attack them in matters of religion, they have the liberty to defend themselves. *Inq.* How long have you been married? Was your wife a widow, or a maid, when you married her? *Mart.* My lord, she was a widow, and had two children; and I have been married about seven years with her; [which he knew as well as I; but was always sifting me, and hardly ever looked in my face.] *Inq.* What quarrels have you had with people? Do you remember their names? If you do, name them. *Mart.* I named four or five that I had words with. *Inq.* You think that those people are your enemies; tell me, what reason you have to think so? *Mart.* My lord, at my first arrival at Malaga, three Irishmen went to the bishops court, to acquaint them that I was a Jew; they hardly knew my name, nor what religion I was of. Your lordship has heard of it, I suppose; all the time that I lived at Malaga, they, upon divers occasions, shewed themselves my enemies. My friends oftentimes told me that they spoke ill of me behind my back; sometimes saying that I was a Jew, and sometimes that I was a heretic; and that they would play me a trick one day, that I should not carry much money along with me, if I left the place; and I find, my lord, that they have accomplished their design. *Inq.* Have you had no words about religion? Have not you blasphemed against our holy faith? *Mart.* No, my lord, I am a better bred man than that. My religion does not permit any such things. It is true, that I have had high words about religion, when I have been attacked; but not to blaspheme your religion. *Inq.* Well, but what is the reason that you have so many enemies? Can you tell? *Mart.* I know no other reason, my lord, but that I am an English protestant, and had better business than they had, which caused them to envy me ever since

I have

I have lived at Malaga. [He speaks to the secretary, and tells him, that there is some likelihood in what I said; but it could be remedied.] *Inq.* Well, but Isaac, have you no inclination to be a good Christian, and to be in the right way of salvation? You are a man of age, and of reason, and have a family; it is time to think of your soul. *Mart.* My lord, I hope God will save me in the religion that I have been brought up in. I have no inclination to change my religion. Jesus Christ allows of no persecution. I hope, my lord, there is none here. *Inq.* No, Isaac, it is all voluntary. I would have you think upon it for the good of your soul, and of your family. Don't you believe in the holy father the pope, that he is infallible, and that he can absolve people from their sins? *Mart.* No, my lord, I believe that he is no more than another bishop; and can absolve no more than another clergyman can do. *Inq.* Don't you believe in purgatory? *Mart.* No, my lord, I believe in no such thing. *Inq.* What! don't you believe that there is a place called purgatory, where the souls of those that die are retained to be purified before they can go to heaven? *Mart.* No, my lord, I believe that the blood of Christ is sufficient to cleanse us from our iniquities. *Inq.* Poor man! you have been brought up in heresy and ignorance from your youthful days. I am sorry for you; you will find yourself mistaken when it is too late; you have time to consider upon it, and I would advise you to do it for your own good. Can you think of any thing else that you have done that they have sent you here for? *Mart.* No, my lord. I have had some few words with people; but I believe it is inconsistent with this affair. *Inq.* What words had you with the Spaniards at Malaga? *Mart.* My lord, at first, several desired me to speak the lingua for them, to help them to sell their goods to ships that came to load there, and I did; but there came so many that I could not do business for myself, so that I desired them to excuse me, and to take some body else: but they still importuned me so, that I was obliged to tell them that I would trouble my head no more about their business, and that I had business enough of my own to mind: at which they would sometimes fall into a passion, and generally reflect upon my religion, which I could not bear at all times, so that we sometimes quarrelled very much. *Inq.* Very well, Isaac. Have you any thing else to say relating to your affair? *Mart.* My lord, I don't know what to say. *Inq.* Well, go to your dungeon, and think upon what you have done; for it will be a great help to your releasement. I will do you what service I can; but you must do what you can to serve yourself, and think upon what I have said to you.

I was called to audience three different times more about the same subject; and he, still admonishing me to change my religion, gave me to understand, though he did not speak downright, that it was the only way to get out of my troubles, which made me very uneasy in my mind, seeing what he aimed at.

You must know, that the secretary writes in short hand what I answered to his demands.

A visit of one of the lords Inquisitors, Don Petro Leonor.

Don Fernando, the head gaol-keeper, one morning, told me, that I must get my dungeon very clean, put every thing under the bed, and dress myself as well as I could; gave me some aniseed to throw in the fire, when I should hear him come again, with one of the lords of the Inquisition, who was to come to see me. Some time after, he came, and I threw the aniseed in the fire, to take away the stink of the dungeon. His lordship's name was Don Petro Leonor. He was the second inquisitor, and thus he begun to speak to me, as if he had never heard talk of me.

Inq. How do you? What is your name? *Mart.* My lord, my name is Ifaac Martin. *Inq.* Well, is the gaol-keeper civil to you? Do you want for any thing? Have you your allowance? *Mart.* My lord, the gaol-keeper is very civil, and I believe that he allows me what is allowed; but if I had more I could eat it. [He fpeaks to the gaol-keeper, and afks him if he gave me my allowance; the gaol-keeper anfwers, that he did.] *Inq.* Well, then you have enough, [faid he to me.] *Mart.* My lord, it is not that which troubles me, it is my being detained here. I can live upon the allowance, though it is fhort. *Inq.* Well, can I ferve you in any thing? The fecretary fhall write it down. What have you to fay? Tell me *Mart.* My lord, I have nothing to fay but what I have faid. [You muft know that there is always a fecretary with them, who carries pen, ink and paper.] *Inq.* Hark ye, you have been brought up in herefy; it is a pity. You were all good people and good Chriftians in England till Henry the eighth came; and that was your firft lofs. Then came queen Elizabeth, and fhe was a very wicked woman, that every body knows; and here of late, you have had one, that you call king William; he had no religion; what he aimed at was to get the crown, and fo you have been led away. [And thus he run on a long while.] *Mart.* My lord, I believe that king William lived and died as a good proteftant Chriftian; and he received the facrament from one of our bifhops a little before he died. *Inq.* I am very well affured that he had no religion, for I read it in a French book; and as for your bifhops and clergymen, they are a ftrange fort of men to marry and live fuch lives as they do. *Mart.* My lord, I believe they live very well. *Inq.* Hold your tongue, you know no better; you are here for the good of your foul. Now is a very good time for you to renounce that herefy which you have been brought up in, and to become a good Chriftian, as your forefathers were. You have time to think of it; there is nothing to disturb you. Do you say your prayers sometimes? *Mart.* Yes, my lord, I say my prayers. *Inq.* Very well; you must pray to God to enlighten you in the true faith of the church of Rome, without which no man can be saved. It has been said that you are a Jew, but I don't believe it, though you look something like one; but it does not go by looks always. It may be some of your relations formerly were Jews. *Mart.* My lord, I never heard that any of my relations were Jews; as for my looks at present, I believe they are like a Jew's or a Turk's. [Durst I to have spoken, I had told him that he looked like one, for his lordship had a tallow wainscotted look.] *Inq.* Well, think what I have said to you for the good of your soul; and don't be hardened in your opinion, but believe what I say is for your good. You Englishmen mind eating and drinking, and your pleasures, more than religion. And so he went away, and glad was I to be rid of his visit.

Some days after Don Fernando told me I must go to the audience. Coming into the room, my lord begun to speak to me thus.

Inq. Well, Isaac, have you any thing now to tell me relating to your affair? *Mart.* No, my lord, unless I tell you the same thing over again, and I believe it will not signify any thing. *Inq.* What, then you have nothing else to say, Isaac? *Mart.* No, my lord, I have nothing to say. [He rings a bell to call the gaol-keeper, and bids him call another secretary, which came with some writings in his hand, makes me sign what I had said in my examination; and orders the secretary to read aloud the papers that he had in his hand, which were my accusations. After that he spoke to me thus.] *Inq.* Well, what have you to say for yourself? You have heard what you are accused of? *Mart.* My lord, there are some accusations that are true, and some are false. *Inq.* Can you answer to them all? *Mart.* Yes, my lord, one after another. *Inq.* So you shall; but you must take your oath that you will answer true, to the best of
your

your remembrance. *Mart.* My lord, I will. [After he had given me my oath as before, he said.] *Inq.* Do you think that you know any of those people that have sent their accusations against you? *Mart.* My lord, I do know a great many, if not all. I wish your lordship would send for them, that I may see them face to face. *Inq.* There is no such thing practised here; don't be hasty; answer just, and declare the truth. *Mart.* So I will, my lord.

1. Accusation. That at your first coming to Malaga, you went and scolded at the school-master for teaching your children the Christian doctrine: telling him that you will teach them your religion; and that you sent them to school to learn to read and to write, and not religion.

Mart. My lord, I confess the truth. I hope your lordship requires nothing else. I did go to the schoolmaster, and told him, that I sent my children to learn to read and write, and not to learn prayers; that I would have them brought up in my religion, and would teach them how to pray; but I did not scold at him. I believe, my lord, I have the liberty to bring up my children in my own faith, without being called to an account for it. *Inq.* No, since you live in a Christian country, you must let your children be brought up in the Christian faith. [Bid me hold my tongue; and bid the secretary write down what I had said, and that I was guilty in so doing.]

2. *Acc.* That at divers times it was remarked, that I did not pull my hat off, nor pay any homage to images, but turned my back to them.

Mart. My lord, in my religion we pay no respect to graven images. I profess myself to be a protestant, and it is against my conscience to bow to any; and am not obliged by articles of peace so to do. I believe your lordship knows what the word protestant means. *Inq.* You live in a country where people do so; and it gives ill examples if you don't do as the rest. Whether you believe it is proper or not, to do, you must do it. *Mart.* My lord, consider that I am an English

lish proteftant, and that I have not the liberty of confcience, if I am obliged fo to do. [He bids the fecretary write down what I have faid.]

3. Acc. You have faid, walking in your room with an Englifh captain, a heretic like yourfelf, that purgatory was but an invention of the church of Rome to get money; for there was one that could fpeak the language that heard you fay fo.

Mart. My lord, I can't remember every thing that I have faid during four years time. It may be that I have faid fuch a thing; but if I did, it was not to a Roman catholic. If there was one in the room that heard me fay fo he muft be an Irifhman, who was not very welcome there; for they come more to fpy than for any thing elfe. *Inq.* Do you think that you know his name? *Mart.* Yes, my lord, I believe his name is R. M. *Inq.* But how came you to fay fuch things in thefe countries? *Mart.* My lord, my religion admits of no purgatory, as I told you before, and being in my own houfe, amongft people of my own religion, not minding that Irifhman, I believe I did fay fo. *Inq.* Are you not forry for having faid fo? *Mart.* My lord, if I have faid amifs, I beg your lordfhip's pardon. *Inq.* To be fure, you ought not to fpeak fo in thefe countries. Write down fecretary, that the heretic begs pardon to the third accufation.

4. Acc. That going along with a perfon, he pulled his hat off to a crucifix; and you afked him for what reafon he pulled off his hat? He told you, to the crucifix; and you anfwered him, we have no fuch thing in our country, and went away without pulling off your hat.

Mart. My lord, I remember the time very well, it is very true. I never pulled off my hat to a crucifix, unlefs they are carried in proceffion, and then I ufed to pull it off; but not in refpect to the image, but to caufe no fcandal. *Inq.* Don't you find yourfelf in a fault for fo doing? For if every body fhould do fo, the Chriftian religion would fall and come to nothing. *Mart.* My lord, if I was a Roman, or, if by articles

of

of peace between my king and the king of Spain, there were such things mentioned, that English protestants were obliged to pay homage to all the crucifixes, images and saints; I should reckon myself guilty; but as there is no such thing, I reckon myself no ways guilty, and desire your lordship to try me by the articles of peace, that I may know whether I am guilty or not.

5. *Acc.* That you have spoken several times against the church of Rome, disputing of religion, and had been admonished several times to embrace our holy faith, without which no man can be saved; but you never would give ear to it.

Mart. My lord, at my first arrival in the Inquisition, you granted me, that a man might defend his religion; it is what I have done. As for being admonished to change it, it has happened very often; but I have no inclination to change. *Inq.* Could not you defend your religion without speaking against the church of Rome? *Mart.* My lord, I can't tell how to do that; for in disputing, as people spoke against my religion I spoke against theirs, and gave proof of scripture for what I said. *Inq.* Hold your tongue with your scripture; there are other things beside scripture that you must believe that are revealed to the church. You are in the wrong; you must take care what you say in these countries. It was for the good of your soul that you were admonished; and I would have you consider of it at present, for your own good.

6. *Acc.* That being aboard an English ship with your wife, and others in company, a certain person, of the female sex, was admonishing your wife to be a good Christian, and to change her religion; and you bid her hold her tongue and mind her own religion, and not trouble herself to make converts; and you scolded at her very much. It was on a Friday, and you eat meat. Do you remember that, Isaac?

Mart. Yes, my lord, we were very merry drinking of Florence and punch, and that woman was always talking

ing of religion to my wife, though she hardly knew what she said, and at best knew but little of the matter. I desired her to be quiet, and told her we did not come abroad to talk of religion, but to be merry; which she, continuing to talk of, made us all very uneasy, so that I bid her hold her tongue, and mind her own religion; and so we quarrelled. As for eating meat of a Friday, I generally do, and so did she, though she is a Roman catholic. *Inq.* You are in the wrong; that woman gave good advice to your wife, and might have converted her if it had not been for you; but I suppose that you don't care that she should be a Christian; you will have her remain as she is. *Mart.* My lord, I hope she is a Christian already, and has no mind to change her religion. *Inq.* If it was not for you your family would be all good Christians, but you hinder them. Write down, secretary, what the heretic says.

7. *Acc.* That being in company with some English heretic captains at a church, there were some people kneeling and praying to the image of the virgin Mary, and the captains asked you if they prayed to the image, to which you answered, Yes; that they were brought up in that way of worshipping from their infancy, and that they knew no better, being brought up in ignorance.

Mart. My lord, I have been divers times walking with captains; I don't remember this particular time; it may be that some body heard me say so; but I am sure I spoke English, and it must be an Irishman that heard me say so. *Inq.* You think that no body understands what you say; but you are mistaken, and people hearing you talk so, may believe that they are brought up in ignorance, and not in the right way. *Mart.* My lord, I did not say it designedly to make them believe so, neither did I know that any body understood me, but those captains that are of the same religion as I am; if I have said amiss, I beg your lordship's pardon. It

was

was through ignorance, not knowing that such things might not be said in these countries. *Inq.* You have more malice than ignorance in what you say. You know too much of what you should not know, and you won't know what you should know. Do you beg pardon of this holy tribunal for having said so? *Mart.* Yes, my lord, if I have said amiss. [He speaks to the secretary, shaking his head, Write down what the heretic says; I wish begging pardon may do.]

8. Acc. That being a walking with several merchants, the holy host passed by, they all pulled off their hats, and some kneeled down, but you did not so much as pull your hat off, which caused a great scandal; insomuch, that some people had a mind to stab you, for seeing you so irreverent in a Christian country.

Mart. My lord, it is false. I have lived several years in Roman countries, and know that by articles of peace I am obliged to have my hat off; and during my living at Malaga I always took care to cause no scandal. But for bowing or kneeling I did not, nor am obliged to it, for it is against our religion. As for people stabbing me, I have run those hazards many a time upon the account of my religion. *Inq.* But these people would not accuse you if it was not true. *Mart.* My lord, they accuse me of being a Jew, must that be true? I wish your lordship would let me see my accusers; for whilst I am here, they may accuse me of murder, and I must answer to a thing that I know nothing of. I don't understand this way of justice; let the secretary write down what you please. *Inq.* Don't you be in a passion, Isaac. *Mart.* My lord, it is very hard to be accused of things that one knows nothing of. In other courts one sees their accusers. I don't understand this way of justice, my lord. It signifies nothing to me to make any defence; let your secretary write what you please. *Inq.* I believe you don't understand this justice; but you deny the accusation, don't you? *Mart.* Yes, my lord, I do, for it is false.

9. Acc.

9. *Acc.* You have been threatened divers times with the pope's authority in these countries; and you have said that you did not value him, and that he had no authority over you.

Mart. My lord, it is true, I have said so. *Inq.* How came you to say so? Don't you value the holy father, which is God on earth? *Mart.* My lord, talking with some people, which were very troublesome about religion, they have threatened me with the pope's authority; and being an English protestant, not belonging to the church of Rome, I thought that he had nothing to do with me. *Inq.* What! Then you value no body. *Mart.* I beg your lordship's pardon. I value all mankind as being fellow-creatures. I value the pope as bishop of Rome, but not for what authority he has over me, for I believe he has none. *Inq.* You are mistaken, Isaac. Who is the head of your church? *Mart.* My lord, I see to my sorrow that I was mistaken. Christ Jesus is the head of our church. *Inq.* What! Then you allow no head upon earth? *Mart.* No, my lord. *Inq.* Hold your tongue, you are an unbeliever; he is God upon earth.

10. *Acc.* That being a walking with some captains of ships, there was a procession going by, and you bid them to retire, and not to mind it, though it was their design to see it, but you hindered them out of disrespect to it.

Mart. My lord, processions are very frequent in Malaga. I have oftentimes been in company with captains that never were in Roman countries, and they not knowing that people went there for devotion, would laugh, and some would not pull their hats off; so that I often bid them retire, to cause no scandal; I hope there is no harm in that, my lord. *Inq.* Have you no respect for our processions? *Mart.* My lord, living in a Roman country, that I might cause no scandal, I used to pull off my hat, but not in respect to the images that were there.

11. *Acc.*

11. *Acc.* That the procession went by, and all the people kneeled down, and worshipped, and you stood with your hat on and took no notice of it, which caused a great scandal.

Mart. My lord, I remember nothing of the accusation, but I believe it is false; and if I did not pull my hat off, it was because the host was not there: but for kneeling or bowing, as I told your lordship before, I never do. Your lordship tries me as if I was a Roman; I am a protestant. I gave a small account of my religion to your lordship at my first coming; if I was a Roman I should be guilty. *Inq.* Well, but though you have the liberty to live in these Christian countries, you have not the liberty to do what you please. *Mart.* My lord, I hope that English protestants have liberty of conscience in these countries, by articles of peace, or else they would not live here. The Spaniards are not molested in England upon the account of their religion. *Inq.* You ought to conform yourself to the country that you live in.

12. *Acc.* That being in your house, an English captain speaking to you, asked you if you was a Jew, and you fell a laughing, and said, that you did not value what such scandalous people said; that you was ready to give an account of your religion.

Mart. It is true, my lord, I little valued what such scandalous people said, and was always ready to give an account of my faith; and little thought I should be sent here to be examined, to know whether I was a Jew or no; there are clergymen enough at Malaga. *Inq.* This is the properest place to be examined, and it is no laughing matter in this country to bear the name of a Jew. *Mart.* My lord, before I came to Malaga I had lived in several parts of Spain and Portugal. I knew that Jews are not allowed to live in those countries, and are burnt if they don't change their religion, if taken up by the Inquisition. Had I been a Jew I should not come here to live with a wife and four children to run these hazards. I

believe

believe your lordship knows very well that I am no Jew.

Inq. Your name is Isaac, and your son's name is Abraham, and you say that you are no Jew! *Mart.* Those names signify nothing, my lord. I thank God I am a good Christian, and hope to have a share in the merit of that precious blood that Christ has shed upon the cross, for the redemption of mankind, and hope to die in the same faith.

13. *Acc.* That you never gave any thing to those that beg for the souls that are in purgatory, but huffed them, sending them to the devil.

Mart. My lord, it is true, but he does not mention the reason why I did so. *Inq.* Well, let us hear; but speak the truth; how was it? *Mart.* My lord, the person that comes to beg, knows me very well to be a protestant; he comes generally every night at my door. I often desired of him to excuse me; that I gave no alms for the souls that are in purgatory; but the more I excused myself the more he insisted; insomuch that he called me heretic dog, telling me that I was damn'd, and should go to the devil. I refrained as much as I could speaking to him; but at last gave him as good as he brought. I allow myself that I was to blame in putting myself in a passion with such a man; but one is not master of one's self at all times; and though I lived in a Roman country, I don't think that I am obliged to take all the abuses that I have received upon the account of my religion. I have given sometimes alms to people that asked me in a civil way, but not to pray for souls departed. *Inq.* What! Then you don't believe there is a purgatory? *Mart.* No, my lord, I don't believe there is any such thing. *Inq.* Have you declared the truth? *Mart.* Yes, my lord. *Inq.* Well, hold your tongue, say no more.

14. *Acc.* That people being in company, have heard you say that you feared no justice; and they asked you if you did not fear the Inquisition, and you answered, No; that you were no Jew nor Roman catholic,

Catholic, that you was an English Protestant; and that the inquisition had nothing to do with you. *Mart.* My lord, I have oftentimes said so. *Inq.* What, are you under no laws, because you are an Englishman? *Mart.* My lord, an honest man fears no justice. I know, that let me live where I will, I am subject to the civil laws of the country; but I did not believe the ecclesiastical law, as I suppose you call this, had any power over English Protestants. *Inq.* You think, that because you are an English Protestant, you may say or do what you please. This is a country where people must take a great deal of care what they say. *Mart.* My lord, I lived such a life at Malaga, that I feared no justice; if I have said amiss, I beg your Lordship's pardon. *Inq.* Do you beg pardon of the holy office, for what you have said? *Mart.* My lord, if I have said amiss, I beg pardon. *Inq.* Secretary, write down that the heretic begs pardon to that accusation; I wish it may do.

15th Acc. That you have had Jews in your house, without giving notice to the commissioner of the Inquisition, that they might be taken up, and prosecuted according to the laws of the country. How durst you to do such things? Do you remember any such things?

Mart. Yes, My Lord, I do very well. *Inq.* Let us hear what you have to say for yourself? *Mart.* My Lord, there came a ship bound for Leghorn, that had a passenger that came to my house. He spoke very good Spanish; and I believe, by his looks, he was a Jew. He stayed with his captain about two hours at my house. I never saw him before nor since; he might be a Christian, for what I knew; but being bound for Leghorn, and speaking good Spanish, I thought he was a Jew. That is all that I know of the man. God knows what religion he was of. *Inq.* Do you know the person that has sent his accusation against you? *Mart.* Yes, my lord, his name is A. H. a man of a sorry character.

16th Acc. That it is confirmed by feveral people, that the faid heretic, Ifaac Martin, during his living at Malaga, has, at divers times, fhown himfelf very difaffected againft the holy faith of the church of Rome, and has hindered fome people from embracing it; and, had it not been for the fake of his family, he had been murdered long ago; and we recommend him to your holy office, as a dangerous and pernicious man againft the holy faith of the church of Rome, and as one of its greateft enemies; and a great many report, that he is a Jew. We defire your holy tribunal will examine him, with a great deal of ftrictnefs, according to the cuftom of your holy office; and give him fuch chaftifement as your lordfhips fhall think fit, as well in body, as in chattels.

Inq. Well, what have you to fay for yourfelf? See what a character people give you? Sure, you are a very wicked man! *Mart.* My lord, I fuppofe thefe are very good Chriftians that give me this character! God knows beft what to do with them. There is none of them that can fay, that I have wronged any body at Malaga. I have always profeffed myfelf to be a Proteftant; and for that reafon, and no other, I have been brought here. I hope God will enable me to go through thefe afflictions. I am very well affured, that your lordfhip knows that I am no Jew. As for what character they give me, God knows beft whether I deferve it or no. I have anfwered, to your examination, the truth, to the beft of my remembrance; and I believe your lordfhip knows it to be fo; and knows, that thofe people which informed againft me, are but people of a very indifferent character, who have always envied me, ever fince I lived at Malaga. *Inq.* Moft of your accufers are your countrymen. Sure, they would not fpeak againft you, if it was not fo! *Mart.* My lord, thofe whom you reckon my countrymen, are the worft enemies I have. I deny them for countrymen. They are Irifh. It is true that Ireland belongs to the
crown·

in the INQUISITION at GRANADA. 355

crown of England; but thefe people have deferted from our army, and are enemies to my religion, king, and country, and the worft that an Englifh Proteftant can have abroad. I wonder, my lord, that there is never a merchant, or a man of any good repute, that has declared any thing againft me. *Inq.* Hold your tongue. Do you think that I will believe all you fay? To be fure, you have been a very wicked man, by what is mentioned here; and you deny a great many things, and are fo malicious, that you give what turn you pleafe to things. I have heard of you four years ago. You are a fly man. But we have tortures to make people fpeak the truth, if they do not. *Mart.* My lord, you may do what you pleafe with me. I cannot help myfelf. Your lordfhip knows that I have declared the truth. *Inq.* You fhall have a lawyer to defend your caufe; but I believe it is very bad. [The lawyer is called in; my lord tells him that I am a ftrong heretic; that he has examined me; that I deny a great many things of which I am accufed. He bids him write to Malaga, to know what they fay of me: tells him that my cafe is very bad, but might be remedied; but I would not.] Go, you are guilty. You may repent of what you have faid, if you do not take care. Sign thefe papers, which is what you confefs. [The lawyer faid yea, and nay, to what my lord faid, and fpoke not a word to me, nor I to him; fo I went away to my dungeon.

Don Fernando had oftentimes told me, that if I would go to audience, I might, if I defired it. Finding that I was a fortnight without being called, I told him, that I defired audience; which was granted me two or three days afterwards. Coming into the room, my Lord begun thus.

Inq. Well, Ifaac, What have you to fay in your defence? You have demanded audience. *Mart.* My lord, I have nothing to fay, but what I have faid already. I come to beg the favour of your lordfhip to difpatch dispatch me. I believe you have done examining of me. I remember, that they desired your lordship to chastise me in body and wealth. I believe that my body has been chastised enough, in suffering what I have suffered; and to be locked up in a dark dungeon, by myself, where I am used worse than a dog. As for what wealth God has given me, your lordship is welcome to it. If I am such a bad man, as people report, fetter me, and send me, with my family, aboard any ship; let her be bound where she will, God will provide for us. *Inq.* Hold, hold, Isaac, things are not done so soon as you think for. You have broken the articles of peace, by your own confession. *Mart.* My lord, I am very sorry if I have. I desire your lordship would shew them to me; that I may know in what I am guilty. *Inq.* I have them. You shall see them another time. There is a great deal to be said in your affair. Have you any thing else to say? *Mart.* No, My lord, I desire to be tried by them. You was pleased to tell me, that you would quickly dispatch me. *Inq.* Go, go to your dungeon, and think upon what you have done.

When I came to my dungeon, I was resolved to ask for no more audience; and wondered that such a man, who sits upon a throne betwixt two crucifixes, attributing to himself holiness and infallibility, should tell me so many lies; and found that there was no way of redemption, but by praying to God, to give me strength to overcome the miseries that I was in, and in his mercy, to deliver me from their hands.

Some days after, Don Joseph Equarez, the third inquisitor, came with a secretary to my dungeon, and thus he begun.

Inq. How do you do, Isaac? Have you any thing to say in your defence? Can I serve you in any thing? Tell me. *Mart.* My lord, I have nothing to say, but what I have said already. I think it is very hard to be kept here so long. *Inq.* Hark ye, you think, you

you Englishmen, that we aim at your wealth; but you are mistaken: there is no such thing. You have confessed, that you did not pull your hat off at our images. You ought to do it, living in these Christian countries, whether you believe in them or no; for it shews ill examples, if you do not. *Mart.* My lord, we Protestants never do such things; it is against our religion and against our conscience so to do. *Inq.* You must all do it in this country, and it is a thing that ought to be done. See if I can serve you in any thing? *Mart.* If your lordship would be pleased to get me out of this misery, I should be very much obliged to you. *Inq.* There is time for all things. You have been brought up in heresy; you are here for the good of your soul; you must enlighten yourself in the true faith. I will do you all the service I can. Have you any thing else to say? *Mart.* My lord, I hope to be saved in the faith that I am in. *Inq.* Well, think upon what I have said to you. Fare you well.

DESCRIPTION of the INQUISITION of GRANADA.

In my dismal solitude, having no comfort of the world but to see Don Fernando and Don Baltazar, when they came to light my lamp mornings and nights, I studied, as much as I could, to get into their favour, that I might have some small comfort in speaking to them. They were both pretty civil in their way; but especially Don Fernando, who told me, he had been a passenger aboard an English ship, and the captain was very civil to him; and that he loved the English very well; that he would do me all the service that he could; bidding me to take patience; that he believed my case was not mortal; and he believed, that if I would change my religion, I should soon be at liberty: that he thought I was wise enough to see what I was there for; that the holy Inquisition had a mind to make me a good Christian.

Christian. I told him, that I thought their lordships aimed at that; but it was a thing that I could not do; that it was against my conscience; and I desired him to let me have as much of his conversation as he could. He told me, that he was not allowed to talk to the prisoners, but would come now and then to talk a little to me; which he did sometimes, opening the close door, and through the grated one, we used to talk together for two or three minutes; which was a great deal of satisfaction to me in my dismal solitude. I aimed to learn of him what I could, relating to the secrets of the Inquisition. But as they are sworn to keep secret the ways they have, I could get but little out of him.

The Inquisition is like a palace, till you open the doors of the dungeons; and then it looks very dismal. It is built much in the same manner as a convent, with galleries all round it. There are dungeons on the ground floor, up one pair of stairs, and up two pair of stairs, all in the same nature. They are about fifteen foot long, and ten in breadth; two doors to each dungeon, well bolted, and well locked; light enough to see to read, in some parts where the light gives. There are three lords Inquisitors; but there is but one that examines at an audience. They have their apartments in the Inquisition. There are five secretaries, two gaol-keepers, which receive salary from the king. The king names the Inquisitors, and the pope confirms them. Don Baltazar, the under-gaol-keeper, told me, there were about a hundred dungeons, and each person is in one by himself. The prisoners are let out but one at a time, to fetch their allowance, or to throw out their dirt, which is twice a week each, and then they are locked up. Every prisoner is allowed five pence halfpenny a day, English coin, for all necessaries. The gaol-keeper comes and asks you twice a week, what you will have to eat or to drink, as far as it would go. I was allowed between four and five pound of bread a week;

a week; two pound and a quarter of meat, which I used to make six boilings of; and on a Friday, boiled some bread with a little oil and greens together for my dinner. I was best provided with wine; for I had about six pints of our measure per week. Greens I had plenty to put in my pot. I had at breakfast a piece of bread, as big as a couple of eggs, a glass of wine and a glass of water mixed together, and at supper the same; but at dinner I had always my six ounces of meat (except Fridays) and a great deal of greens boiled along with it; so that my belly was pretty full at dinner. The first day my meat was sweet; but the second it smelt, and the third it stunk, and was green in summer-time: but I used to eat it, having nothing else. At first I thought it very hard to be reduced to such an allowance, having lived in plenty; but sometime after I was used to it; but grew very lean, though, I thank God, I enjoyed my health almost all the time I was there.

The Inquisitors are respected by every body; but more for fear than for love. They all keep their coaches. I asked Don Fernando one day, if the prisoners were kept long there; for I had heard that they were kept sometimes ten years; to which he answered, ten is nothing, for sometimes they are kept twenty and thirty years, and sometimes three or four before they are examined. Hearing these words I was troubled very much, so that I was afraid to ask him any thing else at that time. The prisoners are allowed earthen plates, and pipkins, and an earthen stove to light fire in; pitchers to hold water, three baskets to put their bread and necessaries in, a wooden spoon, a broom; and a bason to do what one has occasion in. There are no shelves nor tables allowed, nor any thing to sit upon but some boards, that are fastened in the wall which your bed is upon. You are allowed no knife nor fork; so that they are obliged to part their meat with their teeth and fingers as well as they can. I had heard, many years before

fore I was taken up, that they gave meat without bones to the prisoners that were in the Inquisition; but to my sorrow, when I came there, I found the contrary: for sometimes out of six ounces, I believe, I had but three or four of meat. The prisoners are not allowed books, pen, ink, nor paper; and if they are there ever so many years, they can never hear from their family or relations. They are not allowed to hear sermons, or mass, nor to take the sacrament; and if they pray, it must be so softly that no body can hear them, upon pain of being chastised.

I was one day singing to myself very softly, thinking no body heard me, the sixth psalm, which was very *à propos* for the condition I was in; but Don Fernando came and threatened me, and bid me hold my tongue. I asked his pardon, and I found it out afterwards, that they walked softly, to hear if the prisoners made any noise, or spoke one to another. They are so secret in their ways, that several friends and relations may be in the same Inquisition, and not know of it.

If a person dies there, he is buried without any ceremony: but he is allowed to confess to a priest before he dies. If after he is dead he is found guilty, his bones are brought in a box to be burnt, when the *Auto da Fé* is celebrated, when they deliver people out of the Inquisition, to receive the punishment to which they have been condemned. The prisoners are not to know their accusers, nor what they are accused of; they must guess it, and accuse themselves: and if they do not, they torture them to make them confess; and by these violences many are made to confess things that they were never guilty of, in order to confiscate what they are worth in the world, which they take care to have in their own hands; for when they seize a person, they seize all that he has. His family may starve, they do not mind that. And if the person should complain, after they have made him take the oath to keep the secret, and not

to

to discover what has been done to him during the time he was in the Inquisition, if they find it out, and retake him, he is burnt, or sent to the gallies, without remission; for having complained against the Inquisition, after he had confessed he was guilty: so that people, to save their lives, very often confess what they are not guilty of; and when they have got out of their hands, though they have suffered the torture, and lost what they had, are obliged to say, that the holy Inquisition is just, for fear of being retaken. Thus it happens very often, that people are accused of being Jews who were very good Christians; and, by being tortured, confess they are Jews, though they never were; and by confessing, they save their lives, though they lose what they are worth in the world. Others rather chuse to suffer death. There have been frequent instances of persons, who have declared at the place of execution, that they died Christians, and never were Jews; and hoped that Christ would have mercy on them; for they chose rather to die than to deny the Christian faith. But when any person dies in the Roman faith, he has the benefit of being strangled, before he is put in the flames.

I could recollect a great many such examples, which I have heard from Roman Catholics themselves, who complain of that way of justice, but durst not speak it publicly for fear of being taken up. It is certain that there is not such a court in the world, nor any that takes such titles as they do; for they call themselves the Holy Tribunal of the Inquisition, the Holy House, the Holy Office, and do what they please under the name of justice; and people are obliged to speak well of it, and to say that they are infallible, though a great many in their hearts believe the contrary, and know, by woeful experience, that their families and themselves have been ruined by them, but durst not complain: for there are so many familiars belonging to them, that give

them

them an account of what they hear say, that people are forced to keep silence.

The word familiar means properly a spy or informer, who gives an account to the Inquisition of what they hear and what they see. It is a place of honour, but of little benefit; except in one thing, that is, if they owe money, no body dares to touch them. There are of all sorts of them, from a duke to a tradesman, and when the Inquisition has a mind to take up any body, they give them orders to do it, and they can command who they please to assist them; for no body dares refuse, upon pain of being taken up themselves; so great is the power of the Inquisition.

I asked Don Fernando one day, how many familiars he thought might belong to the Inquisition of Granada? He told me, he could not very well tell, but he believed there might be about a thousand in all, beside commissioners and secretaries, which are in less number, but spread all over the country, as well as familiars.

There are several Inquisitions in Spain; but the chief is at Madrid, and by what I could learn by Don Fernando, they all give an account, in some measure, of what they do, to the Inquisition of Madrid. I asked Don Fernando another time, whether they put people of quality in the Inquisition? He told me, that the King was subject to it, and that the Inquisition was above him, and that there was a bishop in a little while ago. I asked him for what? He told me, that he had committed some errors in the holy faith. I was allowed a lawyer to defend my cause; but he was not allowed to speak to me, nor I to him.

The holy tribunal, as they call it, is almost as large as our house of parliament, where the lords sit, very finely adorned with pictures. There is also a fine altar: the throne is garnished with red velvet. There are three very fine armed chairs where the Inquisitors fit; behind them there is a large crucifix, embroidered with gold; at the right-hand of it is the triple crown, and the crofs keys under it; and at the left-hand a naked fword, and the king's arms under it, all finely embroidered upon red velvet, with gold and filver. The table is alfo covered with red velvet, with a crucifix upon it, about two foot high, of gold or filver gilded: the fecretary fits at the end of the table, and the prifoner fronting the two crucifixes, and my lord. There is a large filver ftandifh, and fome filver bells upon the table, to call the fecretaries or the gaol-keepers; for there muft no voices be heard.

After I had been there about thirteen weeks, I was called to audience again, which rejoiced me very much, thinking that now I fhould know my doom. When I came into the room, my lord begun thus.

Inq. Well, Ifaac, have you thought of any thing elfe in your affair, befide what you have already declared? *Mart.* No, my lord, I have nothing to fay, unlefs I repeat what I have faid already; I believe it will fignify nothing. *Inq.* Here are feveral more accufations come againft you, that you muft anfwer to. *Mart.* It is very well, my lord. I will anfwer to them as well as I can. [He reads them over, and I believe there were as many again as before; fome I have fet down here that I remember.] *Inq.* Well, Ifaac, what have you to fay now? *Mart.* My lord, this is the fame thing over again, only the accufations are fomething altered and mifplaced. I can quickly anfwer to them; and as for thofe that are added to them, they are almoft all falfe, and the devil has invented them. *Inq.* Hold, Ifaac, you talk ftrangely. *Mart.* My lord, I fpeak the truth. Your lordfhip was pleafed to tell me, at my firft coming, that you would difpatch me very foon. I have been here above three months, and am no likelier to get out than the firft day. *Inq.* Hold, hold; do you think that juftice is done here, as in your country, at random, and I don't know how? Here things are well
exa-

examined, and juftice is done as it ought to be done. *Mart.* My lord, I believe we have good juftice done in England; but I beg your lordfhip's pardon, I do not underftand this way of juftice. *Inq.* I believe you do not. It is no matter. Remember that you are upon your oath, and anfwer to thefe articles. *Mart.* Muft I anfwer to them that I have anfwered already? *Inq.* Yes, you muft; and take care what you fay. *Mart.* It is very well, my lord. [I quickly ran over them, and then he began with the frefh ones.]

17th Acc. That I hindered my family from being brought up in the Chriftian faith; and that if it was not for me, they would be all Romans, and it is againft the laws of the country to hinder them.

Mart. My lord, it is falfe that my family had any inclination to be Romans; neither can any laws oblige them to be fo, or hinder me from bringing them up in my religion. Your lordfhip, five weeks ago, told me, that you would fhew me the articles of peace, and that I had broke them; pray let me fee them, my lord. *Inq.* You fhall fee them another time. Anfwer to thefe articles. *Mart.* My lord, all my family are as I am. I could never perceive that they had a mind to change their religion. *Inq.* What! Do you deny this Accufation? *Mart.* Yes, my lord, I do. It is all falfe.

18th Acc. That I ufed to fhut my window-fhutters when the proceffion went by, to hinder my children from kneeling down; and ufed to beat them, if they fhewed any inclination to be Roman Catholics.

Mart. My lord, it is true that I have fhut my fhutters feveral times; for fometimes I have had captains of fhips in my houfe, that would not pull their hats off when they faw them. As for my children, they went to the window generally to laugh, and I oftentimes bid them not to fhew themfelves when they went by, that no fcandal might be given. And if I had beat them, as it is faid, I believe that I have

have the liberty to do it, if I pleafe. *Inq.* No, you have not, in fome cafes. How old are your children? *Mart.* One is fifteen, the other is eight, and the other is five years of age. *Inq.* They are of age to be brought up in the Chriftian faith. *Mart.* I hope they are, my lord; but as for the two youngeft, they can be brought up to any religion. *Inq.* Your daughter, and your fon Abraham, are of age; and you are but their father-in-law. They may be brought up in the Chriftian faith. You have nothing to do with them. *Mart.* My lord, I hope that they are Chriftians, and I look upon them as if they were my own children. *Inq.* So that you would have them brought up in your religion? *Mart.* Yes, my lord.

19th Acc. That my daughter being of age, had often faid in the neighbourhood, that fhe would be a Roman Catholic; but fhe was afraid that I fhould beat her if I knew of it; and that I had oftentimes beat her upon that account.

Mart. My lord, I have nothing to anfwer to fuch lies. It is as falfe as the devil is falfe. *Inq.* What! Have you nothing to fay, Ifaac, to this article? *Mart.* No, my lord, I never knew my daughter inclinable to be a Roman; and I never did beat her upon that account; it is all falfe; and you may order your fecretary to write down what you pleafe.

20th Acc. That in Lent, and other faft-days, I caufed my family to eat meat, and forbid them to keep any faft-days that were appointed by the church of Rome; and beat them if they did.

Mart. My lord, thofe are poor accufations, and they are all falfe. I thank God, my table afforded flefh and fifh all the year round: I never troubled my head to fee what the fervants ufed to eat; and as for my wife and children, we eat meat all the year, without fcruple of confcience, your lordfhip knows that. *Inq.* You Englifh mind nothing but eating and drinking, and living at your eafe, without doing any

any penance. *Mart.* My lord, I beg your pardon; we have fouls to be faved as well as other nations. We are born in a plentiful country; and, I believe, we live as well as any nation, and ferve God as well. *Inq.* Your country was a good country formerly; it produced a great many faints: but now it produces no fuch thing. *Mart.* My lord, I believe, there are no faints now; but I am perfuaded it produces as many good men as ever it did. *Inq.* Hold your tongue. You are all loft men. You are fallen from the holy church, and there is no falvation for you if you do not come into it again.

21ft Acc. That my children had often been at mafs, and at prayers, in the neighbourhood, and would do it every day if I would let them; but I beat them, and hindered them from being Chriftians, and was the occafion of lofing of their fouls.

Mart. My lord, I never knew my children go to mafs, nor prayers, in the neighbourhood, nor ever beat them upon that account. I hope God will fave their fouls in the religion they are brought up in, though the church of Rome condemns them; and the accufation is falfe. *Inq.* Why! you deny every thing almoft. *Mart.* I deny nothing but what is falfe, my lord. *Inq.* Well, but you may forget, Ifaac. *Mart.* No, my lord, I have nothing elfe to think of; and I do think that thefe are very infignificant articles to allege againft me, if they were as they fay; but they are falfe, and I believe, they are fcandalous people that have invented them. *Inq.* Hold your tongue. How durft you fpeak fo? *Mart.* It is very well, my Lord. Let your fecretary write down any thing, what you pleafe; it is all falfe.

22d Acc. That living at Lifbon, I had several difputes about religion. That I hid myfelf for fear of being taken up by the Inquifition, as being a Jew.——Come anfwer, What have you to fay to this article? It is of confequence.

Mart.

Mart. My lord, let your secretary write down what you please; I have nothing to answer to such scandalous reports. God knows that I am no Jew, and your lordship knows it very well. The devil has invented this to frighten me; but God, that knows every thing, will revenge my cause. *Inq.* Well, but Isaac, you see what they write against you, and all your family's names are antient, and of the Mosaical law. *Mart.* My lord, you have oftentimes reflected upon my name being Isaac, and my son's name being Abraham; but you do not talk of a child that I buried at Malaga, whose name was Peter, and one that I have, whose name is Bernard; they are saints names. *Inq.* Those are all Christian names. *Mart.* And so are the others, my lord. We do not mind whether we give our children names out of the Old or New Testament. Beside, my lord, neither Abraham, nor Isaac, nor Jacob, were Jews. *Inq.* Yes, they were Jews. Sure you are mistaken. *Mart.* I beg your lordship's pardon, I am not mistaken. *Inq.* What were they then? Let us hear. *Mart.* My lord, they were Hebrews; they lived under the law of nature, as God inspired and spoke to them; but were dead many hundred years before God had given his laws to Moses. *Inq.* Hold your tongue. Methinks you understand something of the Mosaical laws. *Mart.* My lord, thank God, I understand some of the Old and some of the New Law; but not so much as I should. We have always the Old and the New Testament in our families; and we read in them, to instruct us in our religion. *Inq.* Hold your tongue; you give a wrong sense to scripture. Your knowing so much has brought you here. You had better know less, and believe the true faith. *Mart.* My lord, I hope to be saved in what I believe: and if at Lisbon I was disputing of religion, it was not defending the laws of Moses; for several Jews were burnt, whilst I was there. Therefore, my lord, it

proves

proves that the accufation is falfe, and that I would not run fuch hazards.

23d Acc. That I bred fchifms among the people, perfuading them to turn heretics, and to leave the church of Rome; out of which no man can be faved.

Mart. I wifh your Lordfhip, or any body elfe, would tell me who I perfuaded to change their religion. You may accufe me of any thing: hell cannot invent greater lies. I cannot think, my lord, who could have fent fuch accufations againft me. When I talked of religion, it was generally with clergymen, and not with common people; for I knew that they are not allowed to talk of religion, and they are not capable of it, and know but little of the matter. *Inq.* They know enough; it is believing that faves us, and you will not believe, but deny almoft every article. Hold your tongue.

24th Acc. That my name being Ifaac, and my fon's name Abraham, I muft be a Jew, or related to Jews.

Mart. My lord, I have fufficiently anfwered upon this matter; this is nothing but repetitions. The Roman Catholics which are in Holland and Flanders, do not much mind whether their children have names out of the Old, or out of the New Teftament. And I know a man at Malaga, who is a Flanderkin, and a Roman Catholic, whofe name is Jacob. As for my parents, I never knew any of them Jews; let your fecretary write what you pleafe.

25th Acc. That I had offered to difpofe of my houfe, and to retire for fear of being taken up by the Inquifition.

Mart. My lord, it is true, that I offered to difpofe of my houfe; but not for fear of the Inquifition: for I never thought that they had any thing to do with Englifh Proteftants. If I had been afraid of it, I would not have come to live in this country. I had opportunities enough to go aboard of Englifh fhips, and retire, if I had been afraid. *Inq.* What, then

then you thought the Inquisition had nothing to do with English Proteſtants? You are miſtaken. *Mart.* My lord, I ſee I am, to my ſorrow. *Inq.* What did you deſign to do, after that you had diſpoſed of your houſe? *Mart.* My lord, to go to my own country; for I was tired of living abroad, eſpecially at Malaga, where I could have no reſt, but was daily affronted on account of my religion. *Inq.* You have a tongue, that you made uſe of to defend yourſelf. *Mart.* My lord, I could not always bear their inſolences; but I find they have accompliſhed their deſign. *Inq.* Well, hold your tongue, you may help yourſelf ſtill, if you will.

26th Acc. That you was always making game of the religion of the church of Rome. Well, what have you to ſay to that?

Mart. My lord, I do not deny, that being in company with ſome Roman Catholics, as they made game of my religion, I made game of theirs; but it was joking, and not in a profane way. *Inq.* Religion ought not to be mocked. *Mart.* It is very true, my lord; but I never ſcandalized them, as they did me, upon the account of my religion. *Inq.* What did they uſe to ſay to you? Let us hear? *Mart.* My lord, you know that the church of Rome does not allow the heretics (as you call them) to be ſaved. In our faith, we have charity for all men; we condemn nobody. I have oftentimes been told, that I and my family were damned, and that it was impoſſible for us to be ſaved. My lord, it is very hard to hear ſuch words, ſo often as I have: I have ſometimes given them an anſwer that they did not like; for I could not always bear what they ſaid. I hope to be ſaved, through God's mercy, as well as they do. *Inq.* So, you ſay, that when they made game of your religion, you made game of theirs; is not that what you ſay? *Mart.* Yes, my lord. *Inq.* Well, hold your tongue; you are a ſly man; you give what turn you pleaſe to things, and deny almoſt every thing:

you will repent of this, if you do not take care; we have ways to make people confess when they will not. Sign these papers, which are the articles you have confessed, and what you deny. But I will not believe you. I have heard of you a long while ago, and know now that you are a cunning pernicious man against the holy catholic faith. *Mart.* My lord, I find that all my defences signify nothing. You have oftentimes bid me defend my cause, and when I would have defended it more than I have, you have often bid me hold my tongue, for you will not believe what I say. I have declared the truth to the best of my knowlege; do with me what you please. I hope God will deliver me from the misery I am in. He knows that I have confessed the truth, and your lordship knows it very well too. *Inq.* Hold your tongue, and say no more. [In comes the lawyer, and sits down. My lord speaks.]

Well, seignor lawyer, I have examined this heretic again; he answers much as he did before: but denies almost all the new articles. I hope you writ to Malaga, that there might be an exact account taken of his life and conversation during the time he lived there. *Law.* Yes, My lord, I did. *Inq.* He has been brought up in heresy; I believe we shall make nothing of him: he follows the steps of Luther and Calvin, who are burning in hell fire, with abundance of their followers. [The secretary and the lawyer spake thus, *To be sure, they are all damned.*] *Mart.* I hope they are not, my lords. *Inq.* Hold your tongue, they are; and every body that does not believe in the holy church of Rome. Are not you sorry for what you have said, during your living at Malaga? *Mart.* My lord, in what I have said amiss, I am sorry for it. Pray tell me, my lord, if the people who have accused me are all upon their oath? *Inq.* Most of them are; they would not say a thing that is not. *Mart.* My lord, it is very well; God is just, and he will be even with them. *Inq.* Well, hold

hold your tongue; you beg pardon of this holy tribunal for what you are guilty of, and defire to be ufed with that mercy and clemency as is accuftomed in this holy office. Is not that what you mean? *Mart.* Yes, my lord, what you pleafe. He fhook his head, and faid I wifh that may do; get you gone to your dungeon.

I had been there about four months, and had had fifteen audiences during that time. Some lafted half an hour, fome an hour, and fome above two hours, full of repetitions. Sometimes he ufed to fpeak very fmoothly to me, and fometimes very roughly, threatening oftentimes to punifh me; and always giving me to underftand, in a crafty jefuitical way of fpeaking, which they have, that if I would change my religion, I might eafily get out of my troubles. It made me very uneafy to fee what he aimed at; but, I thank God, it had no effect upon me: though, I muft confefs, that the flefh being weak, and he frightening me, together with the mifery I was in, fometimes drove me almoft to defpair, fo that I was in fufpence, whether I fhould change my religion or no. But I ftill prayed to God to give me ftrength to overcome all my troubles, and to go through thofe pains wherewith I was threatened, without renouncing the Proteftant religion, which, in his great mercy, he had enlightened me withal.

Whitfun-eve, I was fhaved againft my will; for you muft be fhaved three times a year, whether you will or no, but no oftener. Don Fernando gave me a piece of frankincenfe to put in the fire; bid me clean my dungeon, and drefs myfelf very clean, to receive a vifit from the lords of the Inquifition, who came a little while after. There were two of them, and a fecretary. The head lord, who had examined me, fpoke to me thus.

Inq. Well, Ifaac, how do you? You look very well in health. Can I ferve you in any thing, tell me? *Mart.* My lord, I am, I thank God, well in health;

health; but very much troubled in mind, to be detained here so long from my family. Your lordship has done examining of me; I beg you would dispatch me out of this misery, that I am in. *Inq.* I will do you all the service I can; but you must do what you can to serve yourself. *Mart.* My lord, I do not know what to do; I would do any thing to get out of this misery: I am almost in despair. Your lordship told me, that I should have a lawyer to defend my cause. *Inq.* So you have had one, Isaac, did you not see him? *Mart.* My lord, there was a man that you called a lawyer; but he never spoke to me, nor I to him. If all your lawyers are so quiet in this country, they are the quietest that are in the world; for he hardly said any thing, but yea, and nay, to what your lordship said. *Inq.* Hold, Isaac, the lawyers are not allowed to speak here. He has writ to Malaga for you, and has done what should be done in your case. You do not understand this way of justice. *Mart.* It is very true, I do not understand it at all. [The secretary, and the gaol-keeper, were forced to go out of the dungeon, to laugh; and the two lords smiled to hear me talk as I did: and I scarce knew how to keep my countenance, to think what a lawyer I had to defend my cause, who was not allowed to speak to me, nor I to him.

Inq. Isaac, you know what day it is to-morrow. I would have you think of enlightening yourself in the holy faith; this is a proper time, and I believe it would facilitate your getting your liberty. *Mart.* My lord, if I had no light of divinity, or religion, before I came here, I could get none where I am; for I am locked up without seeing any body to speak to, neither have I any books to read to instruct me; I have hardly day-light, to eat what little victuals are allowed me.

Don PETRO LEONOR, the second INQUISITOR, speaks.

Inq. If you will, you shall have a Jesuit to enlighten

lighten you. *Mart.* You may send one if you please; but I believe it will signify nothing.

Don JOSEPH VILEOT, the HEAD INQUISITOR, speaks.

Inq. No, it must come from himself. It signifies nothing to send him any body. *Mart.* My lord, I hope you allow that the holy scripture is perfect. *Inq.* Yes, I do, Isaac. *Mart.* My lord, I believe in it, and believe it is sufficient to save my soul, if I believe according to it. *Inq.* There are other things that you must believe, beside scripture; that are revealed to the holy church. *Mart.* My lord, I have been brought here for defending my religion; if your lordship would give me leave to speak, I could, by scripture, prove to you, that it is sufficient to believe in it; but I durst not. *Inq.* Well, Isaac, hold your tongue; it is no matter. You must pray to God to enlighten you in the holy faith. *Mart.* So I do, my lord, and hope he will deliver me from my troubles. *Inq.* It is for your good, that we admonish you. It is time for you to take care of your soul. It is a pity that such a man as you, have been brought up in heresy. We would have you consider upon it, for your own good, and it would be a great help to get out of your troubles. *Mart.* I thank your lordship for your advice. I gave you, at first, a short account of my religion. I hope that God will save me in the belief I am in. I beg your lordship's pardon; I cannot change.

Speaks Don PETRO LEONOR, the Second INQUISITOR.

Inq. You must forget what you know, and believe what we say; and that is your only way to get out of your troubles. *Mart.* I beg your lordship's pardon. I am too old to forget what I know. *Inq.* Well, think upon what we have said to you; it is for your

your own good. *Mart.* It is very well, my lord. *Inq.* Good by'e.

And so the door was shut; and I was as likely to get out as the first day, which made me very uneasy in my mind.

About a fortnight after, Don Fernando and Don Baltazar, the two gaol-keepers, came and told me, that I must remove and go to another dungeon. I begged of them to let me remain where I was; but it signified nothing; for they told me the lords had given them orders. When I came to my new dungeon, I thought myself better than where I had been; for I had more light, and could hear some dogs bark, and cocks crow, which was a great satisfaction to me in my dismal solitude; and I did not hear those bitter groans and cries of prisoners, as I used to do sometimes, which terrified me very much. What they did to them, God knows; but I believe they gave them the torture; for it is frequent in that holy place, as they call it. Women with sucking children I could often hear cry and lament. But I had not been there above three or four days, but I wished myself in my old dungeon; for I was so tormented with bugs, that I could not sleep at nights; so that I slept in the day as well as I could. I complained to Don Fernando; but he told me he could not help me; and that I must have patience. Some time after, Don Baltazar came and bid me empty a bason of the prisoners, which I refused, and we had high words about it: but Don Fernando came and told me that I must do it; and if the king was there he should do it. I made no resistance; for I found it was in vain, and that it was to plague me that they had moved me from my dungeon; and then to make me empty basons for others. But I said, I would make my complaint to my lords when I should see them; but I was immediately sent for, and my lord reprimanded me for refusing to do such a thing at the first bidding. I

told

told his lordſhip, that I did not know that he had given ſuch orders; begged his pardon, and ſaid, if he pleaſed I would empty them for all the priſoners. He ſaid, there was no occaſion for that; bid me be gone; but emptying of baſons did not laſt long: for when I had emptied my own, I uſed to aſk the gaol-keeper, whether he had no baſons for me to empty; who, finding that I was ſo forward, would let me empty no more.

Some time after, Don Fernando eſpied a little hole that the mice had made in the wall, and the light came through. He went and acquainted my lord with it, who came in a great paſſion, and called me all to naught, and told me that I had made that hole; that I was a rogue by profeſſion, and that I ſhould pay for all my doings. I begged his lordſhip's pardon, and told him that he might call me what he pleaſed; and that he knew very well that I could not make ſuch a hole, for I had nothing to make it with.

One day I met Don Joſeph Equarez, the third Inquiſitor, at the turn where they give their allowance. He aſked me how I did, as they always do. I told him that I was in health, thank God; but was very much ſurprized to be detained ſo long in priſon from my family; that the law of Chriſt was a law of compaſſion, and merciful, and that it was very hard to be ſerved as I was. I had no ſooner ſpoke thoſe words, but he fell in a rage; bidding me hold my tongue, and mind where I was, and not talk of religion; that if he ever heard me talk ſo again, he knew what to do with me: that there was nothing practiſed but the religion of Chriſt, and mercifulneſs, in the Inquiſition; and how durſt I complain againſt it? I humbly begged his pardon, telling him, that if I had ſaid amiſs, it was for want of knowing better, and that I was ſorry for it. I went to my dungeon, and glad to get off ſo; for he was in a terrible paſſion, and I was very much afraid of him.

I aſked

I asked Don Fernando, some time after, what made him fall into such a passion? He told me that he had reason, and that I must never contradict them in what they say, nor talk of religion; for they were holy men, that knew what they did, and were infallible.

One day, Don Fernando softly, unawares, opened the door, and found me in tears, which happened very often at those times, deploring my hard fate; and praying to God to deliver me from those enemies of the church I was brought up in, and to send me and my family into my native country. He asked me what was the matter? I told him, I had been a praying to God to deliver me from the misery I was in. He told me, that I did not pray to the right God, pitied my condition, and so went away.

Six and twenty weeks after that I had been there, Don Baltazar came to me to go to the audience, and bid me dress myself quickly. I was no sooner out of my dungeon, but he tied a handkerchief about my eyes. I asked him what that was for? He told me, it must be so; and as he was leading me along by the hand, I remembered what the old Inquisitor had told me, that there were torments to make people confess the truth; and how often he had threatened me. I thought it was now going to be put in execution, which terrified me very much; but still trusted that God would give me strength to withstand their torments.

Coming to a place where there are gaggs, that they gagg the prisoners with when they torture them, to prevent their making a noise, I heard a voice that bid me stop, and pull off my cloaths. At which I answered, Must I pull off my cloaths? Yes, said one, pull off your cloaths.

As I was pulling them off, I heard another say, Keep your coat and your waistcoat on and put down your breeches: which accordingly I did, and was twice examined by several examiners; for I could hear several voices, but could see no body. They concluded

cluded that I was not circumcifed; bid me put my breeches up and be gone. Don Baltazar led me back to my dungeon, and glad I was to get off fo; for I muft confefs, I was very much afraid of being tortured; nor did I like fuch audiences.

When I came to my dungeon, I afked Don Baltazar, if that was their way of difpatching of people? That they might, at my firft coming, fee whether I was circumcifed, without ftaying fix and twenty weeks. He fell a laughing, and told me my cafe went on very brifkly; fo fhut the door.

About a month after, one Sunday morning, Don Fernando told me, that I muft get myfelf ready; for I muft go out of gaol, and return to my family. Perceiving that he fmiled, I thought he jefted, and defired him not to jeer me in my afflictions; but fpeaking ferioufly to me, he told me, that the barber would come prefently, and that I muft appear before the lords, and a great many gentlemen.

I cannot exprefs the joy I was in to hear fuch news. I fell a trembling and weeping for joy; fo that for a while I could not put on my cloaths; but recovering a little, I dreffed myfelf as well as I could, and gave God hearty thanks that it had pleafed him to hear my prayers.

Sometime after being fhaved they came for me, but would not let me take my perriwig; but made me go bareheaded. Don Baltazar bid me not be afraid; for they would do me no harm. I was very joyful, and told him, I was afraid of nothing, fo I could but get out of the place where I was; for had they given me my choice to go to the gallies, or to ftay in that difmal folitude, I would have chofen the gallies, where I might have feen, and have fpoken with a fellow-creature.

When I came into the audience-room, I found it full of people, dreffed in ceremonial robes, fome with white wands, and others with halberts. Two men imme-

immediately seized me, and made me kneel down before Don Joseph Equarez. At the same time a rope was put about my neck, which surprized me very much. Don Joseph Equarez, as I was kneeling down before him, spoke these words to me.

Your cause has been seen and examined; go along with those gentlemen: you shall soon be released.

They were about forty that led me in the streets, and then to a church. They placed me at the great altar fronting the pulpit, where a priest or a Jesuit came with a great many writings in his hand, containing my accusations, which he read to the people; but little or nothing of the defence I had made; but that I denied almost every thing: and that the holy Inquisition had done what she could, in admonishing me to embrace the holy faith of the church of Rome, without which no man can be saved; but I was such a pernicious heretic, that I would not hearken to the salvation of my soul, and that the holy tribunal had found me a great enemy to the holy faith. Then he declared, that for these crimes of which he stands convicted, the lords of the holy office have ordered him to be banished out of our Christian kingdoms, upon pain of two hundred lashes, and five years gallies, if ever he returns into any of our Christian dominions; and have given orders that he shall receive two hundred lashes through the public streets of this city.

After he had done reading to the people what he pleased, for there were a great many lies in what he read, I was remanded back to my dungeon.

At night, when Don Baltazar came to light my lamp, I asked him, whether I must receive those two hundred lashes that the priest had spoke of? He told me, that the lords were very merciful, and he believed that I might escape them if I would change my religion. I told him, that since I had endured so much, their lordships might do what they pleased, I would

I would not change. Then he told me that I might change, and when I was at liberty I might live in my own religion.

The next morning, about ten of the clock, I was brought down ſtairs; and as I was there, in came the executioner with ſome ropes and a whip. He bid me take my coat and waiſtcoat off, and pull off my wig and cravat. As I was taking off my ſhirt, he bid me let it alone, he would manage that. He ſlipped my body through the collar, and tied it about my waiſt. Then took a rope and tied my hands together, put another about my neck, and led me out of the Inquiſition, where there were numerous crouds of people waiting to ſee an Engliſh heretic. I was no ſooner out, but a prieſt read my ſentence at the door, as followeth.

"Orders are given, from the lords of the holy office of the Inquiſition, to give unto Iſaac Martin two hundred laſhes through the public ſtreets; he being of the religion of the church of England, a Proteſtant, a heretic, irreverent to the hoſt, and to the image of the Virgin Mary; and ſo let it be executed."

Knowing what was a going to be done to me, I was not ſo frightened as when they blindfolded me. The ſentence read, the executioner mounted me upon an aſs, and led me in the ſtreets; the people huzzaing, cried out, "An Engliſh heretic! Look at the Engliſh heretic, who is no Chriſtian!" and pelting me. The crier of the city walked before me, repeating aloud the ſentence that was read at the door of the Inquiſition, and the executioner whipping me as I went along, a great many people on horſeback in ceremonial robes, with white wands and halberts following of us.

As we paſſed by the market-place, the people's pelting incommoded me very much. I thought I ſhould be knocked off the aſs. I ſpoke aloud, and aſked them what country I was in? They cried out, "a Chriſtian

tian country." To which I replied, " Those ways are practised in Barbary, and not amongst Christians. I am a Christian as well as you are; if I have deserved to be chastised, I am in the justice's hands; let him do it, and not you."

A great many people of the better sort said that I was in the right, and the pelting ceased in a great measure; and a great many would hinder others from throwing at me, and bid me have patience. I thanked them very kindly, and told them, thank God, I had patience. They were surprized to hear me talk Spanish, and pitied me very much. I shall ever thank God for giving me so much patience as I had; for I was not at all concerned, so great was my joy to find that God had graciously delivered me out of their barbarous and cruel hands.

The show being over, which lasted about three quarters of an hour, I was brought back to the Inquisition. Don Fernando received me, and seemed to pity my condition. I asked him, if that was the mercy they practised there? And told him, that I was very well satisfied, and that for the sake of my religion, I was ready to receive a thousand lashes. My cloaths being put on, I mounted up stairs, and he locked me up in my dungeon, where I gave God thanks, that he had given me strength to go through so many severe trials, and had thought me worthy to suffer for the sake of the Protestant religion, in which his holy word had enlightened me; and prayed that he would continually vouchsafe to deliver me from the enemies of the same; and send me to my native country, to enjoy the free exercise of it.

Some time after, Don Baltazar opened the close door, and asked me how I did? I told him, that I was pretty well; but desired him to speak to the lords, to let me have a surgeon to bleed me; for the weather being very hot, I was afraid that my back would putrify, being very much swelled and bruised: for they did not whip me with a cat of
nine

nine tails, but with a scourge made of leathern thongs, three fingers broad, and about the thickness of the soal of a shoe, which draws no blood, but bruises, and makes your back swell very much. For the holy Inquisition is so merciful, that when it delivers a man to be burnt alive, it always gives orders that it must be done without effusion of blood. Don Baltazar told me, that he would do what he could to serve me. At night he came and told me, that the lords would allow no surgeons to bleed me. Then I desired him to get me a little brandy to wash my back, which accordingly he did.

For several nights I could not lie upon my back for the pain that I endured, my body being very much bruised by the pelting of the people. But my greatest pain was, that they did not banish me out of their country, but still detained me.

A fortnight after, Don Fernando bid me get my things ready, that the carrier would come for me, and that I must appear before the lords before I went. I quickly was ready, and felt no pain, hearing those words. Some hours after he came for me, and when I came before the lords, they spoke to me thus.

Inq. Well, Isaac, how do you do? *Mart.* My lord, I am very well, thank God, considering what has passed, which your lordship knows. *Inq.* It is your tongue that is the occasion; you might avoid it if you would. *Mart.* My lord, I am very well satisfied to have suffered what I have. I came here with a great deal of sorrow, but I go with a great deal of joy. *Inq.* Have you heard any prisoners talk one to another since you have been here, in the night, or at any time? *Mart.* No, my lord; but there is an old man in the next dungeon to me, that speaks and talks to himself in the night, and sings sometimes; but I believe he has lost his senses. [And there are a great many that lose their senses by despair.] *Inq.* That old man signifies nothing. You are going to Malaga, where you shall remain in a gaol, till you

you can get aboard of a heretic ſhip; and you are never to return into theſe Chriſtian kingdoms. Do you remember what was read at church the other day? *Mart.* My lord, I remember it very well; and if your lordſhip had not baniſhed me, I ſhould not have lived in a country where I had been ſo uſed. I am very well ſatisfied, my lord. *Inq.* You muſt, before you go, take oath you ſhall keep the ſecret, and not reveal to any body what has happened to you in your caſe, nor what you have heard or ſeen during the time you have been here, and take care of what you ſay, that we hear nothing of it. *Mart.* My lord, it is very well, I will take care. [I took my oath.] *Inq.* What money you have brought here ſhall be returned to you; and when you come to Malaga, your effects ſhall be returned to you.

I thanked his lordſhip very kindly; and ſo, thanks be to God, we parted.

When I came down ſtairs into an office, a prieſt gave me the money my friend had given me, and begun to tell me, that it was pity that ſuch a man as I was blind, and led away in hereſy; that I was certainly damned, without remiſſion, if I remained as I was; and ſo run on.

When I had got my money, I made him a ſhort compliment, told him that I was not blind, and that I was a Chriſtian as well as he, but did not damn any body: that I had been brought here for talking of religion, and that I would take care how I talked; and that I was forbid to talk about religion, or elſe I would give him an anſwer; made him a low bow, and went away with the carrier with a great deal of joy.

Three days after, we arrived at Malaga, where I was put in the common gaol, amongſt the malefactors, with a pair of fetters on. The ſecretary of the Inquiſition, who was a prieſt, and one of them that had taken me up, came to ſee me, and aſked me how
I did?

I did? To which I replied, I was well; but thought it was very hard to be used as I had been; and then to be put amongst the malefactors. I desired him to let me speak with the commissioner that had taken me up; but he stopped my mouth presently, telling me, that I could not speak with the commissioner, that the holy Inquisition had been very merciful to me; and that if he heard that I made any complaints I should be sent back again. I humbly begged his pardon, and desired him to let me go aboard of some English ship, that I might be gone out of the kingdom. To which he answered, To be sure you must go. You are not a fit man to live in these Christian countries, I will dispatch you as soon as possible, and so went away.

My wife, whom I had not heard of since I was taken up, came to see me. I desired her to go to some French merchants, which were my friends, and had great interest with the clergy, to desire them to speak to the commissioner of the Inquisition in my behalf, that I might go aboard some ship, which accordingly they did: so that the secretary came, and bid me pay what was owing to the gaol-keeper, and then conducted me to the water-side, forbidding of me, upon pain of going back to the Inquisition, to set my foot on shore, or go aboard of any ship, unless a heretic one: for I was a dangerous man against the holy faith; and that he would have spies to watch me. I made him a compliment, and told him, I would observe what he said, and desired him to return my effects (that had been taken from me) to my wife. He told me, he would see what could be done. I went aboard of an English ship, but had not been there above five or six hours, but the rupture happened between England and Spain, and the ship that I was in taken, with many others that were there at anchor, waiting for the vintage; upon the account of our fleet, under the command of Sir George Byng, who destroyed the Spanish fleet near Sicily.

Sicily. I was carried with the ſhip's company almoſt naked to the ſhore, into a priſon, where I was put into the ſtocks all that day. One of the mates of the ſhip, who had received a wound on board by one of the Spaniards, was carried to the hoſpital, where he died of his wounds. But the Iriſh prieſt, whom I mentioned before, took care to make him die a good Chriſtian, as they call it, as he had done by ſeveral before; but eſpecially by an Engliſh gentleman who had lodged at my houſe, and to two of my ſervants who were Proteſtants. This was by perſuading them, when they were juſt a dying, and could hardly ſpeak, or make any defence for themſelves, that if they do not change their religion before they die, they are damned, and will certainly go to hell; but, on the contrary, if they die in the faith of the church of Rome, without which no man can be ſaved, they will infallibly go to heaven.

The ſame ſecretary of the Inquiſition, who had taken me out of gaol, and ſent me on board, came to ſee me. He told me not to trouble myſelf, nor to be afraid, that I ſhould not remain as priſoner of war; that he would ſpeak to the general who commanded all the coaſt, to let me go on board of another ſhip; that my caſe was independent from what had happened between the two crowns; that I ſhould not ſtay in Spain upon any account: that I was baniſhed by the Inquiſition, which is above the king, and was not a fit perſon to live in a Chriſtian country. He ſpoke to the priſoners that were Roman Catholics, forbidding them to have any converſation with me; for I was a ſtrong heretic, and a dangerous man. I was very glad to hear him talk as he did; for before, I was very much afraid I ſhould be ſent back to Granada, or on board of ſome of their gallies. I told him, there were ſome Hamburgh ſhips in the road; that if he pleaſed I would go on board one of them. He told me, that he would ſoon diſpatch me; and accordingly he came two days afterward,

afterward, making a fad complaint, and telling me, that the English were very bad people, to ufe their fleet as they had done. He led me to the water-fide, forbidding me, as before, to go on board of any ship but a heretic one; which accordingly I obferved, and was very glad to get off fo.

The ship I went aboard of was a Hamburgher, where I ftayed about fix weeks in the road, expecting that the clergy would return my effects to my wife. But they ftill put her off, and at laft began to threaten her; telling her, that I came off very well, and that the Inquifition had been very merciful to me, and bid her not to be fo troublefome. I afked advice of my friends that ufed to come on board to fee me; and though there were Roman Catholics, they faid very fevere things againft the Inquifition, and told me, as friends, that I might thank God I was fo well delivered from their hands: that in the fame Inquifition they burnt a French Proteftant alive, who would not change his religion: and I have fince feen and fpoke with a man that was at Granada at that fame time, and faw him executed.

My friends advifed me, not to let my wife afk the clergy for any thing, for fear of fome other misfortune. As they had threatened to take away one of my children, which my wife was forced to fend to England whilft I was in the Inquifition, left falling into their hands, fhe fhould never hear of it more; I defired her to come on board with the reft, for fear of the worft. They did return fome fmall matter, and fo we came away. And they gave out that they returned us every thing.

Whilft I was in the Inquifition, the clergy were very bufy about my family to make them change their religion. They fent from the church for my children, and finding that my wife had fent one of them to England, [which was that, which fhe was informed, they had a mind to keep, and had he fallen into their hands, God knows whether we fhould ever have heard of him again; for I have been told that they ufually fend them into convents up in the country:] they gave her a fevere check, afking how fhe durft fend one of her children away without their knowlege? and told her, that I had changed or would change my religion; which was all the talk at the time at Malaga, as well among the proteftants as Roman catholics; it being a very difficult thing to get out of that holy tribunal, as they call it, without changing one's religion. I have known fome that have got out; but they all outwardly profefs themfelves to be Roman catholics; but were not fo when they were put in. They told my wife that if fhe would change her religion fhe fhould have the effects returned to her, and I fhould be fet at liberty: but fhe, remembering what I had oftentimes told her, that I hoped God would give me ftrength to fuffer death before I would change; defired them to excufe her, and that when fhe fhould fee me fhe would refolve them, but not before. Then they attacked the children, and they faid they would do as their mother did.

Some time before I got out there was a great noife fpread that my picture was to be burnt upon the market-place at Malaga; and at the fame time my body was to be burnt at Granada; which frightened my wife very much. But fome good people affured her of the contrary, and told her what would happen to me, and that fhe fhould fee me in a few days, which happened accordingly, after I had been eight months in their hands. God grant that thefe happy kingdoms may never feel the difmal effects of popifh government and arbitrary power.

This narrative is attefted by the Englifh merchants at Malaga, where Mr. Martin lived for four years, as before mentioned; to which is added, a recommendation of him as a proper object for the charity of his countrymen, figned by the archbifhops of Canterbury and York, and by feveral of the bifhops.

As the man was an English protestant residing in Spain, under the protection of treaties subsisting between the two crowns, his commitment and detention were a manifest violation of those treaties, and of the law of nations: accordingly the English consul at Malaga represented the case in a proper manner to the English minister, and the minister in consequence laid the affair before one of the secretaries of state. It was immediately represented to his majesty George I. who was graciously pleased to send a very spirited remonstrance to cardinal Alberoni, Philip V.'s first minister, claiming his own subject, and insisting upon the immediate release of the said Isaac Martin from the prison of the Inquisition; desiring that he might be sent back to England. The cardinal, upon this, applied to the inquisitor-general to know how the case stood: this gentleman, whose name was don Jacinto de Abrana, sent to the inquisitors at Granada for a true account of the case; and then wrote a letter to the cardinal, stating the matter to him; upon which the cardinal gave orders for his release. The original letter which the inquisitor-general wrote to cardinal Alberoni upon this subject, is manifestly a letter written designedly to be shewn to the English ministry, in order to justify the Inquisition in so illegal and inhuman a procedure. There was, no doubt, another private letter written by the same inquisitor to the cardinal, stating the real injustice and indefensible circumstances of this imprisonment; otherwise had the account given in this public letter been strictly true, the poor man had never been released at all. The intercession of George I. did indeed release this unhappy object; but how was he released? He received, upon his enlargement, two hundred lashes, was whipped and pelted for three quarters of an hour through the streets of Granada, stripped and plundered of all his effects, sent back to Malaga, and then put aboard a ship, with his wife and children, to shift for themselves.

selves. ——Upon a view of this case, one cannot help saying, that the tender mercies of the Inquisition are cruel.

But now, thank God, these sanguinary acts of faith seem to be growing out of vogue in Spain. There has not been an *auto de fe* at Madrid for these twelve years; which was owing to this circumstance: a Jew, and his wife, and a daughter of about thirteen years of age, being condemned to be burnt; while the father and mother were burning, they set the child loose from its fetters, and the priests got round it, with a view of converting it by the united force of their rhetoric, and the terrors of immediately undergoing the same cruel death. The child, after seeming, to listen a while to their oratory, gave a sudden spring, and vaulted into the midst of the fire; giving a shining example of the force of early piety, of an heroic fortitude equal to that of the most resolute Roman, or the most unshaken martyr.

The power of this tribunal is now declining very visibly, and seems hastening to its fall; for the present king of Spain has taken a bolder step to humble the Inquisition, than any of the Philips or Charles's who went before him. The inquisitor-general having thought proper, last year, to prohibit a liturgy which the king had licensed, without consulting his majesty about it; the king, with a proper spirit, put the inquisitor under an arrest, and immediately sent him, guarded with a file of grenadiers, into exile, in a convent, at a great distance from Madrid. So determined and resolute a measure as this, alarmed the whole body of the clergy; they moved heaven and earth to obtain the inquisitor's recal; but for some time their endeavours had no effect: the king was inflexible. The common people were taught by their priests to say, that his catholic majesty was no good catholic in his heart. At length, however, the king restored the inquisitor to his liberty: but in such a manner, as that prelate had no reason to triumph.

Mr.

A Man going to ye Flames by ye Sentance of ye Inquisitors.

Mr. Clarke gives us the following account of his journey from London to Madrid.—" I left London, in company with two other gentlemen, on Saturday the 10th of May 1760, set sail from Falmouth on the 20th, and arrived at Corunna on the 26th of the same month.

The harbour of Corunna presents you with a fine prospect as you sail into it; on your right are the Tower of Hercules, the fort, and the town; before you the shipping; all terminated by an agreeable view of the country: on your left you see Cape Prior, the entrance of Ferroll, and a ridge of barren mountains, with a large river running between them. Corunna is well built and populous, but, like most other Spanish towns, has an offensive smell. Their method of keeping the tiles fast, on the roofs of houses, is by laying loose stones upon them. The Spaniards, to my great mortification, have quitted that old dress, which looks so well on our English stage: the men wear a great flapped hat, a cloke reaching down to their feet, and a sword, generally carried under the arm: the women wear a short jacket of one colour, a petticoat of another, and either a white or black woollen veil. We stayed at Corunna a whole week, because we could not procure a vehicle to convey us to Madrid, nearer than from Madrid itself: nor could we travel on the straight road to Astorga by any other convenient method, than riding on mules or horses, for we rejected the litter, as disagreeable and fatiguing, and no other carriage could pass the mountains that way: we wrote therefore to Madrid for a coach to meet us at Astorga, which is about 150 miles from Corunna.

The poorer sort, both men and women, at Corunna, wear neither shoes nor stockings. We lodged at the best inn; but all inns throughout Spain afford miserable accommodations: it was kept by an Irishman named Obrien. We were well entertained by the Spanish governor don Louis de Cordouva, and the English consul Mr. Jordan.

We set out from Corunna the 3d of June, being honoured with a discharge of guns from the packets in the harbour. You must carry your provisions and bedding with you in Spain, as you are not sure of finding them in all places. We seldom met with any thing to eat upon the road, or a bed fit to lie upon. After having passed the fertile mountains of Gallicia, and the barren rocks of Leon, we came to Astorga the 8th of June. Here we rested till the 11th, and then set out in a clumsy coach, drawn by six mules, with ropes instead of traces: this surprised me at first, but I found afterward, that the grandees, and people of rank in Madrid, use ropes constantly at the Prado and Promenade, places of airing, somewhat resembling the old ring in Hyde Park.

After passing over the immense plains of Old and New Castile, which seem more like seas than plains, we arrived at Madrid the 18th of June, being the 7th day from our leaving Astorga. Though we travelled so long a tract of country, we saw few cities or towns that were confiderable for their extent, strength, riches, manufactures, or inhabitants. Villa Franca in Leon is extreamly beautiful, and stands high; Ponferrada neat, anciently called *intra fluvios*, because it was between the rivers Sil and Boega; and afterward stiled *Pons Ferratus*, from its bridge on the hard rock. Medino del Campo in Castile, is an agreeable situation; there is a large square in the middle of it, and some of the nobility reside there.

Lugo in Gallicia is a remarkable ancient city, surrounded with a most singular fortification; as near as I could judge, a square; and at the distance of about every twenty feet a circular bastion of thick and lofty walls: the city fortified on every side in the same manner, has rather a tremendous appearance, and must have been extreamly strong, before the use of that villainous saltpetre, as Shakespeare calls it. It stands near the source of the Minho; the turnips here are said to be so large, as to weigh fifty pounds each:

each: but who can believe it? Its ancient name was *Lucus Augufti*, and thence corruptly called Lugo.

The city of Aftorga in Leon is fituated in a wide plain; the moft remarkable thing in it is the cathedral, which is a noble Gothic building: a bafilica, confifting of fix pointed arches, fupported by tall, light, neat pillars, in a good tafte; the portal a large round arch, with a vaft number of mouldings; and with feven or eight fine altars. But the high altar is exceedingly magnificent; it confifts of twenty compartments of marble-fculpture in alto relievo, the figures as large as life; the fubject the hiftory of our Saviour; at the fummit God the Father crowning the blefled virgin. The glory is well expreffed; for being cut through the frame, and a lamp placed behind it, the light fhews the rays. We happened to attend at the vefpers; the mufic of the organ was fine; the number of tapers, the richnefs of altars, in fhort, the whole fcene was ftriking. This city gives the title of marquis to the family of Oforio, inferior to few, either for antiquity or valour.

Benevente in Leon is encompaffed by three rivers, and remarkable for little more than giving the title of earl to the family of Pimentel. Vallalpando is in a pleafing plain, has a large fquare, and contains a palace of the conftable of Caftile, to whom the town belongs. The only river we paffed of note was a branch of the Minho; a noble current, almoft as broad as the Thames at Windfor, and to appearance deep; finely wooded on each fide, the trees larger and taller than you ufually meet with in Spain. The place where we paffed it was called Hofpital de Efchemofo.

The ftorks nefts upon the tops of the churches, with the birds hovering over them, or juft peeping out, are pleafing as you pafs. It was fo in old Rome: the ftorks built their nefts in great numbers on the fummits of their temples, as their poets often tell us.

We paffed fome forefts; but the trees are dwarf and poor, not refembling the timber of Great Britain; you will in vain look for thofe ftately woods, which not only afford fuel, fhade, and wealth to their owners, but fend forth fleets, which give laws to the ocean. Tho' I loft my watch on the top of one of the higheft mountains near the Zebreros, yet, by extraordinary good fortune, it was found by the *Marigatti*, or mule drivers, and carried to the Padre Abbad of Zebreros, who fent it me in lefs than a month.

The new Stone-caufeway, which joins the two Caftiles, and extends to Guardarama, is a moft magnificent public work: it was done by an order of Ferdinand VI. the late king, as appears by the following infcription on a pillar erected on the caufeway: *Ferdinandus* VI. *Pater Patriæ. Viam Vtrique Caftelliæ Superatis Montibus fecit. Ann. Salutis* M DCC XLIX. *Regni Sui* IV. It is really a noble road, and feems owing rather to the labour and activity of a Roman, than to the flow induftry of a Spaniard.

Some parts of the Caftiles are pleafant; but are ill cultivated; have no wood of any moment; this makes fuel incredibly dear in Madrid; the expence of one fingle fire there for the winter has been known to coft fifty pounds! an amazing article! The charcoal confumed in their kitchens, and braziers, comes chiefly from Gallapagar, at the diftance of thirty miles, which is far enough in that country to make the carriage of it very expenfive. The principal timber they ufe, is fir, the growth of the country; their houfes, churches, carriages, and furniture, are chiefly of deal; there are fometimes no lefs than fourteen large girders in the cieling of a fmall apartment. One would not imagine from this circumftance, that timber was fcarce. As to the water in this country, I do not think it in general good; that of Madrid is excellent, which is plain by the court's being at much expence to have it conveyed to diftant places. There are two fine rivers in the Caftiles, the Tagus and the Guadiana;

Guadiana; as to the Manſanares, which runs cloſe by Madrid, it is but a poor ſtream, and falls into the Xarama, about ſix leagues diſtant from the Tagus. I was told in London, that the ſituation of Madrid was upon a plain, but it is a great miſtake: it is built upon a chain of little hills, and, becauſe there are higher mountains. round it, at a diſtance, has been ſuppoſed to be in a plain.

The Spaniards erect pillars at proper diſtances upon the cauſeways, to direct travellers during the ſnows: we ſaw ſeveral of them in Leon, and other parts. The firſt comer to a Spaniſh inn, be his rank what it may, has the firſt choice of the accommodations: this occaſions a ſort of conteſt between the travellers in this country, who ſhall get firſt to the inn. It is a common practice to ſend a man on an hour or two before: we diſtanced one Don Joſeph, a Biſcayner, in this way; finding that he was going to the ſame *poſada*, or inn, we detached our faithful Antonio, who, as fleet as an Arab, ran over the mountains in bye-baths, and arrived at the inn long before the Don and we came to it. This conteſt ariſes from there being ſeldom more than one inn in a village; at which, if diſappointed, you muſt probably ride eight or ten miles before you can find another, which, at the end of a long day's journey, and in the dark, would be fatiguing, and perhaps dangerous.

Upon a review of the whole country from Corunna to Madrid, one may ſay, that Gallicia is a fine fertile province; that ſome parts of it are equal to many in England; but as to Leon, it is a naked, dreadful, barren rock, except where it is covered with a few pitiful firs, or ſhrubs, ſuch as are about Benevente and Villalpando, and except ſome few plains after you have paſſed Aſtorga. I turned round to take a view of Leon from one of the higheſt mountains, and was almoſt frightened at the ſight; a brown horror, as Mr. Pope expreſſes it, was ſpread over the whole; ſands, rocks, and craggy precipices, formed as ſavage a prospect as can be imagined. And yet this country was probably once fought for; the inhabitants surely must find a charm in it unknown to us. In one of these villages we found a set of people, dressed in a whimsical manner, dancing to rude music; the whole appearance was entertaining and grotesque; the dance artless and odd; its natural simplicity shewed the people in their true character.

The road from Corunna to Madrid is certainly not so bad as it is generally thought in England. The mountains of Gallicia are very passable; the only difficult parts which I saw, were the descent at La Fava, and about twelve miles, as you come out of Serrarias. The mountains of Leon are rather disagreeable than dangerous, and all the rest is easy. Be it as it may, our English messengers find no difficulty in it. The accommodations, indeed, are miserable: I have said you must absolutely carry your provisions and bedding along with you; and even then, unless you can bear fatigue well, lye down in your clothes, eat eggs, onions, and cheese; unless you can sleep while your mules rest, rise the moment you are called, and set out early in the morning, before the heat comes on, you will fare ill as a traveller in Spain. It is a good method to carry dried tongues with you, hard eggs, not hams, for they will not keep, as we found by experience; some portable soup; tea, sugar, and spirituous liquors; not forgetting even pepper and salt: and whenever you meet with good bread, meat, fowls, or wine, always to buy them, whether you want them or not, because you know not what to-morrow may produce. A knife, fork, and spoon, are absolutely necessary, for you will find none; nor should you omit a pair of snuffers, a candlestick, and some wax-candles. Take care only not to carry any tobacco or rum; for they are all contraband, and may occasion the detention, if not the seizure of your baggage. Particularly bring with you as few books as possible, for the Inquisition will seize them. My baggage

baggage was detained a fortnight on account of my books; and the earl of Briftol was obliged to fpeak twice to general Wall, before he could releafe the captives. Many of thefe circumftances feem trifling, but they are fo material, that thofe who happen to travel without them in this country, will find, by dear-bought experience, all thefe trifles become real inconveniences.

The town of Madrid, for as it is not an epifcopal fee, I think we cannot call it a city, is built on fome little hills in the neighbourhood of a very indifferent ftream called the Manfanares; which occafioned much wit, when Philip II. built that great bridge over it, called the Puente de Segovia: fome faid the king fhould fell the bridge to buy a river, &c.

Charles V. having recovered here of a quartan ague, firft made this a royal refidence; but how injudicioufly, needs not be remarked. The capital of fo great and extended a kingdom, ought doubtlefs to be at Seville; where, by means of the port, all the conveniencies and neceffaries of life, and every article of foreign commerce might be had with eafe.

Madrid is furrounded with very lofty mountains, whofe fummits are always covered with fnow. It has no fortifications to defend it; it has no ditch, but is environed by a mud wall. Its gates, according to the tafte of that country, have their locks upon the outfide. There are very few good ftreets, except thofe of the Calle Mayor, the Calle d'Atocha, the Calle Alcala, and the Calle Ancha: the reft are long, narrow, and extreamly dirty. The only good fquare is the Plaça Mayor, which is large and regular enough; but there being balconies to every window, it takes off much of its beauty.

The houfes in Madrid are moft of them brick, with dry walls, lime being there very dear and fcarce; ftone is ftill more expenfive, becaufe it muft be brought from fix or feven leagues diftance. Houfe-rent is at an exorbitant price; but that is not all,

furniture

furniture is scarce to be had, without paying extravagantly for it; and if you would have glass windows to your house, you must put them there yourself, for you will not find them.—The houses in general are wretchedly ill built, for you will seldom see any two walls upon the square: they are laid out chiefly for shew, convenience being little considered: thus you will pass through usually two or three large apartments of no use, in order to come at a small room at the end, where the family sit. This is the general state of the houses there; not but there are some very magnificent palaces, built chiefly by viceroys, returned from their governments, and by the principal grandees: these have courts, and *portes cochers*, though the others have not. The houses in general look more like prisons than the habitations of people at their liberty; the windows, beside having a balcony, being grated with iron bars, particularly the lower range, and sometimes all the rest. A single family is not the sole tenant of an house, as is usually the case in England; they are generally inhabited by many separate families, who notwithstanding are for the most part perfect strangers to each other. Those who can afford it, have a distinct apartment for summer and winter. Foreigners are very much distressed for lodgings at Madrid; there being only one tolerable inn, the Fontana d'Oro; and the Spaniards are not fond of taking strangers into their houses, especially if they are not catholics. There is no such thing as a tavern or coffee-house in the town; they have only one news-paper, which is the Madrid Gazette: their places of diversion are the amphitheatre, built for the exhibition of the bull-feast, and the two theatres of La Cruz, and del Principe. The noise made by the itinerant bodies of psalm singers in the streets, or the *rosarios*, as they call them, is very disagreeable in the evening; the frequent processions, particularly those of the Host, troublesome; at Easter especially, when the sight of those bloody disciplinants, the *flagellantes*, is extreamly shocking.

Next

Next to the king's palaces, one of the beft buildings in Madrid is the Imperial College of Jefuits, which is indeed a very noble ftructure. There is no paffing the ftreets there commodioufly without a vehicle; for as they practife the Scotch, or Edinburgh cuftom, of manuring the ftreets by night, they would be too offenfive to your feet, as well as your nofe, without a chariot by day.

Madrid is governed by a principal officer called the corregidor, who is fomething like our lord mayor, though he is not chofen by the city, but by the king, and is not a merchant or tradefman, but a gentleman well verfed in the law. He acts as a fuperior judge, and has under him forty-one regidors, not unlike our aldermen, who compofe his council, acting as inferior magiftrates under him.

At the end of the city is a famous place for airing and recreation, called the Prado or Pardo de St. Hieronymo; a delightful plain fhaded by rows of poplar-trees, and adorned with twenty-three fountains, from which it is fprinkled every evening when the nobility and gentry repair thither in their coaches, or on horfeback.

At the extremity of the Prado is the palace called Buen Retiro, or the Good Retreat. This is a very indifferent quadrangle, and is not fo good a royal manfion as St. James's. It was defigned as a place of retreat for the king, from the hurry of the court and town. It, however, contains a great number of ftately rooms and noble apartments, adorned with the moft coftly furniture and paintings, executed by the greateft mafters; but it is only built of brick. The gardens are faid to be a perfect paradife, and abound with the moft delightful fhady walks, water-works, and the moft curious productions of art and nature.

Cafa del Campo is a royal feat ftanding on the other fide of the river, to the weft of the city, directly facing the king's town-palace, and was a very delightful place with a fine park, but is now much neglected.

Florida

Florida is another royal pleasure-house, seated near the former in an enchanting situation. The palace of Aranjuez, about thirty miles from Madrid, has a fine front, and is agreeably situated in a pleasant vale at the confluence of two rivers, the Xarama and the Tagus. Though the gardens are only a dead flat, and the walks plantations of trees in straight rows; yet there is something chearful and refreshing in this cool and shady spot. St. Ildephonso is a palace about sixty miles from Madrid, in a delightful lonely country; part of it is also a convent. The building is not grand, nor in a good taste; but the gardens are very fine, and the fountains the noblest in Europe. The gardens are said to have cost five millions sterling. Here king Philip V. retired on his resignation of the crown in the year 1724, and caused the relics of some saints, which were highly revered, to be brought from the Escurial into this chapel.

We now come to the palace, or convent, of the Escurial, so called from the village in which it stands, which is situated seven leagues to the north of Madrid. Philip II. the founder of this palace and the convent belonging to it, made a vow at the battle of St. Quintin against the French, on the frontiers of Picardy, to build a convent at the Escurial for monks of the order of St. Jerom, which he preferred from his being obliged to cannonade a convent of Jeromites during the siege of St. Quintin. The battle being gained on St. Lawrence's day, he called the convent after the name of that saint; and as he was burnt upon a gridiron, this prince immortalized the very manner of his martyrdom; for he not only stuck gridirons, either of paint, wood, metal, or stone, all over the convent, but built the very convent itself in the form of a gridiron. That part of the building which forms the palace is the handle of this gridiron, and the rest being divided into a great number of square courts, the buildings are so ranged as to form the sides and bars. But in building this structure he gave

great

great difguft to the Spanifh cortes: for Philip having affembled them to afk fupplies for carrying on the war againft France, the ftates very freely voted a large fubfidy of fome millions; which the artful monarch, as foon as he had once fecured in his own coffers, applied to the building of this convent. This mifapplication of the public revenues gave fuch vexation to the cortes, that they afterward affembled with more reluctance, being unwilling to be cajoled out of their money by the tricks of defigning princes.

This royal monaftery of St. Laurence is built on the declivity of a mountain, part of the Segovian chain, which feparates the two Caftiles. It is of a beautiful white ftone, veined with blue and brown, of a very fine polifh, and is furrounded with the moft delightful profpect.

The monks here have a higher opinion of Philip II. the founder, than even of St. Laurence and St. Jerom: this indeed is only a decent part of gratitude; for as he thought that, by raifing this fuperb fabric, he fhould atone for all his fins, fo he fpared no expence to render it complete. It coft during his reign twenty-eight millions of ducats, which is about three millions three hundred and fixty thoufand pounds fterling. He lived here chiefly during the laft fifteen years of his life; and when he died, ordered himfelf to be brought out in his bed to the foot of the high altar, that he might die in fight of it; and thus he expired. The place where his bed ftood is fince railed off, as facred.

The Pantheon chapel, the fepulchre of the princes of Spain, is one of the fineft in the world. The principal members of the portal are of black marble, regularly veined and fpotted with white. In the leffer parts gems, gold, filver, and bronzes, unite their luftre. On the fides are two pillars in relievo, with their bafes and capitals, befide the jambs and lintels, formed out of one block of marble. Over this is the frize, and figures to the number of ten, fupporting the crown. The pedeftals, capitals, &c. are of brafs gilt;

gilt; and before the door is a baluftrade of gilt brafs, of moft beautiful workmanfhip.

From this portal you defcend a ftair-cafe compofed of the fineft Tortofa jafpers and Toledo marble, beautifully variegated, finely polifhed, and joined with fuch art as to appear only one fingle piece, fixty-four feet in length, confifting of thirty-four fteps, divided into three flights, by the like number of landing-places. The baluftrades are of beautiful jafper marquetry, with marble mouldings. In the middle hangs a gilt luftre with fix cornucopias. At the third landing-place is the Pantheon door, adorned with four pilafters, two of jafper, and two of bronze. The pavement between the pilafters is of polifhed jafper, and the ceiling reprefents Jacob's ladder.

Upon entering this auguft cemetery, you are ftruck with the beauty of its feveral parts. The order of its architecture is the compofite. Its circumference is one hundred and thirteen feet, and the diameter from wall to wall is fomething more than thirty-fix feet; the height from the pavement to the central ftone at the top is thirty-eight feet, and its figure is perfectly circular. The pavement reprefents the figure of a ftar, the rays of which are formed of innumerable jems, jafpers and different kinds of marble, with a fleuron in the center, glittering with gems. The whole is furrounded with a beautiful pedeftal or bafe, on which ftands fixteen fluted Corinthian pilafters of jafper, the bafes and capitals of gilt bronze. The farcophagi or coffins are placed in niches all round the Pantheon; and the marble of which they are made, is remarkable for the finenefs of the grain, the beauty of the colour, and the ornaments beftowed on them.

The ring in the cieling, in the middle of which is the key-ftone, forms a fplendid fleuron, eighteen feet in circumference, and is of brafs gilt, and the defign and workmanfhip very fine. From this fleuron hangs a large iron-rod, to which is faftened a large gilt luftre lustre of beautiful workmanship. At the lower end are the four evangelists in demi-relievo; over these are twenty-four cornucopias, along the edges of which are cherubins; and above these eight angels holding flambeaus; and the other eight are fixed to the heads of as many seraphs. It is every where embellished with festoons, &c. and surmounted by a splendid crown. When the tapers in these cornucopias, the flambeaus held by the angels, and the candles on the altar are lighted, no words can express its grandeur.

On the right-hand, going out of the Pantheon, a door opens into a vault, which may be called the secondary Pantheon, where those of the royal family who are not entitled to a place in the principal structure are interred. On every side are three rows of niches, to the number of fifty-one, for the coffins; and on the wall next the door is an altar-piece, in which is a good copy of Christ on the cross, from Titian.

The Spaniards have in general an olive complexion, are of a middle stature, rather lean, but well made; they have fine eyes, glossy black hair, and a small well shaped head.—Their cloaths are usually of a very dark colour, and their cloaks almost black. This shews the natural gravity of the people. This is the general dress of the common sort; for the court, and persons of fashion, have most of them now adopted the French dress and modes.

As their natural air is gravity, so they have consequently great coldness and reserve in their deportment; they are therefore very uncommunicative to all, and particularly to strangers. But when once you are become acquainted with them, and have contracted an intimacy, there are not more social, more friendly, or more conversible beings in the world. When they have once professed it, none are more faithful friends.

——They are a people of the highest notions of honour, even to excess, which is a still visible effect of their antient love of chivalry, and was the animating spirit of that enthusiasm. They have great probity and integrity of principle. As they persevere with much fidelity and zeal in their friendships, you will naturally expect to find them warm, relentless, and implacable in their resentments.

They are generous, liberal, magnificent, and charitable; religious without dispute, but devout to the greatest excesses of superstition. What else could induce them to kiss the hands of their priests, and the garments of their monks?

If the Spaniards have any predominant fault, it is, perhaps, that of being rather too high minded; hence they have entertained, at different periods, the most extravagant conceits; such as, that the sun only rose and set in their dominions; that their language was the only tongue fit to address the Almighty with; that they were the peculiar favourites of heaven, insomuch that when the arms of protestants have prevailed over theirs, they have been ready to call God himself an heretic. They formerly thought, that wisdom, glory, power, riches and dominion, were their sole monopoly; but the experience of two or three centuries past has contributed to shew the fondness of all these delusions. The open and avowed attempts of its Austrian princes, grasping at universal monarchy; the secret and more concealed ambition of the Bourbon line, with all their plans of refined policy, have been, as Shakespear calls it, like the baseless fabric of a vision. It has been owing to these lofty conceits, that they are still possessed with the highest notions of nobility, family and blood. The mountaineer of Asturias, though a peasant, will plume himself as much upon his genealogy and descent, as the first grandee; and the Castilian, with his coat-armour, looks upon the Gallician with sovereign contempt.

Nothing can shew the *sang froid* of the Spaniards more strongly than the following circumstance, which, though it hath been often related, is perhaps not known

known to every reader. In the war that enfued between Spain and Portugal, upon the revolution in favour of the duke of Braganza, the Portuguefe plundered the village of Traigueros, and left a centinel in it, while the troops paffed on.—The centinel, to amufe the time, played on his guitar, which happened to be out of tune. A Spaniard belonging to this plundered village, offended with the diffonance of the foldier's mufic, came to the centinel, and civilly begged him to lend him the guitar; which being done, he tuned it, and returned it to the Portuguefe, with this fhort fpeech—Now, Sir, it is in tune, —*Aora fta templada.*

The profeffion of arms is their chief delight; to this darling paffion, commerce, manufactures, and agriculture have been always facrificed. It never appeared more evident than in the fucceffion war; the peafant voluntarily forfook the plough, and ran to the Auftrian or the Bourbon ftandard. There was no occafion for an haranguing ferjeant, or for an officer and a prefs-warrant, to call him to the field of action. *A la guerra, A la guerra,* was all the cry.

It has been imagined, from the event of the late war, that the Spanifh are not good troops; but it is a great miftake; there are no foldiers in the whole world that are braver than the Spanifh. Thofe who fay otherwife only fhew their ignorance of hiftory. They have had the dukes of Berwick and Bitonto, the counts de Gage and Schomberg, the prince of Heffe, the marquis De Las Minas, the generals Stanhope, Peterborough, and Stahrembergh, the eye-witneffes of their bravery. That they make but an indifferent military figure at prefent, is no juft argument againft them; long peace, long difufe, and bad generals, will entirely damp the martial fpirit of any people. They bear all hardfhips with the moft unremitting patience, and can endure heat, cold, and even hunger, with fome degree of chearfulnefs. They have courage and conftancy fufficient for the moft hazardous undertakings; and though naturally flow, yet when once put in action, pursue their object with great warmth and perseverance.

The Spaniards frequently breakfast as well as sup in bed; their breakfast is usually of chocolate, tea being very seldom drank by them. They drink little wine. Their dinner is generally a *pochero*, or beef, mutton, veal, pork, and bacon, greens, &c. all boiled together. If it be a richer, or more expensive mixture of meats and delicacies, it is then stiled an *olla podrida*, or what we call an olio. Temperance in eating and drinking is doubtless one of their virtues; you may see it in their proverbs; *Unas azeitunas, una salada, y ravanillos, son comida de los cavalleros*; that is, Olives, salad, and radishes, are food for a gentleman. They are great devourers of garlic; they seldom change the knife and fork, but eat every thing with the same individual weapon; delicacy, in many instances, not being their character.

The taste for gallantry and dancing prevails in Spain universally; they are the two ruling passions of the country. Jealousy, ever since the accession of the house of Bourbon, has slept in peace. It is observable, that in proportion as manners become more civilized, that furious passion always loses its force. Dancing is so much their favourite entertainment, that their gravest matrons never think themselves excluded by age from this diversion. You may see the grandmother, mother, and daughter, all in the same country dance: the English, on the contrary, give dancing to youth, and leave cards to age. The two most favourite and universal Spanish dances are the *sequedillas* and the *fundungo*: the first is something like our hay; the second is a very ancient dance, and though originally Roman, yet the Spaniards have mixed somewhat of the Moorish along with it: they are excessively fond of it; it is danced by the first of the nobility, as well as by the common people.

Most of the Spaniards take their *siesto*, or sleep after dinner; mass in the morning, dinner at noon, and

and the evening's airing generally finish the round of their day. Tho' it is the *etiquette* of the country for the men and women to wear in the streets, and at mass, all the same dress, yet the ladies in private visits, wear as much variety of dress, and of a much richer sort, than those in England: but to a people of gallantry, the advantage of all wearing the same uniform in public, is easy to be conceived. The married ladies in Spain have each their professed lover, just as the Italian ladies have their cicesbeo. Their evening's airing is insipid to the last degree; you see nothing but a string of coaches following one another, filled with people of fashion: here a duke and his confessor; there a couple of smart young abbes *tête a tête*; here a whole family grouped together, just like a Dutch picture, husband and wife, children and servants, wet nurses and dry all together.—When they take their airing on *gala*, or court days, all their footmen are then dressed in laced liveries, with plumes of feathers in their hats. —The number of servants kept by the grandees, and people of the first fashion, is immoderate. Some of the Spanish grandees retain to the number of three or four hundred domestics; the English ambassador here, in compliance with the taste of the country, keeps near one hundred. As they go with four mules usually, they have consequently two drivers, or postilions; generally four, and sometimes six footmen behind their coaches, beside an helper to take off a pair of mules, when they enter Madrid, as they are not permitted to drive with more than four there. In the hot weather they take out the sides and backs of their coaches, for the sake of the air. They use sedan chairs but very little, and when they do, they have always two footmen, who go on each side the hindmost chairman, in order to hold him up, lest he should fall; and two of each side the sedan, and two who follow behind with lanthorns, though it be in the middle of the day: that is to say, they have

generally

generally nine servants with a coach, and ten with a sedan, beside those who go before.———

Among the diversions and pastimes of the Spaniards, the bull-feast is the most distinguished: we shall give Mr. Clarke's description of that exhibited in the Plaça Mayor at Madrid, upon occasion of his catholic majesty's public entry into his capital, on the 15th of July 1760. The square, which is large, was thronged with people, and all the balconies ornamented with different coloured silks, and crouded from the top to the bottom of the houses: the avenues to the square were built up into the balconies, and a sloping scaffold placed round for the common people, and raised about eight or nine feet from the ground.

First came the coaches of the cavaliers, four in number, of a singular make, with glasses at the ends, and quite open at the sides: the cavaliers were placed at the doors of their coaches, from whence they bowed to the people in the balconies as they passed round the square, and were accompanied by their sponsors, the dukes of Ossuna, Banos, Arcos, and Medina Cæli. Before the royal family came a company of halberdiers, followed by seven or eight of the king's coaches, preceding his coach of state, which was extreamly rich, with red and gold ornaments, and beautiful painted pannels. Then came a coach with some of the great officers; and next the king and queen in a very sumptuous coach of blue, with all the ornaments of massive silver, and a crown at the top: the trappings of the horses were likewise silver, with large white plumes. These were followed by the coaches of the prince of Asturias, the two infantas, and Don Lewis, with their attendants.

Their majesties seated themselves opposite to the balconies of the English ambassador, in which was our author, in a gilt balcony, with a canopy and curtains of scarlet and gold. On the right hand of the

king's

king's balcony were placed the reſt of the royal family, and on the left the gentlemen of the bedchamber in a row, all dreſſed in a very fine uniform of blue and red, richly embroidered with gold. The halberdiers marched from the king's balcony, which was in the center of one ſide, and forming themſelves into two lines fronting different ways, cleared the ſquare of the croud, who retired into the ſcaffolds erected for them; after which the halberdiers formed themſelves into a line before the ſcaffold under the king's balcony. Two companies of boys, dreſſed in an uniform, with caps and red taffety jackets, came with buckets of water in their hands, and watered the ſtage as they croſſed over it to the oppoſite ſide: the ſix chief alguazils of the city now came mounted on fine horſes, covered with trappings, and dreſſed in the old Spaniſh habit, black, with flaſhed ſleeves, great white flowing wigs, and hats with plumes of different coloured feathers. They advanced toward the king's balcony, under which they were obliged to ſtay the whole time to receive his orders, except when they were frightened away by the bulls.

At length the troops belonging to the cavaliers aſcended the ſtage in four large companies, dreſſed in ſilk Mooriſh liveries, richly and elegantly ornamented with lace and embroidery: theſe firſt bowed to the king's balcony, and then went in proceſſion round the ſquare; and from the elegant ſingularity and variety of their uniforms appeared extreamly beautiful. After them came the four knights in the old Spaniſh dreſs, with plumes in their hats, mounted on fine horſes: each held in his hand a ſlender lance, and was attended by two men on foot, dreſſed in light ſilk of the colour of his livery, with cloaks of the ſame: theſe never forſake his ſide, and are his principal defence. The cavaliers then diſpoſe themſelves for the encounter, the firſt placing himſelf oppoſite to the door of the place where the bulls are kept, and the other at ſome diſtance behind him.

At a signal given by the king the doors opened, and the bull appeared, to the sound of martial music, and the loud acclamations of the people: when seeing one of the attendants of the first cavalier spreading his cloak before him, he aimed directly at him; but the man easily avoided him, and gave his master an opportunity of breaking his spear in the bull's neck. In the same manner the bull was tempted to engage the other cavaliers, and always with the same success, till having received the wounds with their lances, he was encountered by the other men on foot, who, after playing with him with incredible agility as long as they thought proper, easily put an end to him by thrusting a sword either into his neck or side, which brings him to the ground, and then they finish him at once, by striking a dagger, or sword, behind his horns into the spine, which is always immediate death. After this the bull is hurried off by mules finely adorned with trappings.

After the knights were sufficiently tired with these exploits, the king gave them leave to retire; bulls were then let out, one at a time, from another door: these were of a more furious nature, and were encountered entirely by men on foot, who were so far from fearing their rage, that they strove to increase it, by darting at their necks, and other parts, little barbed darts ornamented with bunches of paper; some of which were filled with gun-powder, and were no sooner fastened to the bull than they went off like a serpent. Nothing can be imagined more tormenting than these darts, but the amazing dexterity with which they are thrown, takes off the attention from its cruelty. They also dress up goats skins, blown up with wind, and increase the fury of the bull by placing them before him, which makes a very ridiculous part of the entertainment. Many of the bulls, however, would not attack them; and one of the most furious that did, shewed more fear than in encountering his most sturdy antagonist. They also

baited

baited one bull with dogs, which shewed as much courage as any of the bull-dogs in England.

My apprehensions, says our author, were at first principally excited for the men on foot; but the knights are in much more danger, their horses being too full of fire to be exactly governed; they cannot therefore so well avoid the aim, and are liable to be every moment overthrown with their horses, if their attendants by their side do not assist them. Two beautiful horses were nevertheless gored; one of which was overthrown with his rider, but fortunately the man escaped any mischief from his fall. The courage of these horses is so great, that they have been often known to advance toward the bull, when their bowels were trailing on the ground.

This spectacle is one of the finest in the world, whether it be considered merely with respect to the splendor of the sight, or as an exertion of the amazing agility and dexterity of the performers. The Spaniards are so devoted to it, that even the women would pawn their last rag to see it. Nothing can be imagined more crouded than the houses even to the tops of the tiles, and dearly enough do they pay for their pleasure, pent together in the hottest sun, and with the most suffocating heat that can be endured. This is certainly a remnant of Moorish, and perhaps Roman barbarity, and will not bear the speculations of the closet, or the compassionate feelings of the tender heart: but, on the other hand, it has all the good effects of chivalry, in exciting in the minds of the spectators a disposition to hardy actions, without the horror that prevailed in former times, of distinguishing bravery to the prejudice of our own species.

The bull-feast in the Plaça Mayor is never exhibited but upon some extraordinary occasion, as the accession or marriage of their kings, and is attended with very great expence, both to his majesty and the city. But there is a theatre built without the walls, where there are bull-feasts every fortnight, which to
connoisseurs

connoisseurs are greatly preferable to the others, the bulls being more furious, and the danger greater to those who fight them: but there is little difference in their manner of engaging them.

We shall now give some idea of the Spanish theatre, which our author visited at the season for acting the autos, or plays, in support of the catholic faith. The theatre made a good appearance with respect to its size and shape; but was rather dirty and ill lighted, and, what was worse, had an equal mixture of daylight and candles. The prompter's head appeared through a little trap-door, above the level of the stage; and he read the play loud enough to be heard by the people in the boxes. The pit made a motley appearance, many standing in their night-caps and cloaks; while officers and soldiers were interspersed among the dirtiest mob. The side and front boxes were filled by persons well dressed, and that which answered to our two shilling gallery was filled with women, all in the same uniform; a dark petticoat, and a white woollen veil. The actors were dressed in richer cloaths than those in England, and these they are perpetually changing, in order to shew the expensive variety of their wardrobe.

After some tedious and insipid scenes, came on an interlude of humour. One of the comedians addressed a lady who sung very prettily, and offered her a purse of money: in the mean while a man brought in three barber's blocks which he placed upon the stage: these he first dressed in mens cloaths; but then undressing them, dressed them in womens apparel, after which came in three men who had a fancy to tempt these three ladies; but they were inflexibly coy, and it was not long before their gallants discovered their mistake. At length, after some long tiresome uninteresting scenes, full of fustian and bombast, an actor, dressed in a long purple robe, in the character of Christ, preached to the four quarters of the world in their proper dresses; Europe and America heard him gladly,

gladly, but Afia and Africa remained incorrigible. Our Saviour was foon after blind-folded, buffeted, fpit upon, bound, fcourged, crowned with thorns, and compelled to bear his crofs; when he kneeled down and cried, *Padre mi! Padre mi!* " Father, Fa-" ther, why haft thou forfaken me?" After this the fellow placed himfelf againft the wall, with his hands extended, as if on the crofs, and there imitated the expiring agonies of the bleffed Saviour; upon this one of the actreffes unbound him, took off his crown and fcarlet robes, and he having put on his wig and coat, joined the reft of the actors in a dance. After this one of the actreffes, in a very long fpeech, explained the nature, end, and defign of the facrament; and the play was concluded by Chrift appearing in a fhip triumphant.

Soon after our author went to fee a regular comedy, and there were two other Englifh gentlemen in the fame box with him. They underftood very little of the defign of the firft act; they faw a king, a queen, an enchantrefs, and many other pretty delightful fights; but the interlude with which it was concluded was extreamly low. The fcene was intended for the infide of a Spanifh inn, during the night: there were three feather-beds, and as many blankets brought upon the ftage; the queen and her maids of honour perfonated the miftrefs of the inn and her maids; and accordingly fell to making the beds. After this fix men came in to lie there, and one of them being a mifer, had rolled up his money in twenty or thirty pieces of paper. They then undreffed before the ladies, by pulling off fix or feven pair of breeches, and as many coats and waiftcoats, and got into bed two by two: when behold, the jeft confifted in feeing them kick the cloaths off one another, and then fight, as the fpectator is to fuppofe, in the dark. The abfurdity of this fcene, and the incomprehenfible ridiculoufnefs of it, made us, fays our author, laugh immoderately. The fight of the feather-beds,
the

the men kicking and sprawling, the peals of applause
that echoed through the house, were truly inconceivable; though, I believe, our neighbours in the next
box thought we laughed at the wit and humour of the
author. It was a scene that beggars all possible description, and I defy any theatre in Europe, but that
of Madrid, to produce such another.

When this interlude was finished, there succeeded
some other scenes between the king, queen, enchantress, and the rest of the actors. Five or six of them
all at once drew their swords upon the enchantress,
who parried them with her wand, and, to their great
amazement, retired unhurt into her cell. At other
times the enchantress killed with a look, and restored
to life with a second. In short, after several ridiculous incidents, the enchantress renounces the devil
and all his works, and in the conclusion embraces the
catholic faith, and declares she will adhere to that
alone. But it can hardly be supposed, that these absurd dramatic pieces are the best of the kind; and
indeed they are said to have some that are excellent, as
those of Lopez de Vega, which come nearest to our
Shakespeare.

Mr. Clarke tells us, that he has informed himself
from good authority, that our trade with Old and
New Spain is full one third less than it was about
forty years ago; and that the balance and exchange,
between Spain and Great Britain, are every day more
and more turning against the latter kingdom. The
causes of this decrease are indeed not at all difficult to
be discovered or accounted for. Part of it is owing
to the extream avarice and extortion of our own merchants, who, not contented with moderate profits,
have kept up the prices of their goods beyond their
just proportion, and thereby opened a door for the
French and Dutch to undersell us at the Spanish
markets. Another reason is, that the price of labour
in those two countries, is considerably lower than
in our own, which enables them likewise to afford

their

their goods to the Spaniards at a much cheaper rate than we can do. A third reason is, the alteration introduced during the Spanish war in queen Anne's time; when the French crept into that trade, and deprived us of a greater share of it than we shall probably be ever able to recover. A fourth reason may be, the progress which the Spaniards themselves have made in some branches of manufacture: for the encouragement which the kings of the house of Bourbon have given to manufactures and arts, has excited some few Spaniards to apply themselves to industry and trade. For several years past, the ministry in Spain have endeavoured, by means of foreign workmen, to set on foot various manufactures; and the great attention they have given to that object, has not been altogether without effect. But at present, by a strange infatuation, the minister to whose department the care of the manufactures belongs, not only neglects, but discourages them; and they consequently decline very fast.

But notwithstanding the arts of French insinuation, our traffic with Spain is very considerable, and chiefly in the following articles.—We export to that country large quantities of dried and salted fish, called by them *bacalas*; likewise broad cloaths and woollen stuffs of various kinds to a great amount; silk stuffs, cutlery ware, warlike and naval stores, particularly cables and anchors; also watches, wrought brass, and prince's metal, toys, mathematical instruments, cabinet work, particularly of mahogony; wrought and unwrought tin, leather, lead, corn, dry and salted meat, cattle, butter, cheese, beer, hats, linen, vitriol, pepper, rice, and other products of our American colonies: and, if we attended to it, we might supply them with great quantities of timber from those colonies, as the Spaniards, though they have in some parts fine woods of excellent oak, yet from their inexpertness in felling trees, and want of roads, are in a manner entirely deprived of the use of them.

From Spain we receive the following articles: wines, oil, vinegar, fruits of various kinds, viz. olives, raisins of the sun, raisins dried with ashes, called by them *passas de lexia*; raisins from Almunegar, a city on the coast of Andalusia, famous for that produce; chesnuts, almonds, figs, citrons, lemons, oranges, cocoa-nuts, Spanish pepper, pomegranates, fine wool, indigo, cochineal, materials for dying, kali, or barillia, and sofa, for the making of soap and glass, chiefly from Alicant; quicksilver; some wrought silks, particularly from Valentia; and of late raw silk, balsam of Peru, vanillas, cake-chocolate of Guajaca, salsaparilla, salted sea-brizzle, saltpetre, salt from Cadiz, salt from Port St. Mary's, woollen counterpanes, and a remarkable fine sort of blankets from Segovia; iron from Biscay, sword blades, particularly from Toledo, gun and pistol barrels from Guipuscoa and Barcelona, vermilion, borax, hams, snuff from Seville and the Havannah, soap, formerly a considerable article, but as we now make it ourselves, only a trifle, though there is still much of it annually run into Scotland; and several roots and drugs of the growths of Spain and America, employed in medicine.

The trade between Spain and her colonies in America, is the most considerable part of their external commerce, and the great support of their navy; for, till our late breach with France, very few of their ships navigated into foreign parts; and the chief source that supplied the balance of their trade with other nations, arose from this branch. Their internal traffic is by no means proportionate to the numbers of their people, the natural advantages of their situation and climate, the abundance of raw materials which the country produces, and their Indies supply them with; especially when we reflect on the many years of peace which they have enjoyed, and that commerce were never so much considered by the several European states, as it is in the present age.

The

The great error of the Spanish policy seems to be this; they never sufficiently attended to the truth of the following political maxim, That industry, manual labour, and the arts, are more beneficial, and truer sources of wealth to a state, than the richest mines of gold and silver. Dazzled with the spoils of America, they turned their whole attention to seize the exclusive possession of those seeming riches; they neglected agriculture and manufactures, and contracted a contempt for the mechanic and even liberal arts; in consequence of which, the country becoming daily less populous, their maritime and military strength soon declined. Of late years the Spanish ministry hath been fully sensible of this fatal mistake, and hath endeavoured to raise a spirit of industry among the people, by promoting the establishment of manufactures, in various parts of the kingdom: but though they have tempted the people, by exemption from taxes, and many other privileges, yet the progress they have made is not so considerable as might have been expected.

We shall now attend Mr. Clarke on his journey from Madrid to Lisbon.—" As his catholic majesty did not think proper to give the earl of Bristol any answer, in relation to the question put to him by the court of Great Britain, we, who all held ourselves in readiness for an abrupt departure, made the necessary dispositions for an immediate return to England: accordingly the requisite passports being obtained, Stanier Porten, Esq; the English consul-general at Madrid, led the way, and set out, on the 16th of December, on his route for Portugal. We should have been obliged to return that way, because the war prevented our going through France, and the road to Corunna being not practicable for a coach, unless we had made a very wide detour, and taken the road to San Jago de Compostella.——But his Britannic majesty fixed that route, by ordering that a ship (the Portland man of war, captain Richard Hughes commander)

commander) should sail directly for Lisbon, and bring home the English ambassador and his retinue.————
The consul having gone the day before, in order to prepare the way for the ambassador, procure him the best accommodations, and to give notice of his coming; his excellency set out on the 17th of December, without taking leave of the court of Spain.

As the whole nation were averse to a war with England, the Spaniards beheld the ambassador's departure with the utmost regret; it being their opinion, as well as the constant maxim of Patinho, *Con todo el mundo guerra, y paz con Ynglaterra,* " War with all the " world, but peace with England." Some said, *Es por neustros peccaos*; and others, *Es uno golpe politico*; that is, " It is for our sins;" and, " It is a political " stroke;" that is to say, the court's doing, not a national war.

Though the ambassador returned, without taking leave of the court, yet he received, on his departure, all the honours and civilities which were due to his rank and character. General Wall sent orders to all the governors, and commandants of every city or town the ambassador was to pass through, that they should shew him all the accustomed honours and respects due to the ambassador of Great Britain.—Accordingly, at every place, the governor waited on his excellency, at his arrival, with a polite Spanish compliment; the soldiers were drawn up under arms, the drums beating, colours flying, and the cannon on the ramparts fired at his departure.

We were to travel sixty-three leagues before we could get out of Spain, and pass the Guadiana at Badajos, which is the last frontier city toward Portugal; and then we had 29 leagues remaining to Aldea Gallega, a little village on the south side of the Tagus, where we were to pass that river to come at Lisbon. We were to pass two thirds of this way in an enemy's country, and the remainder in a dreary, barren,

rocky

rocky foil, fomewhat, indeed, more fertile than Spain, but very little better in its accommodations. Befide this, the feafon of the year, which is ever unfavourable to travellers, was moft particularly fo to us at this juncture, as it rained almoft that whole fortnight without intermiffion; infomuch, that fome of the rivers were fo increafed, as to prevent a paffage: this happened to thofe who conducted the baggage-waggons, which were retarded fome days by the floods.—Add to this, the rigour of the feafon, and the cold, the ftormy winds to be naturally expected in that part of the year; and, at thofe feafons, the reftlefs toffings of the bay of Bifcay. All which circumftances frequently put me in mind of thofe remarkable words of fcripture, *And pray that your flight be not in the winter.*

The firft place worth notice in this route, is the town of Talavera de la Reyna, in the kingdom of New Caftile, on the banks of the Tagus. It is the greateft manufacture of filver and gold filks, perhaps, in the whole country. The late king Ferdinand protected and encouraged it much; but it is now finking, as moft of the reft of their manufactures are, under the uncommercial afpect of the minifter Squilacci. There is likewife a curious manufacture of earthen ware. Its ancient name was Talabriga. It was called De la Reyna, becaufe it belonged to queen Mary, wife of Alonzo XII.

There is one hill, of a long, winding, and difficult afcent, before you come to Jarayfejo; it is dangerous in fome parts; it employed us almoft a whole morning to furmount it; and one baggage-waggon fell down fome part of the precipice, but was got up again entire. There is likewife a very dangerous pafs of a mountain, about two leagues before you come to Truxillo: your coach muft here be drawn up by oxen, and fupported by men, otherwife it is impoffible to get it over the mountain.——Truxillo is a city in the province of Eftremadura, ftanding on a hill,

hill, on the top whereof is a caftle, the country about it fruitful.——It was founded by Julius Cæfar, and after him called Turris Julia, hence corruptly Truxillo.

The next place of note is Merida, the capital city of the province of Eftremadura, built on the banks of the Guadiana, over which there is a moft noble bridge, the work of that great emperor, as well as builder, Trajan. There are here ftill to be feen many fine remains of Roman antiquity: in the marketplace is a large column, built entirely of infcription and fepulchral ftones, crowned on the top with an antique ftatue; the walls for the moft part Roman; there are fome remains of an amphitheatre, aqueduct, circus, &c. all Roman. It was built by Auguftus, given by him to veteran troops, and called Emerita Augufta, whence corruptly Merida.

Four leagues farther, on the banks of the fame river, ftands Lobon, where there is a caftle. It was antiently called Lychon, in Greek, fignifying a wolf, which its prefent Spanifh name does likewife.

The laft city in Eftremadura, on the frontiers of Portugal, is Badajoz, well fortified, has a fine bridge, a caftle, and was antiently called Pax Augufta; whence its prefent name.——Here we took our laft adieu of Spain; and were not a little pleafed to find ourfelves on Portuguefe ground the next morning, at Elvas; where the ambaffador ftayed all day, though it was only three leagues to it, in order to forward a meffenger to England, and fend his difpatches to the honourable Mr. Hay, his Britannic majefty's minifter plenipotentiary at the court of Lifbon. — Elvas is a city in the province of Alentejo in Portugal. Being the frontier to Spain, it is the beft fortified place the Portuguefe have: it is alfo a bifhopric. There is a good cathedral, with a moft elegant chapter-room. The dean, who was a very polite ecclefiaftic, was fo obliging as to fhew it us himfelf.

Six

Six leagues farther, you come to Eftremos, another fortified place, about two leagues from Villa-Vizofa; where is a caftle on the hill.—The fituation is beautiful, and the town has a clean, neat, pleafing appearance; it is remarkable for a fine manufactory of earthen ware.—It is moft memorable for a victory obtained by the Portuguefe, under the command of count Schomberg, in 1663, over the Caftilians, whofe general was Don John of Auftria, in their laft invafion of that kingdom.—They found in that prince's cafket, after the battle, very compleat lifts of the Spanifh army, artillery, and other offenfive munitions of war.—The court of Lifbon, diverted at this incident, bad their fecretary of ftate write at the bottom of one of thefe lifts, " We certify, that the " above lift is very exact, having found it after the " defeat of Don John of Auftria, near Eftremos, " 8th June 1663."—The diftance of time between the laft and the prefent invafion being only one year fhort of a century.

The next place of note is Arroyolos, ftanding on an eminence, with a good fort to it; it gives the title of earl to the family of Caftro.

The 31ft of December we arrived at Aldea Gallega. Here our difperfed parties united again with the greateft joy, having the beautiful profpect of that fine river the Tagus before us, which is no lefs than twelve miles broad at that place, and which we were to pafs at fix o'clock the next morning, becaufe of the tide. And here we were glad to reft from all our fatigues; fome of us having fuffered very much from the length and labour of the journey.

We arrived at Lifbon about eight o'clock the next morning; where the honourable Mr. Hay received the ambaffador, and his retinue, and conducted him to his own houfe."——

Portugal was formerly called Lufitania; but its boundaries were then different from thofe it has at prefent. The name of Portugal is by fome thought to arife from Portus Gallus, or Portus Gallorum, from the multitude of French which came to the city of Porto, on the river Douro, in order to affift the Chriftians againft the Moors. But the more general opinion is, that it is derived from a town on the river Douro, by the ancients called Cale; but by the moderns changed to Gaya: oppofite to this place a new town, with a harbour, was built by the inhabitants, who gave it the name of Portucale, or the Port of Cale, which, by its profperity, proved the origin of the prefent flourifhing city of Porto; and the whole country from hence received the name of Portugal.

This kingdom is bounded on the north by the Spanifh province of Galicia; on the eaft by the provinces of Leon, Eftremadura, and Andalufia; and on the fouth and weft by the Atlantic ocean: fo that it is the moft wefterly part of the continent of Europe. It extends from 36° 50′ to 42° 3′ north latitude, and between 7° and 10° weft longitude from London. Its length from Valença, the moft northern town in it, to Sagres, the moft fouthern, near Cape St. Vincent, is about 310 miles; and its greateft breadth from Peniche, a fea-port in Eftremadura, to Salvaterra, on the frontiers of Spain, is 112.

The climate is much more temperate than in Spain, though it is a little different in the feveral provinces. The northern parts feel a kind of painful cold in winter, though this is chiefly owing to the rains which fall at that feafon; and in the fouthern the fummer heats are very great. However, both winter and fummer are very fupportable; for cooling fea-breezes, during the latter, refrefh the country, and the feafon of fpring is extreamly delightful.

Though the foil is very fruitful, agriculture is fo much neglected, that above half the country lies wafte, and the inhabitants are fupplied with a great part of their corn by the Englifh and Dutch, and have Indian corn from Africa. Portugal, however, abounds

abounds in excellent wine and oil; the greatest part of the latter is made in the province of Alentejo, for the olive-trees thrive better here, near the sea, than up in the country. Here are also abundance of oranges, lemons, figs, pomegranates, raisins, almonds, chesnuts, and other fruit. It produces great plenty of fine honey, and consequently of wax. The best honey found in the fields is almost of a white colour, and of a most agreeable flavour; and the wood-honey is more agreeable to the taste than in other countries.

As Portugal has some excellent pastures, particularly in the country about Montestrella and near Ourique, the grazing is in some places very considerable, and there are seen an uncommon number of horned cattle and sheep; but in most places it is at so low an ebb, that the greatest part of their oxen come from Spain. Their horses are not large, but very fleet; and they have fine mules, which sell for a great price. The Portuguese breed more asses than horses, the latter being clandestinely imported from Spain.

From the mountains issue several streams and small rivers, which fertilize the vallies and fields, and either join the great rivers in their course, or discharge themselves separately into the sea: but all the great rivers of Portugal have their sources in Spain. All these rivers abound in fish; and the three principal, namely the Douro, the Tagus, and the Guadiana, divide the kingdom into three parts.

With respect to the government of Portugal, the king is, in many respects, an unlimited monarch; but, on the imposition of new taxes, the settlement of the succession, and other important concerns, the consent of the cortes, or states, which consist of the clergy, the high nobility, and the commons, is necessary. The clergy are here represented by the archbishops and bishops; the high nobility are the dukes, marquisses, counts, viscounts, and barons; and the representatives of the commons are chosen by the cities and towns. Among them are also reckoned the lower nobility, and the masterships of the order of knighthood. This assembly never meets but by the king's proclamation; and though the crown is hereditary, yet the consent of the several states is necessary to the succession of a brother's children. The crown too devolves to the female line; but this right is forfeited, if they marry out of the kingdom.

The highest office is the council of state, in which all the great affairs of the kingdom are transacted, with the disposal of all ecclesiastical and temporal offices; as the nomination of all archbishops and bishops, viceroys, captain-generals, governors of the provinces, with every thing relating to peace and war, embassies, alliances, &c.

For the inferior administration of justice, each of the six provinces of the kingdom have inferior courts.

The king's revenue arises first, from the hereditary estates of the royal house of Braganza, to which belong fifty villas. Secondly, from the royal domains. Thirdly, from the customs, of which those of Lisbon are the most considerable. Fourthly, from the taxes. Fifthly, from the excise, which is very high, and paid even by the clergy. Sixthly, from the monopoly of Brazil snuff, which, in 1755, was farmed for three millions of crusadoes. Seventhly, from the coinage. Eighthly, from the sale of indulgencies, which the Pope renews to the king every three years by a special bull. Ninthly, from the grand masterships of the order of knighthood, which the king holds in his own hands. Tenthly, from the ecclesiastical tithes in foreign countries. Eleventhly, from the duty of the fifth part of all gold brought from Brazil, which annually amounts to three hundred thousand pounds sterling; and lastly, from the farm of the Brazil diamonds.

The military forces, in time of peace, when compleat, amount, according to Dr. Busching, to no more

more than fourteen thousand men; and the same author obferves, that the Portuguefe navy in 1754, confifted only of twelve fhips of war, and thefe but weakly manned.

The provinces of Portugal, beginning at the foutheaft, are the following: Eftremadura, Beira, Algarve, Alentejo, Eftremadura, Beira, Trazos Montes, and Entre Duro e Minho.

The Portuguefe foreign dominions, which were formerly extreamly confiderable, are now greatly diminifhed.——They at prefent poffefs, in the Atlantic Ocean, the Cape de Verd Iflands, St. Thome, &c. In Africa, fort Magazan on the coaft of Morocco, Cacheo on the Negro coaft, feveral forts in the kingdom of Congo, Loango, Angola, and Monomotapa; a fort in Monoemugi; the town of Mofambique in the kingdom of that name, and the town of Sofala. In Afia, the towns of Diu, Goa, Onor, Macao, &c. In America, Brazil, part of Guiana, and Paraguay.

Emanuel de Farca, a Portuguefe writer, defcribing his countrymen, fays, " The nobility think themfelves gods, and require a fort of adoration; the gentry afpire to equal them; and the common people difdain to be thought inferior to either." This pride is the characteriftic both of the Spaniards and Portuguefe: and here the grandees and their ladies carry their haughty fpirit to fuch an extravagant height, that they ftand upon the niceft punctilios with refpect to rank and titles. The ladies of quality are ferved by their maids and flaves on the knee; and indeed the women of quality will fcarcely be fpoken to by mean people in any other pofture: a degree of haughtinefs practifed in no other Chriftian country, and which they probably received from the Moors. But this is far from being the worft part of their character; for it is become a proverb, that a Spaniard, ftript of all his good qualities, makes a perfect Portuguefe. Indeed they are generally characterized, as being cruel, treacherous, malicious, and revengeful, both to one another and to strangers; crafty in their dealings, and the meaner sort addicted to thieving. But to this general character, there are many noble exceptions.

The Portuguese gentlemen commonly wear black, and those of the court frequently follow the French fashions.

With respect to their houses and furniture, they have usually a great many rooms on a floor. The floors and ceilings are formed of a plain white plaister, that looks like polished marble. They change their furniture and apartments according to the season of the year; and upon the lower floors of their summer apartments they usually throw water every morning, which soon dries up, and leaves a refreshing coolness. Upon these floors they spread fine mats, and cover the walls with them chair-high; above these are hung pictures and looking glasses, and all round the rooms of the ladies apartments, cushions of silk or velvet are laid upon the mats, which they sit upon crofs-legged, as hath been already observed with respect to the Spanish ladies. Between these cushions are fine tables and cabinets; and, at certain distances, vases of silver, in which are orange or jessamine-trees, and in their windows they have frames of straw-work, to keep out the scorching beams of the sun.

The houses of the nobility are crouded with domestics; but their wages are very low, they having only eight-pence or ten-pence per day to purchase diet, cloaths, and every thing else; and a gentleman belonging to a grandee has only about fifteen crowns a month, though he is obliged to dress in velvet in winter, and silk in summer. Indeed the servants lay out the greatest part of their salaries in cloaths, living upon onions, pease, beans, and other pulse. One reason of the Portuguese nobility having such a number of servants, is a custom which prevails among them, of keeping all in their pay who have served

their

their anceſtors; ſo that ſome of the grandees have four or five hundred of both ſexes, the greateſt part of whom are meerly for ſhew, and ſeldom appear but on days of ceremony.

The quality, beſide their ordinary ſervants, retain abundance of dwarfs of both ſexes, who are dreſſed as fine as poſſible; they have alſo a number of ſlaves, who are Moors, and are valued at four or five hundred crowns apiece. Over theſe they had formerly the power of life and death; but at preſent the government will not permit their killing them. Where two ſlaves marry, their children are ſlaves; but if a freeman marries a ſlave, the children are free.

Theſe ſlaves are their beſt ſervants, for the others will ſometimes pride themſelves on having as good blood as their maſters. The very beggars rather demand than ſupplicate an alms, alleging their being deſcended from old Chriſtians; and if you give them no money, they muſt be diſmiſſed with a compliment, upon which they go away contented.

The food of the Portugueſe is nearly the ſame with that of the Spaniards, and they are equally ſober and abſtemious. The men mix water with their wine, and the women generally drink only water. It is cuſtomary with the Portugueſe to betake themſelves to ſleep about noon, on account of the heat, and to tranſact moſt of their buſineſs in the morning and evening, or even at night.

The method of travelling here is much the ſame as in Spain, except their having fewer coaches, and travelling more by water than the Spaniards, from their country lying along the ſea-coaſt, and its being croſſed by many great rivers that riſe in Spain. The mule or the litter are generally uſed on a journey; their horſes, which are ſprightly and well made, ſerve indeed for ſhort viſits, to prance at a proceſſion, or before the windows of their miſtreſſes; but the mules being ſtronger and ſurer footed, are fitteſt to climb their mountains; but have only a ſlow pace.

Their

Their language is a compound of the Spanish, Latin, Moorish, and French.

With respect to the religion of the Portuguese, they are the most bigotted Papists; but though the exercise of the Jewish religion be prohibited by the fundamental laws of the kingdom, yet all authors agree, that great numbers of secret Jews still remain among the Portuguese; and these too among the nobility, bishops, prebends, monks, nuns, and the very inquisitors themselves: and when unable to conceal themselves, escape to England or Holland, and there openly profess Judaism. The inquisition, which was introduced by king John III. and has since been set up in all the Portuguese dominions, except Brazil, is very active in detecting them, and those they call heretics; and are no less rigorous in punishing them. Impious, cruel, and inhuman, as this tribunal is, yet its festivals or solemn burnings, called *auto de fe*, or the act of faith, afford the highest delight to the infernal bigots, who, while their fellow-creatures are burning in the flames, cry aloud, " Oh, what great goodness! Praised be the holy office." King John IV. in some measure, however, curtailed the power of the inquisition, commanding that all its sentences should be laid before the parliament, and that the accused should be allowed council for making their defence; and enacted, that only blasphemy, sodomy, heresy, sorcery, pagan customs, and the conversion of the Jews should come under their cognizance.

The number of convents in Portugal is said to amount to nine hundred, and most of them are very rich; but the Jesuits, who in multitude and opulence surpassed all the other orders, have lately been banished.

With respect to the ecclesiastics, there is a patriarch of Lisbon, who must always be a cardinal, and of the royal family. Next to him are three archbishops, who rank with marquisses; and the first of them the archbishop of Braga, who is primate of the kingdom,

kingdom, and lord spiritual and temporal of his city and the neighbouring country. The bishops hold the rank of counts. Beside those in Europe, the Portuguese have archbishoprics and bishoprics in the other three parts of the world.

With respect to the state of learning in Portugal, it is at as low an ebb as possible. Indeed there are universities at Coimbra and Evora. At Lisbon is a royal academy for the Portuguese history; at Santarene is an academy of history, antiquities, and languages; and at St. Thomas an academy of sciences, on the same footing as that of Paris: but while bigotry continues here at its present enormous height, it is impossible for science to flourish. An Italian capuchin, in 1746, published a work in the Portuguese tongue, on the true method of study, in four volumes quarto, which he dedicated to the king of Portugal; and he there asserts, that the schools of this country are places of retreat for those errors, which by Newton and Des Cartes, were driven out of the other parts of Europe: and according to him Galilæo, Des Cartes, Newton, and Gassendi, are considered in Portugal as atheists and heretics, not to be mentioned but with some marks of execration.

The Portuguese not only neglect agriculture, but all arts and manufactures, though the country has the finest materials; the greatest part of these are disposed of unwrought to foreigners, and when worked up, are purchased again, at a high price. The Portuguese, indeed, make a little linen, a variety of strawwork, and candy several kinds of fruit, particularly oranges. They have likewise some coarse silk, and woollen manufactures; but these are trifling articles that support only a very small part of the nation.

The Portuguese, however, carry on a very extensive trade; but from this they reap little profit, being obliged to vend, not only their own produce, but all the merchandize and riches brought from their settlements in other parts of the globe, and especially

from

from America, to the Europeans, particularly the English, in exchange for corn and manufactured goods of all kinds, with which they supply both Portugal and its possessions abroad. The chief commodities of the Portuguese consist of imports from their own colonies, particularly from Brazil, as tobacco, cacao-nuts, sugars, spices, drugs, ivory, ebony, brazil-wood, hides, gold, pearls, diamonds, and other valuable gems.

All sums of money are reckoned in Portugal by reis and crusadoes, which are not real, but only imaginary coins. The gold coins of Portugal are, the double moedas, of one pound seven shillings value; the quarter of which is called a millrei, or a thousand reis, and has therefore the number one thousand marked upon it: and the Johns, worth three pound twelve shillings, which are subdivided into halfs, quarters, eighths, and sixteenths. The silver coins are the vintain of twenty reis; the half teeston of fifty; and the whole teeston of one hundred.

" The city of Lisbon, says Mr. Clarke, built, like old Rome, on several little hills, is one of the finest views from the water that can possibly be imagined: as you approach nearer to it, the tragical effects, the havock of that dreadful earthquake, cannot but touch every beholder with sentiments of pain. After landing, we passed through some streets, near a mile in length, where the houses were all fallen on each side, and lay in that undistinguished heap of ruin, into which they sunk at the first convulsive shocks. Not that the reader is to imagine, that the greatest part of that fine city fell on that fatal morning; so far from it, that I believe, not above one fourth part of it was destroyed: for it prevailed more in one particular quarter than the rest; and there the desolation was almost universal, scarce an house or building that was not thrown down. In the other parts of the city, some single ill-conditioned, or ruinous buildings fell, but the rest stood.——And there is scarce a street but you will see shores and props fixed to the buildings on each side, to prevent their falling even now; they having suffered so much from the shock they had received.——Considering how much time has elapsed since the earthquake, very little has been rebuilt in proportion.——They have built a custom-house, an arsenal, a theatre, and some few other buildings. All agree, that the fire occasioned infinitely more havock than the earthquake. Thousands of the inhabitants, unhappily, in the first confusion of their fear, taking the ill-judged step of thronging into the churches, the doors of which being sometimes shut by the violence of the crowd, and sometimes locked by mistake, when the fire seized the roofs of those buildings, these unhappy sufferers were most of them destroyed; some by sheets of lead, that poured like a molten deluge upon their heads; others mashed by the fall of the roofs, and the rest burnt alive. Imagination can scarcely form a scene of confusion, horror, and death more dreadful than this.——After the shocks were over, the fire continued burning for many weeks; and it is thought, was one principal cause of their escaping the plague, as the putrefaction of the bodies was by that means much less.——The calculation of the number that perished, as they kept no registers, must be in great measure conjectural; but that thousands and ten thousands were destroyed, there is no doubt. The morning on which it happened was most remarkably serene and pleasant, particularly about 10 o'clock, and in one quarter more, all was involved in this dreadful scene of terror and destruction.——As this event produced many changes, those among the commercial parts of the city were not the least remarkable. One who yesterday was at the eve of a bankruptcy, found himself to-day with his books cleared; and hundreds, who lived in ease and affluence, as soon as they had recovered from their first panic and dismay, saw want and poverty stare them in the face.

The calamities of Portugal in general, and those of the city of Lisbon in particular, within the space of so few years, cannot, I think, be paralleled in all history.——An earthquake, a fire, a famine, an assassination-plot against their prince, executions upon executions, the scaffolds and wheels for torture reeking with the noblest blood; imprisonment after imprisonment, of the greatest and most distinguished personages; the expulsion of a chief order of ecclesiastics; the invasion of their kingdom by a powerful, stronger, and exasperated nation; the numerous troops of the enemy laying waste their territory, bringing fire and sword with them, and rolling, like distant thunder, toward the gates of their capital; their prince ready almost to save himself by flight.— The Spanish ministry had already decreed the doom of Portugal, and nothing was to be heard at the Escurial, but *delenda est Carthago*. Carthaginian, perhaps, or Jewish story, may possibly afford a scene something like this; but, for the shortness of the period, not so big with events, though in their final destruction superior. From that, indeed, under the hand of Providence, the national humanity and generosity of Great Britain has preserved the Portuguese: and it remains now to be seen, in future treaties, how that people will express their gratitude.

Those who are able to search deeper into human affairs, may assign the causes of such a wonderful chain of events; for my own part, I cannot ascribe all this to so singular a cause as that which a Spaniard hath done, in a famous pamphlet, printed lately at Madrid, and which the baron de Wassenaer sent me this summer. It is intitled, *A Spanish Prophecy*, and endeavours to shew, that all these calamities have befallen the Portuguese, solely because of their connection with the heretic English. The great ruler and

and governor of the world undoubtedly acts by universal laws, regarding the whole system, and cannot, without blasphemy, be considered in the light of a partizan. The rest of the pamphlet tends to shew, that his catholic majesty carried his arms into Portugal, solely to give them liberty, and set them free from English tyranny.

Some of the churches, the arsenal, the theatre, and above all, the aqueduct at Lisbon, deserve the attention of every traveller; the center arch, for its height, being one of the noblest, perhaps, in Europe. One thing is remarkable, that during the earthquake this building stood the attack, though it received so much shock, as that many of the key-stones fell several inches, and hang now only because a small part of the base of the key-stone was catched by the center's closing again.

The theatre is an elegant building, and judiciously disposed; their actors excel in the mute pantomime; they played the *maestro di schola* incomparably well; the scenes had sentiment, character, connection with one another, and carried on the general design. Though the scenery and machines of our theatres are admirable, yet our pantomime farces seem to have little or no meaning. Nor do I much wonder at it; Mr. Garrick, who is certainly the greatest actor that ever trod the stage, must be too warm an admirer of Shakespeare and Nature, to have any relish for these extravagancies, and therefore cannot stoop to give much of his attention to them.

The streets of Lisbon are cleaner than those of Madrid, but disagreeable, from the continual ascents and descents you are obliged to make. Most of the houses have the jalousie, or lattice. The women, though more beautiful, are not so much seen in public as the Spanish, and their head-dress is much prettier. There are few fires in chimnies in the rooms at Lisbon; the want of them is supplied by wearing a cloak a cloak conſtantly in the houſe, or perhaps by a brazier; though the cold is ſometimes very piercing.

The view of the Tagus, from thoſe windows of the town which command it, is remarkably pleaſing: the bean-cods, or ſmall boats, which ſail with any wind or tide, and are continually paſſing; the river crouded with ſhipping of all nations; the coming in of a Bahia or Braſil fleet; the opening of the river toward the bar, with the caſtle of Belem on the right, the king's palace, and the caſtle of St. Julian's on the left; all together form a fine and agreeable view. The paſſage of the bar is ſometimes very dangerous, either in coming in or going out of the river, by the bank of ſand which is thrown up by the winds and ſea. We paſſed it, however, with no difficulty, on the 19th of January, landed at Falmouth on the 28th, and arrived at London the 5th of February, 1762."

The trade of this place, and the navigation to and from it, is ſo very conſiderable, that the cuſtom-houſe which lies on the Tagus, is the principal ſource of the king's European revenues; and this is the grand magazine of all the goods which the Portugueſe fetch from their foreign colonies. The harbour is very large, deep, ſecure, and convenient; and has two entrances, that on the north, called the Corredor, lies between the ſand-bank, the rock of Cachopos, and fort St. Julian: the ſouthern entrance, which is much broader and very convenient, is between Cachopos and the fort of St. Laurence. The city is walled round, having ſeventy-ſeven towers on the walls, and thirty-ſix gates. It has ſo encreaſed by degrees, particularly toward the weſt, that the old walls now divide the two dioceſes. In the center of the city, on one of the hills, ſtands a citadel that commands the whole place, and has caverns in it, in which four regiments of foot are conſtantly quartered. Cloſe by the ſea, at the diſtance of about ten miles

miles from the city, both the entrances to the harbour are defended by two forts; that on the north stands on a rock in the sea, and is called St. Julian; the other to the south is built on piles, on a sandbank, and is named St. Laurence, but is more commonly called Bogio. Two Portuguese miles from St. Julian, and one from Lisbon, stands the fort of Belem, which commands the entrance into the city, where the masters of all ships coming up the Tagus must bring to, and give an account of themselves; and directly opposite to it, on the south side, is the fort of St. Sebastian, commonly called the Old Fort, which stands on the angle of a mountain, along which, a little way on the other side of the city, the passage is defended from the beginning of the harbour by a chain of twelve forts.

If a view of Lisbon is taken from the river, or from the opposite shore, it affords an admirable prospect; for the city being built in the form of a crescent, and the palace, churches, convents, and other buildings rising gradually from the river, one above another, we command the whole city at one prospect.

AN ACCOUNT

Of the EMPIRE of

RUSSIA:

Collected from the OBSERVATIONS of Mr. HANWAY; and other Writers.

THE Russian empire is of an amazing extent: toward the north and east it is bounded by the main ocean, and toward the west and south its limits are settled by treaties, concluded with several far distant powers: with the Swedes, the Poles, the Turks, the Persians, and with the Chinese; by whose dominions this immense empire is bounded. Voltaire justly observes, that " it is of greater extent than all the rest of Europe, or than the Roman empire in the zenith of its power, or the empire of Darius subdued by Alexander: for it contains more than eleven hundred thousand square leagues. Neither the Roman empire, nor that of the Macedonian conqueror, comprized more than five hundred and fifty thousand each; and there is not a kingdom in Europe the twelfth part so extensive as the Roman empire. In length, from the Isle of Dago as far as its most eastern limits, it contains very near a hundred and seventy degrees; so that when it is noon-day in the west, it is very near mid-night in the eastern part of this empire. In breadth it stretches from south to

north

north three thoufand werfts, which make eight hundred leagues."

As this empire confifts of a great number of provinces, many of which are very extenfive, both the foil and temperature of the air, muft be extremely various in different parts. In thofe which lie beyond 60° of latitude, there are few places where corn will grow to maturity; and in the northern parts of the empire, which reach beyond 70°, no garden-fruits are produced, except in the country about Archangel; where many bufhes and fhrubs grow fpontaneoufly, and yield feveral forts of berries: horned cattle are alfo bred, and there are plenty of wild beafts and fowls, and feveral forts of fifh in the neighbourhood of that city. In the provinces fituated in the middle of the empire, the foil produces moft kind of trees and garden-fruits, corn, honey, &c. They are likewife well-ftocked with horned cattle; the woods abound with game; the rivers are navigable, and full of the beft forts of fifh. In the fouthern provinces the climate is hot; and though in fome parts there are many barren waftes, yet in others the land is covered with verdure and flowers. Tobacco, wine, and filk, might be there produced, as the two firft are at Aftracan and the Ukraine; and they are well watered with rivers, which afford plenty of fifh; nor are they deftitute of game in proportion to the extent and number of the woods.

In the middle, and more particularly in the northern parts of the empire, the cold is very fevere, and the days extremely fhort in winter; but the fummers are warm and delightful, and even in the fhorteft nights the twilight is very luminous. At the winter folftice, when the day is at the fhorteft, the fun rifes at Archangel at twenty-four minutes after ten in the morning, and fets at thirty-fix minutes after one. At Peterfburgh the fun rifes at fifteen minutes after nine, and fets at forty-five minutes after two: but at Aftracan the fun rifes at forty-eight minutes after seven, and sets at twelve minutes after four. At the summer solstice, when the day is at the greatest length, this order is reversed, and the sun rises at Astracan at twelve minutes after four, and sets at about forty minutes after seven; and at Archangel rises at thirty-six minutes after one, and sets at twenty-four minutes after ten.

It is a common observation, that the eastern countries are much colder in winter, and hotter in summer, than the western that lie in the same latitude: this is particularly true with respect to Russia; for the river Neva, at Petersburgh, is in some years covered with ice so early as the 24th of October; and in other years, when latest, about the 22d of November; but it generally thaws by the 26th of April, old style.

The reader cannot fail of being pleased with seeing the progress of the seasons at Petersburgh, which is situated in 59° of latitude; as given by Mr. Hanway.

February generally brings with it a bright sun and a clear sky; every object seems to glitter with gems, and the nerves become braced by the cold. There is then no small amusement in riding in sledges upon the snow, to those who, from the length of the winter, have forgot the much superior pleasure which nature presents when cloathed in all her verdure. March is frequently attended with showers, which, with the heat of the sun, penetrate the ice: this is generally three quarters of a yard thick on the Neva, and in some great rivers to the north-east much thicker. This renders it like an honey-comb, and about the end of that month it usually breaks up. The month of April is frequently very warm; summer seems to precede the spring; for it is sometimes the 1st of June before any considerable verdure appears, and then the intense heat brings it on so fast, that the eye can discover its progress from day to day. Till the middle of July it seems to be one continued day, the sun not entirely disappearing above

two

two hours in the twenty-four. September generally brings rain and froft; the feverity of both is increafed in October; and in November the Neva is always frozen. Then comes on the feafon for the eafy and fpeedy conveyance on the fnow, which brings frefh provifions to market, a thoufand Englifh miles by land; when the beef of Archangel is often eaten at Peterfburgh. In December and January the cold is fo very intenfe, that the poor who are overtaken by liquor, or expofed to the air in open places, are frequently frozen to death. But the abundance of birch and alders with which the Ruffians are fupplied, and the commodioufnefs of their ftoves, enable them to introduce any degree of heat into their houfes.

Not one-tenth of the Ruffian empire is fufficiently peopled, and not a tenth part of it properly cultivated: for, notwithftanding its prodigious extent, the number of inhabitants who pay the poll-tax, is computed only at five millions one hundred thoufand; and the reft, including the females, amount to about ten millions, exclufive of the inhabitants of the conquered provinces.

The principal rivers of Ruffia are as follow: the Wolga, in Latin *Volga*, which has its fource in the foreft of Wolconfki, and is one of the largeft rivers in the world; for it runs a courfe of above two thoufand miles before it falls into the Cafpian fea. Its banks are generally fertile, and though not fufficiently cultivated, on account of the frequent incurfions of the Tartars; yet the foil naturally produces all kinds of efculent herbs, and in particular afparagus, of a very extraordinary fize and goodnefs. It receives feveral confiderable rivers, among which are the Occa and Cama, and difcharges itfelf through feveral mouths into the Cafpian fea, by which means it forms many iflands. The Don, the Tanais of the ancients, called Tuna or Duna by the Tartars, which has its fource not far from Tula in the Iwano Offero, or St. John's Lake. It firft runs from north to fouth, and

and after its conflux with the Sofna, directs its course from west to east, and in several large windings, again runs from north to south; but at length dividing into three channels, falls into the sea of Asoph. The Don, in its course, approaches so near the Wolga, that in one place the distance between them is but one hundred and forty wersts, or about eighty English miles. The Dwina is a very large river; the name signifies Double, it being formed by the conflux of the Sukona and the Yug. This river divides itself into two branches or channels near Archangel, from whence it runs into the White Sea.

The Nieper, the ancient Borysthenes, arises from a morass in the forest of Wolconski, about 120 miles above Smolenski, and forms several windings through Lithuania, Little Russia, the country of the Zaporo Cossacs, and a tract inhabited by the Nagaian Tartars; and after forming a marshy lake of sixty wersts in length, and in many places two, four, or even ten wersts in breadth, discharges itself into the Black Sea. The banks on this river are on both sides generally high, and the soil excellent; but in summer the water is not very wholesome. The Nieper has no less than thirteen water-falls within the space of sixty wersts; yet in spring during the land-floods, empty vessels may be hauled over them. There is but one bridge over this river, and that is a floating one, at Kiew, one thousand six hundred thirty-eight paces in length. This bridge is taken away about the end of September, to give the flakes of ice a free passage down the river, and is again put together in spring. There are to be seen on this river a great number of mills erected in boats.

The lake of Ladoga, situated between the gulph of Finland and the lake of Onega, is esteemed the largest lake in Europe, and is supposed to exceed any other for its plenty of fish, among which are also seals. It is 150 miles in length, and 90 in breadth. This lake is full of quick-sands, which being moved

from

from place to place, by the frequent storms to which it is subject, cause several shelves along its course, which often prove fatal to the flat-bottomed vessels of the Russians. This induced Peter the Great to cause a canal, near seventy English miles in length, seventy feet in breadth, and ten or eleven deep, to be cut at a vast expence from the south-west extremity of this lake to the sea. This great work was begun in the year 1718, and though vigorously prosecuted, was not compleated till the year 1732, in the reign of the empress Anne. This canal has twenty-five sluices upon it, and several rivers run into it. At the distance of every werst along its banks, is a pillar marked with the number of wersts; and it is the constant employment of a regiment of soldiers to keep the canal in repair.

The most fertile part of Russia is near the frontiers of Poland, where the inhabitants are able to supply their neighbours with corn. The northern parts are not only extreamly cold, but marshy, and over-run with forests, chiefly inhabited by wild beasts. Beside domestic animals, there are in Russia wild beeves, rein-deer, martens, white and black foxes, ermines, and sables, whose skins make the best furs in the world; as also hyenas or gluttons, bears and wolves.

Before the time of Peter the Great, the Russians were little better than savages; but that wise prince, by incredible application, and a proper mixture of severity and mildness, wrought so happy a change in their manners, as in a great measure sets them on a level with the other civilized nations of Europe.

The Russians are, for the most part, of the middle stature, though many of them are tall and comely. The common people are fond of their ancient customs; and though the majority of them have been gradually brought to submit to modern improvements, many chuse to suffer great inconveniences, and to pay additional taxes, rather than cut off their beards,

beards, and conform to some regulations with respect to religion.

The Russian women are extremely fond of paint, and consider a ruddy complexion as the very essence of beauty; so that in the Russian language, red and beautiful are synonimous terms. Even the poorer sort among the women, in order to mend their complexion, will beg money to buy paint. By this means they daub themselves so much, as to conceal the graces which nature may be presumed to have bestowed on them: for they generally profess, that if they had sufficient plumpness, they can procure themselves beauty. The dress of the common people in Russia is mean; they are cloathed with long coats, made of dressed sheep-skins, with the wool toward their bodies; their legs and feet are swaddled with a coarse cloth, secured by a cord of reeds, and their sandals are of the same materials; their caps are lined with fur, and cover the ears and neck, as well as the head: they wear sashes round their waists, and double gloves, one of woollen, and the other of leather, which take in the hand without any distinction, except the thumb, and these are an essential part of their clothing. However, people of any rank generally dress as we do in England, except wearing a full great-coat lined with fur, with a deep quilted or fur-lined cap, when they go abroad. The women of the lower class, beside their petticoats, wear sheep-skins like the men; but those who move in a higher sphere, wear flowered silk-cloaks, lined with furs. Persons of both sexes hang on their breast a cross, which is put on when they are baptized, and this they never lay aside as long as they live. The crosses of the peasants are of lead; but those worn by persons of wealth, are of gold or silver. The Russians seldom fail of bathing twice a week; for which purpose, almost every house-keeper is provided with a bath; and he that has none of his own, goes to those that are public. It is remarkable, that they often

often sally out naked from the warm bath, run about in the cold, roll themselves in the snow, and then plunge again into the warm water; and this vicissitude of heat and cold they consider as beneficial to the constitution, by rendering them hardy and robust.

The most usual method of building, both in the towns and country villages, is to lay one beam of wood upon another, and fastening them at the four corners, fill up the crevices between the beams with moss. The house is afterward covered with shingles, and holes are made in the timber for doors and windows. A brick stove or large oven is commonly made in the houses of the peasants, and takes up a fourth part of the area: this is flat at the top, and boarded; upon it, and on a kind of shelves round the room, the whole family sleep without beds.

Their furniture consists of three benches, an oblong table, and the picture of a saint or two. Instead of candles or lamps, the Russian peasants usually burn long splinters of deal. The apartments are as black as so many chimneys; for the fire-hearth being within the stove above-mentioned, which has no other vent for the smoke but into the room, the walls are covered with soot. It is no sooner dark, than the houses swarm with a species of insects, called tarakans, which are a kind of goat-chaffers. The best method of keeping them out is burning a light in the room till break of day.

The insatiable eagerness of the common people after spirituous liquors, and other strong drink, especially in the carnival time, is in a great measure owing to the severity of the winter, the rigorous fasts they observe, and the slender diet they live upon throughout the year. Their food chiefly consists of turnips, cabbage, pease, large cucumbers, onions, and coarse ill-tasted fish. Their drink is quas, a kind of small mead; and even among the gentry, brandy always makes a part of every repast. Among the lower class, it is generally the men who give themselves

selves up to these excesses, though it is not uncommon to see at Peterſburgh a drunken woman ſtaggering along the ſtreets. Some authors indeed ſay, that drunkenneſs is ſo far from being conſidered as a crime, that they make it part of their religion, and that they do not think they have kept a holiday as they ought, if they are not drunk before night. Mr. Perry affirms, that if you paſs through Moſcow on a holiday, you will ſee both prieſts and people lie drunk upon the ground; and if you go to help one of them up, he will tell you, by way of excuſe, " It is a holiday." He adds, that their ladies of quality are ſo little aſhamed of drinking to exceſs, that they will frankly acknowlege their having been very drunk, and return thanks for the favour to their friends who made them ſo.

Not only the common people, but the whole nation, are much more uſed to fiſh than fleſh; for their faſts take up near two-thirds of the year, during which they are abſolutely prohibited by their religion to taſte of animal food ; which is obſerved with the utmoſt ſtrictneſs.

A perſon may travel cheap, and with great expedition in Ruſſia, both in ſummer and winter: the poſt-roads leading to the chief towns are very exactly meaſured, with the werſts marked, and the poſt-ſtages fixed at proper diſtances; for throughout the whole empire, and even in Siberia, a pillar, inſcribed with the number of werſts, is erected at the end of each. The expence of travelling in this manner, is ſo eaſy, that between Riga and Peterſburgh, the hire of a poſt-horſe for every werſt is no more than two copeiks and a half, which is one penny three farthings ſterling; between Novogrod and Peterſburgh only one copeik ; and between Novogrod and Moſcow but half a copeik. Nothing can be more accommodated to eaſe and diſpatch than travelling in ſledges during the winter, when the earth is covered deep with ſnow, and impaſſable for wheel-carriages: for in the journey Mr. Hanway made in that season from Moscow to Petersburgh, he slept in his sledge, without waking, while he advanced 100 wersts, or 66 English miles. The whole road between those two cities was marked out in the snow by young fir-trees planted on both sides, at the distance of twenty yards, which, at a moderate computation, amount to 128,480 trees. At certain distances were also great piles of wood, to be set on fire, in order to give light to the empress and her court, if they passed by in the night. On these occasions her imperial majesty is drawn in a kind of house that contains her bed, a table, and other conveniencies, where four persons may take a repast. This wooden structure, which has a sloping roof, and small windows to keep out the cold, is fixed on a sledge, and drawn by twenty-four post-horses; and if any of them fail on the road, others are ready to supply their places. Our author observes, that the late empress was generally no more than three days and nights on the way, notwithstanding her having several small palaces at which she sometimes stopped to refresh herself, though the distance is 488 English miles. Peter the Great once made the journey in forty-six hours, but did not travel in the same carriage. Mr. Busching observes, that it is not uncommon to go it with post-horses in seventy-two hours; and that a commodious sledge, drawn by a pair of post-horses for that journey, may be hired for fourteen or fifteen rubles.

The Russian language derives its origin from the Sclavonian, but at present it is very different from it; and, with regard to religious subjects, is enriched with a great number of Greek words. The alphabet consists of forty-two letters, most of them Greek characters, as they were written in the ninth century: but as the latter did not express every particular found in the Sclavonian language, recourse was had to several Hebrew letters, and to the invention of some arbitrary signs. In the different parts of the Russian empire various dialects are used, as the Muscovite,

covite, the Novogrodian, the Ukrainian, and that of Archangel.

The Ruffians profefs the religion of the Greek church, which was firft embraced by the great duchefs Ogla, fovereign of Ruffia, in the 955th year after the birth of Chrift. The external part of their religion confifts in the number and feverity of their fafts, in which they far exceed the Romifh church. Their ufual weekly fafts are on Wednefdays and Fridays. In lent, they neither eat flefh, milk, eggs, nor butter; but confine themfelves to vegetables, bread, and fifh fried in oil.

The Ruffians are great enemies to the worfhip of graven images, and yet are fo abfurdly inconfiftent, that, in their private devotions, they kneel before a picture of our Saviour, the Virgin Mary, St. Nicholas, or fome other faint, which is an indifpenfible piece of furniture in their clofet. To this they bow feveral times, making the fign of the crofs with their thumb, fore-finger, and third-finger, on the breaft, forehead, and fhoulders; at the fame time repeating, in a low voice, the Lord's Prayer, and fome fhort ejaculations; particularly, "Lord be merciful to me." Indeed they feldom pafs by a church without uttering of thefe words, at the fame time bowing and croffing themfelves, without paying the leaft regard to any perfon who happens to be prefent.

Many of the common people, and even fome perfons of rank, either by way of penance, or from other motives of humiliation, proftrate themfelves on their faces at the entrance of the churches; and thofe who are confcious of having contracted any impurity, forbear entering the church, but ftand at the door. The church bells are often rung; and as ringing is counted a branch of devotion, the towns are provided with a great number of bells, which make, as it were, a continual chiming. The divine fervice is entirely performed in the Sclavonian tongue, which the people do not underftand, as it is very different from the modern Ruffian; and this fervice confifts
of

of abundance of trifling ceremonies, long masses, singing, and prayers; all which are performed by the priests, the congregation only repeating, " Lord " be merciful to me." They sometimes add a lecture from one of the fathers; but there are few churches in which sermons are ever delivered, and even in those they preach but seldom.

There are a great number of convents for the religious of both sexes in the Russian empire; but Peter I. prudently ordered, that no person should be allowed to enter on a monastic life before fifty years of age: but this regulation has been repealed since his death, it being thought proper to shew a greater condescension to the monasteries: however, no man is permitted to turn monk till he is thirty, nor no woman to turn nun till she is fifty; and even then not without the express approbation and licence of the holy synod.

Learning was but little known in Russia before the reign of Peter the Great; but that illustrious monarch spared neither expence nor trouble to dispel the clouds of ignorance which overspread his empire, and to inspire his subjects with a taste for the arts and sciences: he founded an academy of sciences, an university, and a seminary at Petersburgh; beside other schools in the different parts of his empire: invited persons of learning from England, Germany, France, and Holland, to settle at Petersburgh: collected a great number of books; and encouraged his subjects to travel into those countries where the arts and sciences flourished. These wise and laudable measures were continued after his death, and the empress Elizabeth erected an university and two seminaries at Moscow.

All the mechanic arts and trades are continually improving in Russia, and these improvements are far from being entirely owing to the foreigners who reside among them; for the natives being spurred on by emulation, frequently equal, and sometimes exceed their masters. They were formerly almost solely employed in agriculture, feeding of cattle, hunting, and fishing. They excelled indeed in making Russia leather,

leather, which had been long practised by them; but they were entirely unacquainted with the more ingenious mechanic arts. Great numbers of excellent artificers, invited by Peter the Great, settling in his dominions, the Russians shewed that, with proper instructions, they did not want the capacity of being taught; and they have now flourishing manufactures of several kinds.

Russia affords a variety of articles of commerce, that are of great use to foreigners; and, as the exports of this country far exceed its imports, the balance of trade is considerably in its favour. The Russian home commodities are sables and black furs; the skins of blue and white foxes, ermines, hyenas, linxes, squirrels, bears, panthers, wolves, martins, wild cats, white hares, &c. Likewise Russia leather, copper, iron, ising-glass, tallow, pitch, tar, linseed oil, train oil, rosin, honey, wax, potash, salt-fish, hemp, flax, thread, calimancoes, Russia linen, sail-cloth, mats, castor, Siberian musk, mammonts teeth and bones, as they are called; soap, feathers, hogs bristles, timber, &c. to which may be added the Chinese goods, rhubarb, and other drugs, with which the Russians partly furnish the rest of Europe.

The trade to China is chiefly carried on by caravans, and partly by private adventures. The most valuable commodities, and those in the greatest quantity, carried by the Russians to China are furs; in return for which they bring back gold, tea, silks, cotton, &c. The trade to Persia, by the way of Astracan and the Caspian sea, is considerable; and the returns are made in raw silks and silk stuffs. The trade with the Calmucs, which is entirely in private hands, consists of all kinds of iron and copper utensils; in return for which they receive cattle, provisions, and sometimes gold and silver; but this trade is of no great importance. The trade to Bochara, one of the chief towns of Usbec Tartary, is either for ready money or by bartering of goods for cured lamb skins, Indian silks, and sometimes gems brought to the yearly fair of Samarkand. The traders in the Ukraine fell all kinds of provisions to the Crim Tartars; and also carry on a trade with the Greek merchants at Constantinople. The inhabitants of Kiow trade to Silesia in cattle and Russia leather.

The English enjoyed considerable privileges in trade so early as the reign of the czar Iwan Basilowitz, to whom captain Chancellor delivered a letter from Edward VI. in 1553, and received a licence to trade, which was renewed by Peter the Great. In 1742, a treaty of commerce was concluded between Russia and England, by which it was stipulated, that the English should be allowed the privilege of sending goods through Russia into Persia: but captain Elton, an Englishman, having entered into the service of Nadir Shah, and built ships on the Caspian sea for that monarch, the Russians, together with the troubles in Persia, put a stop to this trade. The English, however, still carry on a considerable trade with Russia, which exceeds that of any other nation.

The Dutch carry on the greatest trade, next to the English, with the Russians. Bills of exchange are drawn at Petersburgh on Amsterdam only; on which account the traders of other countries, who give commission for buying Russian commodities at Petersburgh, are obliged to procure credit, or to have proper funds at Amsterdam.

The trade to Petersburgh is now carried to a great height, for the number of ships which entered that port in 1751 from England, Holland, France, Norway, Denmark, Lubec, Hamburgh, Stetin, Rostoc, Kiel, Prussia, Sweden, and Dantzic, amounted to two hundred and ninety. Indeed there is no nation in the world more inclined to commerce than the Russians are at present; but they are so full of chicanery and art, that a foreigner cannot be too much on his guard in his dealings with them.

All the Russian coins, ducats excepted, have inscriptions in the Russian tongue. The gold coins are imperial ducats; and the largest silver coin is the ruble,

ruble, the value of which rises and falls according to the course of exchange. A ruble in Russia is equal to an hundred copeiks, or four shillings and sixpence sterling. The other silver coins are half rubles, which are called poltinnics and quarter rubles. A graphe, or griwe, is of the value of ten copeiks; and ten griwes are equal to a ruble. The copper coins are a copeik, which is of the value of about a halfpenny: a denga, or denushka, two of which make a copeik; and a polushka, which is a quarter of a copeik. There are no other foreign pieces current in Russia than ducats, Holland rixdollars, and Albert dollars.

The antient sovereigns of Russia stiled themselves great dukes, and afterward czars; but Peter the Great assumed the title of emperor, and that title is now given him by all Europe. The titles of the emperor at full length are, Emperor and sole sovereign of all the Russias, sovereign lord of Moscow, Kiow, Wlodimiria, Novogrod; czar in Casan, Astracan, and Siberia; lord of Pleskow; great duke of Smolensko; duke of Esthonia, Livonia, and Carelia; of Tweria, Ingria, Permia, Wiatkia, Bulgaria, and lord of several other territories; great duke of Novogrod, in the low country of Tshernickow, Reisan, Rostow, Iaroslaw, Bielo-sero, Uldoria, Obdoria, Condinia; emperor of all the northern parts; lord of the territory of Juweria; of the Carthalinian, Grewzinian, and Georgian czars; of the Kabardinian, Circassian, and Gorian princes; and lord and supream ruler of many other countries and territories.

Since the reign of Iwan Basilowitz, the arms of Russia have been, or, an eagle displayed sable, holding a golden scepter and monde in his talons: over the eagle's head are three crowns, and on its breast it bears a shield, with the arms of Moscow in the center, encompassed by six others, which are those of Astracan, Siberia, Casan, Kiow, and Wlodimiria.

The power of the Russian emperor is as absolute and unlimited as possible. Peter the Great published an ordinance, by which the succession was entirely to
depend

depend on the will and pleafure of the reigning fovereign; and this is the only written fundamental law in relation to the fucceffion.

The Ruffian court has always been very numerous and magnificent, it being filled, particularly on folemn occafions, by the bojars or privy counfellors; and by the nobles and gentry, who are obliged to pay a conftant attendance, by titles of honour and diftinction, without any falary: as the carvers, who are always two of the firft nobility, and whofe employment is efteemed extreamly honourable; the fewers, who carry meffages of importance, receive ambaffadors, &c. and the gentlemen of the bed-chamber. Thefe two laft titles are given to a great number of perfons, and defcend from father to fon, though they are generally confirmed by the prince; and laftly, by the chief merchants.

The revenues of the Ruffian empire are varioufly computed, fome reckoning that they amount to fixty millions of rubles, others to twenty millions, and others again to no more than eight millions a year: but Mr. Voltaire fays, that, according to the Ruffian finances in 1725, they amounted to thirteen millions of rubles, reckoning only the taxes and duties paid in money, exclufive of what is paid in kind; and he adds, that this fum was then fufficient to maintain three hundred and thirty-nine thoufand five hundred foldiers and failors; and that both the revenue and troops have increafed fince. It is, however, very certain, that the imperial revenues bear no proportion to the vaft extent of the Ruffian dominions; that they do not all confift of ready money, the country in many places furnifhing recruits for the army inftead of it; and moft of the inhabitants of Siberia pay their tribute in furs.

According to the ftate of the Ruffian forces drawn up by Van Hoven in the year 1746, the army then confifted of two hundred and forty-fix thoufand four hundred and ninety-four regulars, and a hundred and twenty thoufand irregulars. The fleet confifted of twenty-four ships of the line, seven frigates, three bomb-ketches, and two flat boats, beside the galley fleet at Peterſburgh, conſiſting of a hundred and two gallies. The fleet has continued pretty nearly the ſame ſince that time; for though ſome new ſhips have been built, others have become unfit for ſervice. The men of war are laid up at Revel and Cronſtadt, and the gallies at Peterſburgh. The Ruſſians indeed have no very good harbour in the Baltic; the water at Cronſtadt, by being too freſh, does conſiderable damage to the ſhips that lie there; beſide, the mouth of the harbour is too narrow, and ſurrounded with rocks and dangerous ſands, and is ſeldom clear of ice before the end of May: nor have they now any conſtant fleet in the Caſpian ſea.

The government of Moſcow is the beſt cultivated and the moſt populous in the whole empire, and may be called the garden of Ruſſia. It contains eleven provinces, the principal places in which are the city of Moſcow and Yaroſlawl.

Moſcow, the antient capital of the Ruſſian empire, and the reſidence of the czars, is ſituated in the circle of its own name, in 55° 40′ latitude, and 38° eaſt longitude; 1414 miles north-eaſt of London. It ſtands in a pleaſant plain on the banks of the river Moſkwa, from which it derives its name. Mr. Hanway ſays, that river runs through it, and, making many windings, adds a very ſtriking beauty to the city; but in ſummer it is in many places ſhallow and unnavigable. Several eminences, interſperſed with groves, gardens, and lawns, form the moſt delightful proſpects. It is built ſomewhat after the eaſtern manner, it having but few regular ſtreets, and a great number of houſes with gardens. The number of the churches in the city is computed at ſixteen hundred, among which are eleven cathedrals, and two hundred and ſeventy-one pariſh churches; the reſt either belong to convents, or may be conſidered as private chapels. Near the churches are hung up ſeveral

veral large bells, which are kept continually chiming. One of thefe is of a ftupendous fize, and, our author obferves, affords a furprifing proof of the folly of thofe who caufed it to be made; but the Ruffians have from time immemorial been extreamly fond of great bells. This bell is 443772 pounds weight, and was caft in the reign of the emprefs Anne: but the beam on which it hung being burnt, it fell, and a large piece is broke out of it. Many of the churches have gilt fteeples, and are magnificently decorated within with paintings; but indeed moft of thefe are miferable daubings, without fhade or perfpective.

The number of public edifices and fquares at Mofcow amount to forty-three. The mean houfes are indeed much more numerous than thofe that are well built; the latter are, however, daily increafing; but, as only a part of the ftreets is paved, they are very dirty.

The city is divided into four circles, one within another. The interior circle, or the Kremelin, which fignifies a fortrefs, contains the following remarkable buildings: the old imperial palace, pleafure-houfe, and ftables, a victualling-houfe, the palace which formerly belonged to the patriarch, nine cathedrals, five convents, four parifh churches, the arfenal, with the public colleges, and other offices. All the churches in the Kremelin have beautiful fpires, moft of them gilt, or covered with filver. The architecture is in the Gothic tafte; but the infide of the churches richly ornamented. From the above circle you pafs over a handfome ftone bridge into the fecond, which is called Kitaigorod, or the Chinefe-town. There are here five ftreets, two cathedrals, eighteen parifh churches, four convents, thirteen noblemen's houfes, and nine public edifices: thefe are the chief difpenfary, from which place the whole empire is fupplied with medicines: the mint, which is a fuperb ftructure: a magazine, or ware-houfe, to which all goods are brought before they have paid duty: the cuftom-houfe: the ambafsador's palace, which is now converted into a silk manufactory: a printing-house: a court of judicature: the physic garden, and the exchange. The third circle surrounds the former, and is named Belgorod, or the white Town, from a white wall with which it is encompassed. It is also called the Czar's Town. It includes seventy-six parish churches, seven abbeys, eleven convents, and nine public edifices: these are two palaces, a cannon foundery, two markets, a brewhouse, a magazine of provisions, the salt-fish harbour, and the Basil garden. At the timber-market are sold new wooden houses, which may be taken to pieces and put together again, where the purchaser pleases.

The fourth circle, called Semlanoigorod, that is, a town surrounded with ramparts of earth, incloses the three preceding parts, and its ramparts include an area of great extent. The entrance was formerly by thirty-four gates of timber, and two of stone; but at present only the two last are standing. Over one of these gates is a mathematical school, and an observatory. This circle contains a hundred and three parish churches, two convents, an imperial stable, an arsenal for artillery, a mint, a magazine for provisions, and a cloth manufactory. Round these principal parts of the city lie the suburbs, which are of great extent, and contain sixty parish churches and ten convents.

The number of inhabitants are supposed to amount to about a hundred and fifty thousand.

Moscow has greatly declined since the building of Petersburgh, and its being made the seat of the empire. It has often suffered by fires, and in 1737, 1748, and 1752, a considerable part of it was reduced to ashes, especially by the last fire, which consumed above half the city, together with the noble dispensary and the czarina's stables. But the houses are always soon rebuilt after such a calamity, they being for the most part formed of very mean materials.

We

We shall now give a particular description of Peterſburgh, one of the capitals of the Ruſſian empire. The beginning and increaſe of this great city were very extraordinary; for, till the year 1703, the only buildings on the ſpot where it ſtands were two ſmall fiſhing-huts. But Peter the Great having in that year taken the town of Nyenſhanze, ſeated on the Neva, and made himſelf maſter of this country, its commodious ſituation for the Baltic trade induced him to build a town and fortreſs here, and he immediately began to put his project in execution.

It was indeed firſt deſigned only for a place of arms, to which all kinds of military ſtores might be conveniently brought from the interior parts of the empire, by which means the war with Sweden might be carried on with more vigour and diſpatch. Hence the public edifices and private houſes were built only with timber, and neither the dock nor the town had any other fortifications than a mean rampart of earth, nor were the ſtreets paved. But the victory at Pultowa, and the conqueſt of Livonia, inſpired Peter with the hopes of being able to preſerve his conqueſt, and to render Peterſburgh the capital of his empire. His fondneſs for maritime affairs, a deſire of perpetuating his name by having it called by that of St. Peter, and his averſion to Moſcow, where, in his younger years, he had received much ill treatment, were the chief motives that induced him to lay the foundation of a new city that might become the capital of his dominions.

Peter had no ſooner formed this deſign, than he ordered the caſtle to be built of ſtone, the admiralty to be walled in with the ſame materials, and all the buildings to be erected in a more handſome and durable manner.

In 1714 he removed the council to Peterſburgh, and noble edifices were erected in a ſtreight line for the public offices, which, in 1718, were alſo removed thither. The principal families of Ruſſia were likewiſe ordered to reſide there, and build houſes according to their abilities. But this occasioned some irregularity in the buildings; for the nobility and burghers had been directed to build their houses on the island of Petersburgh, and many public and private structures were accordingly erected there; but, in 1721, the emperor determined that the whole town should stand on the island of Wasili. The streets were marked out, canals were dug, the island was fortified with 57 bastions, and the nobility were to begin their houses a second time: but the death of the emperor put a stop to the execution of his plan; and the stone buildings that had been erected went to ruin.

The Russian nobility were naturally averse to settle in Petersburgh, as they could neither live there so cheap, nor so commodiously as at Moscow. The country about Petersburgh is not very fertile, so that provisions are brought thither from a great distance, and must be paid for in ready money; which was no small grievance to the nobility, who chiefly subsisted on the produce of their estates; but seldom abounded in cash. Beside, Moscow seemed much fitter for being the imperial seat, as it is in the center of the empire, from whence justice might be more easily administered, and the national revenue be received and disbursed with more convenience and dispatch. Beside, Petersburgh seemed to them to lie too near the frontiers of Sweden. However, this city in the time of Peter I. became large and splendid, and under his successors received additional improvements, so that it is now ranked among the largest and most elegant cities in Europe.

Petersburgh is partly seated on the continent of Ingria and Finland, among thick woods, and partly on several small islands formed by the branches of the Neva, in 59° 57′ north latitude, and 31° east longitude from London. The low and marshy soil on which it stands has been considerably raised with trunks of trees, earth, and stone. However, its situation is pleasant, and the air salubrious. The city is about six English miles in length, and as many in breadth

breadth. The river Neva is about eight hundred paces broad, and near Peterſburgh; but has not every where a proportionable depth of water, ſo that large merchant ſhips are cleared at Cronſtadt, and the men of war built at Peterſburgh are alſo conveyed thither by means of certain machines called camels.

It is ranged on both ſides of the Neva, extending near two Engliſh miles from eaſt to weſt. At the upper end of the north ſide is the citadel, which is more famous for the number of lives it coſt in building, than for its ſtrength. It contains a ſtately church, in which are depoſited the remains of its founder, Peter the Great, and his empreſs Catharine; and it is alſo a priſon for offenders againſt the ſtate. The city has neither walls nor gates; but the marſhy land near it to the north and ſouth, and the gulph of Finland to the eaſt, render it difficult of approach for an army. As Peter the Great took Amſterdam for his model, it is divided by ſeveral canals; but from the reluctance with which it was originally begun by his ſubjects, and from errors in the plan, a part of it ſtill remains unexecuted, and in others the houſes are too near the canal; but there are ſome regular, broad, and well built ſtreets, and ſeveral very noble edifices. The empreſs's fondneſs for building has contributed to the beauty of the city; for beſide the two royal palaces already mentioned, ſhe has built a noble one ſaid to be intended for the Great Duke. Theſe edifices are moſtly of brick plaſtered over, ſo as to make an elegant appearance; but the work is generally done in a hurry, and the materials are not very durable. An Italian architect being eſtabliſhed in Ruſſia, notwithſtanding the difference of climate, the taſte of Italy is adopted in almoſt all their houſes, and though the ſeverity of the cold is ſo great, they abound much more in windows than our houſes in England. The number of people in Peterſburgh is generally computed at 250,000, including the garriſon, which is numerous: but in reckoning the ſubjects throughout the whole empire, it is laid down as a rule, that the hundred and seventy-fifth male raises an army of near 50,000 men, and consequently, supposing an equal number of females, the whole may be reckoned 17,500,000; but the tributary Tartars, the Russian Ukraine, and the conquered provinces are not included in this account.

What is truly deserving admiration in Russia, are the labours of the immortal Peter, who still lives not only in every part of the government, but in every work of art and design. We can hardly say too much of this prince; his character is admired by the world in general, but particularly by the part of it that he governed, and which must ever revere his memory, so long as they retain any traces of his vast genius and indefatigable labours. If, in the revolutions of ages, they should again decline into their ancient barbarity of manners, they never will give a stronger proof of that barbarity, than by ceasing to venerate his name.

It has been imputed to this prince, that he was cruel. The exact rule of mercy and justice cannot always be observed by every mortal man; and least of all by princes, who cannot search to the bottom of every thing. A man of his strength of resolution, cannot be supposed to have a heart of the melting sort; and the ingratitude and insensibility of his subjects, their repugnance to accept the terms of their own felicity by the means he sought it for them, means so obviously productive of the end, and yet so obstinately resisted, could not but fire him with some resentment, and might also persuade him they could be ruled only by a rod of iron. Thus he might commit some acts of severity, but that he put men to death with his own hand, Mr. Hanway is persuaded is not true.

An amorous disposition, and a cruel one, are compatible in the same person, as experience often evinces; but cruelty and greatness of mind, such as this prince demonstrated, are not compatible. His great foible was the love of women; he was not however profuse, nor even generous in his amours,

if

if one may believe the reports of Miſs Croſs, who was diſtinguiſhed in her way, by the emperor's favour in England. In Holland he was ſeen with a girl in his arms at a common drinking-houſe, of which repreſentation there is now an excellent picture in the palace at Peterhoff. A gardener once threw a hough at him for his amorous advances to a girl who was working in a garden. In ſhort, for a king he was as little elegant as expenſive in his amours: as in things of the higheſt moment, ſo in this he acted according to his inclinations, without any regard to forms.

He was often ſeen to weep when he ordered executions. Miſs Hambleton, a maid of honour to the empreſs Catherine, had an amour which at different times produced three children: ſhe had always pleaded ſickneſs; but Peter being ſuſpicious, ordered his phyſician to attend her, who ſoon made the diſcovery. It alſo appeared that a ſenſe of ſhame had triumphed over her humanity, and that the children had been put to death as ſoon as born. Peter enquired if the father of them was privy to the murder; the lady inſiſted that he was innocent, for ſhe had always deceived him, by pretending they were ſent to nurſe. Juſtice now called on the emperor to puniſh the offence. The lady was much beloved by the empreſs, who pleaded for her; as to the amour it would have been pardonable, but not the murder. Peter ſent her to the caſtle, and went himſelf to viſit her: the fact being confeſſed, he pronounced her ſentence with tears, telling her that his duty as a prince, and God's vicegerent, called on him for that juſtice which her crime had rendered indiſpenſably neceſſary; and therefore ſhe muſt prepare for death. He attended her alſo on the ſcaffold, where he embraced her with the utmoſt tenderneſs mixed with ſorrow: and ſome ſay, that when her head was ſtruck off, he took it up by the ear whilſt the lips were yet trembling, and kiſſed them: a circumſtance of an extraordinary nature, and yet not incredible, conſidering the peculiarities of his character.

How generous was his conduct to the Swedish prisoners after the battle of Poltowa! He struck one of his own officers for speaking disrespectfully of the king of Sweden, and said to him, " Am I not a king, " and might not my fortune have been the same " as that prince's?" But what a profusion of sound politics was displayed in his taking his sword from his own side, and presenting it as a token of his favour to the Swedish general Renchild, upon the occasion of that general's saying, " Though the king my mas- " ter acted contrary to my opinion, yet I thought " myself bound, as a faithful subject, to obey his " commands."

As it is the custom with us to interrupt conversation by drinking healths at table, in Russia they add also another impertinence, by their servants offering wine whether you ask for it or not. Peter was in warm dispute with admiral Apraxin, when the vice-admiral Senavin presented him with a salver of wine; the emperor impatiently threw back his arm, which necessarily overset the salver, and struck the admiral: he then pursued his discourse as if nothing had happened; afterward recollecting himself, he asked the admiral Apraxin if he had not struck somebody? " Yes, says he, your majesty has struck the vice- " admiral Senavin; it is true, he was in the wrong " for interrupting your majesty, but he is a very ho- " nest man and a brave officer." Peter then reproached himself for striking an officer of that rank, sent for him immediately, begged his pardon, kissed him, and the next day sent him a present.

We must not be surprised that this prince, while he was only a pupil in the school of greatness, condescended to menial offices or low mechanic employments, when only personal labour and personal knowlege could answer the end he had in view. In the height of his glory, and after the completion of his conquest he had so entire a contempt of those external circumstances which sometimes constitute the
whole

whole of a king, except the power annexed to royalty, that he feemed ambitious only of a fovereignty in foul, and to act rather than appear the king. He had an extream diflike to rich cloaths, and was never fo well fatisfied as in his regimentals: he never wore but one fuit of embroidery, and that for a fingle day only. In the fummer time it was his ufual cuftom to drive about the ftreets of St. Peterfburg in a chair with one horfe, without any other attendance than one foldier on horfeback. In winter he has been feveral times feen in a common hackney fledge. It would fometimes happen that he had not the value of three pence in his pocket to pay the fare; and has more than once afked the loan of this money of any perfon whom he knew, and accidentally met; yet notwithftanding thefe feeming improprieties, the fuperiority of his genius fupported the dignity of a great monarch; and it was by laying afide pomp and fplendor, which were uneffential to his glory, that he appeared fo much like a deity, in every place, almoft at one and the fame time. He was generally at his tribunals and public offices in the winter feafon by five in the morning, and thus his perfonal attendance, and knowlege of bufinefs, taught his fubjects their refpective duties, confined them to thofe duties, and made the ftate flourifh. He was not contented without going to the bottom of things, and therefore, inftead of making his people wait on him, he watched them; fo that he was feldom to be found in the palace. Prince Menzikoff had the charge of public feafts for foreign minifters, fo that Peter fpent no time in vain ceremonies; and as to his own diet it was rather coarfe than elegant.

After what has been obferved of the condefcenfions familiar to Peter the Great, the reader will not be furprifed that he converfed with all forts of people of whom he could learn any thing ufeful; among whom fome of the Englifh and other foreign merchants were frequently his companions. He ate and drank with them, and was often godfather to their children; if his godchild died, he has even more than once attended their funerals. He was very inquifitive about trade, yet he confeffed it was what he leaft underftood: but his eftablifhment of the commerce in St. Peterfburg, and bringing the greateft part of it from Archangel; the premiums he offered to thofe who fhould find out new branches of trade; his fetting up and encouraging new manufactories of linen and hemp in his own country; the great countenance he gave to foreign merchants, and many other fuch like circumftances, are certain indications that he underftood, in many inftances, the means of advancing commerce as well as the great end of it.

This prince made even his pleafures and amufements fubfervient to the important ends of his government. He had more than once received very melancholy proofs of the impatience of his fubjects under the reformation which he had planned, and was now accomplifhing: this rendered him extreamly fufpicious of them. As mens hearts are generally moft open in their cups, he often drank with them liberally, fometimes at court, and oftener at their own houfes. His manners feemed to be rude, in requiring even the ladies, upon certain occafions, to fwallow goblets of wine, or other ftrong liquors; but in this he had his views: drinking is ftill the vice of Ruffia, but in a more elegant manner than in paft times.

He had frequent convulfive diftortions of his head and countenance, contracted by a fright in his youth, upon an occafion when his life was in danger; but in fuch cafes it was always the rule of the company he was in, to look down, or a different way, and purfue their difcourfe without feeming to regard him.

To prevent a furprife or any attempt on his life, he would never lie alone: when he was not with the emprefs or other companion, he ordered one of his chamberlains to fleep with him: which was an uncomfortable fituation to them, as he was very angry

if

if they awaked him; and in his sleep he often grasped them very hard.

What compleated his character as a master of exquisite art and acute judgment, he diverted his people into a contempt of that sordid ignorance which for so many ages had reigned in this country, and which he made it his task to banish. This could not be done more effectually than by ridiculing a superstitious reverence of the customs of their forefathers. With this view he ordered a great number of dresses of the several officers of the crown and court as worn in past ages; and in these himself and his whole court appeared in masquerade: thus exhibiting themselves to the people under several comic figures, they diverted them into a persuasion that they were at least as wise in their age, and in their appearances, as their fathers had been before them."

To what Mr. Hanway relates, we shall add the following remarks from Mr. Bell, who attended the czar in an expedition to Derbent in Persia.

" Several foreign writers have misrepresented and traduced the real character of Peter the Great, by relating mean stories, picked up at alehouses, and circulated among the lowest class of people, most of them without the least ground of truth; whereby many people of good understanding have been misled, and, even to this present time, look on him to have been a vicious man, and a cruel tyrant; than which nothing can be more the reverse of his true character.

Though he might have had some failings, yet it is well known, to many living at the time of the writing this, which is above thirty-seven years after his demise, that his prudence, justice, and humanity very much over-balanced his failings; which principally, if not solely, arose from his inclination to the fair sex.

I shall here, says Mr. Bell, take the liberty to insert a passage or two, which, though trifling, yet as so great a personage is the subject, will not be altogether unacceptable or unentertaining to the reader, as they are instances of his assiduity,

About the middle of October 1714, I arrived at Cronstadt in an English ship. The czar having notice of the ship's arrival, came on board the next morning, from St. Petersburg; being attended only by Dr. Areskine, who was his chief physician at that time, and, on that occasion, served him as interpreter. After his majesty had enquired news about the Swedish fleet, &c. he eat a piece of bread and cheese, and drank a glass of ale, then went on shore to visit the works carrying on at Cronstadt; and returned the same evening in his boat to St. Petersburg, distance about twenty English miles.

The first winter after my arrival at St. Petersburg, I lodged at Mr. Noy's, an English ship-builder in the czar's service. One morning, before day-light, my servant came and told me that the czar was at the door. I got up, and saw him walking up and down the yard, the weather being severely cold and frosty, without any one to attend him. Mr. Noy soon came, and took him into the parlour, where his majesty gave him some particular directions about a ship then on the stocks; which having done, he left him.

His majesty's person was graceful, tall, and well-made, clean and very plain in his apparel. He generally wore an English drab-colour frock, never appearing in a dress-suit of cloaths, unless on great festivals, and remarkable holidays; on which occasions he was sometimes dressed in laced cloaths, of which sort he was not owner of above three or four suits. When he was dressed, he wore the order of St. Andrew; at other times, he had no badge or mark of any order on his person. His equipage was simple, without attendants. In summer, a four-oared wherry was always attending, to carry him over the river, if he should want to cross it, which he frequently did. When he went about the town, by land, he always made use of an open two wheeled chaise, attended by two soldiers, or grooms, who rode before, and a page, who sometimes stood behind the chaise, and often sat in it with his majesty, and drove

drove him. In winter, he made use of a sledge, drawn by one horse, with the same attendants. He found these to be the most expeditious ways of conveyance, and used no other. He was abroad every day in the year, unless confined at home by illness, which rarely happened; so that seldom a day passed but he was seen in almost every part of the city.

I have more than once seen him stop, in the streets, to receive petitions from persons who thought themselves wronged by sentences passed in courts of judicature. On taking the petition, the person was told to come next day to the senate, where the affair was immediately examined, and determined, if the nature of it would admit its being done in so short a time. It will naturally follow, that such free access to his person was not only productive of great relief to many poor widows and orphans, but also a strong check upon judges; and tended very much to prevent any sort of influence prevailing on them to pronounce unjust sentences, for which they were so likely to be called to account.

His majesty might truly be called a man of business; for he could dispatch more affairs in a morning than an houseful of senators could do in a month. He rose almost every morning in the winter-time, before four o'clock, was often in his cabinet by three o'clock, where two private secretaries, and certain clerks, paid constant attendance. He often went so early to the senate, as to occasion the senators being raised out of their beds to attend him there. When assembled, after hearing causes between subject and subject, or public affairs, regarding the interior of the empire, read by the secretary, and the opinion of the senate recited thereupon, he would write upon the process, or upon the affair under deliberation, with his own hand, in a very laconic stile, " Let it be according " to the decree of the senate;" and sometimes would add some particular alterations, such as he thought fit to mention, and under wrote PETER.

His

His majesty knew so little of relaxation of mind when awake, that he never allowed his time of rest to be broke in upon, unless in case of fire. When any accident of that kind happened, in any part of the town, there was a standing order to awake him on its first appearance; and his majesty was frequently the first at the fire, where he always remained, giving the necessary orders, till all further danger was over. This example of paternal regard of the czar for his subjects was, of course, followed by all the great officers, and those of the first quality; which was frequently the means of saving many thousands of his subjects from utter ruin, whose houses and goods, without such singular assistance, must have shared the fate of their ruined neighbours.

In acts of religion he appeared devout, but not superstitious. I have seen him at his public devotions in church many times. I have been present, when his majesty, not liking the clerk's manner of reading the psalms, hath taken the book from the clerk, and hath read them himself; which he did very distinctly, and with proper emphasis. His majesty was allowed, by the best judges of the Sclavonian and Russian languages, to be as great a master of them as any the most learned of his subjects, whether churchmen or laics. He wrote a very good hand, very expeditiously, yet the characters distinct enough; of this I myself am some judge, having seen many of his letters, all wrote with his own hand, to Mr. Henry Stiles, and others. As to his stile, some of his secretaries, and other competent judges of the language, affirmed, that they had never known any man who wrote more correctly, or could comprise the sense and meaning of what he wrote in so few words, as his majesty.

The following I had from a certain Russ gentleman, of very good family, and who was a general officer of unexceptionable character in the army, who had attended his majesty from his very youth, in all his expeditions. This officer being an old friend of mine,

mine, I went to pay him a vifit one evening, long after the death of Peter the Great; when he told me, that fuch and fuch officers, naming them, had dined with him that day, and that the principal fubject of their converfation turned on the actions of their old father (as he termed him, by way of eminence) Peter the Great. He told me further, that though his majefty feemed to be fevere, on certain occafions, yet not one of them all could produce or recollect one fingle inftance of his having punifhed an honeft man; or, that he had caufed any perfon to fuffer any punifhment who had not well deferved it.

He hath been reprefented as making too frequent ufe of fpirituous liquors to excefs, which is an unmerited afperfion; for he had an averfion to all fots, and to thofe too much given to drink. It is true, he had his times of diverfion, when he would be merry himfelf, and liked to fee others fo; this may have been neceffary, and proper for the unbending his mind from affairs of great weight; but fuch amufements occurred generally during holidays, and feftival times, and was, with him, at no time of long continuance. It hath been imputed to him, and not without fome appearance of reafon, that he had political views in encouraging drinking at thefe times of merriment; for, on thefe occafions, he mixed with the company, and, converfing with them on the footing of a companion, had better opportunities, at fuch times, of difcovering the real fentiments of thofe about him, than when they were quite cool.

Thofe, who by their offices about the perfon of Peter the Great, might be fuppofed to be the beft acquainted with his difpofition, always difavowed his drinking to excefs; and infifted on his being a fober prince. During the campaign of the expedition to Derbent in Perfia, he was not guilty of the leaft excefs, but rather lived abftemioufly. In this point I could not be miftaken, as the tent of Dr. Blumentroft, his majefty's chief phyfician, with whom I lodged,

lodged, was always the nearest tent to that of his majesty.

One instance occurs in proof of the temperance of this great man, viz. in our third day's march, on our return from Derbent, when we were kept in continual alarm by considerable bodies of mountaineers, both horse and foot, whom we saw hovering on the tops of the adjacent hills: though they dared not to come down to the plain, to attack any part of our army, yet it was necessary to be watchful of them; which, in some measure, impeded our march. The evening of that day, we had a hollow way to pass, which took up much time, and obliged the greatest part of the army to remain there all night; so that none reached the camp, except the guards, and some light horse who attended their majesties. On my arrival there, about midnight, I found only his majesty's tent set up, and another small one for Mr. Felton, the czar's principal cook, and master of his kitchen. I went into Felton's tent, and found him all alone, with a large sauce-pan of warm grout before him, made of buck wheat with butter; which, he told me, was the remains of their majesties supper, who eat of nothing else that evening; and who were just gone to bed.

During the whole march, his majesty, for the most part, rode an English pad, about fourteen hands high, for which he had a particular liking, as it was very tractable and easy to mount. His picture is drawn by Caravac on this horse. He did not wear boots, as he very often walked on foot. In the heat of the day, when the army halted, he used to go into the empress's coach, and sleep for half an hour. His dress, during the march, was a white night cap, with a plain flapped hat over it, and a short dimitty waistcoat. When at any time he received messengers, from the chieftains of the mountaineers, he put on his regimentals, as an officer of the guards, being lieutenant colonel of the Preobrashensky regiment.

During

During the whole courſe of his life, his majeſty avoided all ſorts of ceremony, except on public occaſions. His manner of living, in his houſe, was more like that of a private gentleman than of ſo great a monarch. I was once at court on a holiday, when the emperor came home from church to dinner, with a large attendance of his miniſters, general officers, and other great men. His table was laid with about fifteen covers. As ſoon as dinner was ſerved up, he and the empreſs took their places; and his majeſty addreſſing himſelf to the company, ſaid, " Gentle-" men, pleaſe to take your places as far as the table " will hold, the reſt will go home and dine with their " wives."

On ſuch occaſions, the princeſſes, his children, dined in another room, to whom he ſent ſuch diſhes, from his own table, as he thought proper, for their dinner.

This great monarch took all the pains, and uſed all the means poſſible, in order to be intimately acquainted with every thing proper for a man, who ruled a mighty empire, to know. He entered into the detail of every branch of the arts uſeful to mankind; into that of all the manufactures which regarded the conſtruction of ſhips, and fitting them for the ſea; into that of the making of arms, artillery, &c. If he had a ruling paſſion for any part of theſe acquirements, it muſt have been for ſhip-building; into which he entered himſelf very early, in the quality of a common workman, with his hatchet, and proceeded regularly through all the degrees, to the rank of maſter-builder, which he attained but a few years before his death. After he got that length in the art, he made the draughts, formed the mouldings, and directed the building of ſeveral men of war, of the ſecond and third rates, himſelf; and he duly demanded and received his ſalary as a maſter-builder. The day of launching the ſhips, which he himſelf built, he celebrated as a holiday, and put on laced clothes; but before he went to work, to ſtrike away ſtanchions, blocks, &c. he always put off his fine coat.

He was very frugal in what regarded his perſonal expences, and thoſe of his houſhold. Notwithſtanding his frugality in what related to himſelf, he ſpared no coſt, in whatever concerned the public, in the ſtructure of his men of war, in the artillery, fortifications, arſenals, canals, &c. all which bore marks of very great magnificence. Nor was he ſparing in his buildings, and the decorations of his gardens with ſtatues, grottos, fountains, &c. of which the buildings of the ſummer palace, and the gardens at St. Peterſburg, at Peterhoff, Strealna, Czarſky Sealo, and many others, are ſufficient proofs. I ſhall not detain the reader longer, on the ſubject of this very great man's character, or way of living, than to acquaint him, that, as his majeſty was very early up in the morning, he went abroad generally without breakfaſt; came home to dinner about eleven o'clock; after dinner went to ſleep for about an hour; after which, if buſineſs did not intervene, he ſometimes diverted himſelf at his turning loom; then went to viſit thoſe he had a regard for, as well foreigners as Ruſſians, with whom he would be very ſociable, and eaſy in converſation. He ſometimes ſupped with them; which, generally in his latter days, was on hare or wild fowl, roaſted very dry, drank ſmall beer, and ſometimes a few glaſſes of wine; and generally was in bed before ten o'clock at night. He neither played at cards, dice, or any game of chance.

The reader will pleaſe to take along with him the following obſervation, viz. that this monarch was at no time, even during maſquerades, feaſtings, aſſemblies, or any other diverſions or amuſements, by day or night, without the attendance of ſome or other of his miniſters, and of thoſe who poſſeſſed his confidence; by which means buſineſs, and ſuch affairs as were of the greateſt conſequence, went on regularly; and ſome of them even concerted during thoſe times of relaxation."——

A brief ACCOUNT of the Kingdom of

PRUSSIA;

With some Anecdotes of King FREDERIC II.

From Mr. HANWAY, &c.

THE kingdom of Prussia, which has been called Ducal Prussia, and belongs to the house of Brandenburg, is divided from the other dominions of its sovereign by Polish Prussia, and is bounded on the north by Samogitia, on the east by Lithuania, on the south by Poland Proper and Masovia, and on the west by Polish Prussia and the Baltic. Its greatest length, from its northern extremity to Soldau, is about a hundred and ninety miles, and its breadth, from the borders of the great duchy of Lithuania, near Shirwind, to the western coast of Samland, is a hundred and fourteen miles; but in other places it is much narrower.

With respect to the climate and temperature of the air, the two last months of the spring and the two first summer months are temperate, warm, and pleasant, and the weather generally favourable for bringing the fruits of the earth to maturity; but before and after these months the air is cold and piercing: autumn is often wet, and the winter severe. The air is, however, well purified by high winds. As to the distempers which most prevail in Prussia, the inhabitants are more subject to the gout and stone than to the scurvy. The soil produces great plenty of corn, fruit, excellent herbs, and pasturage. Prussia likewise abounds with flocks and herds, and exceeding fine horses; its chief commodities are buck-wheat, wool, flax, hemp, wax, honey, hops, pit-coal, and pitch.

pitch. Vast quantities of amber are found on the coasts of the Baltic, in Prussia, particularly on the Samland shore.

The number of inhabitants in this kingdom were in the year 1755 computed at 635,998 persons capable of bearing arms, and consist of native Prussians, who, from their language and manners, appear to be descended from the Germans; of Lithuanians, who have their peculiar language; and of Poles.

With respect to the religion of Prussia, the inhabitants are in general Lutherans; but as a great number of the colonists are Calvinists, they have also their churches, not only in the cities and towns, but in some villages they have a particular church appropriated to their use, and in other places they perform divine service in the Lutheran churches. The papists have a few churches in this kingdom; here are also some Mennonites, and a few congregations of Socinians.

The manufactures in Prussia are daily improving and increasing, particularly the glass and iron works, manufactures of silk, cloth, camblet, linen, and stockings; paper, powder, copper, and brass mills. Prussia is conveniently situated for trade, and to promote it a college of commerce and navigation has been erected, which takes a cognizance of all disputes and proposals relating to trade and commerce.

The commodities of Prussia and great Lithuania, sold to foreign merchants, and annually exported, are all kinds of grain, to the amount of twenty thousand lasts; pine trees for masts, deal boards, and timber; tar, wood-ashes, pot-ash, elk skins, leather, furs, amber, about twelve thousand five hundred stone of wax, honey, manna, linseed oil, flax, hemp, linseed, and hemp-seed; also yarn, hogs bristles, stags horns, and elks hoofs; oat-meal, mead, dried fish, sturgeon, caviar, lampreys, sausages, butter, and tallow, of which last three thousand four hundred stones are exported every year.

Frederic, the son of Frederic William the Great, and the grandfather of the present king, raised the duchy

A brief ACCOUNT of the Kingdom of

PRUSSIA;

With some Anecdotes of King FREDERIC II.

From Mr. HANWAY, &c.

THE kingdom of Prussia, which has been called Ducal Prussia, and belongs to the house of Brandenburg, is divided from the other dominions of its sovereign by Polish Prussia, and is bounded on the north by Samogitia, on the east by Lithuania, on the south by Poland Proper and Masovia, and on the west by Polish Prussia and the Baltic. Its greatest length, from its northern extremity to Soldau, is about a hundred and ninety miles, and its breadth, from the borders of the great duchy of Lithuania, near Shirwind, to the western coast of Samland, is a hundred and fourteen miles; but in other places it is much narrower.

With respect to the climate and temperature of the air, the two last months of the spring and the two first summer months are temperate, warm, and pleasant, and the weather generally favourable for bringing the fruits of the earth to maturity; but before and after these months the air is cold and piercing: autumn is often wet, and the winter severe. The air is, however, well purified by high winds. As to the distempers which most prevail in Prussia, the inhabitants are more subject to the gout and stone than to the scurvy. The soil produces great plenty of corn, fruit, excellent herbs, and pasturage. Prussia likewise abounds with flocks and herds, and exceeding fine horses; its chief commodities are buck-wheat, wool, flax, hemp, wax, honey, hops, pit-coal, and pitch.

pitch. Vaſt quantities of amber are found on the coaſts of the Baltic, in Pruſſia, particularly on the Samland ſhore.

The number of inhabitants in this kingdom were in the year 1755 computed at 635,998 perſons capable of bearing arms, and conſiſt of native Pruſſians, who, from their language and manners, appear to be deſcended from the Germans; of Lithuanians, who have their peculiar language; and of Poles.

With reſpect to the religion of Pruſſia, the inhabitants are in general Lutherans; but as a great number of the coloniſts are Calviniſts, they have alſo their churches, not only in the cities and towns, but in ſome villages they have a particular church appropriated to their uſe, and in other places they perform divine ſervice in the Lutheran churches. The papiſts have a few churches in this kingdom; here are alſo ſome Mennonites, and a few congregations of Socinians.

The manufactures in Pruſſia are daily improving and increaſing, particularly the glaſs and iron works, manufactures of ſilk, cloth, camblet, linen, and ſtockings; paper, powder, copper, and braſs mills. Pruſſia is conveniently ſituated for trade, and to promote it a college of commerce and navigation has been erected, which takes a cognizance of all diſputes and propoſals relating to trade and commerce.

The commodities of Pruſſia and great Lithuania, ſold to foreign merchants, and annually exported, are all kinds of grain, to the amount of twenty thouſand laſts; pine trees for maſts, deal boards, and timber; tar, wood-aſhes, pot-aſh, elk ſkins, leather, furs, amber, about twelve thouſand five hundred ſtone of wax, honey, manna, linſeed oil, flax, hemp, linſeed, and hemp-ſeed; alſo yarn, hogs briſtles, ſtags horns, and elks hoofs; oat-meal, mead, dried fiſh, ſturgeon, caviar, lampreys, ſauſages, butter, and tallow, of which laſt three thouſand four hundred ſtones are exported every year.

Frederic, the ſon of Frederic William the Great, and the grandfather of the preſent king, raiſed the duchy

duchy of Pruſſia to a kingdom, and in 1701, in a ſolemn aſſembly of the ſtates of the empire, placed the crown with his own hands upon his head and that of his conſort; ſoon after which he was acknowleged as king of Pruſſia by all the other chriſtian powers. His ſon Frederic William, who aſcended the throne in 1713, peopled his country by the favourable reception he gave to the diſtreſſed and perſecuted Saltzburghers; and rendered his reign glorious by many uſeful and magnificent foundations. This monarch was ſucceeded in 1740 by his ſon Frederic II. his preſent majeſty, who has annexed to his dominions the greateſt part of Sileſia and Eaſt Frieſland, rendered his kingdom formidable by his valour and uncommon prudence, and promoted the happineſs of his ſubjects by an amendment and reduction of the laws, the increaſe of commerce, and many other wiſe regulations.

Berlin is airy and elegant: the ſtreets are regular and clean, and the houſes uniform. In going toward the palace on the Pont Neuf, or new bridge, which is of ſtone, over the Spree, is an equeſtrian ſtatue of Frederic William the Great, which is eſteemed a piece of exquiſite workmanſhip; it was erected by Frederic I. king of Pruſſia, who alſo built the palace, which is very magnificent.

It is a pleaſure to obſerve the great œconomy of this court, the apartments in the palace are adorned with ſilver in every ſhape; but theſe ornaments are ſo maſſy, that the faſhion is not more than 7 l. per cent. ſo that four millions of dollars might be realized with great eaſe. The king's particular apartments are elegant, but have nothing extraordinary; the prevailing taſte is white ſtucco and gilding. Several of the private apartments have tables, with pens, ink, and looſe papers, which indicate the diſpatch of buſineſs, more than the regularity and elegance one naturally expects to find in a royal palace.

Mr.

Mr. Hanway obferves, that at the time of his being at Berlin, the king of Pruffia was confidered as no friend to Great Britain; but adds, there is a pleafure in praifing the worthy, whether they happen to be our friends or not. Frederic II. king of Pruffia and elector of Brandenburg, was born on the 24th of January 1712, and was the fon of king Frederic William, by Sophia Dorothea, the fifter of king George II. He afcended the throne on the 21ft of May 1740, and was therefore 28 years of age when his father died. He had an early tafte of literature and the polite arts, and diftinguifhed himfelf by the delicacy of his manners, in oppofition to the inelegant cuftoms that prevailed at his father's court.

There is one circumftance in favour of his Pruffian majefty beyond any other prince in Europe; which is the great œconomy of his government and perfonal expence. The allowance of his table is but 30 crowns, or 5 l, 5 s. a day, fifh and wine excepted, in which he is at no great expence. Potfdam is the favourite refidence of the king of Pruffia, who here avoids the empty ceremonies of a court. He entertains at his table twelve perfons: thofe of his minifters moft in favour are firft invited, with thofe of foreign princes who happen to be at Potfdam, and his officers, even to an enfign, fill up the vacant places. His converfation is free and eafy, even to jefting; but he paffes from the gay to the ferious in an inftant, and fupports his dignity both from the fear and the affection of thofe about him. So little does he obferve ufelefs forms, that he has rifen from his chair at his writing-table, and caufed his fecretary to take his place, and write down the orders which he dictated ftanding.

END of the FIFTH VOLUME.

www.ingramcontent.com/pod-product-compliance
Lightning Source LLC
Chambersburg PA
CBHW051843300426
44117CB00006B/249